UNITED STATES DIPLOMATIC HISTORY

UNITED STATES DIPLOMATIC HISTORY

From Revolution to Empire

Volume 1
To 1914

GERARD CLARFIELD
University of Missouri-Columbia

PRENTICE HALL   Englewood Cliffs, New Jersey 07632

Library of Congress Cataloging-in-Publication Data

Clarfield, Gerard H.
    United States diplomatic history : from revolution to empire /
Gerard Clarfield.
        p.   cm.
    Includes bibliographical references (v. 1, p.   ) and index.
    Contents: v. 1. To 1914
    ISBN 0-13-029190-0 (v. 1)
    1. United States—Foreign relations.   I. Title.
E183.7.C59   1992
327.73—dc20   91-20218
                                                           CIP

Acquisitions editor: Stephen Dalphin
Editorial/production supervision and
    interior design: Barbara Reilly
Copy editor: Ann Hofstra Grogg
Cover design: Wanda Lubelska Design
Prepress buyer: Debra Kesar/Kelly Behr
Manufacturing buyer: Mary Ann Gloriande
Editorial assistant: Caffie Risher

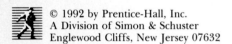 © 1992 by Prentice-Hall, Inc.
A Division of Simon & Schuster
Englewood Cliffs, New Jersey 07632

Printed in the United States of America
10 9 8 7 6 5 4 3 2 1

ISBN   0-13-029190-0

Prentice-Hall International (UK) Limited, *London*
Prentice-Hall of Australia Pty. Limited, *Sydney*
Prentice-Hall Canada Inc., *Toronto*
Prentice-Hall Hispanoamericana, S.A., *Mexico*
Prentice-Hall of India Private Limited, *New Delhi*
Prentice-Hall of Japan, Inc., *Tokyo*
Simon & Schuster Asia Pte. Ltd., *Singapore*
Editora Prentice-Hall do Brasil, Ltda., *Rio de Janeiro*

For Leslie and Joe,
who fully appreciate what W. C. Fields
had in mind when he said, "On the
whole, I'd rather be in Philadelphia."

CONTENTS

PREFACE

We live during a particularly exciting moment in world affairs. The cold war, America's fixation for more than four decades, has given way to a new and unpredictable international situation. Eastern Europe and the Soviet Union are suffering from grave economic and political problems; a united Germany is predominant in Europe; and Japan has become a global economic power. The Middle East and Africa are aflame. And, as I write, the war in the Persian Gulf has just come to a close, leaving in its wake widespread instability throughout the region.

The American people and their leaders have emerged from this conflict exultant, filled with hubris, and confident, as they have not been since the Vietnam War, that this country can shape the course of world history. Whether that is true is problematic. Notwithstanding the United States's impressive showing in the Gulf War, Washington's position in the world has eroded—along with its once overwhelming economic strength. One thing seems certain, however. We are at one of those moments in world affairs that bears the earmarks of a watershed. All in all, it is a fine moment to take stock, to look back. I hope that students will want to do that and that this volume will help.

It wasn't too long ago (before the proliferation of good, relatively inexpensive paperback books) that students were required to depend upon a textbook as their main source of information in history courses. These books were by and large extremely thorough, and of course, students received a solid grounding in the major issues. But they also spent a good deal of time unraveling the mysteries surrounding obscure boundary disputes, quarrels over fishing rights, and pelagic sealing controversies, all matters of less than earth-shaking consequence.

As teachers I think we are more sensitive today. We know that a good teaching tool does not need to be, indeed probably should not be, encyclopedic. At the same time I think we are also wise enough to know what should be remembered. My hope is that this book lives up to that standard.

Like all syntheses, this book is based in large part on an extensive reading of the work of others. I have, through the use of notes and the section on supplementary reading, acknowledged many but by no means all of my debts. I would therefore like to take this opportunity to thank those whose names do not appear in these pages but whose work has nevertheless contributed so much to my understanding of our diplomatic history. I would also like to express my profound appreciation to Michael Barnhart of the State University of New York at Stony Brook and to Manfred Jonas of Union College for their careful reading of this work in manuscript and the many helpful suggestions they have offered. I am also deeply grateful to Mrs. Patty Eggleston for her help in preparing the manuscript for publication. Last, but by no means least, I thank my editors, Barbara Reilly, who has been a joy to work with, and Ann Hofstra Grogg, whose extraordinary labors on my behalf have been an enormous asset.

INTRODUCTION

When I began writing these volumes on the course of United States diplomatic history over the past two-and-a half centuries, I had no particular interpretive axe to grind. Nor do I now. Yet two basic themes do emerge from the narrative. The first of these, which reveals itself quite early, is a persistent contradiction that existed between the political hopes of American policy makers and certain fundamental economic realities.

The idea that the United States should "steer clear" of European political affairs and wars was articulated by John Adams and Thomas Paine as early as 1776, and written indelibly into our history by James Monroe in his famous 1823 doctrine. That was all well and good except that while the United States was seeking what amounted to political isolation, it was at the same time an important member of the international economic community with an ever-increasing stake in world trade. Could America stay politically unentangled while at the same time playing an important role in the global economy? Early policy makers grappled with this dilemma but were confronted with repeated crises and humiliations, the result of attempting to play the role of a neutral trading nation during the wars of the French Revolution and Napoleon. Finally, in 1812, James Madison felt he had no option but to fight. The nation's honor, the credibility of the Jeffersonian Republican party, and his own personal political interest required it.

The years that followed the War of 1812, while replete with many problems, saw no repetition of the crises that had plagued the founding fathers. But that was not because succeeding generations had resolved their dilemma. It was simply that the political settlement arranged at the Congress of Vienna in 1815 ushered in a century of relative peace in Europe.

Nonentanglement remained a hallowed tradition, an unquestioned verity for most Americans well into the twentieth century. Yet long before that, the United States had in fact sidled up to and taken a seat at the table where the high-stakes game of international diplomacy was played. In part this dramatic break with tradition was a reflection of the fact that the United States had become a great power and that an increasing number of Americans believed it should act like one. Moreover, the country had reached a point in its economic development when foreign trade, and therefore foreign markets, had become exceptionally important. With England, France, Germany, Russia and Japan expanding through Africa, Asia, and the Pacific, Washington either had to join in the race for empire or risk being left behind, a second-rate power. Given these alternatives and the nationalist as well as economic pressures at work in the United States, it is hardly surprising that Washington resolved its long standing dilemma by abandoning its commitment to nonentanglement.

Expansionism is the second theme that permeates the history of American foreign policy. The Declaration of Independence stands as the first great expansionist document in our national history. Here the revolutionary generation claimed the right, indeed the duty, to throw off despotism and establish a society based on libertarian principles. In the process they changed forever the map of North America, creating a nation that extended from the Atlantic to the Mississippi, from the Great Lakes almost to the Gulf of Mexico.

When, almost thirty years later, Thomas Jefferson violated his own strict constructionist convictions to acquire the Louisiana Purchase, he believed first that he was securing the "empire for liberty" begun in 1776, that this vast area would guarantee America's agrarian future for all time. He also believed that by eliminating France as a neighbor and securing total control over the Mississippi River he was protecting America against the danger of being dragged into future European wars.

The reasons behind the United States's expansionist thrust changed with its geopolitical situation. In 1846, when James K. Polk decided on war with Mexico in order to secure California and the southwest for the United States, rabid expansionists explained this territorial grab in Jeffersonian terms as "expanding the area of freedom." In fact, however, Polk was not motivated by ideological passion. He was the first in a succession of policy makers who thought in terms of acquiring Pacific coast ports and an Isthmian canal in hopes of securing a "passage to India." Such a development, he imagined, would at once lead to the growth of a valuable Pacific trade and be vastly encouraging to the internal economic development of the United States.

Once Polk had secured ports on the Pacific, the next logical step was to move into the Caribbean and the Pacific. But at that point in time, America's expansionist thrust was blunted first by the sectional controversy and the Civil War, and later by domestic economic and political considerations as well as the fact that the idea of acquiring overseas holdings ran directly contrary to the powerful tradition of nonentanglement. In the aftermath of the war a succession of policy makers dreamed the same dream. Still, no administration developed a clear-cut policy of overseas expansion until Benjamin Harrison entered the White House in 1889. Even then it took another ten years before the vision acquired substance.

In the 1840s, President Polk envisioned what Professor Norman Graebner has called an *Empire on the Pacific* (1955). In 1899, President William McKinley secured an empire *in* the Pacific. His successor, Theodore Roosevelt fulfilled another aspect of the vision when he took the Panama Canal Zone and undertook to transform the Caribbean into an American lake, a process completed by President Woodrow Wilson.

Looking back on this earlier time from the vantage point of the late twentieth century, the basic themes that appear to have dominated America's foreign policy during its rise to great power seem clear enough. There is a danger, however, in thinking that these themes were as obvious to those who made history as they are to those of us who are privileged to look back upon it. Historians attempt to make sense of the past. In the process they decide which evidence is important and which is not. In some ways a historian is like a paleontologist picking over old bones. The bones, as we all know, can be assembled in different ways to create different impressions. So can the facts of history. This book represents my way of looking at the evidence. Readers should understand that and retain a critical perspective.

John Paul Jones raided the Irish Coast almost at will during the Revolutionary War. Americans viewed him as a naval hero. It is obvious from this cartoon, however, that the British saw him in an altogether different light.

1

AMERICA'S REVOLUTIONARY DIPLOMACY, 1775–1783

On the second of July 1776, the Continental Congress, meeting in Carpenter's Hall in Philadelphia, approved a resolution offered by Virginia's Richard Henry Lee, "that these United States are, and of a right ought to be free and independent."[1] Two days later, the delegates approved Thomas Jefferson's ringing declaration. It was the beginning of a new era in Western history. The "contagion of liberty" had been loosed, and nothing would ever be quite the same again.

Although for a century and more the thirteen Atlantic coast colonies grew and evolved as parts of the British empire, there had been from the very beginning an almost schizophrenic quality about their attachment to Britain. The colonists had been proud to proclaim themselves "freeborn Englishmen," subjects of the most enlightened nation in Europe. Yet at the same time they saw American society as unique—different from and in an ethical and spiritual sense superior to Old World cultures. It had been so from the very beginning of the American experience. The purpose of the earliest Puritan immigrants, after all, had been to establish a new Godly commonwealth at a time when England seemed to be descending into what they feared might be a permanent state of heresy and corruption. Thus in the spring of 1630, as he stood on the deck of the ship *Arabella* and felt the gentle swell of the sea beneath his feet, John Winthrop explained to his fellow immigrants that their purpose was to establish a society superior to the one they were leaving behind, "a Citty upon a Hill," a virtuous community that would stand as an example for the rest of humankind to wonder at and emulate.[2]

If the religious fervor of the Puritans was one factor that contributed to the shaping of a unique American character and society, another deserving of mention here was the availability of cheap and virtually limitless expanses of land. This led to the growth of a fundamentally agrarian, socially mobile society in which Europe's rigid class system could not take root.

In the later part of the eighteenth century, a young Frenchman who first crossed the Atlantic to serve with the French army in Canada observed life in this new society. J. Hector St. John de Crèvecoeur traveled widely in British North America before settling in rural New York. There, in the last decade of the colonial era, he wrote of his delight at witnessing the evolution of a people largely untainted by Europe's corrupt hand. A new sort of person was emerging in America—one who knew nothing of aristocratic pretensions or a repressive clergy but who cherished simple republican principles and enjoyed a bountiful life earned by hard labor on the land.

If Americans took pride in their virtuous society, the other side of the coin was the fear that European corruption would, like some dread contagion, reach across the Atlantic to engulf them. John Dickinson, later a leading Pennsylvania revolutionary, was a student living in London in the early 1750s. Impressed by the grandeur of the great city, he was at the same time appalled by the corruption of British politics. "I think the character of Rome will equally suit this nation," wrote Dickinson, "Easy to be bought, if there was but a purchaser." Many years later, while serving as America's envoy to France, Thomas Jefferson made the same point. He urged James Monroe to join him in Paris not so much to indulge in the pleasures of the Old World as to rejoice in the advantages of the New. "My God! how little do my countrymen know what precious blessings they are in possession of, and which no other people on earth enjoy. The comparison of our governments with those of Europe is like a comparison of heaven and hell."[3]

These feelings, the sense of uniqueness and the fear that too close an association with the nations of the Old World might lead to the destruction of republican virtue in the New, are clearly reflected in the earliest American approach to foreign policy. Thomas Paine, idealist, moralist, and a masterful political essayist, had been in America for less than two years when he published the influential pamphlet *Common Sense* in 1776. Yet he was aware of the importance of these attitudes and used them to argue for both independence and a foreign policy based on the principle of nonentanglement in Europe's political affairs.

Paine focused on the ideological divide that separated Europe, where monarchies held sway, from North America, where a republic was emerging. He argued that war, the scourge of Europe, was a product of monarchy itself—the original sport of kings as it were. But America, where a republican system was taking shape, had no reason for involvement in Europe's dynastic

In 1776 Thomas Paine published *Common Sense*, a pamphlet in which he advocated a foreign policy of political nonentanglement in Europe's political affairs and trade expansion for the United States.

squabbles. Republican governments were by their very nature peace loving. They could not suffer from the princely ambition for conquest and glory since they were or should be concerned with the well-being of the people, and the people's interest was never served by war.

Paine also contended that the "alliance" with England had produced only a succession of wars, none of which had been in America's interest. Once separated from the mother country, he went on, America could live in peace with the other European states that would have no reason to quarrel with an independent North American republic. On the other hand, he warned, "Any submission to, or dependence on, Great Britain tends directly to involve this continent in european [*sic*] wars and quarrels, and set us at variance with nations who would otherwise seek our friendship, and against whom we have neither anger nor complaint." "It is the true interest of America," Paine concluded, "to steer clear of European contentions, which she never can do, while, by her dependence on Britain, she is made the makeweight in the scale of British politics." Paine's views were seconded in the Continental Congress, where the mercurial John Adams warned that America should "avoid all obligations and temptations to take any part in future European wars."[4]

Yet if nonentanglement in Old World politics was a clear priority, powerful forces were at work driving all sections of the new nation into a close economic relationship with Europe. New England's prosperity depended on its continued access to the fisheries of the North Atlantic as well as markets that stretched from the West Indies to the Azores and included the Catholic countries of southern Europe. Moreover, its merchant ships roamed the globe in search of profitable cargoes. In the Middle Atlantic states, where pork, beef, wheat, and other food grains sought foreign markets, the story was much the same. And the South, with its staple-producing plantation economy, was more dependent upon world markets than any other section. Finally, all sections looked to Europe for manufactured and luxury goods available nowhere else.

Could the United States hope to remain an integral part of the Atlantic trading community and at the same time avoid becoming entangled in Europe's wars? This was the problem, and John Adams, who took the lead in directing congressional thinking on the subject, obviously had his doubts. Like his friend Thomas Jefferson, Adams enjoyed fantasizing about an America isolated economically from Europe. That would, of course, have been an ideal solution. But he knew that his countrymen, as "aquatic as the tortoises and sea-fowl," would never consent to stay at home economically. Because economic isolation was not feasible, Adams advocated negotiating a network of reciprocal trade treaties with the nations of Europe. The object was to create an international competition for advantage in the American marketplace that could be manipulated by American policy makers to preserve the young nation's sovereignty, peace, and neutrality while at the same time expanding her share of world trade. Paine had hinted at the same approach when he remarked in *Common Sense* that once independent America would find it relatively simple to maintain her sovereignty since all of Europe's states would want to keep America a "free port." Her trade, he thought, would "always be a protection."[5]

Following the decision for independence, Congress established a committee to lay down the basic principles for a truly American foreign policy. The committee was made up of Adams, Benjamin Franklin, John Dickinson, Benjamin Harrison, and Robert Morris. But Adams, recognized by his colleagues for his keen interest in foreign affairs, did most of the work. Predictably, the Model Treaty, or, as it was sometimes called, "The Plan of 1776," reflected his views. America would seek no political connection with any European state but would arrange bilateral commercial treaties with nations willing to extend recognition and negotiate. Nor did Adams have any doubt that the European states would negotiate. He was convinced that the American marketplace was so extraordinarily valuable that European states would be willing, at least in a figurative sense, to stand in line for the privilege.

In the fullness of its early and as it turned out naive enthusiasm, Congress implemented another of Adams's ideas, adopting a tactic some would label "militia diplomacy." Without first attempting to assess Old World attitudes toward the revolution in America, Congress sent its representatives to the far corners of the European Continent seeking recognition and trade.

Benjamin Franklin, whose long experience in Europe led him to doubt the wisdom of this approach, thought it bad policy, explaining to

Virginia's Arthur Lee that a "virgin state should preserve its virgin character, and not go about suitoring for alliances, but wait with decent dignity for the application of others."[6] As the old philosopher suspected, Congress and its envoys came in for some rude shocks. In the first place, most of Europe's monarchies were appalled at a revolution that challenged royal authority. Nor were they willing to take any step that might result in a war with England. The attraction of the American marketplace was not so powerful as Adams had thought. Congress would have to rethink this earliest approach to foreign policy.

FRANCE OFFERS COVERT AID

Long before the sound of musketry shattered the morning calm on Lexington Green, American leaders understood that the French might be prepared to come to their aid. For the better part of a century Britain and France had been involved in a great struggle for empire. The Treaty of Utrecht of 1713, which ended the War of the Spanish Succession, checked French hopes for further expansion in the Old World and the New. It also left three great rivals, Britain, France, and Spain, in control of vast western hemispheric empires. Spain held all of Mexico, Central and South America (except for Portuguese Brazil and Surinam), Cuba, Puerto Rico, the Floridas and half of Santo Domingo. France controlled all of Canada, the vast Louisiana territory, the other half of Santo Domingo, and both Guadeloupe and Martinique in the West Indies. The British, meanwhile, held the Hudson Bay Colony, Nova Scotia, Newfoundland, the thirteen Atlantic coast colonies, Jamaica, Barbados, and the Leeward islands.

During the decades that followed the peace of Utrecht the struggle for empire continued with Britain playing an increasingly aggressive role. The War of Jenkins's Ear (1739–41) began with a botched British attempt to seize Cartagena from Spain and ended inconclusively when the two belligerents became involved on opposite sides in the War of the Austrian Succession (1740–48) in Europe. France's decision to ally itself with Spain in this European war precipitated an Anglo-French conflict for control of North America known as King George's War (1744–48) which, like the War of Jenkins's Ear, also ended in a draw.

During the next several years the Anglo-French rivalry in North America intensified. The Hudson's Bay Company expanded its fur trading operations into areas claimed by the French while the British government established a fort at Halifax in Nova Scotia to counter the French fortress at Louisbourg. Meanwhile English subjects began migrating from Pennsylvania and Virginia into the upper Ohio Valley, an area also claimed by the French. The formation of the Ohio Company of Virginia as well as other companies with large scale land claims west of the Alleghenies made it clear that Anglo-Americans would soon be pouring across the mountains.

The French countered these developments in a number of ways.

They constructed military strong points along the Great Lakes, seized British traders operating in the Ohio River Valley, and built forts along the Allegheny river and at the forks of the Ohio river further to the south. It was there in July 1754 that French forces fought a skirmish with a small body of Virginia militia led by a young officer named George Washington. This engagement marked the beginning of the French and Indian War (1754–63) which within two years had spread to Europe, Africa, and Asia. In European history it is known as the Seven Years' War. But whatever one chooses to call it, there was no ambiguity about the outcome. France was defeated and humiliated.

The Treaty of Paris of 1763 left Britain dominant in North America as well as in Africa and India, where French influence was virtually extinguished. Under the terms of this agreement, Paris was forced to cede Canada as well as all territory east of the Mississippi river (save for the city of New Orleans) to the British. Only two small islands in the Gulf of St. Lawrence remained of a French empire that had once encompassed millions of square miles. Britain also expanded its holdings in the West Indies at France's expense, although the islands of Martinique, Guadeloupe, and St. Lucia reverted to French control after the war.

Even before the Treaty of Paris was signed it became the purpose of French diplomacy to destroy British power and restore France to a position of primacy in Europe. As early as 1763, Étienne-François, duc de Choiseul, minister of marine in the government of Louis XV, began planning for that glorious day. He devoted himself to rebuilding the French navy and at the same time laid elaborate plans for a bold cross-channel invasion of England.

Alert to the possibility that the restiveness in Britain's North American empire might produce a revolution, Choiseul sent observers to America to study the situation and lend encouragement to America's radicals. The first of these, a naval officer known only as Pontleroy, reported in 1764 that the Americans were "too rich to be obedient, eager to be the sole masters of their fur trade, and restive to shake off the fetters and restraints of their commerce."[7] Another observer sent in the following year arrived at precisely the same conclusions. Johanne, the baron de Kalb, who during the War for Independence fought and died gallantly as a volunteer in George Washington's army, was still another of Choiseul's emissaries to the American Whigs.

Left to his own devices, the impulsive Choiseul might have done more to encourage colonial discontent, perhaps even risking a confrontation with England. But he had to contend with the cautious Louis XV and his minister of finance, Anne Robert Jacques, baron de Turgot, who feared that the French economy would collapse under the strain of another war. The bureaucratic infighting between Turgot and Choiseul continued until 1770, when Louis lost patience with Choiseul and dismissed him from office.

For the next four years French foreign policy was in the hands of Emmanuel-Armand, the duc d'Aiguillon, who sought a rapprochement with England, the better to deal with a growing Russian threat in the East. Not surprisingly, during this period France turned its back on the American situation. Aiguillon's attempt at détente with Great Britain came to nothing as London arrogantly rejected the proffered hand of friendship. That, as things turned out, was a serious blunder. If France had been allied with Britain against Russia during the American Revolutionary War, there would certainly have been no Franco-American alliance. And without that alliance it is very unlikely that the colonists could have secured their independence.

In 1774 a great deal changed very quickly in France. Louis XV died, and his grandson, the shy, dull, Louis XVI, then just twenty, ascended the throne. More comfortable hunting or tinkering in his locksmith's workshop than dealing with affairs of state, Louis was poorly suited to the position he inherited. He did, however, appoint as ministers men of genuine ability. One of these was Charles Gravier, the comte de Vergennes, who took over as foreign minister. Vergennes, a career diplomat who was justly regarded as one of the most subtle, sophisticated statesmen of his age, revived Choiseul's dream of revenge against England. Not so impetuous as Choiseul, however, he approached the possibility of war cautiously.

During the summer of 1775 Vergennes decided that the fighting then taking place between British and American forces in North America could be turned to France's advantage. How he came to this conclusion is an interesting story in itself. It all began when the chevalier d'Eon, a transvestite nobleman and a shadowy figure at court, stole a number of embarrassing documents, among them a plan for the invasion of England. D'Eon fled across the channel and informed France's foreign ministry that if France would not pay for the return of the documents he would sell them to the English. Vergennes immediately sent Caron de Beaumarchais, musician, playwright, and sometime secret agent, to London. History does not record whether this romantic adventurer made contact with d'Eon. One supposes so, however, since the British do not seem to have obtained the stolen papers. What history does reveal is that while in London, Beaumarchais made contact with a number of American radicals and hatched a scheme to funnel secret aid to the American rebels. He returned to France bubbling over with excitement. Conspiracy was in the air, and the forty-three-year-old playwright hoped to be at the center of it.

Soon, with Vergennes's blessings, the playwright was shuttling back and forth between London and Paris developing his plans. His co-conspirator in London was Virginia's Arthur Lee, a radical Whig with close connections to Congress's Secret Committee of Correspondence.

Vergennes, meanwhile, was busy at Versailles attempting to convince the king that a program of covert aid made sense. That wasn't as easy as it might seem, for Louis had serious doubts about supporting a rebellion aimed at overthrowing royal authority. Moreover, the ever-cautious Turgot strongly opposed Vergennes's scheme, fearing it might land France in a war with England. This time, however, it was Turgot who lost—the argument as well as his job. The king approved a secret "loan" of a million livres (about £ 200,000) and King Carlos III of Spain, France's partner in the Bourbon Family Compact, pledged a like sum.

The money was delivered to Beaumarchais. But to keep the English ignorant of its true source, it had to be "laundered" before it could be spent. Swiss bank accounts not having become fashionable, the adventurous author of *The Marriage of Figaro* found another way. The firm of Roderique Hortalez & Company, a fictitious Portuguese trading company, provided a vehicle for sending aid to the Americans.

Since Portugal was a long-time British ally, the Portuguese connection was a nice touch. On the surface it would appear that the Americans were doing business with a legitimate private firm. There would be nothing to connect France or Spain with the trade in contraband of war that quickly developed. The lords of Whitehall might not like it, but there wasn't much they could do about it either.

Of course Beaumarchais hadn't intended to *sell* contraband to the Americans. The money seems originally to have been intended as aid with no strings attached. But when Silas Deane, an agent of the Continental Congress, turned up in Paris empowered to purchase war material, Beaumarchais was more than happy to accommodate him. All told, Hortalez & Company sold war material valued at some 5.6 million livres to the United States through Deane, almost all of it on credit.

Vergennes took a number of other steps to encourage the American rebels as well. Aware that many Americans feared France might take advantage of their rebellion to reclaim Canada, he sent a secret emissary, Achard de Bonvouloir, to Philadelphia to assure them that France not only supported their efforts but had no interest in reoccupying its lost province. Bonvouloir also informed the Americans that their ships would be welcome in French ports and that "the facilities which they would find there for their commerce would soon prove the esteem which we hold for them."[8]

Vergennes went one step further in encouraging the American rebellion, warning London that France would not tolerate British cruisers searching French merchant ships for contraband while in French territorial waters. This move was intended to protect the contraband trade, since cargoes of military material regularly cleared French ports for the French West Indies, where small, swift sailing ships waited to take on these cargoes and run the British blockade. It was indeed a most benevolent neutrality that Charles Gravier had fashioned, a recognition in all but name of American belligerency.

THE FRENCH ALLIANCE

When the war began, it was more or less generally believed, at least in patriot circles, that the British would be unable to sustain a serious military effort in America for any lengthy period of time. Optimists expected that the British, at the end of impossibly long supply lines, would find little or no support among Americans. Needless to say, the optimists were wrong. Much later, a wiser John Adams guessed that no more than a third of the people supported the Revolution. A second third, he believed, remained loyal to the Crown, while the remainder refused to take sides. Whether Adams's estimates are correct or not is immaterial. The point is that the British found plenty of support among the American population and had no supply difficulties during the war.

Nor did the fighting go as so many patriots had hoped. In the campaign of 1776 Washington was defeated at the battle of Long Island and forced into a retreat that did not end until he had put the Delaware River between himself and the advancing English. Worse, the American army, which by the end of the year amounted to no more than five thousand effectives, was shrinking by the day as individual soldiers, their terms of enlistment up, left for home. Only a last-minute call for ninety-day volunteers saved the army from dissolution and the Revolution from disaster then and there.

Under these circumstances, Congress did the pragmatic thing: it began to look for help. A military alliance with France, once considered too dangerous, now seemed to offer the best hope, perhaps the only hope for military success. But would Louis be willing to run the risk of war with England considering the unpromising battlefield situation in America?

Late in 1776 Congress appointed three commissioners to seek increased economic aid as well as a military alliance with France. Silas Deane, already deeply involved with Beaumarchais, was one of these. But Deane played only a small role in the ensuing diplomacy, confining his efforts to purchasing. The second envoy was the acerbic, suspicious, and altogether ungracious Arthur Lee, who spent the majority of his time in Paris trying to prove that Deane and Beaumarchais were what a later generation of Americans would describe as crooked defense contractors. This may have been just as well, since Lee had an uncanny knack for making enemies; nobody at the French court wanted much to do with him.

The dominant figure on the commission was the aged Benjamin Franklin, scientist and philosopher, the greatest man of letters in America, and undoubtedly its best-known citizen. Franklin, who had spent years in England hobnobbing with the great and near-great, was more at home in silk pantaloons than simple homespun. But no sooner had he set foot on French soil than he realized the French expected him to live up to their vision of the virtuous yet simple yeoman, a rustic. He played the role expertly, affecting the plainest clothing topped off by a simple fur cap that he wore almost everywhere during those first weeks in Paris.

The old man was an immediate sensation. Pictures of him sprouted in shop windows throughout the city. Small enamels of the envoy, depicting him in his fur cap of course, sold at premium prices, as did rings and snuffboxes emblazoned with his image. The ladies of the French capital outdid one another in paying homage to "Mon cher Papa," some even doing their hair in a style meant to imitate his cap. Franklin was indisputably a genius at public relations. He was not at all certain, however, that he could convince France's cool-headed foreign minister that an alliance was in their mutual interest.

Benjamin Franklin was not only a great favorite with the ladies of Paris; he represented his country there brilliantly during the struggle for independence.

Much to the annoyance of David Murray, Lord Stormont, Britain's ambassador in Paris, Vergennes received Franklin at the Foreign Ministry almost as soon as he arrived. At his charming best, Vergennes nevertheless made it clear that he had no intention of recognizing the United States, an act that surely would have produced an immediate conflict with England. When the time was right Vergennes fully intended to jump into the war. But first he needed to put the French navy in fighting trim. Aware of recent British victories in America, he no doubt also wanted solid evidence of American staying power before risking war.

During the first half of 1777 Vergennes made a public show of seeming to uphold French neutrality. But behind the scenes he played a different game. He did nothing to stop the trade in contraband, even providing the Americans in Paris with a second subsidy of 2 million livres. He allowed Franklin to purchase and outfit privateers for operations against British shipping and, save when their escapades were too obvious to be ignored, winked at the activities of American privateersmen who regularly brought captured British ships into French ports for sale.

The British were not unaware of Vergennes's double game; Paris was alive with Lord Stormont's spies. But London had no desire to widen the war and so remained content to issue periodic protests and warnings, hoping in this way to minimize French support for the Americans.

This situation remained unchanged until the summer of 1777 when, with the fleet at last in readiness, Vergennes decided that the time had come for action. He pressed the king for a commitment. In a memorandum dated July 23, 1777, he argued that secret aid could not secure French objectives. France, he wrote, must "either . . . abandon America . . . or aid her courageously and effectively."[9] The King quickly agreed, contingent upon the cooperation of the Spanish, who were partners in the Bourbon Family Compact.

The king's insistence on Spanish cooperation was a disappointment to Vergennes, who at that time envisioned a short war with England that would secure American independence in a single campaign. France's military and naval resources alone were sufficient for such a war. Moreover, the foreign minister realized that it would be difficult to persuade the Spanish to cooperate.

Spain would have liked nothing better than to regain East and West Florida, which as a French ally it had lost to the British during the Seven Years' War. Moreover, war with England would provide the opportunity for a Franco-Spanish assault on Gibraltar, held by the British since 1704. These were, no doubt, attractive incentives. On the other hand, Spain had to consider far more carefully than France the effect an independent United States would have on affairs in the New World. There was an empire at stake in the Caribbean, Central, and South America, an empire Spain was increasingly incapable of defending. An independent America would be a threat to that empire. And what of the British? If Spain aided the North American rebels, might not London decide to return the compliment by encouraging revolution in Latin America?

So long as Jerónimo, marquis de Grimaldi, remained Spain's foreign minister there was at least a chance that Spain might decide to take the gamble. War became less likely, however, when José de Moñino y Redondo, the conde de Floridablanca took over at the Foreign Ministry. Floridablanca was notorious for his tantrums, his unwillingness to brook contradiction or even to take advice. Yet he was shrewd. Middle class by birth and a lawyer by profession, Floridablanca was a master of duplicity, and in this sense at least a match for his rivals in the other chancellories of Europe.

Floridablanca hoped to subordinate American as well as French interests to those of Spain. His objectives were entirely territorial. Above all he sought the return of Gibraltar. He also had his eyes on Minorca, Jamaica, and the Floridas, then in English hands. (East Florida was bounded on the West by the Apalachacola river. West Florida ran along the Gulf Coast to the Mississippi river. See map, p. 28) Unconvinced that war was the best way to achieve his ends, Floridablanca refused to follow where Vergennes led.

This situation had become all but intolerable to the French foreign minister when he learned in December 1777 that an entire British army had surrendered to the Americans near Saratoga, New York. At last Vergennes had the leverage he needed to convince the king that, Spain or no Spain, the moment was right to strike. To avoid the prying eyes of Lord Stormont's spies, he held a clandestine meeting with Franklin and Deane at an out-of-

General John Burgoyne's surrender of an entire British army to the Americans at Saratoga was not only important militarily; it had significant foreign policy implications as well, for it encouraged the French to intervene in the war.

the-way house on the outskirts of Paris. There he assured the two Americans that an alliance was a certainty. Perhaps hoping that Saratoga had changed minds in Madrid, he also sent a dispatch rider racing to the Spanish capital with a renewed appeal for cooperation. But whether Floridablanca decided to cooperate or not, Vergennes was determined to act. Toward that end he now began to press the king for a Franco-American alliance.

Rocked by the news from Saratoga, London also made certain moves, hoping to arrange a peace settlement with the rebellious colonies on the basis of what amounted to home rule within the empire. An agent of the British secret service, Paul Wentworth, traveled to Paris to discuss peace terms with the Americans there.

Wentworth remained in Paris for more than three weeks. Early in his stay he met twice with Deane. But Franklin at first held aloof. Under the mistaken impression that Vergennes needed more convincing before he would consent to an alliance, the good doctor thought it wise to have a known spy whose mission was well understood at Versailles, and who was being kept under close surveillance, literally panting for an interview.

At length Franklin consented to meet with Wentworth at his suburban home in Passy. But the British agent learned nothing and left unable to say whether Franklin was interested in pursuing negotiations. "I never knew him so eccentric," he explained to his chief, Sir William Eden. Normally the old man was lucid and to the point. On this occasion, however, "he was diffuse and unmethodical."[10] It apparently never occurred to Wentworth that there might be method in Franklin's verbal games.

Franklin's clever attempt at using Wentworth to manipulate Vergennes was wasted effort. France's foreign minister needed no convincing, a fact that became clear when, only a short while after the Wentworth visit, Conrad-Alexandre Gérard came from the French Foreign Ministry to offer aid and a military alliance. While Franklin had been busy with the English, Vergennes had been equally busy with the king. On February 6, 1778, French and American representatives signed treaties of commerce and alliance. The United States had passed a major milestone on the road to independence.

SPAIN AND THE AMERICAN REVOLUTION

Floridablanca, who distrusted and despised his French counterpart, was determined that Spain would fight only as a last resort and only if France was prepared to pay well for Spain's support. Since Vergennes envisioned a short war in which Spanish aid would be of minimal importance, and considering the fact that the Spanish fleet was not ready to put to sea, he was at first unprepared to make the concessions Spain demanded. Inevitably, the negotiations between these erstwhile partners moved slowly.

A year later, by which time Vergennes realized that he needed Spanish help more than he had at first supposed, he made the concessions necessary to bring Spain into the war. The Treaty of Aranjuez, signed on April 12, 1779, committed France to aid in the capture of Gibraltar, the Floridas, and the island of Minorca. In return the Spanish agreed to join in France's war against England. But contrary to Vergennes's hopes, they refused to recognize the United States. In fact, Floridablanca continued his vehement opposition to American independence. He explained to Armand-Marc, comte de Montmorin, the French ambassador in Spain, that the American states ought to continue as weak dependencies of Britain. Such a condition, he thought, would produce continual strife, weakening England while undercutting the possibility that the United States might ever threaten Spain's holdings in the Western Hemisphere.

Vergennes thus got his Spanish alliance, but as a result he found himself in the awkward position of having one ally, Spain, totally opposed to the war aims of the other. Even this was not the worst of it. Floridablanca also insisted that prior to declaring war he be allowed to offer his good offices to London for the purpose of mediating a settlement to the war in North America. In proposing a forced mediation while threatening war with Britain as the alternative, Floridablanca was at his devious best. He realized that the British would reject his proposal. It was designed to be rejected. But why, then, offer mediation in the first place? Spain's foreign minister hoped that the British would be willing to make a counteroffer to keep Spain neutral. And Floridablanca had his price—Gibraltar. Had London been willing to cede "the Rock," Spain would have abandoned France.

Nor did the beginning of actual hostilities between Spain and England alter Floridablanca's purposes. All of Spain's military activities in the Western Hemisphere were calculated to limit the size and power of the United States. Madrid quickly seized the Floridas from Britain and sent expeditions up the Mississippi to lay claim to all the territory west of the great river as well as all the land bounded by the Appalachians on the east and the Ohio River on the north. If an independent United States did emerge as a result of the war, Floridablanca was determined to see to it that the new nation was confined behind the eastern mountains.

Spain's policy toward the United States notwithstanding, Floridablanca viewed John Jay's arrival in Madrid on April 4, 1780, as particularly fortuitous. Jay, a former president of Congress and chief justice of the New York Supreme Court, came seeking recognition, trade, and economic aid. Of course Floridablanca had no interest in offering any of these. But he was at the time engaged in secret talks with Father Thomas Hussey, a huge man with a degree in theology from the University of Seville, the ear of the British government, and an insatiable taste for intrigue. Through Hussey and later Richard Cumberland, who had connections with the British colonial secretary, Lord George Germain, Floridablanca continued his negotiations with London. He still hoped to squeeze Gibraltar and certain lesser territorial concessions from the British in exchange for peace and the promise that France and Spain would impose a settlement on the Americans that would leave them British dependents.

Jay's presence in Madrid during these talks served a useful purpose. He was a living, breathing threat that if London did not make the concessions demanded, Spain would recognize the Americans. These negotiations continued until late August 1780, when Britain finally made it clear that Gibraltar was not on the trading block. A frustrated Floridablanca then warned Hussey and Cumberland against leaving Spain "without settling matters." If they did, he warned, "he would immediately treat with Mr. Jay and acknowledge him."[11] But of course that was one threat the unhappy foreign minister had no intention of carrying out.

For two frustrating, humiliating years John Jay remained in Spain. One of his primary responsibilities was to seek financial support. But an occasional inconsequential loan was all he was able to garner. During this period he was manipulated, seldom treated with respect, and subjected to the incessant demands of various foreign ministry officials that the United States give up its claim to a boundary on the Mississippi. Jay knew that to do so would set back the settlement of the trans-Appalachian West by decades, for, without the river, settlers beyond the mountains would have no means of moving their surplus crops to market. He therefore conceded nothing, telling Don Diego de Gardoqui that "Americans, almost to a man, believe that God Almighty had made that river a highway for the people of the upper country to go to the sea by" and that to be cut off from markets for their surplus products, as well as from access to foreign manufactures "when they daily saw a fine river flowing before their doors," was out of the question.[12]

Jay arrived in Spain suspicious of Spanish as well as French purposes. Fearing he might not be up to dealing with the unscrupulous European statesmen he expected to encounter, he left the country deeply embittered and more suspicious than ever. This frame of mind was by no means the best for one soon to be involved in the delicate process of negotiating a peace treaty with England. A diplomat is wise to be cautious, but Jay crossed the line into near-paranoia with unfortunate results for the United States.

BRITAIN BESIEGED

The year 1780 began on a grim note for the British ministry. The war in America, which the government once hoped to bring to a swift conclusion, had evolved into a major international contest. Meanwhile Ireland, mired in economic crisis, was again in ferment. Treasury Secretary John Robinson urged quick action to alleviate the suffering there before "French money, French emissaries and French supplies of arms and ammunition have time to get there." In Parliament the Whig opposition was demanding not merely a change of cabinet but a change in the very system of government. Charging the king with "a fixed determination to govern this country" through his own personal influence, Whig leaders called for a return to constitutionalism. Some were even so bold as to remind the king of what befell Charles I, the last king to seek too much power.[13]

Britain's head of government, Lord North, longed for retirement. But the king would not hear of it. "If the house falls about my ears," the minister complained, "I cannot help it. All I can do is not to quit a falling house and to use every means in my power to sustain it as long as possible."[14]

Lord North's profound feelings of despair were more completely justified than even he could have imagined at the time. Before the end of the year, the American war expanded to include not only France and Spain but most of the rest of Europe as well. Six other nations joined the Empress Catherine of Russia in the Armed Neutrality of the North, a league of neutral nations committed to the defense of their shipping against British depredations. A seventh nation, the Netherlands, tried to join the league but was forced into the war as a result of Britain's bumbling diplomacy.

The Dutch Republic was not the great power that it had been a century before. The country was divided internally, and its naval power was sadly diminished. One thing had not changed, however. Canny Dutch traders still knew a good thing when they saw one. And so, almost as soon as the American Revolutionary War began, a significant trade grew up between the rebellious colonies and the Netherlands. Vigorous British protests put an end to the direct trade. But substantial quantities of goods destined ultimately for America continued to move between the Netherlands and the tiny, mountainous island of St. Eustatius, a Dutch holding in the Leeward Islands. Orangetown, the largest port on the island, became a major trans-shipment point. There Dutch ships transferred their cargoes to American blockade runners for the last stage of the voyage.

The British put up with this obvious subterfuge until Dutch ships began carrying naval stores—ships' timbers, tar, resin, and the like—from the Baltic states to France. In fact, this trade had no strategic significance since France had large inventories of naval stores on hand as well as easy access to supplies from Italy and elsewhere. Nevertheless, London demanded that the Dutch call a halt.

For a variety of reasons ranging from national pride to French threats and the arcane maneuvers of the country's own diverse political factions, the Dutch refused to give in. At the same time they searched frantically for some way to avoid war and thought for a moment they had found it when they were invited to join the Armed Neutrality. But, for reasons that are by no means clear, this possibility prompted the British to declare war before the Dutch could act. And so a blundering British Foreign Office added another to the growing list of powers arrayed against it. It did so over an issue of no consequence, a trade in naval stores that could have no bearing on the outcome of the war.

Dutch involvement in the war contributed in a curiously convoluted way to the decisive Franco-American victory at Yorktown in 1781. On learning that England and the Netherlands were at war, Admiral Lord George Rodney sailed from North American waters to seize St. Eustatius and close down the illicit trade emanating from that tiny island. While Rodney remained in the West Indies gloating over the shiploads of booty he had taken, a French fleet commanded by Admiral François Joseph Paul de Grasse entered North American waters. When General Sir Henry Clinton commanding British forces in New York learned of the French fleet, he tried to warn Rodney, but the admiral paid no heed. This oversight proved disastrous, for in October, when a combined Franco-American force laid siege to Lord Cornwallis's army near Yorktown, de Grasse's squadron, unchallenged by the Royal Navy, cut off any possibility of evacuation by sea. On October 19, 1781, Cornwallis surrendered.

News of this disaster reached London in late November. King George took the defeat in stride, insisting that England would persevere. But Lord North knew better. According to Lord George Germain and Lord Stormont, who brought the unwelcome news, he reacted as though he had "taken a ball in his chest." Unable to sit or think he strode about repeating over and over again, "Oh God! it is all over!"[15] He was right. The British public, long divided over the war, now demanded peace. Parliament passed resolutions favoring peace, and three weeks later North resigned.

North's resignation left the king with no choice but to ask the Whig opposition, which had long been critical of his American policy, to form a government. Charles Watson-Wentworth, Lord Rockingham, became the new prime minister. But Rockingham was a doddering old man, a

Lord Cornwallis's surrender at Yorktown was the decisive battle of the Revolution. It led
to Lord North's resignation and opened the way for peace negotiations in Paris.

mere figurehead. Real power was shared by Charles James Fox in the
Foreign Office and William Petty, Lord Shelburne, secretary of state for the
colonies.

These developments put the comte de Vergennes in a quandary.
The American aspect of the war seemed about to wind down. But the
fighting continued in Europe, and Spain's objectives, especially Gibraltar,
remained out of reach. Moreover, with negotiations for a North American
settlement in the offing, he had somehow to reconcile America's territorial
ambitions west of the Appalachians with Spanish claims. Frustrated by his
allies' conflicting ambitions, Vergennes also feared that American policy
makers might be considering a separate peace with England. He was especially
suspicious of John Adams, the man Congress had empowered to negotiate
with London.

ADAMS AND VERGENNES

Adams first appeared in Paris in April 1778, sent by Congress to help
negotiate a Franco-American alliance. When he arrived, however, he found
that work already completed. He spent the next several months studying

French, writing friends in America, and trying to be useful while awaiting instructions. Late in the year Congress dissolved the original negotiating commission. Franklin was appointed minister to France; Arthur Lee was transferred to Spain; and Silas Deane returned to the United States.

Adams, who received no new instructions, interpreted Congress's silence as an indication that he either had been or was about to be dismissed. At this point, his pride a ruin, he began to show signs of a near-pathological envy of Franklin. He became obsessively critical of the older man, showering his friends in America with letters attacking Franklin as indolent, incompetent—even immoral. While doing his best to undermine congressional confidence in his colleague, Adams began to suspect that Franklin was responsible for his own humiliation, that Franklin had conspired with Adams's enemies in Congress to have him dismissed. This conviction grew until it became a fixation that Adams carried with him to the grave.

Franklin never appreciated the depth of Adams's hostility. Yet he did sense that something was askew, observing once: "He means well for his country, is always an honest man, often a wise one, but sometimes and in some things, absolutely out of his senses."[16]

Unable to contain his bitterness and unwilling to wait for instructions, Adams returned to the United States. Hardly had he arrived, however, before he discovered that Congress had not forgotten him after all. On the contrary, he had been chosen minister plenipotentiary to negotiate a treaty of peace, a post of transcendent importance.

Adams returned to Paris on February 9, 1780. But his behavior was now dictated by pride, personal ambition, and the paranoid fantasy that if Franklin learned the purpose of his mission he would, out of sheer envy, do all in his power to assure its failure. He therefore refused to tell his colleague the purpose of his mission. Anxious to begin negotiations with the British before Franklin, "the old conjurer," had a chance to undercut him, Adams informed Vergennes of his instructions while at the same time making it obvious that he was in a great hurry to open the talks.[17]

At this time, early in 1780, the war had reached no decisive turning point in America. Moreover, the economic situation there had been steadily deteriorating. Inflation had so undermined the American economy that the national currency was valueless. Why, Vergennes, wondered, should Adams think the moment opportune for negotiations? Unaware that Adams was being moved by the irrational fear of Franklin, the foreign minister searched for and found what appeared to be a rational explanation for Adams's curious behavior. Conrad-Alexandre Gérard, France's first envoy to the United States, had peppered his official correspondence with repeated references to a growing congressional faction that was agitating for a separate peace with Britain on terms short of independence. Though it was utterly absurd, Gérard named Adams as a prominent member of this group. Given this inaccurate bit of information, Vergennes seems to have tentatively concluded that Adams's early interest in opening talks with Britain stemmed from his desire to betray the alliance.

Vergennes's initial suspicions were reinforced because Adams, who was himself suspicious of French purposes, concealed the fact that Congress had instructed him to work closely with the French Foreign Ministry while negotiating with the British. Vergennes, who received an accurate description of Adams's instructions from Gérard, did not believe that Adams's failure to confide in him was merely an oversight. A man with betrayal in his heart would necessarily want to work alone and unobserved.

Nothing that occurred during the several months following Adams's arrival in Paris served to disabuse Vergennes of these opinions. On the contrary, the two men quarreled repeatedly. By the end of July 1780, their relationship had deteriorated so that Vergennes cut Adams off entirely, refusing to have anything further to do with him.

Given this sad history of mutual suspicion and misunderstanding, it is by no means surprising that Vergennes should have tried to neutralize Adams or that he should have instructed his minister in the United States to see what could be done about gaining control over the course and pace of Anglo-American negotiations. It is surprising, however, that Anne César, the chevalier La Luzerne, who had by this time replaced Gérard in America should have been so successful in carrying out these instructions. By distributing favors and in some cases outright bribes to members of Congress, the French envoy was able to bring about some remarkable changes. First, Adams's authority was diluted by making him but one on a commission of five that included Franklin, Jay, South Carolina's Henry Laurens, and Thomas Jefferson. Even more significant, Congress instructed its envoys to confer regularly with the French during the peace talks and to "undertake nothing . . . without their knowledge and concurrence, and ultimately to govern yourselves by their advice and opinion."[18]

Vergennes was, of course, very pleased, for Congress had in effect given him control of the peace talks. The American negotiators, on the other hand, viewed their instructions as a scandalous abdication of responsibility and refused to be bound by them. To a man those who participated in the negotiations consulted Vergennes only when it suited their purposes.

FRANKLIN AND OSWALD

Lord Shelburne, who made American policy for the newly installed Whig ministry in London, hoped initially that the colonists might be willing to agree to a separate peace on the basis of something less than complete independence. He chose Richard Oswald, a retired merchant with relatives and friends in America, to explore these possibilities with the American representatives in Paris. When Oswald arrived in the French capital, only Franklin was there to greet him. John Adams was attending to affairs in the

Netherlands, and none of the other delegates appointed by Congress had as yet arrived.

In these early discussions Franklin made it clear that independence was absolutely essential and that he would not consider negotiating a separate peace with England. So that there would be no misunderstanding on this point, Franklin escorted Oswald to Versailles, where Vergennes himself lectured Britain's discomfited emissary on the subject of treaty obligations.

If Franklin was at the time unwilling to make a separate peace, he was nevertheless at pains to assure Oswald that he did want to negotiate and, his instructions notwithstanding, that he was not prepared to be governed by the views of the comte de Vergennes. During the talks that followed, as the two men set about outlining the basis of a settlement, the good doctor kept the French Foreign Ministry completely in the dark.

Their work finished, Oswald returned to London carrying proposals that Franklin had divided into two categories: those that were essential and those he thought merely desirable. Franklin's minimums included independence, generous boundaries for the United States, and the freedom to fish off Newfoundland's Grand Banks, deemed vital in New England. The desirable points included reparations for damage done by British forces during the fighting, an admission of war guilt as well as an apology from Parliament, freedom for the United States to trade within the British empire, and last but by no means least, the cession of Canada.

Shelburne was disappointed by the outcome of the talks. The illusion that the Americans might be satisfied with a status short of independence had been shattered. He quickly decided, however, that he would have to work for the next best thing, the creation of a cordial relationship with the United States. He was prepared to accept Franklin's essential terms and at that point even ready to agree to a boundary that gave the United States a large part of what is today the Canadian heartland.

There were two reasons for Shelburne's astonishing generosity. First, he hoped to convince England's European enemies to make peace and believed that an American settlement which would free British forces for use elsewhere would provide the leverage he required. Second, he wanted to preserve and build upon the close economic relationship that had existed between Britain and the colonies before the war. A generous peace settlement would lay the foundation for that.

Lord Shelburne, an early convert to Adam Smith's economic theories, believed the conquest of trade and markets rather than control over colonies per se was crucial to a nation's economic strength. The American colonies had been the diadem of England's empire. But England's power developed because it had been able to exploit America's growing economy. Now Shelburne hoped to author a new policy. By establishing a harmonious relationship with an independent United States, England would be able to continue the exploitation of the markets and resources of America. Nor did he believe that a weak and threatened United States would serve British interests best. On the contrary, a policy that encouraged the growth and prosperity of America would also serve British interests, since it would make the American marketplace increasingly valuable.

THE TALKS ON HOLD—JAY'S BLUNDERS

Richard Oswald returned to Paris in May 1782, empowered to make major concessions to the Americans. An agreement might quickly have been arranged but for the misguided intervention of John Jay, who arrived from Spain in time to play a major role in the negotiations.

The two years that Jay spent in Madrid left him psychologically scarred. He had been more than ordinarily suspicious before going to Europe. His Spanish experience sharpened that suspicious turn of mind, especially with regard to America's erstwhile friends. He knew that Floridablanca would never recognize the United States until England did. He was aware, too, that Spain's territorial ambitions ran directly contrary to those of the United States, especially with regard to control of the Mississippi. And because during his long stay in Spain the comte de Montmorin, France's ambassador there, had been no help to him, he concluded that France, too, was hostile to American interests.

Jay found confirmation for these views during the first several months of his stay in Paris. He quickly discovered that Gérard de Rayneval, Vergennes's private secretary, had formed a united front with the Spanish minister in opposing American claims west of the Appalachians. He also came into possession, courtesy of the British, of a memorandum from La Luzerne's secretary, François Barbé-Marbois, who argued that France was under no obligation to support American claims to the Atlantic fisheries, a view later expressed by Rayneval.

Jay was right to be skeptical and on his guard, but he carried his suspicions too far. Vergennes was not so completely antagonistic to American interests as the New Yorker imagined. Vergennes had his own problems, specifically two allies whose war aims were at cross-purposes. He would have been delighted were it possible to arrange a settlement to the western boundary and Mississippi questions satisfactory to both. Nor was Vergennes particularly anxious to see the United States penned in east of mountains. He believed that no matter where the boundary was drawn, so long as England continued to menace the United States from Canada the new nation would have no choice but to remain dependent upon France.

Suspicious of his allies, Jay was equally skeptical when judging British purposes. Even the wording of Richard Oswald's formal commission set his sensitive antennae to vibrating. Oswald was authorized to treat with representatives of the revolted colonies and not with a sovereign government. Jay wanted Oswald's commission changed to reflect his and Franklin's status as representatives of an independent nation, and insisted that the negotiations be halted until Shelburne agreed. Even after learning that Oswald had been instructed to recognize American independence in the first article of the peace treaty, Jay refused to change his opinion.

Franklin disagreed, and the two men looked to Vergennes for guidance. But the French diplomat only fueled Jay's suspicions by urging them to proceed with the talks. When it became clear that Jay was adamant on the subject, Franklin gave way, agreeing to suspend the talks until such time as Shelburne redrafted Oswald's commission.

Jay's insistence on this point was not only pointless but counterproductive. It made no difference that Oswald's commission did not refer to Franklin and Jay as representatives of a sovereign nation. Although he would have disagreed, it is even arguable that in treating with the American envoys Shelburne was de facto recognizing American sovereignty since their instructions identified them as representatives of an independent nation. More to the point, however, true recognition would come only with the signing of a definitive treaty of peace. In insisting on a delay Jay did not hasten that day; he put it off.

After the Paris talks were suspended, diplomatic action shifted to the other side of the English Channel. Early in September Gérard de Rayneval, Vergennes's private secretary, suddenly dropped from sight. Traveling incognito, he crossed the channel, took lodgings in London, and contacted Shelburne. Rayneval's sudden disappearance did not go unnoticed. Jay, for one, quickly learned of his mission and immediately drew the wrong conclusion. He believed that Rayneval had gone to London hoping to convince Shelburne to join France in denying the United States access to Newfoundland's fisheries while limiting the new nation to the land area east of the Appalachians.

In fact, Rayneval and Shelburne spent only a very brief time discussing the American question. Political developments in eastern and central Europe and Vergennes's anxiety to settle the European aspect of the war occupied the two statesmen almost exclusively.

Perhaps if Franklin had been well he might have been able to dissuade Jay from what he did next. But the old man had fallen seriously ill. Jay was on his own and more suspicious of French purposes than ever.

Fearing betrayal, Jay sent an English friend, Benjamin Vaughan, as his emissary to London. Through Vaughan, Jay informed Shelburne that the prompt recognition of American independence was essential, that he viewed it as "the touchstone of British sincerity."[19] He also wanted Shelburne to understand that he was prepared to negotiate a separate peace, abandoning American commitments to the French in return for a favorable agreement.

Again Jay had allowed his suspicions to get the better of his good judgment. By revealing that he was ready to abandon the French alliance he provided Shelburne with information that could have been used to destroy French confidence in the United States, fragment the alliance, and undermine the American bargaining position at the coming peace talks. Only the fact that Shelburne was not the duplicitous trickster Jay imagined him to be saved the American from what was, in fact, a foolish and potentially disastrous move.

THE PEACE OF PARIS

On September 27, 1782, Oswald received new instructions authorizing him "to treat with the Commissioners appointed by the Colonies, under the title of Thirteen United States." For some curious reason that satisfied Jay— curious because, as Shelburne saw it, the instructions did not constitute "a final acknowledgement of Independence" but only gave "them during the negotiation the title which they wished to assume."[20] Recognition would come as Shelburne had always intended in the first article of the treaty.

In October the Paris talks reconvened, this time with an enlarged cast of characters. Jay and Franklin were joined by John Adams fresh from a successful negotiation in the Netherlands. In November, Henry Laurens also belatedly appeared. More had changed than the personnel of the American delegation, however. Shelburne had originally been willing to offer the Americans extremely generous boundaries including most of the Canadian heartland, excluding only the Province of Quebec. But during the many weeks that the negotiations were delayed because of Jay's quibble over Oswald's instructions, the situation in London changed. The Franco-Spanish siege of Gibraltar was raised and the British garrison there resupplied and reinforced. This victory gave the war faction in Parliament renewed strength, while weakening the government. As a result, Shelburne was able to make fewer concessions than he had at first planned. He sharply reduced the amount of territory he would cede to the Americans. He also sent Henry Strachey, an experienced undersecretary in the Colonial Office, to join Oswald. Strachey's job was to toughen Britain's negotiating posture and come away with a treaty Shelburne could sell to a Parliament that was showing increasing signs of discontent with his conciliatory approach toward the Americans.

Jay, Adams, and Franklin (who had by this time recovered from his illness) agreed that during this last, crucial stage of the peace negotiations they would neither consult with nor be governed by the judgments of the comte de Vergennes. Having decided to violate their instructions in this regard, they also at least tacitly agreed that the treaty of alliance, which bound the United States to make no separate peace, might also have to be circumvented. Expedience in the service of the national interest was clearly the order of the day.

The talks themselves moved rapidly ahead, and on November 30, 1782, the English and American delegates, meeting in Oswald's Paris apartment, signed a "provisional" treaty of peace. While the final treaty officially ending French as well as American participation in the war was not signed until the following year, the provisional agreement of 1782 laid out the terms of the settlement, ended the fighting in North America, and freed British forces for use elsewhere. Only in the most narrow and legalistic sense, then, can it be said that the United States lived up to its commitments to France.

The treaty itself was quite favorable to American interests. Although Shelburne finally decided to hold all of Canada above the Great Lakes, he surrendered the area between the lakes and the Ohio River to the United States and agreed to a Mississippi boundary in the west. The two parties entered into a secret agreement on the southern boundary. Should Spain hold the Floridas after the European aspect of the war was ended, the boundary would be drawn along the thirty-first parallel. But if England reclaimed the Floridas the boundary would be moved north to a line set at thirty-two degrees, twenty-eight minutes. New England's fishing privileges were also secured, although the right to cure fish on Newfoundland shores was lost.

Of course the American delegates made certain concessions as well. Article 4 of the treaty stipulated that British creditors should not be prohibited from bringing court action in the United States to collect debts incurred by Americans prior to the war. It was also agreed that Congress would "recommend" to the states that property seized from loyalists during the Revolution be restored.

When Benjamin Franklin informed Vergennes that the negotiations had been completed and a provisional treaty signed, the foreign minister showed real annoyance. Unimpressed by the "provisional" character of the November accord, he charged that the Americans had not only violated their instructions by not consulting him during the talks but had also disregarded their obligations to France by making what amounted to a separate peace. Yet Vergennes understood how the great game of dynastic diplomacy was played; and if the Americans had shown themselves to be fast learners, he couldn't complain, especially considering the scale of the American success. "You will notice," he wrote in great surprise, "that the English buy the peace more than they make it. Their concessions in fact as much to the boundaries as to the fisheries and the loyalists, exceed all that I should have thought possible."[21]

In fact, Vergennes had little reason to complain. Though the war had gone on longer than he had originally hoped, he had achieved his fundamental purpose—the destruction of Britain's North American empire. Moreover, by abandoning the alliance in favor of a separate peace, the Americans offered him an opportunity to abandon his own commitments to Spain. The siege of Gibraltar had failed. With America out of the war, England would be able to concentrate her forces in Europe. Under these circumstances taking "the Rock" was out of the question. Vergennes could back gracefully out of his commitments to Floridablanca by claiming that France had been betrayed by the Americans. Spain would have to settle for lesser prizes.

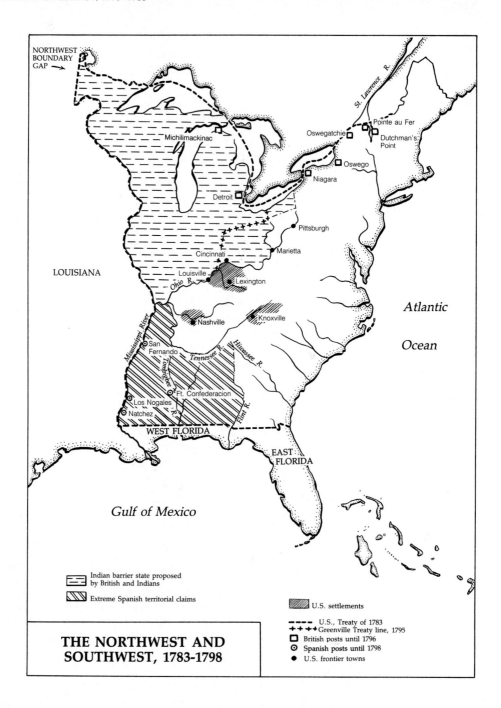

NORTHWEST
BOUNDARY
GAP

St. Lawrence R.

Michilimackinac

Pointe au Fer

Oswegatchie

Dutchman's
Point

Oswego

Detroit

Niagara

Pittsburgh

Cincinnati

Marietta

LOUISIANA

Louisville

Lexington

Ohio R.

Nashville

Knoxville

Atlantic

Ocean

Mississippi River

San
Fernando

Tombigbee R.

Tennessee R.

Hiwassee R.

Ft. Confederacion

Flint R.

Los Nogales

Natchez

WEST FLORIDA

EAST
FLORIDA

Gulf of Mexico

Indian barrier state proposed
by British and Indians

Extreme Spanish territorial claims

U.S. settlements

- - - - U.S., Treaty of 1783
+ + + + Greenville Treaty line, 1795
□ British posts until 1796
⊙ Spanish posts until 1798
● U.S. frontier towns

THE NORTHWEST AND
SOUTHWEST, 1783-1798

ENDNOTES

1. Richard Henry Lee, quoted in *The Journals of the Continental Congress, 1774–1789,* eds. Worthington Chauncey Ford, et al. (Washington, D.C., 1904–1937), V, p. 21.

2. *The Winthrop Papers* (Massachusetts Historical Society, Boston, 1929–1947, 5 vols), I, p. 295.

3. John Dickinson, quoted in Bernard Bailyn, *The Ideological Origins of the American Revolution* (Harvard University Press, Cambridge, Mass.,1967), pp. 89–91; Thomas Jefferson to James Monroe June 17, 1785, *The Writings of Thomas Jefferson,* ed. A.E. Bergh (Monticello ed., Washington D.C., 1904), V, p. 21.

4. Thomas Paine, *Common Sense,* quoted in Felix Gilbert, *The Beginnings of American Foreign Policy* (Princeton University Press, Princeton N.J., 1962), p. 43; *The Diary and Autobiography of John Adams,* ed. Lyman H. Butterfield (Belknap Press of Harvard University Press, Cambridge, Mass., 1962), III, pt.1, p. 329.

5. John Adams to John Jay, December 6, 1785, in *The Works of John Adams,* ed. Charles Francis Adams (Little, Brown and Co., Boston, 1850–56), VIII, pp. 356–357; Thomas Paine, *Common Sense,* in *Tracts of the American Revolution* ed. Merrill Jensen (Bobbs-Merrill and Co., Indianapolis, Ind., 1967), p. 423.

6. Benjamin Franklin, quoted in Samuel Flagg Bemis, *The Diplomacy of the American Revolution* (University of Indiana Press, Bloomington, Ind., 1957), p. 114n.

7. Pontleroy, quoted in Richard W. Van Alstyne, *Empire and Independence: The International History of the American Revolution* (John Wiley & Co., N.Y., 1965), p. 51.

8. Achard de Bonvouloir, quoted in *The Revolutionary Diplomatic Correspondence of the United States,* ed. Francis Wharton (Washington, D.C., 1889), II, p. 21.

9. Vergennes memorandum, quoted in Bemis, *Diplomacy of the Revolution,* p. 16.

10. Paul Wentworth, quoted in Carl Van Doren, *Benjamin Franklin* (The Viking Press, N.Y., 1938), p. 592.

11. Floridablanca, quoted in Richard B. Morris, *The Peacemakers, The Great Powers and American Independence* (Harper & Row, N.Y., 1965), p. 61.

12. John Jay, quoted in *ibid.,* p. 232.

13. John Robinson, quoted in *ibid.,* p. 70; Lord Rockingham, quoted in *ibid.,* p. 71.

14. Lord North, quoted in *ibid.,* p. 68.

15. Lord North, quoted in *ibid.,* p. 251.

16. Franklin, quoted in Van Doren, *Franklin,* p. 694.

17. Adams, quoted in Morris, *The Peacemakers,* p. 264; see also James H. Hutson, *John Adams and the Diplomacy of the American Revolution* (University of Kentucky Press, Lexington, Ky., 1980), p. 56.

18. Instructions, quoted in Bemis, *Diplomacy of the Revolution,* pp. 189–90.

19. John Jay, quoted in Morris, *The Peacemakers,* p. 333.

20. Lord Shelburne, quoted in Jonathan R. Dull, *A Diplomatic History of the American Revolution* (Yale University Press, New Haven, Conn., 1985), p. 148; Morris, *Peacemakers,* pp. 342–43.

21. Vergennes, quoted in *Revolutionary Diplomatic Correspondence,* Wharton ed., VI, p. 107.

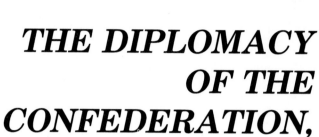

2

THE DIPLOMACY OF THE CONFEDERATION, 1783–1789

As the secretary for foreign affairs during the Confederation period, John Jay made a major contribution to the movement for a new stronger national government with the power to protect and defend America's international interests.

During the Revolution, American policy makers won a greater foreign policy victory than perhaps they deserved. It remained to be seen, however, whether in the postwar era other successes would follow. Certainly the decentralized form of government they created was poorly suited to the conduct of an effective foreign policy.

The Articles of Confederation government had no executive or judicial branches, only a Congress. And while in theory Congress had many rights and responsibilities, it lacked the power to tax, to regulate commerce, and most of all to coerce. Some curious foreign policy anomalies resulted. For example, although Congress had the authority to raise and maintain military and naval forces, it could do so only if the states voluntarily contributed funds for that purpose. In practice, then, the United States could not support its policies or even defend its interests when force was required since the states were seldom in a cooperative mood. Congress also had the authority to negotiate treaties with foreign nations but could not require the states to abide by these agreements. And since Congress lacked the power both to tax and to regulate commerce, it could not retaliate against nations that practiced various forms of economic discrimination against the United States.

This curious system of government was the result of an attempt to avoid the danger to liberty posed by a too-powerful central authority. Having freed themselves from king and Parliament, America's leaders had no intention of establishing the institutional basis for a new homegrown form of tyranny. Unhappily, in their enthusiasm for decentralization they created a government that was incapable of protecting America's vital interests.

For eight long years Americans had been forced to substitute primitive domestic products for the more sophisticated goods of European origin that they had long been accustomed to. At war's end American merchants rushed to meet the pent-up demand. They rushed, ironically, back to England because American consumers preferred British manufactures and because British merchants alone were willing to extend the long-term credit Americans required. The increased demand for British goods was so overwhelming that it soon outstripped available supplies. Complained one British merchant; "Tradesmen and manufacturers are so glutted with orders . . . they must at this present moment be courted instead of commanded to obtain anything out of their hands."[1]

During the colonial period Americans had suffered from a consistently unfavorable balance of trade, importing more than they exported while financing the difference on credit. Following the Revolution, that trade imbalance quickly reappeared. Thus, between 1784 and 1786 Americans imported British goods valued at £ 7,591,935 while exporting to England products valued at only £ 2,486,058. The difference was financed on credit or paid for in specie. But credit had its limits, and payment in cash couldn't go on forever. It wasn't long, therefore, before the American economy began suffering from a serious shortage of specie. As the money supply dried up, debtors found it increasingly difficult to meet old obligations. Credit was soon exhausted, and a wave of bankruptcies swept the Atlantic seaboard. The new nation found itself in the grip of an economic depression. "The scarcity of money in consequence of our excessive importation of British frippery," the Massachusetts businessman Elbridge Gerry complained, "has occasioned stagnation of trade."[2] Gerry was only partially correct. The depression had many causes. But at the time Americans focused on two interconnected explanations: British exploitation of the American marketplace and a discriminatory British trade policy that proved extremely damaging to America's export trade.

Lord Shelburne had intended to negotiate a liberal commercial agreement that would have allowed the United States wide latitude for trade within the British empire while at the same time strengthening Britain's grip on the expanding North American market. Such an accord, Shelburne believed, would not only be economically beneficial to Britain; it would draw the United States and Britain together while driving a wedge between France and America. But Shelburne's free trade policies, years ahead of their time, ran into stiff opposition from shipowners, merchants, and certain Canadian producers who were determined to preserve a closed imperial system that called for the aggressive pursuit of foreign markets, state subsidies for domestic industries, and high tariffs to protect the home market from foreign competition.

Among the most persuasive defenders of this old mercantilist order was John Baker Holroyd, the earl of Sheffield. In his *Observations on the Commerce of the American States* (1783), Sheffield pointed out that Britain had no reason to make any trade concessions to the United States. The Americans had fought to get out of the British empire, he argued, now let them suffer the consequences of lost markets and economic dislocation. The plain truth was that Britain could discriminate against American products and shipping while at the same time dominating the American market. Britain could do this, he explained, because the Americans needed credit that only English merchants were willing to provide, because the Articles of Confederation government lacked the means of retaliating against British trade restrictions no matter how draconian, and because the individual American states lacked the will to cooperate in a coherent policy of economic retaliation. And Sheffield was right. So long as the United States could not retaliate, Britain had nothing to fear.

By the time a bill to authorize the negotiation of a liberal trade agreement with America came before Parliament, the debate was all but over. Shelburne had been driven from office, and few in Parliament were willing to defend his liberal economic ideas.

MERCANTILISM TRIUMPHANT

Reacting to the demands of economic traditionalists, the House of Commons buried Shelburne's trade bill in committee. Parliament then enacted legislation restricting American access to British markets. Canada, the Northern Provinces, and the West Indies were closed to American ships. American salted meat and fish were excluded from the West Indies, formerly a major market. American-built ships were banned from the British merchant marine, while American fish and whale oil were denied former markets in the British Isles. In addition, American ships were prohibited from carrying any manufactured goods or reexports to British ports.

British policy worked just as Lord Sheffield said it would. England's merchants sold freely in the American market while its ships dominated the American carrying trade. Pierse Long, a New Hampshire merchant and shipowner visiting New York in 1785, was struck by the extent of British domination. "It is amazing to see the quantity of vessels . . . from all parts of England now in this Harbour carrying goods to market." "I hope very soon," he continued, "there will be an end put to so diabolical a trade."[3]

Every section of the country suffered as a result of Britain's discriminatory trade practices. In New England the shipbuilding industry languished because American ships had only restricted access to British ports and because the British market for American-built ships had disappeared. The whaling industry, denied its principal prewar market in the British Isles, suffered a similar fate. The loss of markets in the West Indies, Canada, and the Northern Provinces was a disastrous blow to the fishing industry as well. It is true that French holdings in the Caribbean were opened to American fish at this time; but an oversupply of fish drove prices down so that merchants "suffered great losses upon all they shipped thither, and the fishery exhibited . . . extreme symptoms of decline." The Revolution, James Madison complained, "has robbed us of our trade with the West Indies, the only one which yielded us a favorable balance, without reopening any other channels to compensate for it."[4]

The Middle States were also hard hit, and for the same reason; British policy denied them access to their traditional markets. Surpluses of corn and other grains as well as pork and beef soon developed, driving domestic prices down. At Philadelphia, for example, the price of Indian corn declined by almost 50 percent between the summer of 1783 and early 1785, while the price of flour fell by more than a third. Dried meats fared no better. "Pork is not likely to be wanted," one merchant lamented, while "beef is a perfect glut."[5]

Bad though the situation was in New England and the Middle States, the South was even more seriously affected. After the war British shippers quickly came to dominate the carrying trade in southern staples. Freight rates soared, often reaching 14 percent of the value of the cargo. At the same time southern planters, desperate for capital, borrowed heavily from British lenders at high interest rates. Finally, British manufactured goods— often the only sort available—sold at premium prices.

At the same time London took steps to shrink the British market for southern staples. A stiff tax on tobacco resulted in a dramatic reduction in British tobacco imports. Rice, a major export of Georgia and South Carolina in prewar times, suffered a similar fate after the Parliament saddled it with a high, restrictive duty. Indigo, another important prewar export, also went into decline. And North Carolina's naval stores, once supported by a Crown subsidy, lost the British market entirely.

Southerners were caught in an economic vice. Increased costs, shrunken markets, and declining income left them only one option—to go further into debt. And they did. The South's foreign debt, owed almost exclusively to British creditors, stood at approximately £ 2 million in 1783 but soared over the next few years. William Kilty, a Maryland observer, realized that there were many reasons for economic hard times in the South. But he also believed that southerners were the special victims of "old British debts, now pressing on them with an interest nearly equal to the principal, and the addition of new ones which have been, through necessity contracted."[6]

A number of states attempted to retaliate against Britain's discriminatory trade practices. But these measures proved ineffective primarily because they did not apply uniformly in all the states. It was then relatively simple for British merchants to focus their business in those states that, anxious for the trade, refused to join in policies of economic retaliation. Britain's *Gentleman's Magazine* laughed:

> By the latest letters from the American States, the restraint laid upon their trade with the British West India islands has thrown them into the utmost perplexity; and by way of retaliation they are passing laws inimical to their own interest; and what is still worse, inconsistent with each other. . . . Hence the dissentions that universally prevail throughout what may be called the thirteen Dis-United States.[7]

Differences over the Anglo-American economic relationship were complemented during the Confederation period by growing political problems stemming from the failure of both England and the United States to live up to the terms of the Treaty of Paris. Undoubtedly the most serious breach of the agreement was Britain's refusal to surrender seven strategically located frontier military and trading posts along the Great Lakes on the American side of the Canadian border. The decision to retain these posts was based on two considerations. First, the Hudson's Bay Company had for some time conducted a valuable fur trade with the Indians of the Old Northwest from these posts. Their loss would have cut British fur traders off from some of their most important connections. Company leaders therefore urged the ministry to hold the posts at least for a time so that they might make the necessary adjustments.

A far more important reason for London's unwillingness to evacuate the posts had to do with Indian relations. Under the terms of the 1768 Treaty of Fort Stanwix, Britain recognized the right of the northwestern tribes to control the area north of the Ohio River and west of the mountains. When the Revolution erupted, the British urged these same tribes to join in the war against the Americans. The Indians were only too happy to oblige because even then Americans were spilling over the mountains in unwanted numbers. Then, in 1783 England made peace and transferred sovereignty over the Ohio Valley to the United States. But the Indians, who had not made peace, continued to oppose American encroachment. Had the British turned the posts over to the Americans, the Indians would no doubt have considered this transfer a betrayal and would probably have retaliated against British settlements in Canada. "I do from my soul pity these poor people," wrote General Allan Maclean, who commanded at Fort Niagara. He added, "Should they commit outrages at giving up the posts it would not surprise me."[8] For these reasons then, even before the peace treaty went into effect the British government had decided it must find a pretext for holding the posts even though they were clearly in American territory.

As economic and political problems between the United States and Britain multiplied, the importance of opening a dialogue with London became increasingly obvious to American policy makers. At length, in 1785 John Adams, who had lobbied incessantly for the appointment, was sent as America's first minister to the Court of St. James's. It was a triumphal moment for the former provincial attorney, the fulfillment of a driving ambition. But if Adams derived great personal satisfaction from the appointment, his diplomatic efforts proved fruitless.

Even before Adams arrived, ominous portents of rough sledding ahead appeared in the British press. Thus the London *Public Advertiser* cried:

> An Ambassador from America! Good Heavens what a sound—The Gazette surely never announced anything so extraordinary before. . . . This will be such a phenomenon in the Corps Diplomatique that 'tis hard to say which can excite indignation most, the insolence of those who appoint the character, or the meanness of those who receive it.[9]

Adams, who had probably never before been referred to as "it," could hardly have been encouraged by the *Advertiser*'s snide commentary.

On arriving in London, Adams was received in his official capacity, presented to the king, and granted regular access to the foreign secretary, Francis Godolphin, Lord Carmarthen. But Adams was at the same time swiftly disabused of the idea that he might bring about a change in British policy. London's grip on the Northwest posts appeared unshakable. Nor would the foreign secretary consider opening British markets more widely. The British were happy with things as they were. Nothing Adams could do or say shook their resolve. They were calling the shots, and they knew it.

The British were practicing traditional mercantilism, protecting their industries and their markets from foreign competition, selling as much as possible abroad, and importing only what they couldn't produce for themselves. But Adams thought there was more to it than that. Always somewhat paranoid when operating in Europe's diplomatic milieu, he had not been in London long before he concluded that England was prosecuting a carefully orchestrated commercial war designed to "destroy America's maritime industries, discourage the growth of her manufactures, and leave her only the production of agricultural staples." He thought Britain's plan was to transform America into an economic colony to be "fleeced . . . by rapacious foreign factors." It was, he thought, time to be realistic, to fight fire with fire. The states would have to band together matching restriction with restriction, until the British decided to be reasonable. "I would not advise to this commercial struggle," Adams wrote, "if I could see a prospect of justice without it, but I do not. Every appearance is to the contrary."[10]

SPAIN AND THE AMERICAN WEST

Frustrated at their inability to deal with the British challenge, American diplomats of the Confederation period had no more success resolving their difficulties with the Spanish. One of the conde de Floridablanca's principal objectives during the war had been to limit American expansion that otherwise might threaten Spain's weakly defended and sparsely populated North American frontier. The Anglo-American peace treaty, with its recognition of generous boundaries for the United States, was then a serious setback to Spain.

At war's end Floridablanca confronted a potentially aggressive though internally divided neighbor claiming the right to navigate the Mississippi and insisting on a southern border with Spanish Florida at the 31st degree, far to the south of the line claimed by Madrid. Making matters worse, thousands of American settlers were already living in Kentucky and Tennessee, with more pouring through the Cumberland Gap every day. In an effort to stem the flow and reduce the pressure on Spain's holdings, Madrid, claiming the sole right to navigate the Mississippi where it flowed between Spanish banks, closed the river to American traffic. It was a dangerous, not to say provocative move, for it meant that settlers in Kentucky and Tennessee, who counted on the river to move their crops to market, would be cut off and forced either to move their goods over the mountains—an arduous task—or to live a primitive self-sufficient existence.

No one was more aware of the danger that frustrated settlers might mount some sort of filibustering expedition against New Orleans than the governor of Spanish Louisiana, Esteban Miró. Therefore, when the opportunity presented itself, he agreed to an informal alliance with the Creek Indian nation, led at the time by the brilliant Alexander McGillivray. The Choctaw and Chickasaw tribes soon joined in what became a formidable *entente*. Working through Panton-Leslie and Company, a British trading company located in East Florida, Miró supported Indian resistance to American encroachment in the Southwest.

Meanwhile, Floridablanca sought security through direct talks. He sent Don Diego de Gardoqui to New York for discussions with John Jay, secretary for foreign affairs for the Confederation Congress. Gardoqui came empowered to negotiate a reciprocal trade treaty, concede a boundary between the United States and Spanish Florida at the 31st degree, and offer naval protection for American ships trading in the Mediterranean, where they were subject to harassment by the corsairs of the Barbary states. In return the United States would have to surrender the right to navigate the Mississippi. This requirement was a major barrier to any sort of agreement, since Congress had instructed Jay not to cede the navigation rights on the river under any circumstances.

As the talks progressed and Gardoqui unveiled one concession after another, Jay became convinced that some sort of compromise on the Mississippi question was in order. With the country in the grip of a depression and desperately searching for markets to replace those denied them by the British, the commercial concessions offered by the Spanish were very appealing. But Jay was not motivated by commercial considerations alone. He thought it unlikely that Madrid could long resist the pressure brought against Spanish North America by a growing American population in the West. In the long run it seemed certain that the United States would gain control of the Mississippi.

But what of the short term? In a sense Jay believed it was immaterial whether the United States actually had a right to navigate the river, since Congress was in no position to enforce that right and the Spanish were unprepared to concede the point unless forced to do so. "Why," Jay wondered, "should we not (for a valuable consideration too) consent to forbear to use what we know is not in our power to use?"[11] It seemed reasonable to strike a bargain. Unprepared to abandon the American claim to the right of navigation, Jay was nevertheless ready to agree to forgo the exercise of that right for a period of twenty-five years. Spain would gain something in the near term but would in the process be required to admit the legitimacy of the American position.

When Jay asked Congress to allow him to negotiate the agreement he thought was obtainable, seven eastern states, attracted by the possibilities opened by the trade agreement, voted for the change. But five southern states, more directly interested in the settlement of Kentucky and Tennessee, voted no. Since nine states were needed for approval, the proposal was defeated.

The abortive Jay-Gardoqui agreement set off a storm of angry protest throughout the South and West that demonstrated just how fragile the union of states actually was at this time. Virginia's James Monroe, a delegate to Congress who had invested heavily in southwestern lands, denounced Jay as the leader of an eastern conspiracy intent on destroying the settlements in the Southwest and thus eliminating the possibility of new states being created there. This plan, he charged, would keep "the States southward as they now are," a minority section. "In short," he concluded, "it is a system of policy which has for its object the keeping the weight of gov't. & population in this quarter [the Northeast] & is prepared by a set of men so flagitious, unprincipled & determined in their pursuits, as to satisfy me beyond a doubt they have extended their views to the dismemberment of the gov't." Governor Patrick Henry of Virginia, who also held southwestern lands, was equally outraged and is said to have remarked that he would "rather part with the Confederation than relinquish the navigation of the Mississippi." Western sentiment was equally unrestrained. "To sell us, and make us vassals of the merciless Spaniards, is a grievance not to be borne," cried one protester.[12] Committees of correspondence sprung up throughout the West. Soon a full-fledged separatist movement was under way in Kentucky and Tennessee.

Here was a situation ready-made for the conspiratorial talents of one of the great scoundrels of early American history, General James Wilkinson. In 1787, while his co-conspirators kept the separatist movement simmering in Kentucky, Wilkinson journeyed to New Orleans, where he conferred with Governor Miró. The general, who was good at this sort of thing, filled Miró's head with visions of a separate western republic under the protection of Spain—a dependent, nonthreatening satellite. All Miró had to do to, Wilkinson explained, was to grant him and a select group of his friends the right to ship goods down the river. They would do the rest. Delighted, Miró agreed to place Wilkinson's plan before the king. Meanwhile he had Wilkinson swear an oath of allegiance to Spain—a curious rite since the general was loyal only to himself—and authorized him to ship $30,000 in goods downriver annually. The enthusiastic Miró had in effect given Wilkinson and his friends a limited monopoly on trade down the Mississippi.

This negotiation, as things turned out, was the high point of Wilkinson's conspiracy. In 1788, at a convention called to protest Virginia's refusal to grant Kentucky separate statehood, the pleas of Wilkinson and other separatists fell on deaf ears. And in 1789, while in New Orleans, the general learned that the Spanish government was not interested in his plot. Instead, Madrid tried to ease the pressure by opening the river to Americans willing to pay a 15 percent duty on goods shipped to New Orleans. Finally, on returning to Kentucky later that year, Wilkinson found area leaders busy drafting the state constitution under which Kentucky would join the Union three years later. Wilkinson's separatist movement died aborning. But as the Confederation era wound toward its conclusion, Spanish-American relations remained, as before, in a sad state of disarray.

FRANCE AND THE BARBARY STATES

Not even the relationship with France, the wartime ally, developed as many Americans had hoped. The two nations had no political difficulties, but the substantial economic relationship that some had counted upon to make up for lost markets inside the British empire failed to materialize. This failure resulted in part from an American predilection for British goods as well as a dependency on British credit. But it was also a result of French trade policy. When Thomas Jefferson took over for Benjamin Franklin as the American minister to France, he discovered that despite the Alliance of 1778, trade still took place within a tangled thicket of mercantilist restrictions damaging to American interests. French monopolistic practices in the tobacco business alone, Jefferson charged, cost Virginia and Maryland growers upward of £ 400,000 annually. Nor would the French open their West Indian holdings to American trade save on a restricted basis. Thus no American ships with a cargo capacity of more than sixty tons could trade in the islands. American salted fish, a staple of the slaves' diet, was subjected to a heavy duty. And trade in salt pork and breadstuffs was carried on under temporary laws subject to repeal on short notice. While the restrictions placed on American trade by France were less burdensome than those imposed by England, the difference was more a matter of degree than of substance. France, a mercantilist state, continued monopolistic and protectionist practices that, for the most part, left the United States on the outside looking in.

If it was difficult for Americans to accept economic victimization at the hands of Europe's great powers, it was even more trying, not to say humiliating, to be driven entirely out of the lucrative Mediterranean trade by a gang of cutthroats. Yet that is precisely what happened. The Barbary states of Algiers, Morocco, Tripoli, and Tunis had for years demanded and received what amounted to "protection money" from other nations who paid for the privilege of doing business in the Mediterranean. Those who refused to pay had their merchant ships attacked by the swift galleys of the Moorish states. Seamen were enslaved and held for ransom; ships and cargoes were taken.

Before the Revolution, American vessels had been safe, protected by the Union Jack. But after independence sailing the Mediterranean proved too dangerous. Trade there never resumed after the war. Without the financial resources to buy off the Barbary pirates, and lacking naval power to protect American shipping, the Confederation government had no choice but to swallow still another indignity.

A NEW CONSTITUTION

The system of government created under the Articles of Confederation was not responsible for the many foreign problems faced by the republic. But its inadequacies made it next to impossible for policy makers to react effectively. It is no wonder, then, that the Confederation government quickly came under attack. As early as 1783 Alexander Hamilton warned General George Washington that only the creation of a strong central government could "prevent our being a ball in the hands of European powers, bandied against each other at their pleasure."[13]

At first Hamilton, New York's Robert Morris, and a few other conservative nationalists stood virtually alone. But in time others joined a growing chorus of criticism. Thus John Adams, once a strong advocate of decentralization, turned completely about. From London, where he had learned at firsthand that the British would respond only to overt pressure, he made it clear that it was up to "the States to determine whether there is or is not a union in America." Unity, he argued, would bring "respect"; without it "they will be little regarded." Even Thomas Jefferson, whose stand on states rights made him the best-known advocate of decentralization during a later era, attacked the Articles as too much of a good thing. He deplored that "pride of independence" which had taken "deep and dangerous hold on the hearts of individual states." Greater unity was essential. Otherwise, he predicted, the nation would collapse of its own weight. Civil war would result, with the contending states calling on Britain and France for aid. The final cost, he feared, would be American independence.[14]

The United States Constitution, which became the law of the land in 1788, was intended to remedy foreign policy and other defects of the older system. Now the federal government alone, not the states, could regulate trade. This power over trade, combined with the newly acquired taxing power, enabled the new government to retaliate against nations imposing unfair trade restrictions on the United States. Again, because it had the taxing power, Congress could in fact raise and support military and naval forces for the advancement of American rights and interests. Finally, the national government had the right to make treaties that, as the nation's highest law, could not be violated by the states. The national government created under the new Constitution would have power. But how that power was to be used soon produced sharp disagreement in the United States.

ENDNOTES

1. Quoted in James B. Hedges, *The Browns of Providence Plantations: Colonial Years* (Harvard University Press, Cambridge, Mass., 1952), pp. 92–93.
2. Elbridge Gerry, quoted in Curtis Nettles, *The Emergence of a National Economy* (Harper and Row, N.Y., 1962), p. 61.
3. Pierse Long, quoted in Paul A. Varg, *The Foreign Policy of the Founding Fathers* (Michigan State University Press, East Lansing, Mich., 1963), p. 52.
4. James Madison, quoted in Nettles, *The Emergence of a National Economy*, p. 56.
5. A Philadelphia merchant, quoted in *ibid.*, p. 55.
6. William Kilty, quoted in Varg, *The Foreign Policy of the Founding Fathers*, p. 57.
7. *Gentleman's Magazine*, quoted in Frederick W. Marks III, *Independence on Trial: Foreign Affairs and the Making of the Constitution*, (Scholarly Resources, Inc., Wilmington, Del., 1986), p. 83.
8. General Allan Maclean, quoted in Samuel Flagg Bemis, *Jay's Treaty: A Study in Commerce and Diplomacy* (Yale University Press, New Haven, Conn., 1962), p. 8n.
9. *Public Advertiser*, quoted in Gilbert Chinard, *Honest John Adams* (Little, Brown and Co., N.Y., 1964), p. 195.
10. Adams to Jay, August 6, 1785, *The Works of John Adams* ed., Charles Francis Adams (Little, Brown and Co., Boston, 1850–1856), VIII, pp. 289–91.
11. John Jay, quoted in Frank Monaghan, *John Jay, Defender of Liberty* (Bobbs-Merrill and Co., Indianapolis, Ind., and N.Y., 1935), p. 259.
12. Patrick Henry, quoted in Andrew C. McLaughlin, *The Confederation and the Constitution* (Harper and Bros., N.Y., 1905), pp. 99–100; James Monroe to Patrick Henry, August 12, 1786, *The Writings of James Monroe*, ed. Stanislaus Murray Hamilton (G. P. Putnam's Sons, N.Y., 1898–1903), I, p. 150.
13. Alexander Hamilton, quoted in Varg, *The Foreign Policy of the Founding Fathers*, p. 47.
14. Jefferson and Adams, quoted in *ibid.*

As secretary of the treasury in George Washington's government, Alexander Hamilton interfered constantly in the management of America's foreign relations.

3

NEW GOVERNMENT, NEW PROBLEMS, 1789–1796

April 30, 1789, dawned cloudy in New York City; there was a chill in the morning air. But minor inconveniences failed to dampen the enthusiasm of the crowd that had gathered outside the house where George Washington was spending the night. It was a historic occasion. Later that day the general would take the oath of office as the nation's first president.

Washington and his personal secretary, Tobias Lear, rose early that morning to prepare for the remarkable day that lay ahead. The general's hair was carefully powered. He dressed in a new brown broadcloth suit, white silk stockings, and shoes adorned with silver buckles. From his waist hung a fine ceremonial sword.

Shortly after noon Washington emerged from the house and climbed into a waiting coach. In only a few minutes he was in front of Federal Hall, once the home of the Confederation Congress. He stepped from the coach and moved quickly through the large crowd of enthusiastic onlookers. On a second story balcony waited New York's Chancellor Robert R. Livingston who, after administering the oath of office, turned to the crowd and cried out "Long live George Washington, President of the United States." The people cheered and shouted; some even cried. The cannon on the Battery fired a salute that was returned by a Spanish warship anchored in the harbor.[1]

The idol of the people and certainly the hero of the moment, Washington could do no wrong. France's minister, Éléanor-François Élie, the comte de Moustier, thought that "never has sovereign reigned more completely in the hearts of his subjects than did Washington in those of his fellow citizens." And so it may have seemed even to the president on that extraordinary day. But if so, the feeling lingered for only a little while. Washington had seen public opinion shift too often during the Revolution to place much reliance on the lasting power of his personal popularity. He knew that if he did not live up to the people's expectations they would "turn the extravagant (and I may say undue) praises which they are heaping upon me at this moment, into equally extravagant (though I will fondly hope unmerited) censures." He was, of course, correct. Life at the top—even for George Washington—was going to be difficult.[2]

Haunted by self-doubt and aware of his own inadequacies, Washington surrounded himself with advisers of outstanding ability. The bluff Henry Knox who had served him so loyally during the Revolution became the secretary of war. Washington named Edmund Randolph, the son of a close personal friend, to be attorney general. Thomas Jefferson was recalled from Paris to head the State Department. And the brilliant but arrogant Alexander Hamilton was put in charge of the Treasury. These men formed the inner circle of Washington's administration.

The members of the Constitutional Convention viewed with genuine concern the possibility that political factions might develop in the United States. Yet factions did develop. Before the middle of the 1790s, partisan warfare had broken out between Federalists, who coalesced in support of conservative, commercially oriented views often identified with Alexander Hamilton, and a Democratic-Republican opposition led by two Virginians, James Madison and Thomas Jefferson.

Few would have predicted that Madison and Hamilton were destined to become rivals or that international issues could have divided them. They had fought side by side for the ratification of the Constitution and seemed to agree on basic foreign policy issues, especially the problem of how to deal with the English. Hamilton was merely echoing Madison's thinking when in his *Federalist Papers*, number 11, he denounced British trade practices as designed to deprive the United States "of an active commerce in our own bottoms" for the "purpose of preventing our interference in their navigation, of monopolizing the profits of our trade, and of clipping the wings by which we might soar to a dangerous greatness." A strong central government was essential, Hamilton continued, to unite the states behind a system of retaliatory measures that would "oblige foreign countries to bid against each other, for the privileges of our markets."[3]

But a remarkable change came over Hamilton once the Constitution had been ratified. He no longer spoke of bearding the British Lion in his den. On the contrary, the preservation of harmony with Britain became central to his foreign policy views. The importance of this change can hardly be overestimated, for it was a key issue dividing Hamiltonians and Jeffersonians throughout the 1790s.

That Hamilton and Madison were destined to part company became evident during the first session of Congress. With the House of Representatives debating methods of raising revenues, Madison, a leader in the lower house, proposed exactly the sort of discriminatory policy that Hamilton had outlined in his *Federalist Papers,* number 11. Madison called for a three-tiered system of tonnage duties to be paid by ships entering American ports: American vessels would pay very low rates; the ships of nations that had favorable commercial agreements with the United States would pay somewhat higher duties; and ships registered to Britain and other nations that refused to enter such agreements would be heavily taxed. "The policy of Parliament," Madison argued, "has been to seize every advantage which our weak and unguarded situation exposed. She has bound us in commercial manacles and nearly defeated the object of our independence." But now, Madison continued, the young Prometheus, at last unbound, could strike a blow in return. England, he said, must either abandon her discriminatory trade practices or suffer the consequences.[4]

In spite of his earlier advocacy of just such a discriminatory system, Hamilton now led a quiet behind-the-scenes opposition to Madison's proposal. The new government, he thought, required a prolonged period of peace during which to establish itself. A trade war with Britain was the last thing he wanted. Moreover, plans for the financial system that would bear his name were already moving forward. The secretary hoped to establish the public credit by funding the foreign and domestic debt and having the national government assume state debts incurred during the Revolution. This responsibility was going to be expensive. Since all agreed that internal taxes were out of the question, the funds to make this program work could come only from tariffs and tonnage duties on ships entering American ports. Maintaining a cordial relationship with England was vital, then, since fully three-quarters of all goods imported into the United States came from the British empire and were carried on British vessels. Madison's proposed discriminatory trade policies would have reduced revenues at a most inopportune time. The success of Hamilton's financial program and continued friendly relations with England were inextricably linked. That, at least, was the way the secretary of the treasury saw things.

Madison's bill passed the House but was gutted in the Senate, where its key discriminatory feature was abandoned. All foreign vessels would pay the same duties in American ports. There would be no retaliation against the British even though they continued their discriminatory practices. Congressman Fisher Ames of Massachusetts, a staunch Hamiltonian, was exultant. "The Senate, God bless them, as if designated by providence to keep rash and flolicsome brats out of the fire," had saved the situation. A dejected Madison, meanwhile, blamed his defeat on "New York influence."[5]

Not long after this, strong differences of opinion over America's English policy again surfaced inside the government. This time Hamilton's opponent was Secretary Jefferson. Late in 1789 Spanish officials seized a number of British merchant ships anchored in Nootka Sound, a small inlet on the western shore of Vancouver Island. Two great empires, each claiming sovereignty over the western reaches of the continent had clashed, and the reverberations were felt in New York, the temporary capital, where it was thought a general European war might soon erupt.

In August 1790, with the Anglo-Spanish crisis simmering, troop movements in Canada prompted Washington to consult his cabinet on what to do if London asked permission to use American territory as a springboard for an attack on Spanish New Orleans. Hamilton and Jefferson agreed that the president ought to give his approval. The British were likely to do as they pleased in any event, and the United States hadn't the means to stop them. It made no sense to invite humiliation by denying permission only to be ignored.

But Hamilton and Jefferson were worlds apart on the related but far more fundamental question of what the president ought to do if the British took Louisiana and the Floridas from Spain. Anxious above all to preserve harmony with the English, Hamilton believed that so long as London lived up to the 1783 agreement guaranteeing the American right to navigate the Mississippi, the United States had no reason to object. Jefferson, on the other hand, believed the United States ought to fight rather than allow these territories to fall to the British. Spain's grip on its North American holdings was feeble. Jefferson had no doubt that the Floridas as well as New Orleans were destined to become part of the United States. But if Britain replaced Spain in these areas, the geopolitical situation would change for the worse. "If Great Britain establishes herself on our whole land-board," he told James Monroe, "our lot will be bloody and eternal war" or "indissoluble confederacy."[6]

The war scare of 1790 soon faded. The British neither asked permission to send troops across American territory nor moved against New Orleans and the Floridas. But the differences between Hamilton and Jefferson were real enough. Washington's was a house divided. It remained to be seen how long he could hold it together.

Early intra-administration conflicts over foreign policy took on a decidedly ideological flavor once the French Revolution became an issue in American politics. What had been largely an internal dispute involving members of the administration and Congress became by 1793 a raging public debate.

During its earliest phase, most Americans sympathized with the French Revolution, viewing it as an outgrowth of their own struggle. Thus men of otherwise diverse political views including Hamilton, Jefferson, and John Adams, all at one time or another expressed support for the movement. It wasn't until the Revolution entered its more violent stage that significant differences began to emerge inside the American body politic. The execution of Louis XVI and his queen actually set some Republicans to celebrating. "Louis Capet has lost his caput,"[7] gloated one anonymous writer. Though

Thomas Jefferson was more restrained, he wasted no tears on the royal pair who, he observed dryly, were "amenable to punishment like other criminals." The Federalists took an entirely different position. To Connecticut's Chauncey Goodrich the executions seemed "a wanton act of barbarity, disgraceful even to a Parisian mob."[8]

As the long train of aristocrats, clerics, and other enemies of the regime made its way to the guillotine, Federalists, many of whom seem to have considered themselves candidates for execution should the mad contagion make its way across the Atlantic, became increasingly strident. Fisher Ames exclaimed; "Behold France . . . an open Hell still ringing with agonies and blasphemies, still smoking with sufferings and crimes, in which we see . . . perhaps our future state." Hamilton was equally aghast. The Reign of Terror's "horrid and disgusting scenes," he wrote, stood as "proofs of atrocious depravity in the most influential leaders of the revolution." Jean-Paul Marat and Maximilien Robespierre were "assassins still reeking with the blood of their fellow citizens."[9]

Rather surprisingly, considering the liberal but hardly revolutionary nature of the Jeffersonian Republican movement, its leaders took a far different view, arguing in effect that the end—a more perfect society—justified the means. Some of Jefferson's personal friends went to their deaths under the guillotine. Yet he viewed their fate as of less consequence than the outcome of the Revolution itself. The killing, he thought, must have a purpose. And so he insisted that in the end France's torment would benefit all humankind. "The liberty of the whole world was depending on the issue of the contest," he wrote. "And was ever such a prize won with so little innocent blood?"[10]

THE ANGLO-FRENCH WAR AND AMERICAN NEUTRALITY

In January 1793, Jefferson stated flatly his belief that ninety-nine out of every one hundred Americans supported the French revolutionary cause. The majority was not quite so overwhelming, yet it is clear that the nation was awash in enthusiasm for the French cause. American Republicans were itching for something to celebrate when, on December 14, 1792, they learned that a French army had thrown back an invading force of Austrians and Prussians at the battle of Valmy. The Allied attempt to overthrow the French Revolution had failed.

The news arrived first in Philadelphia, where a spontaneous celebration began. Church bells rang, businesses closed, and people drank to the Revolution at inns and taverns far into the night. The celebration was better planned in New York, where according to one newspaper's account an entire day was set aside for "feasting and bell ringing and the firing of cannon." In the evening "the Society of St. Tammany lit up its great wigwam, and the members of the order spent their time till after midnight singing songs."[11]

In April 1793, only a few months after this Republican outburst, Americans learned that France had declared war on Great Britain. For the Federalists, ideology and interest had meshed. England now stood as the defender of conservative constitutionalism against the forces of revolutionary ferment. At the same time the economic relationship with Britain lost none of its importance. It is no wonder, then, that Federalists in general became enthusiastic supporters of England and advocates of a pro-British neutrality. Nor is it surprising that the Jeffersonian Republicans should have taken precisely the opposite view.

None of this was good news to George Washington, whose hopes of maintaining a balanced foreign policy were clearly in jeopardy. At home in Mount Vernon when he learned that France and England had gone to war, he returned immediately to Philadelphia to confer with his cabinet. Two issues were quickly and easily decided. All agreed that the United States should remain neutral and that the president should receive the new French minister, Edmond Charles Genêt, who had recently landed in Charleston and was even then traveling by land toward the capital.

The truly divisive question before the cabinet had to do with the Franco-American Treaty of Alliance of 1778. Hamilton argued that the French treaty should be considered void since the government that negotiated it no longer existed. He soon abandoned that curious position, however, in favor of the only somewhat more defensible view that although the treaty remained in force it should be "suspended" until the revolution in France had run its course and a stable government was established there.

This line of reasoning infuriated Jefferson. Hamilton, he thought, was "panic-struck if we refuse our breech to every kick which Great Britain may chuse to give it." "If we preserve even a sneaking neutrality," the angry Virginian wrote, "we shall be indebted for it to the President & not to his counsellors."[12] Washington did not entirely disappoint the secretary of state. He rejected Hamilton's advice, deciding instead to interpret America's obligations to France in the narrowest way commensurate with good faith. Whether that would be enough to preserve peaceful relations with France or England remained to be seen.

THE GENÊT AFFAIR

While the president and his cabinet were debating policy in Philadelphia, far to the south a much different scene was unfolding. On April 8, 1793, the French frigate *Embuscade* with Minister Genêt on board put in at Charleston. After receiving a hero's welcome from local Republicans, Genêt began putting plans into effect that jeopardized Washington's policy of strict neutrality. First, because at this time Spain was part of the coalition fighting France, he ordered the French consul in Charleston to develop plans for an attack on Spanish Florida using American territory as a base of operations and employing American volunteers. Genêt, meanwhile, began commissioning privateers to prey on British shipping. During his brief stay in Charleston the envoy commissioned only four such vessels. But he had a suitcase full of commissions, and there was no lack of American merchants willing to turn their ships loose on the many rich British prizes to be taken in North American and Caribbean waters.

Paris neither expected nor wanted the United States to declare war against England. The French did hope, however, that Philadelphia would adopt a benevolent neutrality, looking the other way while Genêt commissioned privateers and organized the military expedition against Spain's North American holdings. They also seem to have assumed that French war vessels and privateers would be allowed to operate from American ports and that American merchants would supply the French West Indies with food and other essentials. This cooperation was vital since the Royal Navy controlled the seas and made it impossible for French merchant ships to carry on the normal trade.

When Genêt left Charleston, he felt confident that the United States would prove to be the benevolent neutral the Foreign Ministry was hoping for. As he traveled north toward Philadelphia, that belief was repeatedly reconfirmed, for in literally every town through which he passed he was feted by local Republicans. It was then a supremely confident Edmond Genêt who rolled into Philadelphia on May 16, 1793.

Thomas Jefferson viewed Genêt's arrival in the capital as a heaven-sent opportunity. To that point Hamilton's influence had been all too pronounced. The administration, Jefferson feared, was in danger of adopting "a mere English neutrality."[13] Jefferson wanted Philadelphia's Republicans to roll out the red carpet for Genêt. Such a demonstration, he hoped, would awaken the president to the fact that his policies did not reflect the prevailing views of mainstream America.

Philadelphia did not disappoint the secretary of state, staging a massive reception for Genêt. The president, however, was unimpressed. At his first meeting with the youthful minister Washington was studiously correct, nothing more. Later Genêt complained that Washington's demeanor had been a calculated insult. But that was later, after his mission had failed. At the time he made no complaint. Indeed, there was nothing to complain about. Washington's behavior was entirely in keeping with his neutral policy.

Genêt quickly established a warm personal relationship with Jefferson, who was charmed by the younger man's often flashing conversation and deeply impressed by his passionate commitment to republican principles. Nor could Genêt be anything but awed by the author of the Declaration of Independence whose pro-French sympathies were so obvious. In spite of this cordiality Genêt and Jefferson were destined to clash, for in his official capacity Jefferson represented a policy that was bound to infuriate the ardent young envoy.

Genêt came to the United States virtually penniless. He had been instructed to request that the United States pay in its entirety the debt it owed France for loans advanced during the Revolutionary War. These funds were to be used to finance the expedition against Spanish North America and purchase supplies for the French islands in the Caribbean that were threatened by famine as a result of the British blockade. But Washington rejected Genêt's request. The government, he said, hadn't the means to pay more than the regularly scheduled payment. This explanation might have satisfied the envoy. But in a subsequent conversation Hamilton told him bluntly that the administration believed prepayment of the debt would constitute a violation of its neutral policy. Furious, Genêt then accused Washington of collaborating with the British in their attempt "to destroy by famine the French republicans and liberty."[14]

Genêt was further angered when the administration objected to the outfitting of French privateers in American ports. He insisted that his right to do this was "incontestable" under the terms of the Alliance of 1778. He also contended that for the same reason the ships and cargoes taken by these marauders could be sold in the United States. To all of this Thomas Jefferson gave a firm but polite no. But Genêt, who believed that the American people were sympathetic to the French cause even if their government was not, refused to stop either the arming of privateers or prize sales.

In off-the-record conversations with the young Frenchman Jefferson conceded that American policy was skewed in a pro-British direction. But he urged his impulsive friend to be patient. Congress would soon reconvene; perhaps then something could be done to alter the situation. Unhappily, Genêt was not a patient man. His revolutionary instincts told him that if a government followed policies that did not reflect popular sentiment, an appeal should be made to the true sovereign authority—the people.

Here was a thought to send a shudder down the spine of even the most staunch American Republican, for to appeal over the head of the great Washington was surely to court political disaster. And yet that is what Genêt threatened to do. Jefferson tried to dissuade him. "I fear he will enlarge the circle of those disaffected to his country," he explained to James Madison. "I am doing everything in my power to moderate the impetuosity of his movements, and to destroy the dangerous opinion which has been excited in him that the people of the U.S. will disavow the acts of their government and that he has an appeal from the executive to Congress & from both to the people."[15] But not even Thomas Jefferson could show Genêt the error of his ways.

The whole awful mess came to a head in July 1793, when Pennsylvania's governor, Thomas Mifflin, reported that *The Little Sarah*, a British ship recently captured and brought into the port of Philadelphia by a French privateer, was being outfitted as a privateer in defiance of administration policy. Jefferson warned Genêt that he was courting disaster and thought he had wrung a promise from him that the ship would not sail at least until after the president, who was out of the city, had returned for consultations. But the ship, renamed *The Petit Democrat*, put to sea before the authorities could do anything about her.

At last Genêt had gone too far. Sensing how vulnerable he now was,

Alexander Hamilton delivered the coup de grace in a series of newspaper essays that he signed "No Jacobin." In the first of these he asserted publicly what Jefferson and others had known for some time, that Genêt had "threatened to appeal from the President to the people."[16] The story had exactly the effect that Hamilton hoped for and Jefferson feared. Genêt's stock plummeted as the people rallied to support the president. With cries of popular indignation ringing in their ears, the Republicans did the sensible thing: they abandoned Genêt. "His conduct," wrote the rueful James Madison, "has been that of a madman."[17]

Considering Genêt's self-destructive behavior, it is not surprising that the administration requested his recall. Nor is it difficult to understand why Paris agreed. Genêt was a Girondist, and the Jacobins had seized power there. A new French envoy, Joseph Fauchet, appeared in Philadelphia in February 1794 with orders recalling Genêt. But the passionate young diplomat never returned to France, where a death warrant no doubt awaited him. Instead he asked for and was granted political asylum. He remained in the United States, married the beautiful Cornelia Clinton, daughter of New York's Governor George Clinton, and abandoned politics in favor of the life of a country gentleman.

BY SEA AND BY LAND: THE ANGLO-AMERICAN CRISIS

Alexander Hamilton had every reason to be smug. The Genêt affair had sent the Republicans reeling. Nor was there any reason to believe that they would be able to recover sufficiently to again challenge the course of administration foreign policy. But Hamilton failed to take the British into account. Their maritime depredations not only restored the political initiative to the Republicans but almost produced a war.

The first indication that things were seriously amiss in Anglo-American relations surfaced in June 1793, when King George III issued an order-in-council (an executive order of the king & Privy Council) directing the Royal Navy to seize all neutral ships carrying corn, flour, or meal to French ports. Food grains had never before been considered contraband of war. News of this order, therefore, came as a shock and was only partially mitigated by the fact that the British announced they would purchase rather than condemn the cargoes they seized. In November the situation became infinitely worse. A second order-in-council authorized the seizure of all neutral ships engaged in the French West Indies trade. American merchants were given no advance warning of what was to come. In fact this latest order was kept secret until the Royal Navy and a band of hastily outfitted privateers were ready to act.

Early in March 1794, news began to trickle into Philadelphia of numerous seizures by British ships operating in the Caribbean. In fact more than three hundred ships were caught up in this British dragnet. American newspapers were soon full of stories of seizures, unjust condemnations by rapacious admiralty court judges, and the abuse and even the impressment (abduction) of American seamen for involuntary service in the Royal Navy.

The depredations were serious enough in themselves. But for the British to act without giving merchants any forewarning was considered unforgivable—literally a case of great power piracy intended to line the pockets of officers in the Royal Navy and their privateering friends who became rich on prize money. The merchants of Charleston, Philadelphia, New York, Boston, and other towns passed resolutions denouncing the seizures. In Congress many Federalists who had only recently fought tooth and nail against any measure the British might find irritating now favored preparations for war. The Marblehead, Massachusetts, militia, three thousand strong, began to drill seriously for the first time in years. The town of Portsmouth sent a message to Congress indicating that the people there preferred to fight rather than put up with any further humiliation at the hands of the English. All along the coast forts were refurbished and earthworks thrown up as the war fever spread.

While Congress debated, President Washington prepared for the likelihood of war by announcing a thirty-day embargo (later extended to sixty days) on all foreign trade. On the day following, New Jersey's Jonathan Dayton, a moderate Federalist, introduced resolutions in the House calling on the states to raise eighty thousand militiamen and authorizing the administration to add twenty-five thousand regular troops to the tiny national army. Another Dayton resolution called for the sequestration of all private debts owed to British creditors by American citizens, the funds thus raised to be used to compensate merchants and others who had suffered losses as a result of recent British seizures. Fearing that the British would declare war if the sequestration proposal was enacted, Alexander Hamilton opposed Dayton's second proposal. "No powers of language at my command," he said, "can express the abhorrence I feel at the idea of violating the property of individuals . . . on account of controversies between nation and nation."[18] The House, however, felt differently, and Dayton's resolutions passed easily. Even the Federalist-controlled Senate came close to passing the bill. There, however, a tie vote gave Vice-President John Adams the opportunity to kill the sequestration proposal.

America's war fever was fed not only by Britain's high-handed maritime practices but also by the role the empire continued to play on the northwestern frontier. The United States had been involved in intermittent warfare with the Miami, Shawnee, Wyandotte, and other western Indian tribes since the Revolution. But until the Constitution gave the national government the power to support an army, little had been done to bring the Indians to terms. The Washington administration was more vigorous but at first no more effective. Two military expeditions, the first in 1790 and a second in 1791, were thrown back by the Indians with heavy losses. Meanwhile, from the seven Northwest posts still in British hands, officers of the British Indian Department gave aid and encouragement to the Indians.

After the second American defeat, London added insult to injury by offering to mediate a settlement on terms humiliating to the United States. The proposal called for the British to withdraw from the Northwest posts, destroying them as they left. The United States would on its part cede the entire Ohio Valley to the Indians. The integrity of the "Indian barrier state" thus created would be guaranteed by both powers. President Washington quickly rejected this insolent proposal. But that left him no closer to a solution to the Indian problem than before.

The situation brightened somewhat in 1793 when the Mohawk chieftain Joseph Brant and other Iroquois intermediaries arranged a peace conference to be held at Sandusky on Lake Erie. The western tribes had long insisted on an Ohio River boundary with the United States. But because thousands of white settlers had already moved into parts of the Ohio Valley, the administration could not cede that boundary. The president was, however, ready to offer the Indians much of what they wanted territorially as well as a generous financial settlement. Secretary of War Knox and his chief negotiator, Timothy Pickering, were convinced that if they could meet the Indians face to face without British interference a settlement was possible.

A delegation made up of Pickering, General Benjamin Lincoln, and Virginia's Beverley Randolph set out for Sandusky in mid-April 1793. But they never reached their destination. Instead they became the unwilling guests of the lieutenant-governor of Lower Canada, John Graves Simcoe, who detained them for weeks at Fort Niagara. The western tribes, meanwhile, met with Colonel John Butler and Alexander McKee of the British Indian Department. The only contact the American delegates had with the Indians took place on Bois Blanc Island near Detroit, where, under the watchful eyes of British agents, they conferred briefly with a tiny group of Indian militants. These Indians made it painfully clear that unless the American delegates were prepared to cede an Ohio River boundary there could be no purpose in holding a conference.

The American negotiators returned to Philadelphia empty handed. The Indian war continued, and for this they blamed the British. Benjamin Lincoln believed that Butler and McKee had convinced the Indians to hold out for an Ohio River boundary knowing this would make a settlement impossible. Pickering agreed. It had been the "craft of the *man* or *men* who control the Indians," he complained, "to keep us at a distance lest by free and daily communications and friendly intercourse we should make some impression."[19]

If Washington had any doubt that the British were responsible for his problems in the West or that they intended soon to declare war, these were erased early in 1794 when he learned of a council recently held between the governor of Canada, Sir Guy Carlton, Lord Dorchester, and the Indians of the Seven Villages of Lower Canada. In his remarks Dorchester predicted war between Britain and the United States and urged the Indians to become his allies. A week later he ordered Lieutenant-Governor Simcoe to begin construction of a fort at the rapids of the Maumee, deep in American territory.

On March 10, 1794, with the crisis in Anglo-American relations about to boil over, four worried Federalist senators, Rufus King of New York, Connecticut's Oliver Ellsworth, George Cabot, and Caleb Strong of Massachusetts, met with Alexander Hamilton to plan strategy. Taking their cue from the Treasury secretary, the senators wrote the president urging him to send Hamilton to London to negotiate a settlement. The president was at first unenthusiastic. Even after he began to see merit in the proposal he remained lukewarm about sending Hamilton because, as he explained in his own wonderfully understated way, the secretary did not "possess the general confidence of the country." When two Republican members of Congress, James Monroe and John Nicholas, objected to a Hamilton appointment, the president turned quickly to John Jay, who was somewhat more palatable to the Republicans. To further allay Republican suspicions and ease the path of the Jay nomination in the Senate, Washington also nominated Monroe to replace the Federalist, Gouverneur Morris, as the American minister in Paris.

Edmund Randolph, who had replaced Jefferson in the State Department, drafted Jay's instructions. But as usual Hamilton had the last word. He revised Randolph's work, eliminating everything that seemed needlessly provocative. "We are still on the path of negotiation," he observed, "let us not plant it with thorns."[20] Obviously Hamilton was still terribly anxious to avoid a war. Yet even after softening Jay's instructions he was not optimistic. Jay would be asking the English to evacuate the Northwest posts, sign a favorable commercial treaty, compensate the former owners for thousands of slaves seized by British forces during the Revolution, and repay merchants who had been victimized by the recent wave of depredations in the West Indies. But he had nothing to offer in return. Nor was he in a position to threaten economic sanctions; the entire Federalist system depended on revenues collected on British imports and from tonnage duties paid by British ships.

In an attempt to provide his envoy with a hint of leverage, Randolph had instructed Jay to warn London that in the event a satisfactory settlement to their differences could not be worked out, the United States might join Sweden and Denmark in a revitalized Armed Neutrality. But the first Armed Neutrality had been something of a joke. Even the Empress Catherine referred to it as the "Armed Nullity." Without Russia a revived combination of neutrals would be even more laughable. In any event, even before the negotiations began Hamilton removed the issue as a factor in the negotiations by quietly informing the British minister in Philadelphia, George Hammond, that the United States would under no circumstances join the new Armed Neutrality. Whatever leverage Jay might have been able to generate from this source was thus eliminated.

Jay then had no bargaining power. He went as a supplicant and could only point out to William Wyndham, Lord Grenville that unless he adopted a more conciliatory policy the result would be either a war that was in neither country's interest or a change of government in Philadelphia that might lead to war.

The latter thought was on more than a few minds as the envoy prepared to sail for England. A deeply frustrated Alexander Hamilton, for example, advised Jay to be cordial but firm during the talks for unless a settlement "could be effected on solid terms . . . it would be better to do nothing."[21] A treaty that made too many concessions, he thought, would be worse than none at all, for it would arouse public anger, put Federalism in a difficult place politically, and in any event probably fail in the Senate.

With Jay handling the negotiations in London, Washington sent South Carolina's Thomas Pinckney, the resident minister there, on a special mission to Madrid to see what could be done about outstanding issues in Spanish-American relations. The president's timing couldn't have been better. Floridablanca's successor in the Foreign Ministry, Manuel de Godoy, was in the midst of arranging a revolution in Spanish foreign policy that was certain to anger Britain and leave Spain's New World empire extremely vulnerable. During the early stages of the Wars of the French Revolution, Spain had forsaken its long-standing alliance with neighboring France to join in the war against it. But before the end of 1794, with French forces across the Pyrenees, Godoy saw no alternative but to change sides. Soon French and Spanish negotiators, meeting in the Swiss town of Basel, began work on an agreement that would transform Spain from an enemy to a military ally of France.

Godoy feared that once Spain changed sides, the British would retaliate by attacking Spain's American empire. It wasn't an appealing prospect. But the alternative—French conquest of Spain proper—was even less appealing.

When he learned of John Jay's mission to London and the possibility of an Anglo-American rapprochement, Godoy concluded that something drastic would have to be done to keep Spain's two potential western hemispheric enemies from joining forces. To accomplish this he was prepared to make concessions to Pinckney across a broad front. But in return he wanted the American to agree to a treaty of alliance and a reciprocal guarantee of territories in the Western Hemisphere. Pinckney, however, stuck to his instructions, refusing to consider an alliance or any other mutual guarantees.

When Pinckney learned that a Franco-Spanish treaty of alliance had been signed on July 22, 1795, he realized that his bargaining position had been vastly strengthened. Godoy, however, continued to spar. At length, in mid-October, Pinckney demanded his passports and threatened to leave without an agreement. At that point Godoy gave in. Three days later the two diplomats signed Pinckney's Treaty. The United States had won a boundary with Spanish Florida at the 31st degree. More important, the agreement guaranteed to American citizens the right to navigate the Mississippi and deposit their goods at New Orleans duty free for shipment elsewhere.

Having failed to negotiate an alliance with the United States, Godoy evidently thought the next best thing was to eliminate possible reasons for the United States to join England in attacking Spain's New World empire. Pinckney's mission had been a remarkable success. Without making a single concession he achieved everything the administration hoped for. Unhappily, the same could not be said for John Jay.

JAY'S TREATY

Jay sailed for London in May 1794. But it was almost a year before administration leaders received an official copy of the treaty he negotiated. When at last they had a chance to study the agreement, Washington and Secretary of State Randolph were both appalled. It was extremely favorable to Britain and, if ratified, was certain to spawn a crisis in Franco-American relations.

To be sure, Britain's secretary for foreign affairs, Lord Grenville, had made certain concessions. He agreed to surrender the Northwest posts by June 30, 1796, and to arbitrate both the claims of American merchants arising out of recent maritime seizures in the Caribbean and the dispute over the Maine boundary that had remained undefined since 1783. But Jay surrendered much more.

The commercial aspect of Jay's Treaty was particularly disappointing. Grenville agreed to open Britain's East Indian holdings to American trade. That, however, was a matter of little economic consequence at the time. Britain's far more important West Indian colonies were opened only to ships with a cargo capacity of seventy tons or less—tiny vessels. To win even this slight concession Jay gave up far more than he received, agreeing that American ships would forgo the right to carry molasses, sugar, coffee, cocoa, or cotton in world trade.

Jay surrendered on another major commercial point as well when, in spite of the fact that Britain's discriminatory trade policies remained unchanged, he agreed to grant Britain most-favored-nation status in the American marketplace. This status meant that for the life of the treaty British products entering the United States would be taxed at the lowest prevailing tariff rates and that British shippers would pay equally low tonnage duties. In effect the agreement prohibited the United States from retaliating against Britain's unfair trade practices.

Jay also made startling concessions relating to America's neutral rights. He agreed that noncontraband goods owned by citizens of a belligerent state (France and Spain) that were found on board American merchant ships could legitimately be seized. This was both a sharp reversal of the principle of "free ships, free goods," which was incorporated into the Franco-American Alliance of 1778, and a serious blow to the French, who depended on American merchant ships to carry goods between the French West Indies and Europe. Under the terms of Jay's Treaty, free ships, it appeared, would mean free goods only when the potential captor was French and the goods in question were English, and not the other way around.

Jay also acquiesced in the so-called Rule of the War of 1756, by which the British claimed that colonies closed to neutral trade in peacetime (the French and Spanish West Indies) could not be opened to neutrals in time of war and that neutral ships engaged in such trade could be taken as legal prizes. Moreover, although the United States had earlier insisted that contraband of war should be defined narrowly to include only those items that were directly applicable to the conduct of military operations, Jay now accepted an expanded British definition that included raw materials and even some foodstuffs. Finally, harking back to the Genêt episode, the treaty also prohibited privateersmen from operating from or selling their prizes in American ports.

Jay's Treaty was so controversial that the president, fearing a popular outcry, kept its terms secret until the Senate could act on it. When the special session convened early in June 1795, Hamilton's friends there sent him a copy of the agreement for comment. The former treasury secretary, who had by this time left government service and was practicing law in New York City, was no more pleased with the treaty than Washington. Nevertheless, he advised the senators to reject Article 12 of the treaty, the commercial agreement, which he considered totally unacceptable, and approve the rest. Senate Federalists followed where Hamilton led. After more than two weeks of rancorous debate, the Senate approved the amended treaty by a strict party vote of 20–10.

Even though he finally supported ratification, Hamilton was hardly enthusiastic about it. The treaty's only saving grace, he thought, was that it was better than war. His sister-in-law's comment, that he thus supported a treaty "he never would himself have deigned to submit to," was not far from the mark.[22] During the legislative debate, the senators met in executive session, which meant that they were barred from making the terms of the treaty public. Even after the Senate approved the agreement, the rules required continued secrecy until the president had decided whether or not to ratify it. But only three days after the Senate voted, Benjamin Franklin Bache's *Philadelphia Aurora and General Advertiser*, a Republican paper, carried a more or less accurate summary of the treaty. At that point Senator Stevens Thompson Mason of Virginia turned an official copy of the treaty over to the gleeful Bache, who promptly printed thousands of copies for national distribution.

Within a few days copies of Jay's Treaty were on sale as far south as Savannah and as far north as Boston, where the first in a series of Republican-sponsored mass meetings was held to denounce the accord. There, fifteen hundred irate Republicans petitioned the president, urging him to reject the treaty. Similar meetings followed in other seaboard cities. In New York, where Hamilton tried to debate the protesters, he was stoned for his trouble and left the meeting with blood streaming down his face. In Philadelphia, after passing a series of antitreaty resolutions, another crowd of fifteen hundred watched as a local Republican leader, Blair M'Clenarchan, waved the treaty above his head and shouted, "What a damned treaty! I make a motion that every good citizen in this assembly kick this damned treaty to hell."[23] They did their best, marching en masse to the British minister's house, where the treaty was publicly burned.

The president, who of course had to decide whether to ratify the treaty, kept his own counsel, refusing to be influenced by the Republican clamor. Unable to decide what to do, he wrote to Hamilton asking his opinion. But before his longtime adviser could reply, the Royal Navy began a fresh offensive against American shipping. Secretary of State Randolph branded this latest outrage completely "irreconcilable" with the terms of Jay's Treaty, and the president agreed. Ratification now seemed out of the question. Over the objections of Attorney General William Bradford, Secretary of War Timothy Pickering, and the new secretary of the treasury, Oliver Wolcott, Jr., all of whom urged ratification, Washington decided he would attempt to reopen negotiations, hoping for a less objectionable agreement.

THE TREATY RESURRECTED

With the treaty sitting dead in the water, fate intervened on its behalf. Much earlier the Royal Navy had intercepted a number of dispatches sent by Joseph Fauchet, the French minister in Philadelphia, to his government. The Foreign Office forwarded certain of these to Britain's American envoy, George Hammond, along with instructions to communicate the information they contained "to well disposed persons in America."[24] One of these dispatches implied that Secretary of State Randolph was a French sympathizer and that in 1794 he had asked Fauchet to help finance the Whiskey Rebellion, a civil disturbance against the national government then brewing in back-country Pennsylvania.

Hammond wondered what effect these disclosures would have on Washington, since Randolph alone among his cabinet advisers opposed ratification of the treaty. With this in mind, Hamilton met with Secretary of the Treasury Wolcott, translated the dispatch orally for him, and gave him the original. Wolcott immediately consulted with Secretary of War Pickering, who produced a labored written translation of the dispatch. At a meeting with the president, Pickering urged him to ratify Jay's Treaty, denounced Randolph as a traitor and left a copy of Fauchet's translated dispatch as proof.

The president was, of course, stunned, his confidence in Randolph badly shaken. With Hamilton and the remainder of the cabinet recommending the ratification of Jay's Treaty, he at last gave in. Only after the treaty had been ratified was the befuddled secretary of state, who could not fathom the President's sudden turnabout, confronted with Fauchet's dispatch.

Randolph tried to exonerate himself. But it was no good. He then resigned, returned to Virginia, and published a *Vindication* (1795), hoping in this way to save his reputation. But that was not any good either. Randolph had been ruined. And the pity of it is, he was innocent. We know this now because of a brilliant bit of historical detective work done by Irving Brant, best known for his multi-volume biography of James Madison. Brant also presents an impressive array of evidence indicating that Wolcott and Pickering knew that Randolph was innocent even as they were destroying him.[25]

The Republicans made one final attempt to kill Jay's Treaty, this time in the House of Representatives. The president needed $80,000 to implement the agreement, and all money bills had to originate in the lower house, where the Republicans, working with a group of moderate nonaligned congressmen, claimed a working majority. As soon as Congress convened in early 1796, House Republicans moved immediately to the attack, demanding that the president forward all documents relevant to the negotiation of Jay's Treaty. On the advice of Timothy Pickering, who had replaced Randolph in the State Department, Washington returned a blunt refusal to the House, charging its leaders with acting unconstitutionally by attempting to interfere in the treaty-making process. A battle was thus joined, one the administration at first seemed destined to lose.

Not only did the Republicans hold the upper hand in the House, they had the British to help them. The Royal Navy's maritime depredations, which had by no means ceased, were regularly highlighted in the press. Making matters worse, in the midst of the treaty fight Lord Grenville let it be known that he would not surrender the Northwest posts on the date agreed upon unless the treaty had been implemented by that time *and* the United States had agreed to a supplementary article to the treaty guaranteeing that after the posts were surrendered British fur traders would be allowed to continue their operations in the American Northwest. "The British ministry are as great fools or as great rascals as our jacobins," Hamilton raged, "else our commerce would not continue to be distressed as it is by their cruisers; Nor would the Executive be embarrassed as it now is by the new proposition."[26] The situation remained deadlocked until about the middle of April 1796. Washington would not forward the diplomatic correspondence, and the House refused to appropriate the money. At that point, however, the situation began to change as a number of Republicans joined the Federalists in supporting the president.

In the West the Pinckney and Jay treaties were viewed as a package. The first guaranteed westerners the duty-free use of the Mississippi River and access to national and international markets. The second eliminated the British from the Old Northwest. Without British support the western Indians would be forced to make peace, paving the way for economic growth and the development of the trans-Appalachian West. But neither treaty was particularly important without the other. As Alexander Addison, an associate of the Republican leader Albert Gallatin, remarked, Pinckney's Treaty was worth next to nothing unless the United States also controlled the Northwest posts. With rumors circulating that Madrid might refuse to ratify Pinckney's

Treaty or that the Federalists would kill it unless the House implemented the British treaty, western Republicans began demanding implementation of both agreements. Under this kind of pressure the Republican majority in the House began to crumble.

Other pressures encouraging to the supporters of the treaty were building east of the mountains, where an economic crisis was developing. As it became clear that Jay's Treaty might not be implemented, maritime insurance companies, anticipating war with England, refused to insure shippers against capture at sea. The overall number of sailings dropped as an actual though undeclared embargo began to take shape. Sailors and dock workers were thrown out of work. At the same time, commodity prices tumbled, and merchants with large stocks of flour and other staples on hand seemed suddenly to be threatened with bankruptcy. Where once there had been mass meetings protesting Jay's Treaty, now even larger meetings demanded its implementation. These developments caused many eastern Republican and nonaligned congressmen, who had earlier opposed implementation of the treaty, to change their position.

During the latter part of April, the Republican majority in the House dwindled until, on April 30, after an impassioned speech by the Federalist orator, Fisher Ames, the bill implementing Jay's Treaty passed. The great debate, one of the most bitterly fought contests in the history of American foreign policy, was over. The precedent it set in eliminating the House of Representatives from the treaty-making function has never been overturned.

Peace with England, though paid for at a high price, was preserved. It remained to be seen, however, how France would react to these changed circumstances.

ENDNOTES

1. Robert R. Livingston, quoted in Douglas Southall Freeman, *George Washington* (Charles Scribner's Sons, N.Y., 1954), VI, p. 192.

2. The comte de Moustier, quoted in *ibid.*, p. 195; George Washington, quoted in *ibid.*

3. Alexander Hamilton, number 11, *The Federalist*, ed. Edward Mead Earle (Random House, N.Y., 1942), pp. 63–65.

4. James Madison, quoted in John C. Miller, *Alexander Hamilton and the Growth of the New Nation* (Harper and Row, N.Y., 1959), pp. 222–25.

5. Hamilton, quoted in Miller, *Hamilton*, p. 224; Fisher Ames to James Minot, May 27, 1789, *The Works of Fisher Ames*, ed. Seth Ames (Little, Brown and Co., Boston, 1854), II, pp. 45–46.

6. Thomas Jefferson, quoted in Arthur Burr Darling, *Our Rising Empire* (Yale University Press, New Haven, Conn., 1940), p. 138.

7. *National Gazette*, April 20, 1793.

8. Goodrich and Jefferson, quoted in Dumas Malone, *Jefferson and the Ordeal of Liberty* (Little, Brown and Co., Boston, 1962), pp. 60–61.

9. Fisher Ames, quoted in *The Works of Fisher Ames*, II, p. 112; Hamilton, quoted in Miller, *Hamilton*, pp. 364–66.

10. Jefferson to William Short, Jan. 3, 1793, *The Writings of Thomas Jefferson*, ed. Paul L. Ford (N.Y., 1892–1905), VI, pp. 153–57.

11. Quoted in John Bach McMaster, *A History of the People of the United States* (D. Appleton and Co., N.Y., 1885–1904), II, pp. 90–91.

12. Jefferson, quoted in Harry Ammon, *The Genêt Mission* (W. W. Norton and Co., N.Y., 1973), p. 52.

13. Thomas Jefferson, quoted in Dumas Malone, *Jefferson and the Ordeal of Liberty*, p. 62.

14. Edmund Genêt, quoted in Miller, *Hamilton*, p. 373.

15. Jefferson, quoted in Ammon, *The Genêt Mission*, p. 74.

16. Hamilton, quoted in Miller, *Hamilton*, pp. 377–78.

17. Madison, quoted in Irving Brant, *James Madison* (Bobbs-Merrill and Co., Indianapolis, Ind., 1953), III, p. 384.

18. Hamilton, quoted in Miller, *Hamilton*, p. 391.

19. Timothy Pickering, quoted in Gerard Clarfield, *Timothy Pickering and the American Republic* (Pittsburgh University Press, Pittsburgh, Pa., 1980), p. 144.

20. Hamilton to Edmund Randolph, April 27, 1794, *The Papers of Alexander Hamilton*, ed. Harold Syrett et al. (Columbia University Press, N.Y., 1962), XVI, p. 347.

21. Hamilton to Jay, May 6, 1794, *ibid.*, p. 381.

22. Quoted in Miller, *Hamilton*, p. 422.

23. Blair M'Clenarchan, quoted in Frank Monaghan, *John Jay, Defender of Liberty* (Bobbs-Merrill and Co., Indianapolis, Ind., and N.Y., 1935), pp. 393–94.

24. Instructions to George Hammond, May 9, 1795, *Instructions to British Ministers in the United States*, ed. Bernard Mayo, American Historical Association Annual Report (Washington D.C.: American Historical Association, 1936), III, p. 83.

25. Irving Brant, "Edmund Randolph, Not Guilty!" *William and Mary Quarterly*, 3d. series, VII (April, 1950), pp. 179–98.

26. Hamilton to Wolcott, April 20, 1796, *Hamilton Papers*, ed. Syrett et al., XX, p. 178.

John Adams, "His Rotundity," was often criticized by his political opponents for putting on aristocratic airs. Here we see why, for he poses in a style characteristic of European monarchs of the age.

4

QUASI-WAR, 1796–1800

Jay's Treaty, which temporarily resolved differences with England, produced new difficulties for the United States, this time with France. Paris had been concerned about developments in Anglo-American relations from the day it was learned that Jay was on his way to London. Foreign Minister Charles Delacroix's worst fears were only confirmed when he learned the details of the agreement. From his point of view the Washington administration had forsaken commitments made under the Treaty of Alliance of 1778. French goods carried on American ships would no longer be protected by the American flag. Moreover, by acquiescing in the so-called Rule of the War of 1756, the administration sent a clear message to America's merchants: trade with France or the French West Indies would be at their own risk. The effect of this message, Delacroix feared, might be to starve the island's inhabitants. Why, after all, should a merchant risk trading with France or its colonies without the protection of his government when there was plenty of money to be made in those areas of the world not declared off limits by the Royal Navy?

In spite of these developments, Delacroix was disinclined to behave provocatively. Acting on the assumption that a Republican president would adopt a pro-French foreign policy, he decided instead to intervene on Thomas Jefferson's behalf in the election of 1796. Delacroix adopted this strategy not only because French observers in the United States had empha-sized the importance of ideology in Jeffersonian thinking, but also because he had been encouraged to do so by James Monroe, the American minister in Paris.

To say that Monroe fell out with the administration over Jay's Treaty would be a gross understatement. His anger was profound. Behind Monroe's fury lay the fear that France might make war on the United States. He certainly believed France had just cause. But he also believed that a war would strengthen Federalism at home while undermining the Republican movement. He therefore tried to convince Delacroix, and through him the Directory (the five-man executive of the French government), that war would only serve to cement the developing relationship between England and America. Monroe urged French leaders to await the outcome of the upcoming presidential election. A Republican victory, he promised, would produce a swift change in American policy.

Pierre Adet, the French minister in Philadelphia and the chosen instrument of Delacroix's policy, worked closely with John Beckley, a key figure in Pennsylvania's Republican party and a shrewd political tactician. Beckley knew that only a few electoral votes would separate Jefferson and Vice-President John Adams in an election that was too close to call. He also believed that the election would be won or lost in Pennsylvania, where the candidates were running neck and neck.

A week before Pennsylvania's voters went to the polls, Adet published a letter in the *Philadelphia Aurora* addressed to the secretary of state but really intended for Pennsylvania's voters. Claiming that the administration had violated commitments made to France under the agreements of 1778, he unveiled a new French maritime decree making American ships fair game for French privateers and warships. Having allowed the British "to sport" with its neutrality, Adet wrote, the American government could not complain "when France, to restore the balance of neutrality to its equilibrium, shall act in the same manner as the English."[1]

Though the envoy made no mention of the election, Adet's message was clear. War with France was likely if the United States continued the policies of the Federalist party. In a second letter, published just before the state's presidential electors voted, Adet increased the pressure by announcing his recall while indicating that no new envoy would be sent to the United States until the government changed its pro-British policies.

Adet's intervention in the Pennsylvania elections seems to have paid dividends, as Jefferson won fourteen of the state's fifteen electoral votes. "We are unfortunate in the election in this state," wrote the Federalist Senator William Bingham. "The most unwearied exertions accompanied by some bribery, and not a little chicane, have been practiced on this occasion by the anti-federal Party. They were essentially aided in their views by some of Mr. Adet's strokes of diplomatic finesse."[2]

Due in no small part to his strong showing in Pennsylvania, Jefferson came within an ace of winning the presidency, losing to Adams by a mere three electoral votes. But in the game that Delacroix was playing, close wasn't good enough. And so with John Adams, another Federalist, about to take the oath of office, Delacroix and the Directory decided to increase the pressure on the diplomatic front. They refused to receive General Charles C. Pinckney, the South Carolina Federalist who had been sent to replace Monroe in Paris. Simultaneously, French warships and privateers began preying on American merchant vessels.

By the time John Adams took the oath of office in March 1797, France and the United States seemed to be drifting toward war. Adams, however, doubted that the Directory meant to carry things that far. He thought it much more likely that Paris would exert increasing pressure along the fault line in American politics that separated Federalists from Republicans, hoping to create an internal crisis. His own strategy was designed to convince the Directory that this approach wouldn't work, that when faced with a foreign threat Americans would stand together.

Adams hoped that a commission representative of divergent regional and political views would be able to negotiate a settlement. He reasoned that when confronted with such a group the French would decide it was useless to pursue their divisive tactics. They might not, of course. But the Republicans would then have to admit that it was the French who were being unreasonable. That admission would, in turn, encourage national unity in the event that war proved unavoidable.

Adams's first choice to represent the Republican and southern point of view on his projected peace commission was Vice-President Thomas Jefferson. The Virginian refused the appointment but was so intrigued by Adams's proposal that he contacted James Madison about going to Paris. But Madison, who feared a trick, also turned the president down. Perhaps this was for the best, since when Secretary of the Treasury Oliver Wolcott learned that Adams was considering the appointment of a ranking Republican to the negotiating team, he threatened to resign and take the rest of the cabinet with him. Had Adams appointed an important Republican to the commission, his administration might well have collapsed.

An angry Adams complained to his wife that if "the Federalists go to playing pranks I will resign the office and let Jefferson lead them to peace, wealth and power if he will. From the situation, where I now am, I see a scene of ambition, beyond all my former suspicions or imaginations."[3] Of course this intensely ambitious political man had no intention of resigning. And so he persevered.

To dramatize the seriousness of the crisis with France, Adams called a special session of Congress for May 1797. In a speech delivered at the opening session he tried to project the image of a leader anxious for peace but ready for war. He announced that he was preparing to send a peace commission to France but simultaneously urged Congress to prepare for conflict in the event the negotiations failed.

Though Adams earnestly desired peace, the Republicans, deeply suspicious, assumed that his real purpose was war and that he intended the talks should fail. After his maiden speech it was, therefore, partisan warfare as usual. But whereas the Republican press had been cautious in its attacks on the revered Washington, it was open season on "His Rotundity," who Benjamin Franklin Bache delighted in pointing out was "President by three votes only."[4]

Irritated but undeterred, Adams set immediately to work organizing his negotiating team. He chose General Charles C. Pinckney, a moderate South Carolina Federalist and the minister recently rejected by the French, to be one of the commissioners. The Virginia Federalist, John Marshall, represented a different southern state and a more conservative point of view. The most controversial member of the commission was Adams's friend Elbridge Gerry of Massachusetts. Gerry was at this time attached to neither political faction but was on good terms both with the president and many Republican leaders, including Vice-President Jefferson.

THE XYZ AFFAIR

Early in the summer of 1797 Gerry and Marshall sailed to join Pinckney, who awaited their arrival in the Netherlands. To those who remained behind in Philadelphia, it must have seemed as though the envoys had sailed off the edge of the earth. Their first five dispatches did not reach the president until March 1798. From these Adams learned that his emissaries had not even been received but had been kept cooling their heels in the antechambers of official Paris. And that wasn't the worst of it. France's new foreign minister, Charles Maurice Talleyrand, had used three intermediaries (designated as X, Y, and Z in the dispatches) in an attempt to extort a bribe of some $250,000 from the envoys. Talleyrand's men also suggested that peace would depend on America's willingness to extend a "forced loan" to France of some $12 million which it was clear was never to be repaid. The envoys were also told that the Directory would no doubt require an official apology for the harsh criticism President Adams had leveled at France in his May 1797 address to Congress.

The envoys, who had no authority to pay bribes, negotiate loans, or make apologies, refused to consider any such concessions. In their final dispatch they indicated that there was no hope for the success of their mission. They would make one last attempt to open talks but, failing that, would demand their passports.

Adams, who was thoroughly infuriated not only with the Directory but also with his own envoys for remaining so long in such humiliating circumstances, wanted to publish the correspondence then and there. He felt certain that the public reaction to what became known as the XYZ affair would silence his domestic opponents and justify a declaration of war. Nor can there be much doubt that at that moment Adams wanted war. Still, he hesitated. If the published dispatches reached France before the envoys left, they might be placed in physical danger. French governments had in the past imprisoned foreign diplomats for less than what his envoys had disclosed.

But Adams was not prepared to keep the documents under wraps indefinitely. As early as March 11, he told Theodore Sedgwick, a Federalist congressman, that he was withholding the dispatches only because he did not want to expose the envoys to "assassination," that he sought only a little extra time to allow them to leave Paris before published copies of their correspondence reached France. Adams sent a special messenger by fast ship to warn the envoys that unless negotiations had actually begun they were to leave France immediately.

On March 19, Adams, speaking generally, informed Congress that the talks had failed, authorized the arming of American merchant ships, and urged the legislators to prepare the nation for war. When House Republicans balked, demanding to see the envoys' dispatches, Adams was happy to oblige. He forwarded the papers and at the same time announced that he would never again send an envoy to France unless first assured that he would be "received, respected and honored as the representative of a great, free, powerful and independent nation."[5] Ten thousand copies of the XYZ dispatches were then printed and distributed nationally.

The effect of these developments was electric. For one thing, the president became more popular than ever before in his long political career. Crowds of patriotic Federalists filled Philadelphia's theater each night, where they cheered and shouted for encore performances of "Hail Columbia." Addresses supporting his policies poured in upon the president from all points on the compass. Early in May twelve hundred young men, all sporting the black cockade, symbol of Federalism, met at the City Tavern in Philadelphia and marched from there to the president's house, where they pledged him their support. Dozens of new lyrics were composed to the tune of "Yankee Doodle."

With the country literally oozing patriotism, Congress rushed to support the president. A law was enacted suspending all trade with France as well as the French West Indies. The treaties of 1778 were abrogated, and the United States Navy was given its sailing orders. The naval war with France had begun.

One of the two Alien Acts passed during that session authorized the president to deport aliens suspected of being dangerous to the public safety or of harboring "treasonable or secret" inclinations. At the same time the Naturalization Law made it more difficult for aliens to gain the protection of United States citizenship. The even more notorious Sedition Act made it a crime punishable by imprisonment to write or speak against the policies of the government if the effect of the action was to bring the government into disrepute. The army was expanded to some thirteen thousand men, and a number of new direct taxes were levied to pay for the increased costs of the growing defense establishment.

Many historians have described the summer of 1798 as a time when a war fever gripped the nation. There is obviously something to this. Yet it is worth noting that even at their most extreme the enthusiasms of that summer produced neither a declaration of war nor national unity. To be sure the Republicans were thrown into disarray by the XYZ disclosures. But they did not support the hostile measures taken against France. Nor did they fold up their tents and steal quietly away. They simply waited for the storm to pass. Moreover, although it is true that the Federalists managed to enact some important legislation, they did not get everything they hoped for. Thus, when Secretary of War James McHenry sought an extra $1.2 million for defense, the House cut his request by a whopping one-third. A bill to establish a twenty thousand man provisional army was totally gutted in the House. Plans to increase the size of the navy also came to nothing. The House, in fact, succeeded in reducing from sixteen to twelve the number of small armed ships to be constructed for convoy duty—this in the middle of an undeclared naval war with France. Most important, those Federalists who hoped for a declaration of war were never able to muster the necessary congressional majority.

Any possibility that Congress would declare war vanished in June 1798, when it was learned that although John Marshall and Charles C. Pinckney had left Paris, the third peace commissioner, Elbridge Gerry, had decided to remain behind. Gerry's decision was widely interpreted to mean that chances for a negotiated settlement still existed. That view was strengthened when the Republican editor, Benjamin Franklin Bache, published a letter from Talleyrand expressing what appeared to be a genuine interest in a reconciliation with America. With peace then still viewed as a possibility, Congress adjourned.

Militant Federalists, those who viewed war as the best security not only against the French but also as a method of destroying the power of the Republican opposition, were in despair. Wrote the Massachusetts merchant Stephen Higginson, "Nothing but an open war can save us, and the more inveterate and deadly it shall be the better will be our chance of security in the future." Abigail Adams, no doubt echoing the thoughts of the president, remarked that although important things had been accomplished during the recent congressional session a declaration of war "ought undoubtedly to have been made." She blamed Gerry for this failure. His decision to divide the commission and remain in France, she thought, had been "wrong, very wrong."[6]

At the time few were more disappointed than John Adams when Congress adjourned without declaring war. During the summer and early autumn of 1798, however, he began to have second thoughts. One development that gave him pause was the fact that he was forced very much against his will to appoint Alexander Hamilton—that "Creole bastard" Adams once called him, referring to the circumstances of his birth—as the de facto commander of the recently enlarged army.[7]

To dramatize the seriousness of the Franco-American crisis, Adams asked the aged Washington to accept an appointment as commander in chief of the army. Never really expecting the old general to take the field, Adams

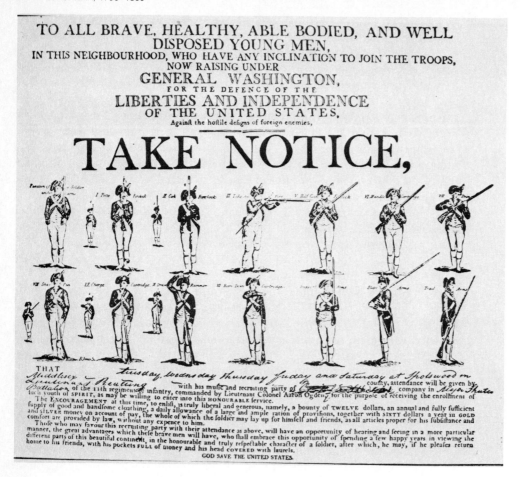

TO ALL BRAVE, HEALTHY, ABLE BODIED, AND WELL DISPOSED YOUNG MEN,

IN THIS NEIGHBOURHOOD, WHO HAVE ANY INCLINATION TO JOIN THE TROOPS, NOW RAISING UNDER

GENERAL WASHINGTON,

FOR THE DEFENCE OF THE

LIBERTIES AND INDEPENDENCE

OF THE UNITED STATES,

Against the hostile designs of foreign enemies,

TAKE NOTICE,

GOD SAVE THE UNITED STATES.

In spite of rosy promises of "a few happy years" soldiering after which the volunteer could "return home to his friends, with his pockets full of money and his head covered with laurels," military recruitment went slowly during the crisis with France in 1798.

explained, "We must have your name, if you will in any case, permit us to use it—there will be more efficacy in it than in many an army."[8] Washington agreed on two conditions: first, that he would not have to become actively involved in military affairs until the army was actually deployed; and second, that he be allowed to select his staff. Adams quickly agreed. Washington then asked Adams to appoint Hamilton his second in command. With Washington a mere figurehead, Hamilton would be in actual control of the army.

The president, who knew that Hamilton had opposed his election in 1796, tried wriggle free of his rather thoughtless commitment. But when Washington threatened to resign if Hamilton was not given the appointment, Adams had no choice but to give in. It was, of course, humiliating for Adams to have Hamilton literally crammed down his throat in that way. His wife

Abigail mourned, too. "Serious people are mortified," she lamented, "and every Uriah must tremble for his Bathsheba."[9]

Whether there existed in the United States any latter-day biblical beauties tempting enough to arouse Hamilton's lusts was a matter of conjecture. President Adams was troubled by other concerns. Congress and the public had approved an enlarged army because they feared war with France and the threat of invasion. But the president knew that Hamilton had other plans. He was involved in a scheme hatched by the Latin American revolutionary leader Francisco de Miranda, in which an American army and a British naval force would collaborate in driving the Spanish from the Western Hemisphere.

Adams had not the least interest in supporting Hamilton's military ambitions. Armies are costly affairs and he was certain that the taxes necessary to finance the fifty-thousand-man force Hamilton envisioned "would have raised a rebellion in every state in the Union. The very idea of the expense of it would have turned President, Senate, and House out of doors."[10]

POLITICS AND PEACEMAKING

While Adams fretted over the implications of an army under the command of Alexander Hamilton, in Paris, Talleyrand was doing everything in his power to arrange a reconciliation. It was widely assumed in the United States that the bishop of Autun himself was responsible for the crisis in French relations. This was no doubt the result of the role he played in the XYZ affair. But Talleyrand saw no advantage in a conflict with America. War would destroy all trade between the United States and France as well as France's continental allies. Worse, since the United States was a major source of provisions for the French West Indies, war would result in starvation for the island populations and probably force them to surrender to the British. It would also give Britain even greater advantages in the American market-place while at the same time adding to its naval strength. America had only a small fleet, but it could provide the Royal Navy with twenty thousand able-bodied seamen. The British, with more ships than seamen to work them, would find these American sailors immensely useful. Perhaps worst of all, war would provide the Americans with an excuse to seize Florida and Louisiana from France's ally Spain. And Talleyrand had ambitions of his own for these vast areas.

At length, but too late to open negotiations with the departed American envoys, Marshall and Pinckney, Talleyrand won the Directory over to his way of thinking. He tried to engage Elbridge Gerry, the lone American envoy remaining in Paris, in serious talks. But Gerry, who had no authority to negotiate singly, refused. He did agree, however, to take any proposals Talleyrand cared to make back to the president. When at length Gerry was allowed to leave Paris, he carried Talleyrand's promise of an honorable peace. Talleyrand also released all of his correspondence with Gerry on the subject of a treaty, making certain that this material reached Republican editors in the United States. The correspondence, which emphasized Talleyrand's desire for serious negotiations, began appearing in American newspapers in August. Matching his words with deeds, Talleyrand also saw to it that privateering operations against American shipping were sharply curtailed and that a long-standing embargo on American ships in French ports was lifted.

Adams may or may not have been impressed by these new French initiatives. The recent history of Franco-American relations had left him deeply suspicious. It was quite possible, he thought, that the French had been taken aback by the effect of the XYZ disclosures and were pretending to be interested in a settlement in order to once again encourage political divisiveness in the United States. On the other hand, Adams could not ignore the possibility that Talleyrand was serious, especially in light of the many indications that popular enthusiasm for war was in decline and that something like an antiadministration backlash was in the making.

Signs of growing domestic opposition to administration policy were clear and unmistakable. Thus, when the Federalists used the Sedition Act to muzzle the Republican press, imprisoning several important editors including Thomas Cooper, William Duane, and James Callender, popular opposition to these repressive measures quickly developed. Nowhere was feeling any stronger than in Virginia and Kentucky. There the state legislatures, encouraged by Thomas Jefferson and James Madison, passed resolutions denouncing the Sedition Act and claiming for the states the right to judge the constitutionality of laws enacted by Congress. But it wasn't just in southern Republican strongholds that these administration policies came under attack. In Vermont, for example, when the Republican congressman, Matthew Lyon, was imprisoned for sedition, he promptly became a popular martyr and was elected to another term in Congress even though he remained in jail.

Before the last autumn leaves of 1798 had fallen, Adams was also aware of growing public dissatisfaction over the increased costs of government under his administration. Britain's Admiral Horatio Lord Nelson had won a smashing victory over a French fleet at the battle of the Nile, and the Directory had acknowledged Britain's control of the seas by abandoning plans for a cross-channel invasion of England. These developments made it difficult to take the threat of a French invasion seriously. As President Adams himself remarked, "At present there is no more prospect of seeing a French army here, than there is in heaven."[11] That being the case, increasing numbers of Americans wondered how long the government would insist on maintaining the enlarged army it had created and the taxes needed to support it.

The political handwriting, though still faint, was already on the wall. Popular support for continued large-scale military expenditures was eroding. That was a fact Adams could ignore only at his own risk. "House and land tax of Congress goes on heavily, causing great uneasiness," wrote the

Massachusetts democrat, Seth Ames. "Silent indignation hath not yet exploded—tho' hard threatened. I fear civil war must be the result of Government measures."[12]

Though it was hardly a civil war, Pennsylvania was the scene of a minor uprising against the direct tax. John Fries, an auctioneer by trade (and a Federalist until the new federal taxes came along) was arrested for his role in the "insurrection" and tried for treason. Sentenced to hang, he was later pardoned by the president. "Fries's Rebellion," as it is sometimes called, was not a great threat to the republic. But it was another indication of the growing discontent with administration policy.

The political appeal of those who advocated peace, the demobilization of the military, and a tax cut was still another clear indication of growing discontent. While passing through Marlboro, Massachusetts, Adams was told by the minister of a local congregation that "a number of his parishioners had . . . voted for" the local Republican congressman only because "he was a great opposer of the land tax."[13] Elbridge Gerry, who returned from Paris trumpeting the view that peace with France on honorable terms was possible, quickly became one of the most popular men in Massachusetts.

Nor could Adams discount the significance of Dr. George Logan's election to the House of Representatives from Pennsylvania. Logan had earlier traveled to France, hoping that in direct talks with Talleyrand he could break the diplomatic impasse and lay the basis for peace. Adams had scoffed at Logan's efforts, and Congress subsequently enacted legislation—the Logan Act—making it a criminal offense for private citizens to interfere in the diplomatic process. The people of Logan's congressional district, however, felt quite differently about the good doctor, whose antiwar views were shared by a majority in the newly elected House of Representatives.

TALLEYRAND OPENS THE WAY

Well before the end of 1798, John Adams knew that substantial numbers of Americans had become disenchanted with his policies. Any doubts he had were surely erased as he rode toward Philadelphia for the opening of the December session of Congress. As he traveled he repeatedly encountered "great prejudices against the land tax." The people, Adams thought, had thus far been quiescent. But, he continued, "their patience" would "not last always."[14]

With Congress about to convene, Adams had to make an important decision. Extreme Federalists, including Hamilton and three of the four members of his cabinet, wanted him to ask for a declaration of war. But Adams realized that to persist in the policies of the spring and summer would be worse than unavailing; it would be foolish. Even if Adams had asked for war, it would have done him no good. He didn't have the votes. On the other hand, Adams's distrust of the French ran deep. He was, therefore, disinclined to reopen negotiations without further evidence of the

Directory's sincerity. And so he attempted a straddle. In his opening address he urged Congress and the people to keep up their guard. At the same time he left the door ajar for renewed talks when he observed that "harmony between us and France may be restored at her option." The president, however, would go no further. He left it to France "if she is indeed desirous of accommodation, to take the requisite steps."[15] Given the state of public opinion, recent French initiatives, and the fact that the House of Representatives would in all probability have refused to vote for a declaration of war, Adams had made a wise decision. Nevertheless, it cost him the support of the extreme Federalists who, led by Hamilton, broke with him and later opposed his reelection.

In February 1799, Adams received several dispatches from William Vans Murray, the American minister at the Hague. Included was a note from Talleyrand addressed to Louis Pichon, a young French diplomat who, like Murray, was stationed in the Netherlands. The letter contained at least in rough outline the assurances Adams had earlier required as the sine qua non of any future negotiation. His envoys would be received, and serious negotiations would soon follow. Adams reacted quickly, nominating Murray to be the new minister plenipotentiary to the French republic.

When a group of "High Federalist" senators threatened to defeat the Murray nomination in the Senate, Adams, still hoping to keep the Federalists united, agreed to a compromise. Murray would become part of a delegation that was to include two "safe" Federalists, Oliver Ellsworth of Connecticut and William R. Davie of North Carolina. Nor would these two envoys sail for France until they also had been assured that they would be received with due courtesy. Bitter dissent within Federalist ranks, then, caused the president to delay the sailing of his commissioners until November 1799. But, much against the inclinations of the extremists in the party, sail they did.

The American delegation arrived in Paris to find the political situation there totally changed. Napoleon Bonaparte had overthrown the Directory in a coup that took place on 18 Brumaire (November 9–10, 1799). A Consulate had been established with Napoleon himself as first consul. On the international front the war that had absorbed Europe for more than a decade was at last drawing to a conclusion.

The French and American delegations quickly hammered out an agreement. The Convention of 1800, however, was no great diplomatic achievement. The two sides did make peace, which was Adams's principal aim. And both sides also agreed to abrogate the Alliance of 1778, which had proven to be much more than a mere thorn in the side of two Federalist administrations. But the Convention did not go beyond these basic essentials.

Years later, when looking back on the turmoil that characterized his presidency, John Adams described his decision for peace as among "the most disinterested and meritorious actions of my life."[16] He meant that by reopening the negotiations he saved the country from war but as a result lost the political support of the Hamiltonian wing of the Federalist party and with it the election of 1800. An appealing story of presidential self-sacrifice, it is unhappily not entirely convincing. For one thing, it fails to take into account the fact that although Hamilton and other extreme Federalists did their best to undercut him, Adams remained the most powerful figure in the Federalist party, its candidate for president in 1800. Moreover, following Adams's decision to reopen talks with France, the Federalist party, or at least that part of it which Adams represented, gained popularity. Finally, it should be noted that although he was defeated in 1800, Adams actually ran a stronger race than he had four years before. He took all of New England's electoral votes, won six more electoral votes in Pennsylvania than he had in 1796, and did just as well in the states south of Delaware. Adams lost the closely contested election in New York, where clever manipulations by Jefferson's ally, Aaron Burr, and Alexander Hamilton's blunders combined to defeat him. Even in New York the average difference between the victorious Republican electors (whose votes spelled defeat for Adams) and their Federalist opponents was a scant five hundred popular votes.

The strength of the Adams candidacy in 1800 even after the apostasy of Hamilton and the conservative wing of the Federalist party points to only one logical conclusion. When John Adams decided to make peace instead of war, he served not only his country but his own political interests. Before the end of 1798 popular enthusiasm for war and the other extreme measures of the summer had subsided. Had Adams persisted in those policies he might have retained the allegiances of the extreme Federalists. But the popularity of the Federalist party as a whole would have continued to decline, and he would in any event have lost the presidency to Jefferson. By steering back toward the political center and away from extremist measures, Adams actually strengthened his chances for winning reelection and, as we have seen, came within a few hundred popular votes of victory.

ENDNOTES

1. Pierre Adet to Timothy Pickering, May 18, 1796, *American State Papers* (Gales and Seaton, Washington, 1832), vol.I, pt.1, p. 650.

2. William Bingham to Rufus King, November 29, 1796, *The Life and Correspondence of Rufus King* ed. C. R. King (G. P. Putnam's Sons, N.Y., 1895–99), II, p. 124.

3. John Adams, quoted in Page Smith, *John Adams* (Doubleday and Co., Garden City and N.Y., 1962), II, p. 920.

4. *Philadelphia Aurora and General Advertiser*, May 23, 1797.

5. *Messages and Papers of the Presidents*, ed. James D. Richardson (Washington D.C., 1900), I, p. 266.

6. Stephen Higginson to Oliver Wolcott Jr., July 11, 1798, in Oliver Wolcott, *Memoirs of the Administrations of Washington and John Adams*, ed. George Gibbs (W. Van Norden, N.Y., 1846), II, p. 71; Abigail Adams, quoted in Gerard Clarfield, *Timothy Pickering and the American Republic*, p. 193.

7. Adams, quoted in Smith, *John Adams*, II, p. 1043.

8. John Adams to George Washington, June 22, 1798, Adams Papers Microfilm (Massachusetts Historical Society, Boston, 1954), reel #117.

9. Abigail Adams to John Adams, January 12, 1799, *ibid.*, reel #393.

10. John Adams, "Correspondence Originally Published in the *Boston Patriot*," in *The Works of John Adams*, ed. C. F. Adams (Little, Brown and Company, Boston, 1854–1856), IX, p. 290.

11. John Adams, quoted in Manning J. Dauer, *The Adams Federalists* (Johns Hopkins University Press, Baltimore, Md., 1953), p. 214.

12. Seth Ames, quoted in Stephen G. Kurtz, *The Presidency of John Adams* (A. S. Barnes and Co., N.Y., 1957), pp. 362–63.

13. William S. Shaw to Abigail Adams, November 25, 1798, *Adams Papers Microfilm*, reel #392.

14. John Adams, quoted in Kurtz, *The Presidency of John Adams*, p. 361.

15. Adams, quoted in John C. Miller, *The Federalist Era* (Harper and Row, N.Y., 1960), p. 244.

16. Adams to James Lloyd, January, 1815, *Adams Works*, ed. C. F. Adams, X, p. 113.

JEFFERSONIAN DIPLOMACY, 1801–1809

Thomas Jefferson came to the presidency committed to peace and commerce with all nations and entangling alliances with none. Experience demonstrated, however, that economic entanglements led to political problems and that neutrality was next to impossible for a nation as deeply involved in the Atlantic trading community as was the United States.

Thomas Jefferson's inauguration was without doubt one of the least pretentious on record. There was no inaugural ball, no planned celebration, not even a coach to carry the president-elect to the steps of the Capitol. Instead, at about noon on inauguration day Jefferson emerged from the boarding house where he had spent the night. Dressed in a plain dark suit and accompanied by a number of friends, he ambled toward the Capitol behind two ragtag companies of local militiamen, while those who had come to Washington D.C., the new national capital, to witness the great event looked on.

This ostentatious lack of ostentation was only a forerunner of things to come. Life inside Jefferson's White House was notoriously informal, a fact that discomfited some in Washington's tiny diplomatic community, who were used to the formality of European court life. The president himself often shambled about dressed in an old bathrobe and worn slippers, even on occasion greeting foreign dignitaries in this attire. Often, one suspects Jefferson of actually enjoying the discomfort he caused. Anthony Merry, the very stuffy British minister who arrived in Washington in 1803, was given the full treatment. Arriving at the White House one fine November day in full regalia, he found the president "not merely in undress, but *actually standing in slippers down at the heels, and both pantaloons, coat, and under-clothes indicative of utter slovenliness and indifference to appearances, and in a state of negligence actually studied.*"[1] It was just the beginning of a long, unhappy relationship.

Jefferson's insistence on projecting an image of republican simplicity was both a reflection of his personal taste and a political statement. Presidents Washington and Adams had both emphasized the importance of ceremony as a method of building respect for the presidency. They had even held weekly levees after the fashion of the European aristocracy. Jefferson believed the Federalists had gone beyond simply aping certain aristocratic customs. He was persuaded that they had been moving toward the creation of a European-style tyranny. The election of 1800, however, changed all that. Jefferson viewed himself as the spokesperson for "as real a revolution in the principles of our government as that of 1776 was in its form."[2]

This "revolution" was just as true in the field of foreign relations as it was in domestic affairs. Jefferson believed that the Federalists had abandoned neutrality in favor of a pro-British foreign policy. In his inaugural address he affirmed his commitment to first principles, to "peace, commerce, and honest friendship with all nations," but "entangling alliances with none." In a letter to Thomas Paine he reiterated the point, explaining that he had no intention of aligning the United States with any foreign government. "Determined as we are to avoid, if possible, wasting the energies of our people in war and destruction, we shall avoid implicating ourselves with the powers of Europe, even in support of principles which we mean to pursue. They have so many other interests different from ours that we must avoid being entangled in them." For Jefferson, then, the Revolution of 1800 was restorative. At home it revitalized republican ideals that had been threatened by the aristocratic proclivities of the Federalists. In the foreign arena it returned America to true neutrality, to "commerce with all nations and political involvements with none."[3]

THE BARBARY WARS

During the partisan struggle of the 1790s, the Federalists tried to saddle Jefferson with a reputation for being incapable of decisive action when the use of force was required. But the facts tell us otherwise. When the issue was important and the odds were right, Jefferson was quite ready to resort to force. He made that clear not two weeks after taking power when, without so much as a by-your-leave from Congress, he authorized naval operations against the Barbary states of Algiers, Tripoli, and Tunis. Two Federalist presidents had paid tribute to these pirate states in return for which American merchantmen were allowed to trade unhindered in the Mediterranean. Now a supposedly pacifist president—a strict constructionist at that—made war by executive order.

On June 2, 1801, Commodore Richard Dale, commanding a squadron of three frigates and a schooner, set sail for the Mediterranean. Administra-

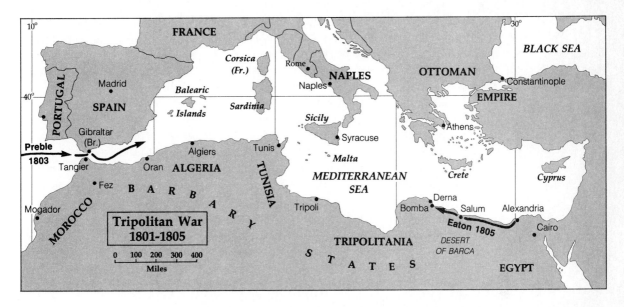

Tripolitan War
1801–1805

0   100   200   300   400
Miles

tion leaders attempted to finesse the fact that they had gone to war without congressional authorization by admonishing Dale to act only on the defensive. Still, war is war no matter how it is defined; and one man's defense can to the unsophisticated eye seem very offensive indeed. So it was with Dale, who was to "protect our commerce and chastise their insolence; by sinking, burning, or destroying their ships and vessels."[4]

To understand why Jefferson acted so decisively against the Barbary States it is necessary to backtrack to the year 1784, when he was the American minister to France and the Articles of Confederation government was in its infancy. At that time Jefferson was part of a commission with instructions to purchase peace treaties from Algiers, Morocco, Tripoli, and Tunis. The commission was also supposed to purchase the freedom of twenty-one American seamen then enslaved in Algiers.

Neither Jefferson nor John Adams, another member of this commission, was enthusiastic about ransoming hostages or buying protection from a gang of unruly cutthroats. But Adams accepted it as a necessary evil because he thought the American people were more willing to demean themselves in this way than go to war. Jefferson, on the other hand, preferred to fight. He felt that if the American Revolution meant anything it stood for the advance of civilization, the triumph of reason and law over blind force. How then could the United States knuckle under to pirates?

At a less ideological level Jefferson doubted that even if the Barbary states could be bought off they would stay bought. He noted that the British, who did pay tribute, always had recourse to the Royal Navy if one or another of the piratical clan should stray from his agreement. A treaty purchased from a nest of pirates, he thought, "would depend on their idea of our power."[5] But since the United States had virtually no power at its disposal, there was little reason to believe the pirates would live up to their agreements.

In 1784 neither Adams nor Jefferson had the opportunity to test their theories. Congress hadn't enough money to ransom the twenty-one enslaved Americans or buy protection save from Morocco, the least predatory of the Barbary states. Frustrated by his government's weakness, Jefferson was in his own words "absolutely suspended between indignation and impotence." "We ought to begin a naval power, if we mean to carry on our own commerce," he explained in a letter to James Monroe. "Can we begin it on a more honorable occasion, or with a weaker foe?" he asked. What America needed in the Mediterranean, he continued, was not a peace emissary but John Paul Jones in command of a half-dozen frigates.[6] At last in 1801 Jefferson was in a position to act. And so Commodore Dale became the first in a long succession of American naval commanders to lead fighting ships into the Mediterranean

By the time Dale's tiny squadron came on station Yusuf Karamanli, the pasha of Tripoli, had sent men to the United States consulate to cut down the flagpole. It was his way of declaring war. The pasha wanted increased tribute. What he got was war and a nearly successful attempt by the Jefferson administration to place his brother Hamet on the throne in a coup d'état.

If the truth be known, it wasn't much of a war. For four years American naval forces engaged in a running battle with Tripolitan corsairs, blockading Tripoli for a time and bombarding coastal fortifications. The most dramatic event of the fighting came when the frigate *Philadelphia*, after having run aground while chasing a Tripolitan cruiser, was taken by the pasha's men and anchored in Tripoli's harbor under the guns of the fortress there. Stephen Decatur, a young naval lieutenant destined for great things during the War of 1812, led a raiding party that set fire to the *Philadelphia*. Decatur escaped without losing a man. On hearing of Decatur's exploit, Britain's Admiral Horatio Lord Nelson, the victor in the battle of the Nile who was destined for death and immortality at Trafalgar, pronounced Decatur's raid "the most bold and daring act of the age."[7]

Tripoli and the United States made peace when Tobias Lear, consul general to all the Barbary states, negotiated an agreement that represented only a partial victory for Jefferson. The United States would no longer pay tribute to the pasha. And presents would be sent only on the appointment of a new consul. But Lear did agree to pay a $60,000 ransom for the officers and men of the *Philadelphia* who had been enslaved.

Lear's diplomacy didn't sit well with Captain John Rodgers, commander of the Mediterranean squadron at the time. He offered to personally raise the money to ransom the *Philadelphia*'s crew if Lear would continue the war. But the consul general prevailed, and the Tripolitan War came to an inconclusive end.

Like Commodore Rodgers, historians since have criticized Lear, claiming he settled for too little. Yet if the Tripolitan War was not a complete victory, it was the opening salvo in a campaign that had by 1816 put an end

On the night of February 16, 1804, Lieutenant Stephen Decatur led a raiding party into the harbor at Tripoli, literally under the guns of the fortress there, in a daring attempt to set the captured frigate *Philadelphia* on fire. He accomplished his mission and escaped without losing a man.

BURNING of the FRIGATE PHILADELPHIA in the HARBOUR of TRIPOLI. 16 Feb. 1804.

to the piratical maraudings of the North African states and made the Mediterranean safe for the commerce of all nations.

By taking a stand against international lawlessness, Jefferson reaffirmed the view of American and European liberals alike that the American Revolution marked the dawn of a new era. The pope himself commented on the significance of what the United States had undertaken when he noted that "with a small force and in a short space of time," Commodore Edward Preble, the most aggressive of American commanders in the Mediterranean, had "done more for the cause of Christianity than the most powerful nations of Christendom have done for ages."[8]

THE FRENCH IN LOUISIANA

If Jefferson viewed the activities of the Barbary pirates as a challenge to the meaning of the American Revolution as well as a serious inconvenience to America's Mediterranean trade, closer to home he confronted an international adventurer whose power vastly exceeded that of the Muslim princes and whose ambitions posed a direct threat to the security of the United States.

The end of the war in Europe led Napoleon Bonaparte to turn his attention to new enterprises in the Western Hemisphere, where empires waited to be conquered. Napoleon sought the return of the vast area known as Louisiana, which France had ceded to Spain in 1762. This region was to serve as the granary for an expanded French empire in the Caribbean, centering on the island of Santo Domingo.

Napoleon had only the slightest difficulty reacquiring Louisiana from Spain. Under terms of the secret Treaty of San Ildefonso signed on October 1, 1800, and a second agreement initialed in March of the following year, the first consul agreed that in return for Louisiana he would place the king of Spain's son-in-law on the throne of the kingdom of Etruria (the provinces of Tuscany and Piombino in Italy). In another part of the agreement, which became significant later, Napoleon also agreed that he would never transfer Louisiana to a third power.

The second of Napoleon's twin objectives was the restoration of French rule over the rich sugar-producing island of Santo Domingo. To accomplish this he would have to deal with "the Black Napoleon," Toussaint L'Ouverture. Toussaint, a self-educated slave, had been freed shortly before a successful slave uprising erupted on the island in 1791. He joined the rebels and quickly displayed his genius both as a political leader and military strategist. By the time Bonaparte cast his eye westward, Toussaint ruled all of Santo Domingo.

Napoleon planned a two-pronged assault on his western hemispheric objectives. One army commanded by his brother-in-law, General Charles Victor Leclerc, would subdue Santo Domingo's blacks, while a second army led by General Claude Victor was to take control of Louisiana. General Victor's mission was of vital importance. Napoleon viewed the Peace of Amiens, which had ended the recent European war, as a mere truce. Once the conflagration broke out again, as it was bound to do, it would be impossible to send forces to defend Louisiana since the British navy would again assert its dominance on the seas. It was, therefore, vital that Victor's army be in control of the colony before war came. Victor could then hold Louisiana against the possibility of an attack by British or American forces.

Governments leaked then, just as they do now. Shortly after France and Spain signed their secret accord Rufus King, the American minister in London, informed the State Department of the rumored retrocession of Louisiana. If the rumors were true, and King believed they were, Pinckney's Treaty was about to become meaningless. French control of the Mississippi could mean that nearly a million western Americans would be cut off from the sea and the marketplace.

The idea of a French army landing in Santo Domingo caused no sleepless nights at the White House. On the contrary, anything the French could do to crush Toussaint's revolution would be deeply appreciated by southern slaveholders. Jefferson himself told Louis Pichon, France's chargé d'affaires in Washington, that he not only approved but would help Napoleon restore white rule on the island. "Nothing would be easier," he explained, "than to supply completely your army and your squadron and to starve Toussaint."[9]

Louisiana, however, was another matter entirely. Jefferson and Secretary of State James Madison agreed that Napoleonic control of New

Orleans would pose a grave threat to the nation's security. Aware that the European wars were likely to begin again at any time, they also feared that the British might take advantage of a renewed conflict to seize Louisiana and control of the all-important river for themselves. It seemed essential that the United States should secure New Orleans and control of the Mississippi as soon as possible

So long as administration leaders had no proof that the French had wrested New Orleans and Louisiana from Spain, they approached the issue cautiously. Robert R. Livingston, the minister in Paris, was instructed to inform the Foreign Ministry that Washington viewed the possibility of a French presence on the Mississippi with grave concern. He was also to hint that if the rumored cession had in fact taken place the United States might be forced into a "closer connection" with Britain. But Livingston was cautioned against making any overt threats.

Once in possession of solid evidence that France had acquired Louisiana, administration leaders became more aggressive. Madison warned Louis Pichon point blank that although France might take possession of the area, "it could not long preserve Louisiana against the United States." To those who believed that France might be able to use its control of the Mississippi to divide the union, Madison replied that "nothing would do more to unite the whole continent than having France in the neighborhood."[10] In a famous letter sent to Livingston in Paris, the contents of which were transmitted to the French government, Jefferson went even further, warning:

> The day France takes possession of New Orleans fixes the sentence which is to restrain her forever within her low water mark. It seals the union of two nations who in conjunction can maintain exclusive possession of the ocean. From that moment we must marry ourselves to the British fleet and nation.[11]

The president's dark warnings did no good. Livingston complained that there "never was a government in which less could be done by negotiation than here. . . . One man is everything. He seldom asks advice and never hears it unasked. Though the sense of every reflecting man is against this wild expedition, no one dares to tell him so."[12]

In October 1802, with the Louisiana question still unresolved, Juan Ventura Morales, the Spanish intendant at New Orleans, suddenly suspended the American right to deposit goods there, thus closing the Mississippi to American trade. Morales's action set off a storm of protest in the West, where access to the great river was vital.

Conventional wisdom had it that Morales was acting on orders from Paris and that closing the river was a prelude to the French occupation of Louisiana. But when both the Spanish governor of Louisiana and Spain's minister in Washington, the young marquis Casa de Yrujo, assured the president that Morales was acting independently and that the port would soon be reopened, Jefferson took these assurances at face value. But that still left him with a problem for the West was in a frenzy. William C. C.

Claiborne, the governor of the Mississippi Territory, recommended the immediate seizure of New Orleans and promised to provide six hundred militiamen to do the job. The Federalists, meanwhile, saw opportunity knocking and were quick to take advantage of the situation. Thus Connecticut's Roger Griswold demanded that the administration force the Spanish to reopen the river. Alexander Hamilton, also on the attack, asserted that closing New Orleans was merely a preface to French occupation of the area and demanded that the government ally itself with Britain and seize Louisiana before it fell into Napoleon's hands. "Such measures," he thought "would astonish and discontent Buonaparte himself . . . and all Europe would be taught to respect us."[13]

THE MONROE MISSION

Clearly, Jefferson had to do something. To pacify the West and make Napoleon understand that he considered the issue of vital importance, the president nominated James Monroe as his special envoy to join Livingston in Paris. Monroe, who had for two decades championed western interests at the national political level, was an excellent choice. With $2 million at his disposal, the envoy was instructed to purchase New Orleans and the Floridas "or as much thereof as the actual proprietor can be prevailed on to part with." "The Floridas and New Orleans command the only outlets to the sea" for western Americans, Secretary Madison wrote. They "must become a part of the United States, either by purchase or conquest." At the same time Madison warned Louis Pichon, the French chargé, that if Napoleon took possession of New Orleans and closed the river, the administration in Washington might well lose control of the situation. There were, he noted, two hundred thousand angry western militiamen who might act on their own. "This consideration," he remarked menacingly, "ought not to be overlooked by France and would be alone sufficient if allowed its due weight to cure the frenzy which covets Louisiana." Before the end of January 1803, Pichon, who noted with concern the growing cordiality between the president and the young British chargé, Edward Thornton, warned his government that "necessity is forcing Mr. Jefferson to give up his pretensions and scruples against an English alliance."[14]

While Jefferson and Madison were doing everything possible to dramatize the impending dangers, in Paris, Livingston at last found a direct conduit to Napoleon. Working through Joseph Bonaparte, Livingston proposed a treaty by which France would cede New Orleans, upper Louisiana, and West Florida as far as the Perdido River to the United States. (The Perdido was deemed important because it, too, offered access to the sea through the port at Mobile.) At the same time he warned Napoleon that the president wasn't bluffing. France might take possession of New Orleans and Louisiana. But when next Europe went to war, it would lose these holdings and much more besides to the combined forces of England and America.

The administration's threats notwithstanding, it was the failure of his own policies that led Napoleon to abandon his western hemispheric ambitions. At first Leclerc's Santo Domingo campaign seemed to go well. Indeed, within three months the French had captured Toussaint, who was shipped off to a French dungeon, where he perished. But Leclerc's men were never able to conquer the interior of the island, where fierce resistance continued. At the same time the "unseasoned" French fell by the thousands to the ravages of a yellow fever epidemic. When Napoleon learned that Leclerc himself had succumbed, he is said to have raged "damn sugar, damn coffee, damn colonies." His mind began to drift back into more familiar patterns and what was beginning to appear the relatively simple task of conquering Europe.

Napoleon's plans to garrison Louisiana before the outbreak of the next European war also came to grief. General Victor's army was unable to sail from Holland for Louisiana before the winter ice locked the ships in harbor. And so, with another great European war in the offing, Louisiana would be left undefended, vulnerable to a British or an American attack.

On April 10, 1803, Napoleon summoned François, marquis de Barbé-Marbois, the minister of the treasury, and Denis Decres, minister of marine and colonies, to a conference at the picturesque sixteenth-century palace of Saint-Cloud located to the west of Paris on the River Seine. There he told the two ministers that, with war only a matter of time, he was considering selling Louisiana to the United States. Once war came, he explained, he feared losing the entire area, including the Mississippi, to the British. By turning Louisiana over to Jefferson he would eliminate the possibility of an Anglo-American alliance and assure himself that Louisiana and the Mississippi would not fall into British hands. At the same time the money derived from the sale of the territory would come in handy in a war with a country as wealthy as England. Decres offered spirited opposition, but it was no use. Napoleon seldom listened to advisers and, as Barbé-Marbois shrewdly guessed, had made up his mind before the conference began.

Two days after this meeting, Barbé-Marbois turned up unannounced at Robert R. Livingston's Paris apartment. The two men discussed the progress, or rather the lack of progress, in the Louisiana negotiations. Barbé-Marbois then asked Livingston to come to his home on the following evening for further discussions. The next night Livingston obliged, only to learn that Napoleon had given the minister of the treasury control over the negotiations. Moreover, Barbé-Marbois informed the now-elated diplomat that his master wanted to sell not only New Orleans but the entire Louisiana Territory.

It was at this point, after the major breakthrough, that James Monroe arrived in Paris. For a moment it seemed that the conflicting personal ambitions of the two American envoys might upset the negotiations. But setting these feelings aside, the two diplomats agreed to cooperate. Though they had no instructions to purchase more than New Orleans and as much of the Floridas as they could get, they quickly decided that Napoleon's offer

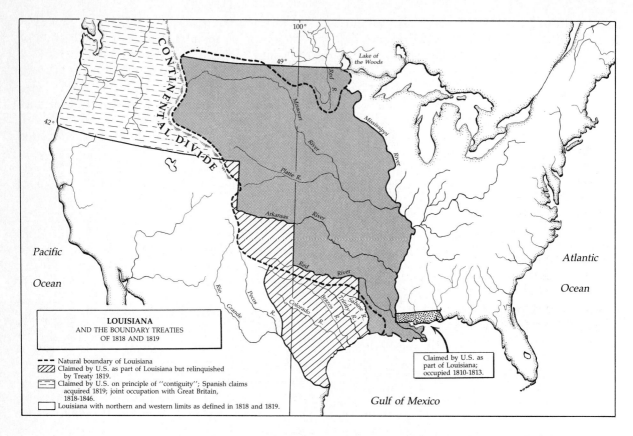

Pacific
Ocean

Atlantic
Ocean

LOUISIANA
AND THE BOUNDARY TREATIES
OF 1818 AND 1819

- - - Natural boundary of Louisiana
Claimed by U.S. as part of Louisiana but relinquished by Treaty 1819.
Claimed by U.S. on principle of "contiguity"; Spanish claims acquired 1819; joint occupation with Great Britain, 1818-1846.
Louisiana with northern and western limits as defined in 1818 and 1819.

Claimed by U.S. as part of Louisiana; occupied 1810-1813.

Gulf of Mexico

was too good to pass up. For a total of $15 million the two diplomats purchased an empire of nearly 830,000 square miles.

On learning of his envoys' accomplishment, Jefferson was first elated and then disturbed. Elated because he believed they had not only secured irrevocable control of the Mississippi but America's agrarian future as well, but disturbed because given his strict constructionist views, he doubted that he had the constitutional authority to make the purchase. He even thought briefly about seeking an amendment to the Constitution granting the government the authority to acquire new territory before going ahead. But he quickly set the idea and his qualms aside. The opportunity that presented itself was too tempting to allow either constitutional scruples or partisan obstructionism to stand in the way. Jefferson took Louisiana and let the opposition rail.

In selling Louisiana to the United States, Napoleon had broken his pledge to Spain that the area would never be ceded to a third power. Madrid protested both in Paris and in Washington. But neither Jefferson nor his successors paid any heed. Undismayed by the charge that they were in effect "buying stolen goods," they insisted that this was an issue to be decided between France and Spain. Since Madrid hadn't the power to block the American takeover, Spain had no choice but to acquiesce.

Nor was it entirely clear just where the boundaries of the vast territory lay. When Livingston asked about the boundaries, Talleyrand, who was then serving as Napoleon's foreign minister, answered enigmatically, "I can give you no direction. You have made a noble bargain for yourselves, and I suppose you will make the most of it."[15] And make the most of it Jefferson did by immediately claiming, with little justification, that the purchase included West Florida. Later the Monroe administration went even further, using the ill-defined western boundary of the purchase as the basis for a negotiation with Spain that extended the national boundary to the Pacific Ocean.

WAR AND NEUTRALITY

In May 1803, the Peace of Amiens collapsed, and Europe plunged once again into chaos and war. The Jefferson administration's policy was to remain uninvolved while taking full advantage of the commercial opportunities opened to neutral commerce as a result of the conflict. Said Secretary Madison, "I hope we shall be wise enough to shun their follies . . . and fortunate enough to turn them by honest means to our just interests."[16] As both the president and his secretary of state were soon to discover, however, trade expansion and noninvolvement were mutually exclusive ideas. The expanding American commercial interest became a target of opportunity for both belligerents, until finally America had no choice but to fight.

The forcible impressment of American seamen into the Royal Navy first became a serious problem during the Wars of the French Revolution. By 1796 the issue had become so significant that the Washington administration felt constrained not only to protest this outrage but to issue official documents to American seamen, certifying that those who carried them were bona fide American citizens. But the British government ignored American protests and paid no heed to these protections. It was too easy, London contended, for British seamen to purchase forged documents and too difficult to distinguish British from American seamen by other means.

The lords of the Admiralty had no intention of allowing the American merchant marine to become a haven for deserters. Had they done so, considering the inhuman conditions that prevailed in the British navy, the desertion rate would have escalated to impossible levels. Moreover, there was a fundamental difference of opinion between British and American authorities regarding the legal definition of American citizenship. The British took the position that an American was someone who had been born in the colonies or emigrated there before 1783. Those who came to the United States after independence remained, as far as the British were concerned, subjects of the king and might legally be required to serve in the military. "Once an Englishman, always an Englishman," remained basic British policy throughout the era.

Impressment became temporarily irrelevant after the Peace of

Amiens in 1801, but returned to plague Anglo-American relations once the Wars of Napoleon began. The British had demobilized rapidly in 1802, releasing some forty thousand seamen from the Royal Navy. Since many of these men found berths in the American merchant fleet, it is not surprising that, with another major European war to be fought, the British began impressing desperately needed seamen from American ships. The argument was always the same, that there was no way to distinguish between Englishmen and Americans. But too many Italians and Swedes serving on American ships were impressed to place much credence in that contention. In all too many instances British commanders impressed men because they needed them, without any consideration for their true nationality.

Secretary Madison insisted that the impressment of any man from the decks of an American ship was a violation of neutral rights. But the Foreign Office rejected outright the secretary's contention as "too extravagant to require any serious Refutation."[17] And so the issue remained unresolved, a festering sore in Anglo-American relations down to the outbreak of war in 1812.

Large numbers of Englishmen were able to find employment in the American merchant service because until 1805 London let stand an Admiralty Court decision rendered four years earlier in the case of the ship *Polly*. This decision allowed American merchants to circumvent the Rule of the War of 1756 and control the carrying trade between the French and Spanish colonies in the New World and Europe.

The *Polly* had been sailing from Marblehead to Bilbao in Spain with a cargo of sugar, cocoa, and other produce of the Spanish colonies, when it was taken by a British cruiser. The case seemed cut and dried, for certainly the ship had been in violation of the Rule of 1756. But Britain's High Court of Admiralty refused to condemn the ship or its cargo on the ground that the *Polly*'s owners had "broken" its voyage by first taking the cargo from the Spanish West Indies to Marblehead, unloading the ship there, paying the customs duties, reloading the ship and then sailing for Europe.

The court intended to discourage American merchants from becoming too deeply involved in the colonial trade by thus adding substantially to their costs. But it didn't work. With Europe again at war after 1803, French and Spanish merchant ships were driven from the seas by the Royal Navy. Paris and Madrid reacted by opening their colonies to neutral ships, and American traders quickly moved in. Over the next two years the value of America's foreign exports—goods imported into the United States and then reexported to Europe—jumped from about $13.5 million to more than $53 million.

Clearly such a situation could not continue forever. It made no sense for the English to drive the French and Spanish merchant fleets from the seas only to see American ships take their place. Moreover, powerful British commercial interests, nonplussed at the growth of American competition in world trade, demanded a change in policy. It came in May 1805 in the form of a second Admiralty Court decision. The ship *Essex* was taken while sailing from Salem to Havana carrying a cargo that had originated in Barcelona. The circumstances were the same as those in the case of the *Polly*. But this time ship and cargo were condemned on the ground that the owners had broken the ship's voyage in Salem as a subterfuge to evade the Rule of 1756 and that the *Essex*'s was in fact a "continuous voyage" from Barcelona to Havana via Salem and was therefore illegal.

Secretary Madison expressed sheer outrage on learning of the *Essex* decision. "From the great amount of property afloat subject to this new and shameful depredation," he predicted that "a dreadful scene of distress may ensue to our commerce." An equally angry James Monroe, then serving as the minister in London, thought this change in policy came about not only for military reasons but also because the British government was anxious to reduce America's increasing power. "No event is deemed more unfavorable to Great Britain than the growing importance of the United States," he wrote, "and it is the primary object of her government to check it, if not crush it."[18]

A crisis in Anglo-American relations soon followed. Over the next several months nearly a hundred American ships were seized by the British. The merchants and marine insurance companies that suffered these losses demanded that Congress do something. Even Federalist merchants talked of war. Theodore Lyman of Massachusetts, for example, predicted "hostile proceedings" if England persisted, while denouncing the government for its failure to arm. Benjamin Goodhue, once a Hamiltonian Federalist senator from Massachusetts, was even more strident. "Rather than have our national rights trampled upon," he stormed, "recourse should be had to arms."[19]

THE GREGG RESOLUTION

Reacting to the crisis, the Pennsylvania Republican, Andrew Gregg, introduced a bill in the House of Representatives calling for the total nonimportation of all English goods. Gregg, like James Madison before him, hoped to force a change in British policy by denying Britain access to the American market. But the Gregg resolution ran into fierce opposition from southern Republicans, who warned that Britain would retaliate by denying southern staple producers their best market, thus bringing about their ruination. Jefferson, too, opposed the bill, not only because he agreed with his southern confreres but also for exactly the same reason Alexander Hamilton had earlier fought trade discrimination against Britain—it would mean a loss of $5 million annually in tariff revenues and force the government to impose unpopular internal taxes to make up the shortfall. All things considered, Jefferson preferred to negotiate.

The Gregg resolution was defeated, and a less stringent bill, the work of Maryland's Joseph Nicholson, was enacted instead. Nicholson's Nonimportation Act was more acceptable to congressional Republicans precisely because it was less provocative to the English. The president, however, who thought even Nicholson had gone too far, convinced Congress to suspend the implementation of the law until he had an opportunity to open talks with the Foreign Office. "No two countries on earth have so many points of common interest and friendship," Jefferson wrote in the spring of 1806, "and their rulers must be great bunglers indeed if with such dispositions, they break them asunder."[20]

Jefferson sent William Pinkney, a prominent Maryland Republican, to London to aid James Monroe in the negotiations. The two American envoys were to seek an end to impressment, restoration of the principle of "broken voyage," compensation for those merchants who had suffered losses as a result of the *Essex* decision, a commercial agreement opening the British West Indies, and greater recognition by the British of America's rights as a neutral. But like John Jay who sought similar concessions more than a decade earlier, Monroe and Pinkney had little to offer in return. It is not surprising, then, that the treaty they negotiated had little to recommend it or that they had little to say on its behalf save that it might be better than war.

The agreement was silent on the vital question of impressment. The Royal Navy's opposition made concessions on this point impossible. Henry Richard Fox, Lord Holland, who represented England at the talks, later wrote that "the atmosphere of the Admiralty made those who breathed it shudder at anything like concessions to the Americans."[21] The commercial articles of the treaty were more disadvantageous than those John Jay had agreed to in 1794. And those, it will be recalled, were rejected by a Federalist Senate. Nor did Monroe and Pinkney win any concessions with regard to the *Essex* decision, the concept of "continuous voyage," or other questions regarding the rights of neutrals. Considering all of the agreement's inadequacies, the real wonder is that Monroe and Pinkney should have thought it worthy of the administration's consideration.

David Erskine, the British minister, was the first person in Washington to receive a copy of the agreement. Well disposed toward the United States and anxious to avoid an Anglo-American war, he rushed the treaty to the Department of State evidently thinking that because American policymakers, too, hoped to avoid war, Madison and Jefferson would view any settlement with England as preferable to none. But when Secretary Madison learned the contents of the treaty, he "expressed the greatest astonishment and disappointment." After discussing the agreement with Madison, a saddened Erskine reported that he did not think ratification "would be possible."[22]

In fact, as the envoy suspected, Jefferson and Madison wanted very much to ratify the agreement. They just couldn't find a sound reason. And so the president refused to submit it to the Senate.

THE CHESAPEAKE AFFAIR

Anglo-American relations continued in a state of disarray until June 22, 1807, when they suddenly turned critical. On that morning, the wind being fair and the tide right, the frigate *Chesapeake*, Commodore James Barron commanding, sailed from Norfolk headed for the Mediterranean. Just beyond the Virginia Capes it was hailed by the British ship *Leopard* and hove to. In a note delivered to Barron, the *Leopard*'s commander demanded that Barron surrender a number of British deserters serving on the *Chesapeake*.

The British, who commonly searched merchant ships for deserters, had never before claimed the right to search national vessels. Barron correctly viewed the British demand as an insult to the American flag and promptly rejected it. At that, the *Leopard* opened fire. In a matter of minutes the *Chesapeake*, completely unprepared for battle, was transformed into a dismasted floating ruin. Barron struck his colors and tried to surrender his ship, but the British commander refused his sword. Instead he sent a boarding party to the *Chesapeake* and removed four men as deserters. The American frigate, with three men killed and eighteen wounded, was left to limp back to Norfolk.

As news of what had befallen the *Chesapeake* spread through Norfolk, tempers flared. The few British officers who happened to be ashore at the time rushed for the safety of their ships. The town's merchants, who had done a thriving business supplying the British squadron that regularly put in there, cut off all supplies and urged other towns in the vicinity to do the same.

As news of the incident spread, so did the anger. In Baltimore, Wilmington, Philadelphia, and New York—even in Boston, where a pro-British sort of Federalism remained fashionable—mass meetings were held at which England was denounced and young men pledged their lives and fortunes in defense of American freedom. Not since 1776, President Jefferson thought, had the country been so aroused.

There is little doubt that at this time Congress would have voted for war had Jefferson so desired. But the president didn't want war. He believed that the *Chesapeake* incident had placed the British in an untenable position and that he could turn the situation to advantage by making menacing gestures while calling for concessions. Jefferson therefore instructed Monroe, who was still in London, to demand reparations, an apology, the return of the seamen impressed from on board the *Chesapeake*, and, most important, a complete end to the practice of impressment. To dramatize the seriousness of the situation, he issued a declaration expelling all British warships from American waters, asked the states to raise one hundred thousand militia, and called Congress into special session. The call for a special session was a dramatic move. But the president had no intention of losing control of the situation to a group of angry legislators. He therefore scheduled the opening of Congress for mid-October. By that time tempers would have cooled, and Monroe would have had an opportunity to negotiate a settlement.

By threatening war, Jefferson hoped to bluff the British into abandoning impressment. But the necessities of war were too compelling for London to give in on this question. Not surprisingly, then, the negotiations between Monroe and the new foreign secretary, George Canning, collapsed.

Canning was willing to make amends for the attack on the *Chesapeake*. But he would not budge on impressment.

By October, when the special session of Congress convened, the legislators as well as the public at large had, as Jefferson suspected they might, calmed down. The president, on the other hand, was now ready to fight. Only after Secretary of the Treasury Albert Gallatin warned him that there was inadequate popular and congressional support for war, that money and military supplies would be a problem, and that the British would take a terrible toll on American commerce while at the same time attacking at will the undefended seacoast cities of the country, did Jefferson decide against seeking a declaration of war that October. Still, he deplored the fact that Congress was "foolishly disposed toward peace."[23] Perhaps Jefferson appreciated the irony. In July, when he might have had a declaration of war, he didn't want one. In October, when he wanted war, he couldn't have it.

JEFFERSON'S EMBARGO

The *Chesapeake* incident flashed like a comet across the night sky, dominating the American perspective on foreign policy. But during this same period no less dramatic events were taking place in Europe. In a series of stunning military victories beginning with the battles of Ulm and Austerlitz in 1805 and ending at Friedland in 1807, Napoleon defeated England's continental allies. Prussia and Austria lay at his feet when he met Czar Alexander I of Russia at Tilsit and signed a truce.

The war had come down to a struggle between France, dominant on the European landmass, and the British who, after Admiral Lord Nelson's 1805 victory at Trafalgar, were dominant on the seas. Unable to strike at England militarily, Napoleon hoped to crush her economically by denying her the vital European marketplace. His Berlin decree (November 21, 1806), the first element in his evolving Continental System, declared the British Isles in a state of blockade. In all parts of Europe under Napoleonic control (and including Russia), trade in British products or the produce of her colonies was prohibited. Moreover, no ship that had first put in at a British-controlled port would be allowed to enter a Continental port. Ships that did so were subject to immediate condemnation.

The British struck back against this declaration of economic warfare on November 11, 1807, with orders-in-council declaring that all areas from which British ships and goods were prohibited were under blockade. Only ships that had first put in at a British port, paid duties, and were specially licensed, could continue on their voyage. The next move was Napoleon's. He reacted with the Milan decree (December 17, 1807), which stipulated that any neutral ships complying with these new British regulations would be considered "denationalized." Such ships along with their cargoes would be seized and sold as British property.

Both belligerents were violating America's neutral rights. But Napoleon's ability to do harm was limited. It was the Royal Navy that forcibly impressed thousands of American seamen. And it was Britain's orders-in-council that denied the United States access to the European marketplace, thus driving commodity prices down and contributing to the economic depression that gripped the South and West in the years after 1807. It is no wonder, then, that first Jefferson and then Madison, while often infuriated with the French, never lost sight of the fact that Britain was the principal despoiler, the major enemy.

The embargo, an administration measure that was rushed through Congress on December 22, 1807, as supplemented by the acts of January 9 and March 12, 1808, forbade all American ships from sailing for foreign ports and prohibited trade across land frontiers as well. Foreign vessels were allowed to enter United States ports and sell their cargoes but could not carry American products abroad. The coastwise trade remained legal. But the merchants involved had to post bond guaranteeing that goods they took on board at one port would be landed somewhere else in the United States.

Although initially Jefferson viewed the embargo as a temporary expedient, Madison convinced him to leave it in effect indefinitely. The secretary of state had long advocated the use of economic sanctions against Britain. England was already feeling the effects of Napoleon's Continental System. Madison believed that if the United States increased the pressure by limiting England's access to the American market while withholding naval stores and grain, which the British needed, London would be forced to make concessions. When he contemplated the effect the embargo would have on the British West Indies, he was even more convinced that Britain would have to give in. Discounting the possibility that Canada and the other Northern Provinces might be able to take up the slack created by the loss of American food and resources, Madison believed the islands were totally dependent on the United States for "the necessaries of life and of cultivation." There was "no other source." Without American supplies, "immediate ruin would ensue."[24]

Madison believed the United States, a fundamentally agricultural society, would stand the stress created by the embargo better than England, a manufacturing and trading nation. He also assumed that the American people had sufficient civic virtue to support government policy even at considerable cost to themselves. Unhappily, neither assumption proved to be entirely correct. Consider first the embargo's impact upon the English. Britain's Tory prime minister, Spencer Perceval, had been guided by two basic considerations in developing the November 1807 orders-in-council. The first was the obvious need to prosecute the war against France. But the second arose from the fact that his Tory party was closely aligned with powerful mercantile and shipping magnets, who were dismayed, not to say infuriated, by the fact that American merchants were taking advantage of their country's neutral status to replace England as the world's principal maritime carrier. Perceval's second aim, then, had been to reduce though not necessarily to destroy America's share of world trade. The November orders were intended to "leave such advantages still to neutral trade as to make it quite clear to be the policy of America to prefer the neutral trade which is left to her to the total stoppage of her trade . . . which a war might occasion."[25]

The embargo did what Perceval hadn't dared to do. France and her allies were denied access to America's resources and the use of the American merchant fleet. At the same time British shipping interests no longer had to concern themselves about American competition. The Americans themselves had taken care of that.

It is true that the embargo sharply reduced Britain's share of the American market, and that proved distressing to British industrialists. But the manufacturing interest was closely identified with the Whig party, which was out of power in London. In any event, because Spanish colonial officials in South America opened the formerly closed markets of the Spanish empire to world trade in 1808, British manufacturers were able to develop new markets there that at least temporarily compensated for the losses they sustained in the United States. It is also clear that American policy makers had underestimated the role Canada and the Northern Provinces could play in supplying both Britain and the West Indies with resources no longer available from the United States.

Madison and Jefferson believed the embargo would create an economic crisis in England. But as far as Perceval and the British Tories were concerned, at least over the short term the embargo could not have been better designed to meet their needs. This evaluation remained true until long after domestic pressures working on the Jefferson administration forced its repeal.

If the embargo failed to have the predicted effect on Britain, it did produce an economic crisis in the United States. Popular discontent with the measure was widespread, but especially pronounced in New England and the Middle States. The Federalists, who hoped to ride the issue back to popularity, were quick to decry the measure. Some, like former secretary of state Timothy Pickering, even charged that Napoleon had ordered Jefferson to implement the embargo as part of his plan to shut Britain out of its world markets. The charge was absurd. But it had a certain vogue among the many who made their living from the sea.

The opponents of the embargo did not confine themselves to mere rhetoric. Smuggling on a large scale soon developed across the land border between the United States and Canada. Those with large quantities of staples on their hands found other ways to evade the law as well, managing in spite of early efforts at enforcement to ship large quantities of America's produce abroad by sea. Aware of this, the administration went to near draconian lengths to stop the smuggling and more or less succeeded, at least with regard to seaborne commerce. The land border, however, was never effectively closed to smugglers.

But the Jefferson administration paid a high price for this partial victory. The federal government assumed police powers that made a mockery of the president's states rights philosophy. At the same time Republican leaders watched helplessly as the unpopular law gave renewed vitality to the once moribund Federalist party. Nor was it long before the Republican party itself began to show signs of fragmentation under the pressure of the government's unpopular and economically disruptive policy.

Political pressures and the inability of the administration to develop an alternative to the embargo led ultimately to paralysis at the highest level. After James Madison's victory in the November 1808 presidential election, a weary, frustrated Thomas Jefferson decided that he had seen enough. Over the strong objections of Madison as well as Treasury Secretary Gallatin, he abandoned his role as legislative leader, leaving the Republicans in Congress to decide what to do next. Not surprisingly, they took the line of least resistance. On March 1, 1809, three days before Madison took the oath of office, Congress repealed the embargo, thus admitting the failure of the fifteen-month effort at economic coercion.

Diplomacy had failed; threats had failed; economic pressure had failed. But because congressional Republicans were unwilling to admit the bankruptcy of past policies, they replaced the embargo with the far less restrictive Nonintercourse Act. This law reopened trade with all nations save England and France and authorized the president to renew trade with either or both belligerents in the event that they stopped their violations of America's neutral rights. The act was a transparent attempt to put the best face possible on the debacle. All sides understood that as soon as the embargo was lifted a vast illicit trade with England, France, and the colonies of all belligerent powers in the Western Hemisphere was certain to develop. At the beginning of James Madison's eight years in the White House, the nation stood humbled.

ENDNOTES

1. Anthony Merry, quoted in *The Founding Fathers: James Madison in His Own Words*, ed. Merrill D. Peterson (N.Y., 1974), p. 248.

2. Thomas Jefferson, quoted in Dumas Malone, *Thomas Jefferson, the President: First Term, 1801–1805* (Little, Brown and Co., Boston, 1970), p. 27.

3. Jefferson, quoted in Arthur Burr Darling, *Our Rising Empire* (Yale University Press, New Haven, Conn., 1940), p. 397; *Messages and Papers of the Presidents*, ed. James D. Richardson (Washington, 1900), I, p. 323.

4. Instructions to Richard Dale, quoted in James Field, *America in the Mediterranean World* (Princeton University Press, Princeton, N.J., 1969), p. 49.

5. Jefferson, quoted in *ibid.*, pp. 34–35.

6. Jefferson, quoted in Dumas Malone, *Jefferson and the Ordeal of Liberty* (Little, Brown and Co., Boston, 1962), p. 123.

7. Horatio Lord Nelson, quoted in Field, *America in the Mediterranean World*, p. 60.

8. Pope Pius VII, quoted in *ibid.*

9. Louis Pichon, quoted in Malone, *Jefferson the President, First Term*, p. 252.

10. James Madison, quoted in Alexander DeConde, *This Affair of Louisiana* (Charles Scribner's, Sons, N.Y., 1976), pp. 112–13.

11. Jefferson to Robert R. Livingston, April 18, 1802, *The Writings of Thomas Jefferson*, ed. A. A. Lipscomb (Washington, D.C., Montecello edition), X, p. 313.

12. Robert R. Livingston, quoted in George Dangerfield, *Chancellor Robert R. Livingston of New York* (Harcourt Brace and Co., 1960), p. 337.

13. Alexander Hamilton, quoted in John C. Miller, *Alexander Hamilton and the Growth of the New Nation* (Harper and Row, N.Y., 1959), p. 559.

14. Madison, quoted in Irving Brant, *James Madison Secretary of State, 1801–1809* (Bobbs-Merrill and Co., Indianapolis, Ind., 1953), p. 106; Edward Thornton, quoted in Dangerfield, *Chancellor Robert R. Livingston*, p. 353.

15. Prince Talleyrand, quoted in *American State Papers, Foreign Relations* (Gales and Seaton, 1832), II, p. 561.

16. Madison, quoted in Malone, *Jefferson the President, First Term*, p. 283.

17. Dudley Ryder, Lord Harrowby, quoted in Reginald Horsman, *The Causes of the War of 1812* (A. S. Barnes, and Co., Cranbury, N.J., 1962), p. 30.

18. Madison to Monroe, September 24, 1805, *The Writings of James Madison*, ed. Galliard Hunt (G. P. Putnam's Sons, N.Y., 1908), VII, p. 190; Monroe, quoted in Burton Spivak, *Jefferson's English Crisis: Commerce, Embargo and the Republican Revolution* (University of Virginia Press, Charlottesville, Va., 1979), p. 18.

19. Theodore Lyman and Benjamin Goodhue, quoted in Gerard Clarfield, *Timothy Pickering and the American Republic* (University of Pittsburgh Press, Pittsburgh, Pa., 1980), pp. 229–30.

20. Jefferson, quoted in Horsman, *The Causes of the War of 1812*, p. 83.

21. Lord Holland, quoted in *ibid.*, p. 87.

22. David Erskin, quoted in Brant, *Madison, Secretary of State*, p. 375; see also Spivak, *Jefferson's English Crisis*, pp. 98-99.

23. Jefferson, quoted in Spivak, *Jefferson's English Crisis*, p. 98.

24. Madison, quoted in J.C.A. Stagg, *Mr. Madison's War: Politics, Diplomacy, and Warfare in the Early American Republic, 1783–1830* (Princeton University Press, Princeton, N.J., 1983), p. 21.

25. Spencer Perceval, quoted in Horsman, *Causes of the War of 1812*, p. 119.

6

WAR AND PEACE WITH ENGLAND, 1809–1815

James Madison, the Father of the Constitution, was reluctant to make war in 1812 and took the first opportunity that offered itself to negotiate peace.

James Madison enjoyed few advantages on entering the White House. The embargo had failed, and it was unlikely that the Nonintercourse Act, which replaced it, would bring either belligerent to terms. The Republican party was divided at home, and the Federalists, once nearly moribund, were making a political comeback. It came as a complete surprise, then, when Britain's minister to the United States, David Erskine, informed the State Department that he was authorized to negotiate the repeal of the orders-in-council.

On learning of this amazing development, a jubilant Madison concluded that the embargo had after all forced the British government to reconsider its policy. But the president guessed wrong. Foreign Secretary George Canning *was* ready to repeal the orders. But in his instructions to Erskine he laid down harsh conditions. First, the United States would have to accept the legality of the Rule of 1756. Canning's second condition was even more unacceptable. According to the terms of the Nonintercourse Act, if Britain ended its restrictions on American commerce the United States would continue nonintercourse against the French. Canning wanted Washington to allow the Royal Navy to enforce nonintercourse by seizing all American vessels attempting to trade with France, its colonies, or its allies.

Had Erskine revealed the true nature of his instructions, there would have been no negotiations, since the president was unprepared to make the required concessions. But Erskine was one of those well-intentioned individuals who do a great deal of harm while intending to do good. Anxious to arrive at a settlement, he deliberately failed to inform Madison of Canning's second condition and during the course of the talks abandoned London's insistence that America abide by the Rule of 1756. The Erskine Agreement of April 1809 was a simple trade. The orders-in-council were to be repealed in return for Madison's promise to reopen trade with Great Britain while continuing nonintercourse against France.

Following the signing of the Erskine Agreement, euphoria reigned in Washington. Without waiting to hear how London would react to the agreement, the president announced that on June 10, 1809, American merchants could once again trade with Britain and its dependencies. During the next several weeks ships were made ready, crews were signed on, and cargoes loaded. On the appointed day some six hundred American merchantmen sailed for British ports.

ERSKINE REPUDIATED

At the time the ministry selected Erskine to represent England in the United States it no doubt seemed a wise decision. The *Chesapeake* affair remained unsettled, and relations between the two countries were seriously deranged. The least London could do was to send someone to Washington who liked Americans. But when Canning first glimpsed the Erskine Agreement, he decided the appointment had been a mistake. Erskine, he thought, had been duped. Madison must have known that the young envoy was violating his instructions even as they negotiated. Canning immediately repudiated the agreement and recalled Erskine. The president, who believed he was the one who had been duped, reinstituted nonintercourse against Britain. And Anglo-American relations hit an all-time low.

No doubt to dramatize his displeasure with Washington, Canning appointed the gruff, arrogant Francis James Jackson to replace the disgraced Erskine. The ship bearing Jackson, his wife and family, his furniture, carriages, and enough table service to entertain the entire Washington diplomatic establishment twice over, arrived early in September 1809. From all appearances, here was a man who had come to stay. Yet he lasted in Washington only a short while.

The blustering Jackson came to the United States not to negotiate but to intimidate. No sooner had he arrived than he began insinuating in his correspondence with the State Department what Canning had alleged privately, that the president had known during the negotiations with Erskine that the former minister was violating his instructions. Madison, who viewed himself as the injured party in the recent negotiations, demanded an apology. When Jackson refused, the president dismissed him and published the entire correspondence that had passed between Jackson and the State Department.

Canning, who took Jackson's side in the dispute, refused to send another minister to the United States for almost a year. The relationship between England and America could hardly have deteriorated further.

Jackson may have been anathema to the administration, but he was a hero to New England's Federalists, who took his cause as their own, defending him in Congress and the press. They arranged what turned out to be a less-than-triumphal tour of the northeastern United States for him and even turned his dismissal into the central issue in that year's New England state elections.

While the Federalists wined, dined, and eulogized a former British envoy whose major achievement was that he had insulted the president, back in Washington the Republicans had a problem. The Nonintercourse Act was scheduled to expire on March 3, 1810. No one in either party wanted it renewed. But neither could the Republicans afford to allow the admittedly unlamented law simply to lapse. To have done so would have been to admit the bankruptcy of their policies. And so, at the suggestion of Secretary of the Treasury Albert Gallatin, and with the approval of the president, North Carolina's Nathaniel Macon introduced a bill that would have freed American ships to trade at their own risk anywhere in the world while closing American ports to the ships of both Britain and France. An old-fashioned navigation bill such as Madison himself might have proposed two decades earlier, Macon's proposal also stipulated that products originating in either England or France could be brought to the United States only in American bottoms.

Macon's Bill No. 1 produced a four-month battle royal in Congress, with the administration's supporters arrayed against a coalition of Federalists, who wanted an end to all economic sanctions against the British, and dissident Republicans, who advocated stronger measures. The bill finally died in a Senate-House conference committee. But that left the Republicans back at square one.

A last-ditch effort by those who felt the need to do something—anything—rather than let the Nonintercourse Act simply die, produced Macon's Bill No. 2. This bill, which was curiously named since Nathaniel Macon had nothing to do with it, reflected the weakness of a Congress that didn't want war, couldn't make peace, and at the same time felt keenly the domestic pressure generated by interests opposed to further economic sanctions. It authorized American ships to go forth into world trade and gave the president the power to reinstitute nonintercourse against one of the belligerent powers if the other stopped violating America's neutral rights.

Madison signed the bill shortly before Congress adjourned. But he recognized this new law for what it was—a humiliating surrender. He saw only one advantage to it. By reopening trade with the belligerents, the law might teach New England's Federalists as well as others who advocated acquiesence in the face of belligerent outrages "the folly, as well as degradation of their policy." The president predicted that Congress's craven surrender would lead to even more serious problems with both Britain and France and that it would soon become clear "that the inconveniences of the Embargo, and non-intercourse, have been exchanged for the greater sacrifices as well as disgrace, resulting from a submission to the predatory systems in force."[1]

MADISON AND FRANCE

During the entire period of crisis from 1807 until the coming of war in 1812, first Thomas Jefferson and then James Madison had been repeatedly embarrassed by the fact that France as well as England made a practice of violating America's neutral rights. In April 1808, for example, after learning of Jefferson's embargo, Napoleon issued his Bayonne decree ordering the seizure of all American ships found in French ports. The cynical explanation offered for this outrage was that since the embargo forbade American ships from leaving American shores, vessels then in French ports flying the American flag must in fact be British ships in disguise. Americans lost some $10 million in goods and ships as a result. Again, on March 23, 1810, Napoleon ordered the seizure of all American ships entering French ports. The Rambouillet decree cost Americans another $10 million in lost property.

These French outrages gave the political opposition at home the opportunity to charge the administration with an extreme form of diplomatic myopia. Why, the Federalists wondered, were the Jeffersonians so indifferent to French attacks on American commerce but sensitive to the least infringement on America's rights when the British were involved? Was it because they had, in fact, become the secret nonbelligerent ally of Bonaparte?

The criticism stung. But both Jefferson and Madison were unswerving in their determination to focus on the British. And with good reason. In the first place, it would have been both ludicrous and ineffective to have attempted to apply pressure against Europe's two greatest powers simultaneously. The only way to achieve any concessions from either was to play one off against the other. But why the British and not the French? There were two good reasons. First, the British were more vulnerable because they relied heavily on American food and raw materials and needed the American marketplace. Second, although Napoleon could be infuriating, from first to last both Jefferson and Madison believed that England was by far the worst offender. And so, in spite of ample French provocation and the embarrassment it caused him at home, Madison stuck to his England-first policy.

The enactment of Macon's Bill No. 2 marked the beginning of a new chapter in the relationship between Bonaparte and the president. Earlier, Napoleon had been pleased by the embargo, for it helped France in its economic struggle against England. He was, therefore, predictably unhappy when the Republicans abandoned their experiment in economic warfare. This new piece of legislation, however, offered another opportunity that the emperor was quick to grasp. France's foreign minister, Jean-Baptiste Nompère, the duc de Cadore, informed John Armstrong, the American minister in Paris, that the Berlin and Milan decrees would be revoked on November

1, 1810, if London repealed the orders-in-council or if in the interim Washington reinstituted nonintercourse against England.

Obviously Napoleon hoped that Madison would ignore the huge loophole he had left for himself and leap at the bait, thus exacerbating the crisis between England and America. Napoleon himself never intended to repeal his decrees. He made that clear on the very day the duc de Cadore delivered his famous letter to Armstrong when he ordered the seizure of all American vessels that had put in at French ports between May 20, 1809, and May 1, 1810.

Not surprisingly, the British refused to change their policy on the basis of Cadore's letter to Armstrong. Two years earlier the ministry had agreed to repeal the orders-in-council if and when Napoleon repealed his decrees. That promise stood. But Britain would make no concessions on the basis of French promises.

The president was no more naive than the British—no more a believer in French integrity than the Foreign Office. Yet in this instance he seemed to take Napoleon's promise at face value. On November 2, 1810, he announced that the Berlin and Milan decrees having been repealed, the United States would immediately reinstitute nonintercourse against Great Britain unless London repealed the orders-in-council within ninety days. It is interesting that only a few days before issuing this proclamation Madison admitted privately that he did not know whether or not the French were serious. "*It is to be hoped*," he wrote, "that France will do what she is understood to be pledged for."[2]

Why, then, did Madison issue the proclamation? And why in the face of mounting evidence to the contrary did he continue to insist thereafter that the French had repealed their decrees? Madison was not "hoodwinked" by Napoleon. The Cadore letter offered him the opportunity to end a humiliating situation in which the United States tamely submitted to the depredations of both Europe's giants. By accepting the fiction that the French had repealed their decrees, he was able to reapply economic sanctions against Britain, the principal violator of America's neutral rights, and restore in some small degree the national honor.

THE POLITICS OF WAR

In a letter to the American Minister in London written in May 1810, Madison observed that the public's attitude toward Britain was becoming increasingly hostile, especially following a sharp drop in commodity prices which many blamed on the fact that Britain's orders-in-council denied Americans access to the European marketplace. Madison continued to hope for peace but predicted that popular indignation would grow as the economic situation deteriorated. He thought it quite likely that Congress, reflecting the popular displeasure with England, would return to Washington for the 1811 session prepared to deal more resolutely with the nation's foreign policy problems.

The president was only half right. The public was becoming decidedly short-tempered, but Congress returned in a fractious and uncooperative mood. The legislators ignored the president's recommendation for increased defense spending and blocked Treasury Secretary Gallatin's efforts to recharter the Bank of the United States, thus denying the government a vital source of funds and credit when war finally did come. At the same time, factional fighting inside the Republican party forced a major shake-up in the administration. Madison fired Secretary of State Robert Smith, who proved to be not only vain and incompetent but disloyal. Smith retaliated by publishing an attack on the president charging that Madison was in collusion with Napoleon. With the administration and the president's party both in a shambles, Secretary Gallatin prevailed on James Monroe, who had himself been sharply critical of Madison's handling of foreign policy, to take over at the State Department, thus reestablishing at least the semblance of order.

But appearances were deceiving. The Republican party remained divided, with powerful factions in rebellion against Madison's leadership. In New York, George and De Witt Clinton were plotting to unseat Madison in the 1812 elections. The powerful William Duane, publisher of the *Philadelphia Aurora*, and Michael Leib, Pennsylvania's influential senator, led another anti-Madison faction. Samuel Smith and his brother Robert, late of the State Department, headed yet another group, called "the Invisibles" that was after Madison. All these influential Republican dissidents attacked the president's foreign policy as weak and ineffective while demanding a stronger more aggressive policy toward Britain.

Madison was also feeling pressure from southern and western farmers and planters, who saw a clear connection between Britain's orders-in-council and the economic depression they were then experiencing. Beginning in 1807 farm prices began to slide. Over the next two years wholesale prices dropped by an average of 20 percent. And that was just the beginning. By 1812 the price of cotton, tobacco, and other staples had fallen so low that in some parts of the country it made little sense to plant crops.

Farmers and planters caught in the throes of depression blamed their predicament on the British, whose orders-in-council denied them access to the European marketplace. By 1811 anger was overflowing. A toast given at a Fourth of July celebration in Frankfurt, Kentucky, that year reflects the mood of agricultural interests in many parts of the country. "Embargoes, nonintercourse, and negotiations, are but illy calculated to secure our rights," said the speaker. "Let us now try old Roman policy, and maintain them with the sword."[3]

With important Republican leaders challenging his leadership while key groups in the South and West demanded a more energetic defense of America's right to trade, it was only a matter of time before the president would have to abandon his commitment to peaceful economic sanctions in favor of war. Still, he waited. The political situation in England appeared to be changing. George III had finally been judged incurably insane. The prince regent now sat in his place. Shortly afterward Washington learned that a new minister, Augustus J. Foster, was on his way to the United States. Perhaps the envoy would come bearing new proposals. Madison would wait and see.

Unhappily for the besieged president, Foster, who arrived in the summer of 1811, brought no relief. The long-smoldering *Chesapeake* matter was finally put to rest. But the British ministry was not prepared to make other concessions. It was a depressed Madison who returned home that summer to mull things over and confer with the other two members of the Virginia triumvirate, Thomas Jefferson and Secretary of State Monroe. These talks evidently produced no new ideas. With public indignation over British trade restrictions at high tide, powerful factions inside his own party demanding a more aggressive policy, and the 1812 elections on the horizon, the president scheduled a special session of Congress for early November. He returned to Washington thinking seriously about seeking a declaration of war against England.

In his opening message to Congress, the president noted that aside from the belated settlement of the *Chesapeake* affair his talks with Augustus Foster had been virtually sterile. Britain was unprepared to make concessions on any of the vital issues. "With this evidence of hostile inflexibility in trampling on rights which no Independent Nation can relinquish," he wrote, "Congress will feel the duty of putting the United States into an armour, and an attitude demanded by the crisis, and corresponding with the national spirit and expectations."[4]

Madison's call to arms came at a time when Congress was finally ready to take strong measures. The recent elections had produced a veritable revolution in Washington. Of the 142 members of the Eleventh Congress, 61 did not return to the Twelfth. The number of Federalist congressmen declined as even in New England some voters tired of their blind commitment to the British. At the same time a new generation of nationalistic Republican leaders rose to prominence in the House of Representatives. From Kentucky came Henry Clay and Richard Mentor Johnson. Tennessee sent the Indian fighter, Felix Grundy. South Carolina produced John C. Calhoun, William Lowndes, and Langdon Cheves. And from western New York came Peter B. Porter. These young "second-generation revolutionaries" quickly won key positions in the House.[5] Clay was elected Speaker. Calhoun, Porter, and Grundy controlled the Foreign Affairs Committee, while Cheves chaired the Naval Committee.

These War Hawks, so named by the antiwar leader of the Old Republicans in the House, John Randolph, were ready—even anxious—for a scrap. They revered Jefferson, Madison, and the other founders of the republic but at the same time felt that the older leaders had become too concerned with preserving what had been accomplished since 1776, too fixated on the past. Impressment and Britain's trade restrictions were insults of such a nature that resistance seemed imperative if the national honor was to be preserved.

The War Hawks were moved by economic considerations, too. Sent to Congress by angry farmers and planters to secure America's rights in the international marketplace, they clearly reflected these feelings when justifying their support for war. On the day Congress took the crucial vote Henry Clay explained, "Today we are asserting our right to the direct trade—the right to export our cotton, tobacco, and other domestic produce to market." Felix Grundy agreed, explaining that the real issue between Britain and America was "the right of exporting the productions of our own soil and industry to foreign markets." As South Carolina's John C. Calhoun explained, the people of the South "see in the low price of produce the hand of foreign injustice."[6]

With Congress in an increasingly militant frame of mind, Madison, who still hoped to avoid war, again hesitated. Recent intelligence indicated that growing internal opposition to the ministry's policies might yet force a change.

By the year 1812 a desperate economic situation prevailed throughout the manufacturing districts of England. Bankruptcies, unemployment, and pauperism had become major problems. Britain's manufacturers and their Whig friends in Parliament contended that because of Napoleon's Continental System, which denied England free access to the European market, the American market had taken on added importance. But because of America's policy of nonimportation—a direct response to the orders-in-council—that market, too, had been lost. The result? British industry was in the doldrums. Parliament was flooded with petitions calling for the repeal of the Orders. "Before these Orders in Council I had a good trade," wrote one Birmingham manufacturer, "and since then my trade is gone." "We have not received American orders in the same way as we used to, since the Orders in Council were issued," complained another.[7]

In the face of growing domestic opposition, the Tory ministry of Spencer Perceval began to weaken. Then, on May 11, as he was entering Parliament, Perceval was shot dead by a madman, John Bellingham. So awful were economic conditions in England that the news of Perceval's murder gave rise to spontaneous celebrations, especially in industrial towns. The assassin, Bellingham, become something of a popular hero. Thousands attended his execution at Newgate Prison in London and cheered him into the next world.

Considering the state of the economy and of public opinion, it is not surprising that the new government, headed by Robert Banks Jenkinson, Lord Liverpool, decided to repeal the orders-in-council. The announcement came on June 23, 1812, three weeks after the president sent his war message to Congress.

Had Bellingham shot Perceval a few months earlier, it might have made a difference. Madison, who obviously didn't want war, might then have considered Liverpool's actions as significant enough to justify further delay. But Bellingham's murderous act came too late. Early in April 1812, Madison took a major step toward war when he announced a ninety-day embargo on trade. The administration was waiting only for late dispatches from Europe before taking the plunge. When on May 19, 1812, the ship

Hornet arrived bringing nothing to indicate a change in British policy, the president decided to act. On June 1, he sent a war message to Congress.

Some historians have wondered how Madison would have behaved had he known that the British were on the brink of repealing the orders-in-council at the very time that Congress was debating a declaration of war. Could the War of 1812 have been avoided? Answers to such speculative questions are, of course, finally impossible. It is probable, however, that British concessions not only came too late but were of too little importance to have swayed Madison, who faced a serious political threat from within his own party.

To be sure, London did repeal the orders-in-council. But the decision resulted from growing domestic pressures (which were bound to dissipate once prosperity returned to the manufacturing districts) and not because the government had changed its opinion of what constituted sound wartime policy. Moreover, the Liverpool government insisted that the orders had been a legitimate exercise of Britain's rights and that similar regulations might be reimposed in the future. Also, of course, the entire question of impressment remained unresolved.

Before the fighting began in earnest, Madison did instruct the American chargé in London, Jonathan Russell, to seek an armistice. But the terms Madison proposed, which included the revocation of the orders-in-council, an end to impressment, the return of all impressed seamen, and an end to all paper blockades, added up to a complete British surrender. Neither Russell nor policy makers in Washington were particularly surprised when London turned the proposal down. It seems quite clear that at this point, having finally crossed the Rubicon, and with the presidential election coming up, Madison preferred war to anything short of a complete diplomatic victory.

It took a divided Congress more than two weeks to vote a declaration of war. The House debated the issue for four days before dividing along partisan lines. Seventy-nine House Republicans were opposed by thirty-three Federalists and a scattering of dissident Republicans. In the Senate the vote was closer but equally partisan in nature. There nineteen Republicans supported war, while six Federalist senators were joined by seven Republican dissidents in opposition.

Even after war had been declared, New England's Federalists, still powerful in the Northeast, did everything they could to undermine the war effort. They began by joining dissident Republicans in support of De Witt Clinton's attempt to unseat Madison in the 1812 elections. During the next two years they opposed the war in ways that bordered on treason. In spite of the federal government's desperate need for funds, most of New England's bankers and investors even refused to purchase government securities.

Those New Englanders who did loan money to the government courted social ostracism and economic retaliation in their home communities. Because the names of those who purchased government securities were regularly published in New England newspapers, the government even

American warships gave a good account of themselves in numerous single-ship actions during the War of 1812. Here the USS *Constitution* leaves HMS *Java* in a sinking condition.

found it necessary to promise New England investors that their identities would remain confidential. In spite of everything the government could do, including the payment of high interest rates, only a tiny fraction of the millions finally borrowed came from New England sources.

Not even the sight of Washington in ruins, most of its public buildings burned by a British raiding party in the summer of 1814, caused the members of New England's Federalist congressional clique to alter their opinions. With one British army known to be on its way to New Orleans while another was poised to attack Sackets Harbor, on Lake Ontario, New Englanders in Congress helped kill an administration plan to call up eighty thousand militiamen. "This system of military conscription is not only inconsistent with the spirit and provisions of the constitution," railed Christopher Gore of Massachusetts, "but also with all the principles of civil liberty. In atrocity it exceeds the conscriptions of the late emperor of France."[8] Federalist New England's opposition was so strident, the implied threat of northern secession from the Union so palpable, that the British did not extend their naval blockade to that region until 1814, hoping in this way to encourage America's fragmentation as a nation.

THE PROMISE OF PEACE

The war went badly for the United States in 1812. The invasion of Canada, which some thought would be a mere "matter of marching," proved a humiliating debacle; the nation was divided internally; and with the national government nearly bankrupt the president wasn't quite sure where the money would come from to continue financing the war. Madison was naturally delighted, then, when early in 1813 he learned that Czar Alexander of Russia had offered to mediate between England and America. In unseemly haste he chose Treasury Secretary Albert Gallatin, the minister in St. Petersburg John Quincy Adams, and the moderate Federalist James A. Bayard as his negotiating team. Before it was known whether the British had accepted the offer, even before the Senate had time to vote on the nominations, Gallatin and Bayard sailed to join Adams in the Russian capital.

Madison's hopes for a quick settlement were dashed when London rejected the czar's offer. Foreign Office officials suspected the Russian emperor of harboring a sneaking admiration for American liberalism; and they knew that he subscribed to the American view of the rights of neutrals on the seas. But if the British did not relish the idea of a Russian mediation, with the European war winding toward its conclusion they were nevertheless interested in ending the American conflict.

A British offer to negotiate directly with the United States arrived in Washington at the same time that American policy makers learned that following his disastrous Russian campaign Napoleon had suffered another major defeat at Leipzig. Peace now seemed especially imperative, for once the war in Europe ended, England would be in a position to concentrate all her naval and military forces on the United States. And so Gallatin, Bayard, and Adams journeyed to the Belgian town of Ghent, where the negotiations were to take place. There they were joined by two additional envoys, Henry Clay and Jonathan Russell.

The American delegation set up housekeeping at the Hôtel d'Alcantara on the rue de Champs and awaited the arrival of their British counterparts. Bayard and Russell, though able men, were clearly secondary figures on a commission dominated by three impressive personalities.

At forty-seven, John Quincy Adams had already served most of a term in the Senate, done a stint as professor of moral philosophy at Harvard, and had a diplomatic career that stretched back over thirty years to the days when he served as his father's secretary in London during the 1780s. The blood of puritans, patriots, and a president flowed in his veins. Cold, dogmatic, and judgmental, Adams never got along with anyone particularly well. His colleagues at Ghent were no exceptions.

Adams knew that he was thought of as "a gloomy misanthropist" but couldn't change that any more than he could tone down the scrappy aggressiveness with which he fought for his views both inside the delegation and across the table at Ghent. In comparing Adams with the rest of St. Petersburg's more or less effete diplomatic establishment, an English observer once called him a "bulldog among spaniels."[9] It was an apt description.

But Adams wasn't the only bulldog at Ghent. The tall, lanky Henry Clay seemed in many ways his exact opposite. He exuded a casual charm, seems to have had enormous sex appeal, and liked nothing better than to stay up all night drinking and gambling. Twice during their stay in Ghent,

Adams, who usually rose before five in the morning, found himself awake and at work before Clay's card parties had broken up. The Kentuckian's carousings, unexceptional on the western frontier, raised more than one pair of eyebrows in the more sedate East. "Isn't it a pity," a New England woman once remarked to Clay's wife Lucretia, "that your husband gambles so much?" "Oh, I don't know," Mrs. Clay replied, "he usually wins."[10] And Clay did usually win, not only at cards but also at politics.

Clay had his own ideas on the conduct of diplomacy. A skilled cardplayer, he explained that he "was for playing *brag* with the British Plenipotentiaries. . . . He said the art of it was to beat your adversary by holding your hand, with a solemn and confidence phiz, [a poker face] and outbragging him."[11] Adams was appalled. The stakes were too high, the dangers too great to risk having one's bluff called.

Strong-willed men playing a dangerous game, Adams and Clay often clashed during the course of the negotiations. But to their credit they never allowed their differences to go beyond the front door of the Hôtel d'Alcantara.

The third major player on the American delegation was Albert Gallatin. Born into an aristocratic Swiss family, Gallatin fled his native land at the age of eighteen. Deeply impressed by the writings of Jean Jacques Rousseau, he sought a life more in harmony with nature and found it on the Pennsylvania frontier. But fate had something other than the bucolic life in store for this romantic youth. In less than a decade he had emerged as a leader among Pennsylvania's Republicans and was sent to Congress, where he fought for the Jeffersonian cause during the 1790s. Gallatin, who combined financial acumen, European sophistication, and strong republican convictions, took over the Treasury Department in 1801 and served as a key adviser to Thomas Jefferson, a role he continued to play during Madison's presidency.

Gallatin has been described as the indispensable man on the American delegation at Ghent, the mediator between the strong-willed Adams and the fiery Clay. To an extent this is true. Gallatin's role as a diplomat working inside the American delegation should not be underestimated. But such a view tends to exaggerate the importance of the divisions among the Americans while ignoring those considerations that bound them together. All were devoted nationalists unwilling to make major concessions. Moreover, all five clearly felt the need to hang together, for they viewed themselves as on the defensive, their country in an exposed and vulnerable position. Because they expected the British negotiators to be arrogant and uncompromising, they also shared the conviction that the talks would probably end in deadlock and the war would continue.

This pessimistic judgment was based on an evaluation of the battlefield situation in mid-1814 as well as what seemed likely to happen in the not-too-distant future. The American navy—sixteen ships at the beginning of the war—had given a wonderful account of itself, winning dramatic victories in a series of heroic single-ship actions. Moreover, during the war American privateers took 1,344 British prizes. But the American war at sea was more an embarrassment than a major problem for England. The British were able to drive American commerce from the oceans. Their blockade of the Atlantic seaboard was in fact so effective that even the coasting trade disappeared. The land war had gone even worse for the United States. Canada remained in British hands, as did portions of northern Maine.

But it wasn't the existing military situation that most troubled the American negotiators. By the time they assembled at Ghent, the war in Europe was over, Napoleon had been exiled to Elba, and the British appeared to be free to apply maximum force against the United States. Madison and Secretary of State Monroe, who shared this estimate of America's weak bargaining position, instructed the delegates to abandon America's war aims and seek only an end to the war on the basis of the prewar status quo. Considering the threatening military situation, they doubted even this could be accomplished.

Fixated on the potentially disastrous military situation, the Americans both in Washington and at Ghent failed to appreciate that Britain, too, had problems. In the first place, the European situation was anything but stable. There were already rumblings of rebelliousness in France, where the restored Louis XVIII sat unsteadily on his throne. Moreover, with Napoleon out of the way, the coalition that had defeated him was showing signs of fragmenting even before the delegates assembled at Vienna to arrange a postwar settlement. And at home the British taxpayer was groaning under a burden no longer willingly borne. London was committed to the American war in the near term. But British policy makers realized that it might not be in their interest to pursue victory in America if it tied them down beyond the current year.

THE TALKS BEGIN

The British representatives, who were a month late in arriving at Ghent, were an unimpressive lot. William Adams was an obscure Admiralty lawyer. Admiral James Baron Gambier's major claim to fame was that he had commanded the British squadron that bombarded defenseless Copenhagen in 1807. Henry Goulburn, was a Foreign Office official of mediocre abilities. It is tempting to argue that one need not pay too much attention to the lack of quality among the frontline British delegates at Ghent since Robert Stewart, Lord Castlereagh, Henry Lord Bathurst, and Lord Liverpool controlled the negotiations from London. Yet this is not entirely correct, since Foreign Office control over the delegates was incomplete, a fact that was to prove embarrassing.

Lord Castlereagh's instructions to the British envoys were vaguely drawn—deliberately so. Goulburn and his colleagues had been sent on a fishing expedition. Their object was to discover what sort of concessions the Americans might be willing to make on a number of questions such as the future of Britain's Indian allies in the Ohio Valley and a possible southward revision of the Canadian boundary. But the negotiators were to behave cautiously in order to keep the Americans at the table. It was clear that much would depend on the outcome of military operations then under way.

Somebody at the Foreign Office should have made certain that the delegates understood the subtle nature of their mission for, as the historian Bradford Perkins has observed, they went to Ghent seemingly unaware of the true intentions of the ministry and determined to impose a humiliating settlement on the United States.[12] At the outset of the talks Goulburn, acting without instructions, insisted that the establishment of an Indian barrier state in the Ohio Valley was absolutely indispensable to the success of the negotiations. When the American delegates pointed out that more than a hundred thousand white settlers lived in the area, the British delegates showed no interest whatsoever. It was not their problem.

Goulburn also demanded an adjustment to the Canadian boundary to allow for the construction of an all-land route from Halifax to Quebec. Reminding the Americans that according to the Treaty of 1783 England had the right to navigate the Mississippi, the British delegates also insisted that in the West the Canadian boundary be moved south to the point where the Mississippi became navigable. They demanded, too, that the United States withdraw its naval forces from the Great Lakes and dismantle its fortifications there while Britain kept its ships and troops on that part of the frontier. They also made it clear that they were not prepared to allow American fishermen to return to their traditional fishing grounds off the Newfoundland Grand Banks unless the United States offered an appropriate quid pro quo. Nor would Britain's delegates consider discussing questions relating to neutral rights.

Whitehall's intention had been to launch a probe, not flail away with a sledgehammer. Above all, it was important to keep the negotiations going until the outcome of that year's military campaigns was known. Only then would it be clear just how far the Americans could be pushed. Now the Foreign Office had a problem, for the American delegates concluded on the basis of Goulburn's opening salvos that there was little point in continuing the talks. "The style of the papers we receive," Adams complained, "is bitter as the quintessence of wormwood—arrogant, dictatorial, insulting."[13] Within two weeks of the opening of talks, the Americans were ready to head for home.

But the negotiations didn't stop. Instead London quickly abandoned the hoary subject of an Indian barrier state and instructed its delegates to keep the talks going. Military operations then under way might still decide a great deal. A large expedition under the command of General Sir Edward Pakenham was preparing to seize New Orleans. Another army commanded by Sir George Prevost was about to strike south from Canada into upper New York State. Meanwhile a third force, commanded jointly by Major General Robert Ross and Admiral Sir George Cockburn, was to raid the Chesapeake Bay area. So while the negotiations continued the war did, too, and the Liverpool government counted on victory in the field to bring success at the bargaining table.

In late September 1814, that tactic seemed to pay off when London learned that General Ross's force had sacked and burned Washington, D.C. Lord Bathurst, secretary of state for war and the colonies, rushed the good news to Goulburn, urging him to use this information to his advantage during the negotiations. But less than three weeks later the tables were suddenly turned when news of major British military setbacks arrived. After burning Washington, Admiral Cockburn and General Ross had set their sights on Baltimore. But there, in an engagement that cost General Ross his life, the American forces stood their ground and drove the British off. Meanwhile, farther to the north, the British suffered another defeat. After Commodore Thomas Macdonough beat the British in a naval engagement on Lake Champlain, Sir George Prevost turned his army of ten thousand northward. The British invasion of New York had failed.

Henry Goulburn considered the Prevost retreat virtually decisive. "If we had either burnt Baltimore or held Plattsburg, I believe we should have had peace on the terms which you have sent to us in a month at latest. As things appear to be going on in America, the result of our negotiation may be very different."[14] London agreed. It would at the very least take another year of campaigning to win the American war. And from the ministry's perspective, the value of a victory was outstripped by the risks involved in attaining it. On the domestic front there was the demand for tax relief to be considered. Europe, meanwhile, was seething. The ministry noted with considerable alarm that the new French government was allowing American privateers to use French ports to refit and sell their prizes. There was also talk of a plot to restore Napoleon. Meanwhile, at Vienna, where a great congress met to arrange a final postwar settlement, Castlereagh and Czar Alexander were at dagger points. There was even talk of an Anglo-Russian war. Under such circumstances, it is not surprising that the British government decided it could no longer afford to remain entangled in the American war. There was too much to be attended to closer to home.

STATUS QUO ANTE

During the third week in October, the British negotiators at Ghent beat a hasty retreat from the advanced positions they had so recently staked out. First one and then another demand fell by the wayside until by November only one substantive issue divided the American and British delegations. Someone, somewhere in Britain's War Office, insisted that the boundary between the United States and Canada be redrawn to conform to the military situation at the time. Since the British held certain salients in American territory around the Great Lakes but, more important, in Maine, such a settlement would have provided England with the all-land route it hoped to establish between Halifax and Quebec.

But Arthur Wellesley, the duke of Wellington, concerned by developing European problems, intervened to eradicate even this modest demand. He pointed out that American forces still held Canadian territory and scoffed at what British forces had achieved along the Canadian-American frontier. "An officer . . . might as well claim . . . the ground on which his piquets stand, or over which his patrols pass." At the time he said, "You have no right . . . to claim a concession of territory."[15] Wellington's opposition to this last British condition cleared the way for a negotiated settlement on the basis of the prewar status quo.

The Liverpool ministry was confirmed in its decision to simply end the American war by news of not military but political developments in America. In August the American delegates at Ghent sent dispatches to Washington detailing the terms first demanded by the English. Madison quickly published these documents. The effect was startling. Not only were the Republicans outraged, but the Federalists, who had long opposed the war, rushed to the colors. Alexander Hanson, whose newspaper, the *Baltimore Federal Republican,* had routinely published the most extreme Federalist views, rose from his seat in the House of Representatives to denounce the "degrading and humiliating conditions" that the British sought to impose. From that moment, he said, the contest ceased to be "a party war" and became "national."[16] All across the country the story was the same. Britain's initial demands at Ghent had done what Madison had failed to do during two years of warfare. The nation was united and unwilling to accept a degrading settlement. It was very clear that if Britain wished to continue the war the struggle would be long, the costs very great, and the outcome uncertain.

On December 24, 1814, the British and American delegates at Ghent signed a treaty of peace reestablishing the prewar status quo. The war was over, but no one on the American delegation felt particularly good about it. A depressed John Quincy Adams described the agreement as nothing more than "an unlimited armistice." The most he and his colleagues could claim was that they had "abandoned no essential right." An even more depressed Henry Clay thought the people would be furious that he and the other envoys had settled for less than victory and feared that "we should all be subject to much reproach."[17]

But Clay and Adams were wrong. Peace was embraced with enormous enthusiasm by the American people. And if they could not claim to have tamed the British Lion, the last important military encounter of the war, General Andrew Jackson's victory at New Orleans, gave an enormous boost to national spirits.

On January 8, 1815, unaware that a peace treaty had been signed fifteen days before, Wellington's brother-in-law, Sir Edward Pakenham, launched a frontal attack against General Andrew Jackson's positions near New Orleans. Pakenham along with seven hundred of his countrymen died that day. All told, the British lost 2,036 killed and wounded in the battle. The Americans, who cut the redcoats to ribbons with artillery fire and never

Andrew Jackson's victory over the British at New Orleans came after the Treaty of Ghent had been signed. Nevertheless, it was a matter of great pride, a rallying point for the sense of nationalism that gripped the nation after the war.

engaged the British at close quarters, suffered only eight killed and thirteen wounded.

Mrs. Pakenham, waiting on board a British transport for the moment when she was to make her triumphal entrance into conquered New Orleans, instead saw her husband's body, preserved in a barrel of rum, hoisted aboard ship. Not long after this the remnants of Pakenham's army, as well as the civil administrators who had come to govern Louisiana, sailed for England.

News of Jackson's victory at New Orleans arrived in New York City on February 5. Six days later HMS *Favorite* sailed into New York Harbor with news of peace. Though a few Federalists, the last of the breed, carped at the administration even then, the nation as a whole took pride in what it had accomplished. The republic had shown that it could act decisively and successfully in defense of its interests. Too many British warships had struck their colors in single-ship actions for the British ever again to scoff at "Yankee pine boards." Lieutenant Oliver Hazard Perry's victory on Lake Erie, Macdonough's success on Lake Champlain, and preeminently Jackson's triumph at New Orleans gave Americans reason to be proud. Albert Gallatin summed things up quite well when he observed:

> The war has been productive of evil and good, but I think the good preponderates. . . . The war has renewed and reinstated the national feelings

and character which the Revolution had given, and which were daily lessened. The people have now more general objects of attachment. . . . They are more Americans; they feel and act more as a nation; and I hope that the permanency of the Union is thereby better secured."[18]

ENDNOTES

1. Madison to William Pinkney, May 23, 1810, *The Writings of James Madison*, ed. Galliard Hunt (G. P. Putnam's Sons, New York, 1908), VIII, p. 99.

2. James Madison, quoted in J.C.A. Stagg, *Mr. Madison's War: Politics, Diplomacy, and Warfare in the Early American Republic, 1783–1830* (Princeton University Press, Princeton, N.J., 1983), p. 56, emphasis added.

3. Quoted in George R. Taylor, "Agrarian Discontent in the Mississippi Valley Preceding the War of 1812," *Journal of Political Economy*, XXXIX (1931), p. 497.

4. *Messages and Papers of the Presidents*, ed. James D. Richardson (Washington, 1900), I, p. 494.

5. Reginald Horsman, *The Causes of the War of 1812* (A. S. Barnes and Co., N.Y., 1962), p. 226.

6. Henry Clay, Felix Grundy, and John C. Calhoun, quoted in *ibid.*, pp. 231–32.

7. British manufacturers, quoted in *ibid.*, p. 253.

8. Christopher Gore, quoted in John Bach McMaster, *History of the People of the United States* (D. Appleton and Co., N.Y., 1884–1905), IV, p. 246.

9. Anonymous, quoted in George Dangerfield, *The Era of Good Feelings* (Harcourt, Brace, and World, N.Y., 1952), p. 7.

10. Lucretia Clay, quoted in *ibid.*, p. 10.

11. Clay, quoted in *Memoirs of John Quincy Adams*, ed. Charles Francis Adams (Lippincott, Philadelphia, Pa., 1874–1877), III, p. 101.

12. Bradford Perkins, *Castlereagh and Adams, England and the United States, 1812–1823* (University of California Press, Berkeley, Calif., 1964), pp. 66–77.

13. John Quincy Adams to Louisa Catherine Adams, September 27, 1814, *The Writings of John Quincy Adams*, ed. Worthington Chauncey Ford (Macmillian Co., N.Y., 1913–1916), V, p. 147.

14. Henry Goulburn, quoted in Bradford Perkins, *Castlereagh and Adams*, pp. 98–99.

15. The Duke of Wellington, quoted in Henry Adams, *The Life of Albert Gallatin* (Peter Smith, N.Y., 1943), pp. 538–39.

16. Alexander C. Hanson, quoted in Gerard Clarfield, *Timothy Pickering and the American Republic* (Pittsburgh University Press, Pittsburgh, Pa., 1980), pp. 257–58.

17. Clay, quoted in Perkins, *Castlereagh and Adams*, pp. 120–21.

18. Albert Gallatin, quoted in *The Selected Writings of Albert Gallatin*, ed. E. James Ferguson (Bobbs-Merrill and Co., Indianapolis, Ind., 1967), p. 351.

During the administration of James Monroe, the nation acquired the Floridas and established a boundary on the Pacific. Guided by Secretary of State John Quincy Adams, Monroe also declared in his famous doctrine that the Western Hemisphere was no longer open to European colonization.

7

THE NATION SPANS THE CONTINENT, 1815–1823

Although the war had ended on a positive note, Americans of all political persuasions believed that the United States and Britain were destined to clash repeatedly in the years to come. Henry Clay predicted a succession of wars "until if the two nations be not crushed, all grounds of collision shall have ceased between them." Rufus King, a close friend of Alexander Hamilton and a onetime Federalist candidate for the presidency, agreed, predicting "repeated struggles . . . upon the ocean before the undisputed Trident reposes in our possession."[1]

The feeling that Anglo-American relations would remain unsettled was enhanced by the carping criticisms of American life and culture that appeared in British periodicals and in the scornful writings of the many British travelers who visited the United States at this time. Characteristic of this sort of writing was a piece that appeared in London's *Quarterly Review* in the autumn of 1814. According to the author, who remained anonymous, Americans were cowards in war and in peace, "the most vain, egotistical, insolent, rodomontade sort of people that are anywhere to be found." They had no history and were irreligious. "One third of the people have no church at all," he exclaimed. "America," this writer concluded, "is all a parody—a mimicry of her parent. It is, however, the mimicry of a child, tetchy and wayward in its infancy, abandoned to bad nurses, and educated in low habits."[2] The *Edinburgh Review, Gentleman's Magazine*, and many other journals quickly joined in the hunt, publishing such a volume of this scurrilous stuff that many in the United States believed the British government had hired an army of "Grubb Street hacks" to attack America in print in order to discourage immigration.[3] American writers, of course, replied in kind.

Surprising to note, the fusillade of acrimonious rubbish that crowded the pages of British and American journals in these years had little effect on Anglo-American relations. Lord Castlereagh, who remained in the Foreign Office until his tragic mental breakdown and suicide in 1822, held consistently to the view that England had much to gain by establishing an amicable postwar relationship with America. The handsome, thoroughly aristocratic lord deplored the growth of republicanism and hadn't much use for any of the Americans he knew. But these were his private thoughts. He made certain that they never became public or interfered with his commitment to improve Anglo-American relations.

Castlereagh's foreign policy was clearly Europe oriented. Nevertheless, he and the prime minister, Lord Liverpool, were the first British statesmen since Lord Shelburne to realize that a friendly relationship with the United States was one of Britain's vital interests. In the years since 1783 the American market for British goods had grown enormously. In the decade after 1815 about one-sixth of all British exports went to the United States. To put it another way, about 40 percent of all American imports were British in origin. In return, Americans sold Britain food and vital raw materials, especially cotton for the textile industry upon which England's industrial revolution was based. The two nations were inextricably linked, a fact that was driven home when the American economy went into a tailspin following the panic of 1819. In a speech given before Parliament in May 1820, the prime minister made this point:

> There is no country more interested than England is, that the distress of America should cease, and that she should be enabled to continue that rapid progress which has been for a time interrupted; for, of all the powers on the face of the earth America is the one whose increasing population and immense territory furnish the best prospects for British produce and manufactures. Everybody, therefore, who wished prosperity to England, must wish prosperity to America.[4]

The important economic relationship then developing was not the only tie that led Castlereagh and Liverpool to seek friendly relations with America. After the War of 1812 British strategists concluded that Canada could only be defended against a well-executed American attack if enormous sums were spent and great pains taken in advance to prepare for the next war. Even then some military men wondered whether a defense of Canada was feasible. Admiral Sir David Milne, for one, thought the province "too distant for us to defend against so powerful a neighbour" and wondered whether it wouldn't be better "to quit . . . Canada altogether."[5] The thought must have occurred to Castlereagh as well, for he spent his time during the trip from London to the Congress of Vienna in 1814 attempting to assess the importance of Canada to the empire. By the time he reached the Austrian capital he had been convinced by the materials he studied that Canada should be preserved. "I have certainly acquired by those researches a very increased notion of the value of our North American provinces to us as a naval power," he wrote.[6] Because military force alone could not sufficiently guarantee continued British control over Canada, it became the responsibility of the Foreign Office to secure that valuable province by diplomatic means.

Finally, because Castlereagh was primarily concerned with Europe, it made sense to secure Britain's rear by maintaining harmony with America. That point grew in importance as the wartime coalition that had defeated Napoleon began to crumble in late 1814. For all of these reasons Castlereagh firmly believed that "there are no two states whose friendly relations are of more practical value to each other, or whose hostility so inevitably and so immediately entails upon both the most serious mischiefs."[7]

Castlereagh's friendly inclinations were at first not fully appreciated in Washington, where deep reservoirs of distrust remained. But it wasn't long before American policy makers recognized the possibility of improved relations with London. Foremost among these was John Quincy Adams, minister to England until 1817 and after that secretary of state in the Monroe administration.

A DIPLOMATIC BONANZA

On May 25, 1815, John Quincy Adams, with his wife Louisa and their young son Charles, arrived in London, where he was to serve as minister to the Court of St. James's. It was the beginning of a long collaboration with Lord Castlereagh, during which a variety of problems in Anglo-American relations were resolved.

Among the issues that threatened Anglo-American harmony in early 1816, none seemed more pressing than the question of naval armaments on the Great Lakes. Castlereagh and Adams were both aware that control of the lakes was a prerequisite to successful military operations in the region. During the war Lieutenant Oliver Hazard Perry's scratch fleet of small warships had given the United States supremacy on the lakes. At war's end, however, a parsimonious Congress put a stop to further naval construction there. London stopped its building program too. But Washington erroneously believed that British construction was continuing. Concerned by British shipbuilding Adams inquired whether Castlereagh was interested in negotiating a naval disarmament agreement for the lakes. The foreign secretary agreed that "keeping a number of armed vessels parading about the lakes in time of peace . . . would be absurd" and that "everything beyond what is necessary to guard against smuggling is calculated only to produce mischief."[8]

Negotiations might have begun immediately. But because Adams had no powers, the talks were transferred to Washington, where the British minister, Charles Bagot, and Acting Secretary of State Richard Rush, worked out the details.

The Rush-Bagot Agreement of 1818 came together easily because British and American views on the question coincided. American policy makers realized that if neither side had warships on the lakes, at the beginning of a future conflict the United States would have logistical advantages that could quickly be transformed into naval superiority there. Castlereagh and the Admiralty knew this, too, but had already decided that in any event the future of North America was for the United States to decide. Britain might try to defend the lakes, but to what end? In agreeing to their demilitarization, Castlereagh acknowledged Washington's supremacy in North America and at the same time contributed to the growing amity that was Canada's best security against an uncertain future.

That perennial favorite in the history of Anglo-American relations— the fisheries question—was another issue that begged for resolution following the war. During the Paris peace talks that led to the Treaty of 1783, old John Adams fought tenaciously to secure New England's right to fish off Newfoundland's Grand Banks. He was forced, however, to settle for the "liberty" to fish. Until the War of 1812 came along, the agreement stood. But when American fishing vessels returned to Newfoundland waters after the war, they were warned away by fleet units of the British North Atlantic squadron. Admiral Edward Griffith, who commanded there, insisted that by declaring war on England the United States had lost the liberty to fish.

A vehement protest from Washington prompted London to authorize American fisherman to return temporarily to their old haunts. But the issue remained to be resolved, as did other questions, including the boundary between Canada and the United States and the question of compensation for the owners of some thirty-six hundred slaves carried off by British forces during the fighting.

Adams, who returned to the United States in 1817 to become secretary of state in the Monroe administration, wanted an omnibus negotiation to resolve as many of these problems as possible. Castlereagh, who was especially interested in resolving the Canadian boundary dispute, readily agreed. The talks began in the summer of 1818 at Castlereagh's country house a few miles outside London. Richard Rush, who had replaced Adams in London, and Albert Gallatin, who was then serving as the American minister in Paris, represented the United States. The British were represented by Henry Goulburn and Frederick John Robinson, president of the Board of Trade.

The Convention of 1818, though it was not all that either Adams or Castlereagh had hoped for, did resolve a number of issues. The fisheries question was again compromised; a commercial treaty first signed in 1815 was renewed; and it was agreed that the question of the slaves taken by British forces during the war would be the subject of arbitration.

On balance, however, the agreement was not considered a major achievement. For example, the Americans were once again disappointed by Britain's refusal to open its West Indian colonies to free trade. Nor were the negotiators able to agree on a Canadian-American boundary beyond the Rocky Mountains. Instead they ran the boundary westward from the Lake of the Woods along the 49th degree as far as the Rocky Mountains. Beyond that point both sides agreed to joint occupancy of the Oregon country for a period of ten years, at which time the issue would again be considered. Other issues including impressment and neutral rights in wartime also remained unresolved.

Since there was no war going on in Europe at this time, a resolution to these last two issues was not vitally important. But it troubled Washington that Castlereagh remained so unwilling to accept the American point of view. Adams and Monroe need not have been concerned, however. The rapprochement stood on the firm foundations of national interest, a truth Lords Castlereagh and Liverpool would demonstrate during the long-drawn-out negotiations between Adams and Don Luis de Onís, Spain's Minister to the United States, over the Floridas and the boundary between the Louisiana Territory and Mexico.

THE FLORIDA QUESTION

The ink was hardly dry on the agreement ceding Louisiana to the United States in 1803 before Thomas Jefferson made a serious attempt to grab West Florida from Spain. Basing his contention on a poorly substantiated claim first advanced by Robert R. Livingston and James Monroe, the men who purchased Louisiana, Jefferson insisted from that time forth that West Florida from the Mississippi to the Perdido River was included in the purchase. The French denied this claim, as did the Spanish. And they had documentary evidence to support their contention. But all evidence to the contrary notwithstanding, Jefferson stood firm.

The president was motivated by two complementary considerations. An expansionist, he was determined that the Floridas and Cuba, too, should one day become part of a rising American empire. He was also acting on what he considered to be a vital national security interest. In the wrong hands, both the Floridas could pose a strategic threat to the United States. But West Florida was most important because it flanked the Mississippi on the east. Whoever controlled this area threatened American control of the river. And if the United States lost control of that great waterway, the future of the transmontane West and of the Union itself would immediately come into question.

So long as Spain held the Floridas, there was no danger. But in 1804, with Europe at war, a weak Spain was liable to lose the Floridas to either France or England. Under the circumstances both Jefferson and Madison felt compelled to do everything possible to acquire the area for the United States. Jefferson first tried the direct approach, sending James Monroe to Madrid to purchase the Floridas. When that failed, Jefferson considered an Anglo-American alliance and military action to achieve the same results, abandoning that option only after British violations of America's neutral rights became too serious to ignore. After that he tried to work through the French but failed once again.

By the time Jefferson left office in 1809, the danger that the Floridas might fall to one of the major belligerents had become quite real. The French had deposed and imprisoned the Spanish king, Ferdinand VII. Napoleon's brother, Joseph Bonaparte, sat upon the Spanish throne. It seemed only a matter of time before either a British force took the Floridas or the French sent an army to secure them (for a map of the Floridas see p. 28). Madison acted quickly to forestall both possibilities. Aware that the overt seizure of West Florida would provoke an outcry from his domestic enemies and foreign critics alike, he acted indirectly. After secretly encouraging those Americans living around Baton Rouge to declare their independence, he absorbed their new "nation" before any other power could do anything about it.

A strong British protest over the seizure of this portion of West Florida only confirmed Madison's fears. Early in 1811, acting on a presidential recommendation, Congress enacted the No Transfer Resolution, which asserted that the United States would not tolerate the transfer of territory bordering the United States from one foreign power to another and would if necessary occupy such areas, leaving their future open to negotiations. Two years later the administration annexed another piece of West Florida between the Pearl and Perdido rivers. During the War of 1812 Congress also secretly authorized the president to seize East Florida. But at the end of the war the area remained in Spanish hands.

Europe's trauma ended in 1815 with the final exile of Napoleon to the island of St. Helena. But Spain's problems in the Western Hemisphere were only just beginning. In 1809, following Joseph Bonaparte's seizure of power in Madrid, the Spanish empire, from Mexico to the tip of Patagonia, rose in revolution. For a brief period beginning in 1814 Spain reasserted its control. But revolution broke out in South and Central America once again in 1817. Spain's feeble grip on its once great empire was slipping. As it did, the country's ability to govern what remained of the Floridas also came into question.

Aware of Spain's growing weakness, Adams and Monroe set out to acquire East Florida for the United States. The Treaty of 1795 between Spain and the United States left the responsibility for controlling the Indians who inhabited Florida to Spain. But warriors of the Seminole and other southwestern Indian tribes operating out of Florida carried on a running battle against an expanding American frontier. At the same time freebooters, operating with impunity from Amelia Island and Galveston, preyed on American commerce in the Gulf of Mexico.

The obvious inability of the Spanish authorities in the Floridas either to control the Indians or to clean out the pirate nests along the Gulf Coast gave President James Monroe precisely the opportunity he needed to exert pressure. He sent a naval force to occupy Amelia Island and began preparations for a descent upon Galveston. The handwriting was on the wall.

Spain could begin serious negotiations on the Florida question or risk losing all of the Floridas and perhaps Texas, too, in a war with the United States. And if the United States did go to war with Spain, wasn't it reasonable to assume that it would recognize the independence of the Latin American states?

Pressed by the Monroe administration, Spain's foreign minister, José Pizarro, turned to Britain for help. He asked the Foreign Office to mediate the dispute between Spain and America, hoping that Castlereagh would be a friendly mediator or, if the United States rejected mediation, that London would take Spain's side in the dispute. But Castlereagh and Adams had built too well in the years following the war. The foreign secretary refused to endanger his American connection for Spain's sake. Castlereagh did inquire whether the United States would be interested in Britain's good offices. But he made it abundantly clear at the same time that he would not be offended if Washington turned him down. Washington's lack of interest in British mediation suited Castlereagh very well indeed. From that point on, he left Spain to deal with the United States on its own. The new Anglo-American relationship thus began to pay dividends in ways that neither Monroe nor Adams had at first considered.

Isolated and under pressure, Pizarro ordered the Spanish minister in Washington, Don Luis de Onís, to open negotiations with Secretary of State Adams. But Pizarro had no intention of bringing the talks to fruition at any time in the near future. His real objective was to keep the Americans talking and await developments.

Onís was an admirable choice for such an assignment. Indefatigable in the pursuit of his sovereign's interests, he spun the negotiations out until events did seem to take a turn in Spain's favor. Early in 1818, General Andrew Jackson, commanding a small army of Tennessee and Georgia volunteers, was sent to clear the Seminole warriors from the Georgia frontier. Convinced that such an offensive would do no good so long as the Indians could retreat into their Florida sanctuaries, he violated Secretary of War John C. Calhoun's instructions by pursuing the Indians into East Florida, where he crushed them. Nor did Jackson stop there. Under the impression that the administration would support such a move after the fact, he seized the Spanish posts at St. Marks and Pensacola.

Along the way, Jackson captured, court martialed, and executed two British subjects. Alexander Arbuthnot was a Scottish merchant who had recently come from the Bahamas and was carrying on a brisk trade with the Indians. Robert C. Ambrister was a young British adventurer who had fought with Wellington at Waterloo, served as part of the Royal Marine detachment guarding Napoleon on St. Helena, and subsequently been cashiered from the service for dueling with a fellow officer. After this, Ambrister went to the British West Indies and then to Florida where, like Arbuthnot, he aided the Indians in their war against the United States.

Whatever these men had been in life, dead they constituted a major headache for the president and his secretary of state. How would the British react when they learned that two Englishmen had been tried and summarily executed by an American general? Was it possible that the British would join forces with Spain to resist the American pressure on Florida? In Madrid, Pizarro thought so, as did Onís, who officially suspended the negotiations until Florida had been returned to Spain and Jackson had been disciplined. More to the point, Onís was waiting until Castlereagh had made his position regarding these new developments clear.

The British reaction was not at all what the Spanish had hoped. Elements of the British press were, of course, furious. But anger was almost universally tempered by caution. Thus the *Caledonian Mercury*, like many other British newspapers, denounced the American outrage while at the same time remarking that the "notion of a war on account of this transaction is, we think, totally out of the question." If Lord Castlereagh was upset he didn't show it. After studying the facts of the case against Ambrister and Arbuthnot, he told the American minister in London, Richard Rush, that he was not even going to make a formal protest. The government had concluded, he explained, that the actions of "the unfortunate sufferers . . . deprived them of any claim on their own Govt. for interference on their behalf."[9]

Unaware of London's reaction, Washington was thrown into a frenzy by Jackson's escapade. The cabinet met five times on five successive days in the middle of July 1818 before a policy was decided upon. Secretary of the Treasury William H. Crawford, glad of the opportunity to attack Jackson, a political rival, demanded that Monroe discipline the general and order him to withdraw from Florida post haste. Secretary of War Calhoun, evidently piqued because Jackson had disobeyed his specific instructions, and also concerned about how Britain might react, joined forces with Crawford. Only John Quincy Adams spoke in Jackson's defense.

Discounting the possibility that the British would make a major issue out of the Ambrister-Arbuthnot affair, Adams argued that the president ought to respond to Spain's protests by defending his general and that he ought further to indicate he would not return the post at Pensacola until the Spanish could guarantee that they would control the Indians in the region. Such forthright action, the secretary believed, would break the logjam in his negotiations with Onís by graphically demonstrating that the administration had reached the limit of its patience.

The cabinet debate came out almost as Adams had hoped. Monroe, who was not anxious to tangle with the popular Jackson, authorized Adams to inform Onís that the administration believed he was completely justified in entering Florida because Spanish officials there had failed to control the Indians. Pensacola would be returned to the Spanish forthwith, but the United States would continue to hold St. Marks until the Spanish could garrison the place with a force large enough to withstand an Indian attack.

Adams had played his hand brilliantly. Madrid now realized that even when provoked London would not act against the United States and that Spain would have to surrender East Florida to the Americans or have it taken by force. Onís reopened the negotiations with Adams and for the first time began serious bargaining. He was now prepared to cede the Floridas in return for a clearly defined southwestern boundary between the United States and Mexico. He also hoped to prevent the United States from recognizing the independence of the Latin American republics.

Onís had been authorized to go so far as to surrender Texas if necessary in exchange for a secure boundary between Mexico and the United States. Adams, who guessed Onís's instructions, was prepared to continue the negotiations until he had forced this concession from the tenacious Spaniard. But when he and Onís came close to an agreement on East Florida and other aspects of the new western boundary line, the president intervened, insisting that Adams end the long-drawn-out negotiations, leaving Texas in Spanish hands. Perhaps Monroe, who was by this time embroiled in the Missouri controversy, feared the effect of adding more land in the Southwest to his cup of woes. Or perhaps he simply wanted to put an end to the extended talks by accepting the enormous concessions Spain had already made. Whatever the case, Adams and Onís signed a treaty on February 22, 1819, that, while it did not include Texas, vastly expanded the continental domain of the United States. The boundary they agreed upon ran from the Gulf of Mexico up the Sabine to the Red River. It then followed the Red River westward to the 100th meridian, ran due north to the Arkansas River, and followed that waterway west to the 105th meridian, where it again struck due north to the 42nd parallel. From there it ran due west to the Pacific. Adams, euphoric over what he had accomplished, later recalled:

> It was near one in the morning . . . when I closed the day with ejaculations of fervent gratitude to the Giver of all good. . . . It was, perhaps, the most important day of my life. . . . The acknowledgement of a definite line of boundary to the South Sea forms a great epoch in our history.[10]

Not everyone was as joyful at the outcome of the talks as Adams, however. Senator Thomas Hart Benton of Missouri was livid when he learned that Texas was not included in the new map of the United States. He insisted that America had a solid claim to the territory and opposed the treaty in the Senate. But it was Congressman David Trimble of Kentucky who spoke most eloquently against the treaty. An early advocate of what Professor Albert K. Weinberg has called "geographic predestination," Trimble pilloried Adams and Monroe for sacrificing America's natural boundary on the Rio Grande.

> The Father of the Universe, in his peculiar providence, had given natural boundaries to every continent and kingdom—permanent, physical, imperishable barriers, to every nation, to shield it from invasion. Man, in his mad career of glory, his thirst for dominion, had rejected as useless the great and permanent boundaries of nature, and sought out ideal, perishable limits of his own creation. . . . It is physical barriers alone that check encroachment, and give repose to feeble nations.[11]

Trimble may have been eloquent, but he was ineffective. The Adams-Onís Treaty passed easily in the Senate.

In spite of his quick Senate victory, John Quincy Adams, an early believer in the adage that if something can go wrong it probably will, fretted over the treaty. Some inner voice told him that the question had not yet been completely settled. Yet what could go wrong? Onís had full powers and His Catholic Majesty, Ferdinand VII, who had been restored to the Spanish throne in 1814, promised "on the word of a king" to approve his emissary's handiwork. Unhappily, however, as Adams and Monroe soon found out, the word of a king is no better than the king himself.

Even by the relatively low standards of the time, it was generally conceded that Ferdinand VII was a poor specimen of a monarch. As a child he had hated and been hated by his parents. In 1807 he was even imprisoned by his father, who accused him of plotting a coup as well as the murder of his mother and her sometime lover Manuel de Godoy. Dull-witted to the point of out-and-out stupidity, Ferdinand was given to long periods of brooding punctuated by frenzied outbursts of brutality. The men who surrounded the king were, with the single exception of poor Pizarro, no better than Ferdinand himself. Self-serving sycophants, they encouraged all of his worst qualities. Once, in a fit of frustration and anger, the honest and long-suffering Onís described them as "ignorant and stupid" fools whose "obstinacy and imbecility" was literally beyond imagining.[12]

In all of their wisdom the king and his Council of State disapproved the treaty Onís had negotiated. Though the envoy had been empowered to cede even Texas in exchange for a firm boundary, they now insisted that he had surrendered too much. They were also distressed that he had not managed to force from the Americans a commitment not to recognize the independence of the rebellious Latin American colonies. Instead, therefore, of signing the treaty, Ferdinand recalled Onís and sent another emissary to Washington to reopen the talks.

As the king should have known, the administration was through talking. Utterly infuriated, Adams advised the president to seize East Florida forthwith. But the cautious Monroe hesitated. And while he considered his options, events took a turn in favor of final ratification. A mutiny that began among Spanish army units quickly spread to Madrid. The king was forced to reinstate the liberal constitution of 1812 and transfer much of his power to the Cortes (the national legislature). Under pressure from the Cortes, the king reluctantly signed the Adams-Onís Treaty on October 24, 1820. Now the United States had, in truth, become a transcontinental power.

LOOKING SOUTH

Throughout the long period during which Adams and Onís struggled to produce their treaty, a major complicating factor in the negotiations was the revolution that then gripped all of Latin America. Onís tried but failed to

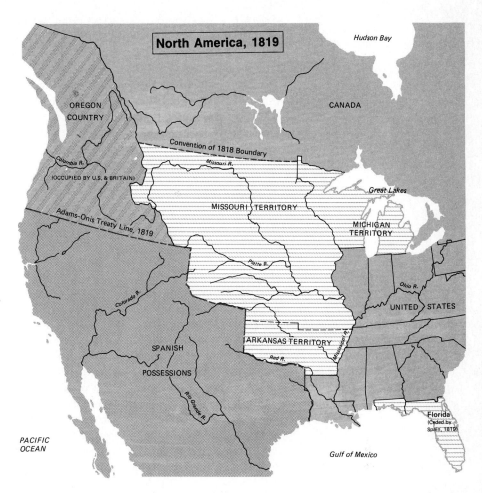

make it a condition of the treaty that the United States would not recognize the independence of the emerging Latin American republics. Still, Adams and Monroe behaved cautiously, holding to a policy of official indifference toward Latin America. Adams maintained that it was inappropriate to recognize the independence of a rebellious people until they had in fact won their freedom. But behind this explanation lay another consideration. Adams and Monroe would do nothing to endanger the ongoing negotiations with Spain.

Beginning in 1817 and continuing until the administration actually did extend recognition to five Latin American republics in 1822, Speaker of the House Henry Clay repeatedly denounced the government's neutral stance as an abandonment of fundamental American principles. He urged Adams and Monroe to act boldly by recognizing the Latin American republics. Clay realized that Latin America's cause had captured the imagination of a great many Americans. The politically astute Kentuckian made the most of that fact.

Whether or not the Spanish-American revolutionary movement was 1776 all over again was, of course, a matter of debate. Adams, for example, scoffed at the idea that the Latin American revolutions had anything to do with liberty, at least as he understood that term. "They had not," he said, "the first elements of good or free government. Arbitrary power, military and ecclesiastical, was stamped upon their education, upon their habits, and upon all their institutions."[13] But not even Adams had the courage to utter such heresies in public. It was good politics to be on the right side of this issue. And that is precisely where Clay positioned himself.

If Clay's advocacy of the Latin American cause was in one sense an act of political opportunism, it is also true that recognition made economic sense, especially following the panic of 1819. The British had dominated Latin American markets from the moment they opened in 1808. Clay argued that the United States ought to fight such an unnatural development and that the best way to begin was by becoming the first to recognize the emerging republics. America, Clay believed, ought "to create a system of which we shall be the center, and in which all South America will act with us." As the leader of a coalition of western hemispheric republics, he argued, the United States would naturally benefit economically, becoming "the place of deposit of the commerce of the world."[14]

Clay was not the only one to offer economic reasons for extending recognition to the Latin Americans. Congressman Joel Poinsett, who had once served as an unofficial agent in South America, argued that recognition would encourage a rise in the standard of living for most Latin Americans and produce "a demand for all the manufactures of this country, and for all the objects of trade." As the historian Arthur P. Whitaker has noted, "The continuance of the economic depression and the loss of other markets made some Americans appreciate more keenly the value of the Latin American market, both actual and potential." It is perhaps not so surprising then that in 1822, with Spanish power virtually eliminated from Central and South America and the Adams-Onís Treaty at last secure, President Monroe extended recognition to five Latin American governments, the United Provinces of the Rio de la Plata, Colombia, Chile, Peru, and Mexico.[15]

NONCOLONIZATION AND EXPANSION

The Fourth Coalition that defeated Napoleon and restored peace to Europe in 1815 began to show cracks and fissures even before the Congress of Vienna convened. Yet in spite of their growing differences, the victorious European powers did manage to redraw the map of Europe and establish the Quadruple Alliance, which committed Britain, Russia, Prussia, and Austria to the defense of Europe's new status quo and to the prevention of a new Napoleonic upsurge in France.

The arrangements made at Vienna, however, did not go far enough for Czar Alexander I. Anxious to organize a league of monarchies committed to the destruction of liberal movements wherever they might arise, he established the so-called Holy Alliance in concert with Prussia and Austria. Austria's Prince Metternich described the Holy Alliance as a "high sounding nothing" and joined only "to please the Tsar." Castlereagh, who warned Lord Liverpool that "the Emperor's mind is not completely sound," refused to initial the agreement, describing it as "a piece of sublime mysticism and nonsense."[16]

Castlereagh and Metternich both understood that the czar's fantasy of a league of monarchs bound together by Christian faith in the defense of the divine right of kings was an absurdity in a rapidly moderizing Europe. But in liberal circles a more sinister interpretation of European developments gained currency. As early as January 1816, Henry Clay warned that the Vienna system constituted a potential threat to republicanism everywhere and that it was "destructive of every principle of liberty."[17] Though no one knew the precise intentions of the Holy Alliance, many in the United States thought it conceivable that an invasion fleet might one day appear off South American shores, come to restore Spain's rule there. And what of the American republic? Would the forces of reaction leave the United States in peace?

At the State Department, John Quincy Adams did not share these concerns. He saw not European unity but the fragmentation of the old wartime coalition. The first clear indication of the split came in 1818, when the European powers, meeting in congress at Aix-la-Chapelle, agreed only to disagree. There the czar, still driven by the mystical vision of a world made safe for absolutism, tried to organize support for Spain in its efforts to regain control of Latin America. But Castlereagh and Metternich together blocked the attempt. In 1820 the czar called for another congress to meet at Troppau. His purpose this time was to organize joint action to crush the Spanish Cortes and restore to power the unhappy Ferdinand VII. Castlereagh refused to attend, pointing out to the czar that the Spanish revolution was a purely internal matter and that Russia's attempt to turn the Quadruple Alliance into a world police force was not welcome. He urged other members of the alliance to keep "within its common sense limits."[18]

These developments, coupled with the cordial relationship between England and America that had grown up after the war, convinced John Quincy Adams of two things. First, he was certain before the end of 1820 that England was going its own way, that its interests diverged from those of the continental powers, and that it would not take a part in the czar's restoration fantasy. Second, because England had growing economic interests in South America as well as a vast market in the United States, it would never allow the continental powers to intervene in the Western Hemisphere. Adams was the first American policy maker to perceive these truths. They served him and the country exceptionally well during Monroe's second administration.

In April 1815, Don Luis de Onís warned his government that if the United States was "permitted to go on growing" it would "be impossible for the powers of Europe to retain a single foot of territory in this continent or a single island in the Gulf of Mexico." Had John Quincy Adams seen this dispatch, he might have advised Onís not to concern himself since there was nothing Europe could do to stop the growth of the American empire in any event. Providence, he believed, had determined that the United States should expand to include all of North America, her "proper dominion." Nor did Adams's vision stop at the shoreline, for he believed that Cuba, another rich prize, beckoned. As Spain's grip on its New World empire faltered, Adams expected that, like a ripe apple falling from a tree, the Pearl of the Antilles would follow the "law of political gravitation" to become part of the United States.[19]

A natural corollary to Adams's view that it was America's destiny to absorb the continent and its environs was his equally firm conviction that the European nations had no future role to play as colonizing powers in the hemisphere. It was, he thought, "a physical, moral, and political absurdity that such fragments of territory, with sovereigns at fifteen hundred miles beyond the sea, worthless and burdensome to their owners, should exist permanently contiguous to a great, powerful, and rapidly growing nation." Since colonial establishments could not "fulfill the great objects of governments in the just purposes of civil society," he explained in his memoirs, "it will be the duty of the human family to abolish them, as they are now endeavoring to abolish the slave trade."[20]

Adams first officially asserted his continental ambitions as well as this new doctrine of noncolonization in January 1821. The occasion was a visit to the State Department by the handsome, dignified, and very straight-laced Stratford Canning, cousin to George Canning, and His Majesty's minister to the United States. The issue that brought Canning hurrying to Adams's office was a newspaper report indicating that the United States was about to establish a settlement in Oregon at the mouth of the Columbia River, an area also claimed by Britain. For two days Adams and Canning wrangled. On the second day of this marathon encounter there took place a brief but extraordinary exchange that Adams later recorded verbatim in his diary:

> "I do not know," said I, "what you claim nor what you do not claim. You claim India; you claim Africa; you claim—" "Perhaps," said he, "a piece of the moon." "No," said I; "I have not heard that you claim exclusively any part of the moon; but there is no spot on *this* habitable globe that I could not affirm you do not claim; and there is none which you may not claim with as much color or right as you can have to the Columbia River or its mouth." "And how far would you consider," said he, "this exclusion of right to extend?" "To all the shores of the South Sea," said I. "We know of no right that you have there." "And in this," said he, "you include our northern provinces on this continent." "No," said I, "there the boundary is marked, and we have no disposition to encroach upon it. Keep what is yours, but leave the rest of the continent to us."[21]

In July 1823, Adams reasserted this noncolonization principle with even greater vehemence. Almost two years, before Czar Alexander I had issued a *ukase* (edict) claiming sovereignty over the Northwest Coast of North America south from Alaska, a Russian province, to 51 degrees north latitude. The *ukase* forbade foreigners from trading in the area or from fishing within one hundred Italian miles of that coast. Britain and the United States immediately protested this extension of Russian claims in North America. Adams told Baron de Tuyll van Serooskerken, the Russian minister, "that we would contest the right of Russia to *any* territorial establishment on this continent and that we should assume distinctly the principle that the American continents are no longer subjects for any new European colonial establishments."[22] Long before President James Monroe announced his famous doctrine, then, Adams made it crystal clear that the United States no longer viewed the Western Hemisphere as open to European colonization. The area was reserved for an expanding American empire.

THE MONROE DOCTRINE

In the autumn of 1823, George Canning, who moved back to the Foreign Office following Castlereagh's suicide, made a startling proposal to Richard Rush, the American envoy in London. Sounding very much like Adams himself, Canning suggested that the United States and Britain jointly state their conviction that Spain had no hope of recovering her colonies, that recognition of the Latin American republics was no longer in doubt but was merely a question of "time and circumstance," and that although the United States and Britain did not object to further peaceful attempts at reconciliation between Spain and its former colonies, they "could not see any portion of them transferred to any other power with indifference." Canning further proposed that London and Washington state publicly that they "aim not at the possession of any portion" of Spain's empire for themselves.[23]

The foreign secretary's timing couldn't have been better. At that very moment a French army, having invaded Spain for the purpose of restoring the monarchy, was advancing on Cádiz, the last stronghold of Spain's liberals. Moreover the Russians had let it be known that once Ferdinand VII was returned to power, they would consider what to do about the Latin Americans. The power of the reactionaries appeared awesome. Liberals in two hemispheres dreaded what might happen. What better time, then, could there have been for the United States to clutch Britain's outstretched hand.

Rush informed Washington of Canning's proposal and while awaiting instructions countered with an offer of his own. The United States had for some time been hoping that Britain would recognize the Latin American republics and so eliminate any possibility of future European-sponsored counterrevolutionary activity in Central and South America. Now here was Canning seemingly on the verge of extending recognition. Rush hoped to take Canning just one step further by promising that he would on his own initiative issue a statement warning that his government "would not remain inactive" in the event of "an attack upon the independence of those states by the Holy Alliance" if Canning would agree to the immediate recognition of the Latin American republics.[24]

Canning wasn't interested in what Rush had to offer. He didn't need an American military commitment to protect Latin America. The Royal Navy could do that without any help. Moreover, because the prince regent, later King George IV, the duke of Wellington, and other powerful conservatives in his party were not yet ready for recognition, he couldn't offer Rush the desired quid pro quo. Finally, Rush had (whether by design or accident is unclear) ignored the most important concession Canning hoped to extract from the United States—a pledge not to acquire any part of Spain's tottering New World empire. Like Adams, Canning had his eye on Cuba and its valuable trade. If England could keep the United States from acquiring the island, it could continue to enjoy trade dominance there.

Rush's refusal to accept Canning's original proposal ended these unofficial talks. The foreign secretary now pursued a Latin American policy independent of the United States. On October 10, 1823, London learned that the French had crushed the Spanish Constitutionalists at Cádiz. To head off any possibility that the French might intervene in Latin America, where Britain had valuable commercial interests, Canning held three days of talks with the French ambassador in London, Prince Jules de Polignac. The confidential Polignac memorandum, a product of these talks, stated categorically that France "abjured . . . any design of acting against" Spain's former Latin American colonies "by force of arms."[25] Since without French aid the Holy Allies were incapable of supporting a counterrevolution in Latin America, the threat there, to the extent that it ever existed, was thus put to rest.

President Monroe, who knew nothing of these later developments, found Canning's original proposal for a joint Anglo-American statement on Latin American affairs very attractive. So, too, did the other members of the once powerful Virginia triumvirate, Thomas Jefferson and James Madison. Both men agreed that Canning's proposal ought to be accepted. Jefferson, who had for years advocated the eventual annexation of Cuba, realized the United States would have to forgo this possibility. But he was willing to pay that price, for England and America together could guarantee absolute security in the Western Hemisphere. Europe would never again be able "to interfere with the affairs of our nations," he wrote. Madison went even further. Caught up in the liberal enthusiasm of the age, he suggested that England and America ought also to denounce the French action in Spain and make a public statement in favor of the Greeks who were then engaged in a rebellion against Turkish authority. "With the British power and navy combined with our own," Madison wrote, "we have nothing to fear from the rest of the nations and, in *the great struggle of the Epoch between liberty and despotism*, we owe it to ourselves to sustain the former in this hemisphere at least."[26]

When the cabinet debated Canning's proposal, Secretary of War John C. Calhoun lent an emphatic amen to the view that cooperation with Britain was in the national interest. But Adams demurred. He was convinced that Canning was using the general atmosphere of hysteria created by recent reactionary successes in Europe to deny America the opportunity of acquiring Cuba. The United States, he insisted, ought "not tie ourselves down to any principle which might immediately afterwards be brought to bear against ourselves."[27] The British, with expanding commercial interests in Latin America, would never allow the restoration of Spanish rule there. Since the United States could count on the Royal Navy to protect the Western Hemisphere whether or not an official relationship existed between England and America, he saw no percentage in playing Canning's game.

A few days prior to this cabinet debate, Baron von Tuyll, the Russian minister, delivered a note warning that if the United States should offer aid to the Latin Americans, Russia, speaking for the Holy Allies and presumably for France, would offer direct support to Spain. Adams thought the Russian note provided a splendid "opportunity for us to take our stand against the Holy Alliance" and simultaneously rebuff Canning's overture. "It would be more candid as well as more dignified," he argued, "to avow our principles explicitly to Russia and France, than to come in as a cock-boat in the wake of the British man-of-war." Monroe, who had earlier made it clear that he opposed "any course which would have the appearance of taking a position subordinate to that of Great Britain," must have been impressed with Adams's views for he now readily agreed.[28]

Shortly after delivery of the State Department's note to the Russian minister, Washington learned that Cádiz had fallen to the French. Still unaware of the secret Polignac memorandum, Secretary of War Calhoun went into a fit of despair. He seemed to believe that if the Holy Allies landed even a few thousand troops in Latin America those countries would quickly collapse. He was, thought Adams, "perfectly moonstruck." Worse, the president seemed to have caught the infection. Adams tried to raise their spirits by pointing out how difficult it would be for the Holy Allies to prevail in a war fought halfway around the world. He told his cabinet colleagues, "I no more believe that the Holy Allies will restore the Spanish dominion upon the American continent than that the Chimborazo [the highest peak in the Equadorean Andes] will sink beneath the ocean."[29]

Clearly Adams and not Calhoun understood the European political situation. Czar Alexander's almost frantic posturing resulted from profound personal insecurity. He lived in constant fear that his own regime might be toppled by a liberal revolution and had little time and less inclination to become militarily involved in western hemispheric affairs. The French government, with more than its share of domestic problems, was in no better position than the czar to support counterrevolution in South America. As for the Austrians, Metternich had taken the British side in opposing any effort to reestablish Spanish rule in South America at the Congress of Aix-la-Chapelle and never changed his mind.

Nor was Adams's judgment based wholly on unsubstantiated analysis. He had hard information. On his return from France in June 1823, Gallatin informed the secretary of a conversation with François René, vicomte de Chateaubriand, the French foreign minister. Gallatin spoke frankly, telling the French diplomat that the United States "would not suffer others to interfere against the emancipation of America." He was categorical, warning of military action and a possible alliance with Great Britain. Chateaubriand assured Gallatin in the most unequivocal terms that "France would not make any attempt whatever of that kind or in any manner interfere with the American question."[30]

Still Calhoun remained unconvinced. When another threat from the czar arrived in Washington only a few days after the news from Cádiz, he told the cabinet, "This confirms me in the view I have taken of the designs of the Holy Allies upon South America." Adams, however, remained equally convinced that the Russians were bluffing. In fact he urged Monroe to use the occasion of this latest Russian threat "to declare our expectation and hope that the European powers will equally abstain from the attempt to spread their principles in the American hemisphere, or to subjugate by force any part of these continents to their will."[31] Monroe quickly assented, choosing as the vehicle for this epochal policy statement his forthcoming state of the union message to Congress.

The first draft of the president's message, an extraordinarily bold statement, affirmed the noncolonization principle, denounced the French for their destruction of Spanish constitutionalism, recognized Greek independence, and recommended that Congress appoint a minister to Greece.

Adams was very unhappy with the president's draft. He did not see how the United States could expect European governments to forgo intervention in the Western Hemisphere if the United States intruded in their affairs. He therefore urged the president to reconsider. Reminding Monroe that the United States had a long-standing policy of nonintervention in European politics, he urged him to take a position "against the interference of European powers by force in South America" while at the same time disclaiming "all interference on our part in Europe."[32]

Once again Adams had his way. The final draft of the Monroe Doctrine, part of the state of the union message of December 2, 1823, made no reference to political developments in Europe but warned "that the American Continents . . . are henceforth not to be considered subjects for future colonization by any European powers." Late in the message the president took note of recent reactionary developments in Europe but only for the purpose of reasserting America's traditional policy of nonintervention. At the same time, however, he warned the European powers that the United States "should consider any attempt on their part to extend their system to any portion of this Hemisphere as dangerous to our peace and safety." The United States, Monroe continued, had no intention of interfering with the western hemispheric colonies of any European state. But Washington would view any attempt by European nations to interfere in the affairs of those

Latin American states that had already secured their independence "as the manifestation of an unfriendly disposition towards the United States."[33]

THE WORLD REACTS

The American public greeted the Monroe Doctrine enthusiastically, as did a few European liberals. Thus the aged Marie Joseph Paul, marquis de Lafayette described the President's message as "the best little bit of paper that God had ever permitted any man to give to the world." Others of a more reactionary bent were naturally less enthusiastic. Prince Metternich, the Austrian chancellor, saw the doctrine as a further extension of the American attack on traditional European institutions, while France's Chateaubriand thought that the noncolonization principle "ought to be resisted by all the powers possessing either territory or commercial interests in that hemisphere."[34]

The Russians reacted scornfully. St. Petersburg viewed the doctrine as stating "views and pretensions so exaggerated, . . . principles so contrary to the rights of European powers, that it merits only the most profound contempt."[35] The czar, like the rest of Europe's leaders, realized the United States had no power to enforce its will throughout the Western Hemisphere, that Britain was the protector of Latin American independence.

The earliest British reaction to the Monroe Doctrine was positive. Canning had already guaranteed Latin America's security first by extracting the Polignac memorandum from the French and then by pointedly refusing to attend an 1824 European Congress called for the purpose of considering an intervention in Latin America. On reading Monroe's message, he remarked, "The Congress was broken in all its limbs before, but the President's speech gives it the *coup de grace*."[36]

But the more Canning thought about the doctrine, the more critical he became, especially of the noncolonization principle. At the same time he realized that British commercial interests might suffer if Latin Americans came to believe that the United States was the guarantor of their security. To counteract that danger, he published the Polignac memorandum, circulated it among Latin American leaders, and fought a successful battle in Parliament to recognize the new western hemispheric republics.

Nor were most informed Latin Americans particularly enthusiastic about Monroe's new policy. In the first place, they were less concerned than were many in the United States over the danger of European intervention. Second, most Latin American leaders realized that it was the British fleet and not the American president's rhetoric that would protect them in the event an intervention was attempted. Finally, even as early as 1823 Latin American resentment toward the United States was quite real. The United States's refusal to aid or even recognize Latin American independence prior to 1822 embittered many. At the same time the Adams-Onís Treaty with

Spain made it clear that the United States would pursue its own interests even at their expense.

It is true that at first a number of Latin American liberals viewed the doctrine with considerable enthusiasm. But disillusionment set in quickly once it became clear that it was not a proclamation of ideological togetherness or the prelude to a network of defensive alliances. The Monroe Doctrine, they soon learned, meant only that the United States would keep its options open and would act in western hemispheric affairs as its own interests dictated.

ENDNOTES

1. Henry Clay and Rufus King, quoted in Bradford Perkins, *Castlereagh and Adams: England and the United States, 1812–1823,* (University of California Press, Berkeley, Cal., 1964), p. 158.

2. The Reverend Samuel Smith, from the *Quarterly Review,* quoted in John Bach McMaster, *A History of the People of the United States* (D. Appleton and Co., N.Y., 1894–1905), V, p. 315.

3. Quoted in *ibid.,* p. 312.

4. Lord Liverpool, quoted in George Dangerfield, *The Era of Good Feelings* (Harcourt, Brace, and World, N.Y., 1952), pp. 258–59.

5. Admiral Milne, quoted in Kenneth Bourne, *Britain and the Balance of Power in North America* (University of California Press, Berkeley, Cal., 1967), p. 15.

6. Lord Castlereagh, quoted in *ibid.,* pp. 53–54.

7. Castlereagh, quoted in Perkins, *Castlereagh and Adams,* p. 201.

8. Castlereagh, quoted in Samuel Flagg Bemis, *John Quincy Adams and the Foundations of American Foreign Policy* (Alfred A. Knopf, N.Y., 1949), I, p. 230.

9. The *Caledonian Mercury,* quoted in Perkins, *Castlereagh and Adams,* pp. 291–92; Castlereagh, quoted in *ibid.*

10. John Quincy Adams in *The Memoirs of John Quincy Adams,* ed. Charles Francis Adams (Lippincott, Philadelphia, 1874–1877), IV, p. 275.

11. Congressman David Trimble, quoted in Albert K. Weinberg, *Manifest Destiny: A Study of Nationalist Expansion in American History* (Quadrangle Books, Chicago, 1963), p. 55.

12. Luis de Onís, quoted in Dangerfield, *The Era of Good Feelings,* p. 144.

13. John Quincy Adams, *Memoirs* V, p. 325.

14. Clay, quoted in Arthur P. Whitaker, *The United States and the Independence of Latin America, 1800 to 1830* (W. W. Norton and Co., N.Y., 1964), pp. 187, 386n.

15. Joel Poinsett, quoted in *Annals of Congress,* 17th Congress, 1st. session, p. 1400; Whitaker, *The United States and the Independence of Latin America,* p. 386.

16. Metternich and Castlereagh, quoted in David Thompson, *Europe Since Napoleon* (Alfred A. Knopf and Co., N.Y., 1957), p. 76.

17. Clay in *The Papers of Henry Clay,* ed. James F. Hopkins et al. (University of Kentucky Press, Lexington Ky., 1961), II, p. 135.

18. Castlereagh, quoted in Thompson, *Europe Since Napoleon,* p. 116.

19. Adams to Hugh Nelson, April 28, 1823, *The Writings of John Quincy Adams,* ed. Charles Francis Adams, VII, pp. 372–73; 381.

20. John Quincy Adams to Edward Everett, January 31, 1822, in *ibid.,* pp. 197–207.

21. Adams, *Memoirs,* V, p. 252.

22. *Ibid.,* VI, p. 163.

23. George Canning, quoted in Bemis, *John Quincy Adams*, I, p. 377; see also Whitaker, *The United States and the Independence of Latin America*, p. 439.

24. Rush, quoted in Dangerfield, *The Era of Good Feelings*, p. 287.

25. Polignac memorandum, quoted in Whitaker, *The United States and the Independence of Latin America*, p. 445.

26. Jefferson to Monroe, October 24, 1823, *The Writings of Thomas Jefferson*, ed. Paul L. Ford (G.P. Putnam's Sons, N.Y., 1892–1899), XII, pp. 318–19; Madison to Monroe, October 29, 1823, *The Writings of James Monroe*, ed. Stanislaus Murray Hamilton (G. P. Putnam's Sons, N.Y., 1898–1903), VI, p. 394.

27. Adams, quoted in Bemis, *John Quincy Adams*, I, p. 385.

28. Adams, *Memoirs*, VI, p. 179.

29. *Ibid.*, p. 186.

30. Albert Gallatin, quoted in Paul A. Varg, *United States Foreign Relations, 1820–1860* (Michigan State University Press, East Lansing, Mich. 1979), p. 53.

31. Adams, *Memoirs* VI, pp. 190, 194.

32. *Ibid.*, p. 198.

33. *Messages and Papers of the Presidents*, ed. James D. Richardson (Washington, 1900), II, pp. 209, 218.

34. Marquis de Lafayette, quoted in Bemis, *John Quincy Adams*, I, p. 403n; François René, vicomte de Chateaubriand, quoted in Dexter Perkins, *A History of the Monroe Doctrine* (Little, Brown and Co., Boston, 1963), p. 57.

35. Quoted in Perkins, *A History of the Monroe Doctrine*, p. 57.

36. Canning, quoted in *Ibid.*, p. 61.

THE AGE OF EXPANSION, 1823–1846

John Tyler, a president without a party, saw expansionism as the issue that might return him to the White House in 1844. He was right about the power of expansionism as an issue but mistaken about his own chances. Before leaving office, however, he did have the pleasure of completing the annexation of Texas, long an ambition of southern expansionists.

For more than a decade after James Monroe left the White House, foreign policy took a back seat to internal developments in the United States. But during the presidency of Martin Van Buren a series of crises in Anglo-American relations threatened to produce a war that neither government wanted. The first sign of trouble ahead came in 1837 when the Canadian rebel, William Mackenzie, led an uprising against the British in Canada. After a series of crushing defeats, Mackenzie and a few followers fled across the border into upper New York State. There, where Anglophobia was practiced as one of the higher arts, Mackenzie was greeted as a hero. Mass meetings were held at Oswego, Ogdensburg, Lockport, Buffalo, and other northern towns, and hundreds pledged their aid and support to the rebels and volunteer companies were organized for the invasion of Canada. Arms, ammunition, food, and other provisions flowed into Buffalo, temporary headquarters of the rebel chieftain.

Heartened by this enthusiastic reception, Mackenzie and a few supporters recrossed the border, seizing Navy Island on the Canadian side of the Niagara River. The steamboat *Caroline*, operating from Fort Schlosser on the American side of the river kept the garrison supplied. But on the night of December 29, 1837, Canadian militiamen crossed the river, seized the *Caroline*, set it ablaze, and sent it drifting down river. One American, Amos Durfee, was killed in the melee.

With both sides of the border aflame, President Van Buren sent General Winfield Scott north to restore order. A first-rate strategist, Scott had also distinguished himself as a diplomat while working with local South Carolina officials to reduce tensions during the nullification crisis of 1832. But not even Scott could cool tempers after the *Caroline* affair. A few months later a number of Americans boarded and burned the Canadian steamboat *Sir Robert Peel*. Other Americans organized secret societies called Hunters Lodges that made armed forays into Canada. How long the British would put up with these actions was anybody's guess, especially since to the northeast of the Niagara frontier more violence portended.

The northeastern boundary dividing New Brunswick from Maine had never been clearly defined. In 1782 the negotiators at Paris agreed that the St. Croix River would be the dividing line. But the 1755 Mitchell's map they used was imprecise, and the exact location of the St. Croix remained unclear. As a result, several thousand square miles of forest land remained in dispute. A number of attempts at compromise, including an 1831 mediation effort, failed to resolve the issue. Then, in 1838, Canadian lumbermen entered the Aroostook Valley, part of the disputed area. Maine authorities sent a land agent, Rufus McIntire, to expel the Canadians. But McIntire was arrested for his trouble. Maine and New Brunswick mobilized their militias. Nova Scotians prepared for war, and in Washington, Congress authorized the president to call up fifty thousand men and appropriated an initial $10 million should war become necessary.

Again President Van Buren interceded to avoid bloodshed, sending Scott on his second peace mission in three years. This time the general was more successful convincing hotheads on both sides of the border to accept a truce.

From Maine to the Great Lakes the situation along the Canadian-American frontier remained tense but calm until late in 1840. This tentative peace was shattered in November of that year, however, when Alexander McLeod, a Canadian, had a little too much to drink at a saloon on the American side of the Niagara and bragged that he was the man who had killed Amos Durfee during the raid on the *Caroline*. When McLeod sobered up he found himself not at home in his own warm bed but in a New York jail charged with murder. He recanted his confession, but it was no good. Warrants had been issued for Durfee's murderer long before. Now the New Yorkers thought they had their man.

THE WEBSTER-ASHBURTON TALKS

Britain's foreign secretary at this time was Henry John Temple, Lord Palmerston. An impulsive, proud, and arrogant Anglo-Irish peer, Palmerston was known for aggressive, often tactless behavior and a rapierlike wit; he was one of the most feared and disliked members of Britain's political elite. It did not take much to bring out the jingo in Palmerston. Still, through the late 1830s he refused to become exercised by England's growing difficulties with the United States. In spite of warnings from Henry Fox, the British minister in Washington, who believed that Van Buren was encouraging the Canadian rebels, the normally fiery Palmerston placed seemingly unflagging faith in the president's sincere desire for peace.

McLeod's arrest changed all that. Palmerston suddenly exploded, informing the American Minister in London that "if McLeod is executed there must be war."[1] Palmerston insisted that McLeod's confession was the raving of a drunk and that even if he had killed Durfee he could not be held accountable since as a militiaman he was acting under instructions from the Crown. The issue, Palmerston insisted, was between Washington and London and could not be settled in a New York state court.

England and America appeared to be headed for a crisis when in 1841 governments changed on both sides of the Atlantic. In Washington the aged William Henry Harrison replaced Van Buren in the White House. The State Department job went to New Hampshire's Daniel Webster, an Anglophile who made peace with England his foremost priority. The nation remained in the grip of the economic depression that followed the panic of 1837. Webster and other like-minded economic internationalists feared that a war, especially one with America's best customer, would disrupt trade and destroy markets that were desperately needed if the country was to find its way back to prosperity.

In London, meanwhile, a Tory ministry headed by Sir Robert Peel took power. Palmerston went into opposition and George Hamilton Gordon, Lord Aberdeen, replaced him in the Foreign Office. Like Webster, Aberdeen wanted a peaceful resolution to Anglo-American differences. But Aberdeen had a problem. Parliament and the British public were up in arms over McLeod. No progress could be made on other issues until McLeod had been freed. And if by some chance he were sent to the gallows, even Aberdeen would have been forced to recommend war.

In Washington, Daniel Webster went to work to defuse this dangerous situation. He took the McLeod case to the New York State Supreme Court, hoping that the court would agree with the British contention that as a Canadian militiaman McLeod could not be tried in a state court and that the real issue was between England and America. When the court rejected Webster's plea, he urged New York's governor, William H. Seward, to pardon McLeod. But Seward refused; the issue was too politically loaded for that. "Public sentiment," he explained, "demands that the law should have its due course."[2]

Seward eased Webster's concern somewhat by assuring him that though McLeod would have to go to trial he would probably never be convicted. This was news to Webster. Yet, as Seward predicted, McLeod was cleared, probably because the governor or persons close to him fixed the outcome. Certainly the circumstances of the trial suggest that someone wanted McLeod cleared. Otherwise there is no way of explaining why the prosecution's two key witnesses mysteriously disappeared before they could testify or why several Americans who had not come forward earlier testified at the trial that McLeod was with them, miles from the *Caroline*, on the night Durfee was killed.

With the McLeod case settled, Webster and Aberdeen could at last begin negotiations. The foreign secretary appointed Alexander Baring, Lord Ashburton, to handle the talks for the Foreign Office in Washington. A partner in the prestigious banking house, the Baring Brothers, Ashburton was known and liked in America. He had married the daughter of Pennsylvania's William Bingham and was well connected with a number of American business and political leaders, including Secretary Webster, who had on several occasions served as the Baring Brothers's legal council in the United States.

All of this was to the good. But Lord Ashburton came to the United States with little to offer. For example, had it been up to Aberdeen, he would have settled the Maine boundary question to the complete satisfaction of the United States. He thought it absurd that the two countries should be at logger heads "for a few miles more or less of a miserable pine swamp."[3] Unhappily, however, it wasn't up to him. First, a settlement had to be defensible before Parliament, where Palmerston and the Whig opposition lay in wait. Second, the aged duke of Wellington, still a power in British politics, demanded that the government secure enough territory in the Northeast for the construction of an all-land route between St. Johns and Quebec. This demand meant, as Webster well knew, that the United States would have to give up a large part of the disputed territory. Nor did Ashburton have much to offer on other issues. Thus, although many in the United States expected at least an apology for burning of the *Caroline*, the envoy had no such authority. If peace was to be made, it was truly up to Daniel Webster to make it.

The first and most troublesome issue that Webster and Ashburton had to address was the northeastern boundary dispute. Webster realized that, before any progress could be made at the negotiating table, the authorities in Maine would have to be convinced that compromise was in their interest. This convincing would be difficult, since Maine had for years taken an extreme position on the boundary question.

To aid in this endeavor, the secretary enlisted the help of one F.O.J. Smith, a Maine politico and newspaper publisher, who lobbied leading Maine officials, including Governor John Fairfield, in support of a compromise. Smith also published essays in the *Portland East Argus*, which he owned in part, to influence public opinion. In return for these good works, he received an annual salary of $3,500 that came directly from the president's secret service funds.

Webster also employed the services of Jared Sparks, a historian, educator, and later the president of Harvard University. Not long before, while conducting research in the French archives, Sparks found a 1746 d'Anville map of North America with the northeastern boundary marked in a strong red line. It was not a Mitchell's map and therefore could not have been used during the 1782 negotiations. But Benjamin Franklin had written that during the negotiations the boundary was marked with such a line. And since the boundary drawn on the map Sparks had found conformed to the extreme British claim, Webster was anxious to believe in it.

Webster also had in his possession a Mitchell's map that had been found among the papers of Baron Friedrich von Steuben, who had fought with American forces during the Revolution. Whether the map had any markings on it in 1838 when it came into Webster's possession we do not know. But when he turned it over to Sparks it, too, had a red line that conformed to the British claim. Armed with the two maps as well as $14,000 provided by Lord Ashburton for unspecified purposes, Sparks set off for Maine. When he returned the money was gone but the news was good. Maine's leaders had seen the light. They would accept a compromise boundary.

By mid-July the most important part of the negotiation—the boundary settlement—had been completed. The United States would receive 7,015 square miles of the disputed land. The British would get 5,012 square miles.

Even after this the talks, which had gone on far too long for Ashburton, who doubted he could survive the suffocating heat of that Washington summer, almost came to grief over the *Creole* affair. This American ship had sailed from Hampton Roads, Virginia late in October 1841, bound for New Orleans with a cargo of 135 slaves. On the night of November 7, nineteen of the slaves took control of the ship, murdered one of their owners, wounded the captain and two members of the crew, and sailed to Nassau, where the British authorities jailed the mutineers but freed the slaves.

Not surprisingly, the *Creole* affair produced outrage in the American South. Proslavery advocates demanded the return of the slaves and the mutineers. "If we may not safely sail on our own coast, with our slave property on board, because Great Britain may choose to deny our right to hold property in slaves," raged John C. Calhoun, "may she not with equal propriety, extend the same rule to our cotton and other staples?"[4]

Webster knew it was unlikely that London would agree to the South's extreme demands. Britain had abolished slavery in 1833, and the antislavery movement in Britain was a powerful political force. He hoped, however, that London might be willing to offer some form of compensation. Otherwise, he feared, proslavery senators and those who opposed a compromise on the northeastern boundary might combine to defeat the treaty he was then negotiating with Lord Ashburton when it reached the Senate.

Personally, Ashburton would have been more than happy to offer compensation, especially if he could get out of Washington before the heat killed him. But he had no instructions. And so he and Webster tried to satisfy proslavery advocates with an exchange of letters in which they established procedures designed to prevent such incidents from happening in the future. They also set up a mixed commission, consisting of representatives from both countries, which a few years later approved $110,330 in compensation for the slaves lost on the *Creole*.

On a related subject—Britain's interest in putting an end to the African slave trade—no progress was possible. The British favored creating a multi-national naval force that would include ships from most of Europe's great powers as well as the United States to patrol the coast of Africa. But opposition from Anglophobes who disputed England's right to "visit and search" American ships in peacetime, as well as many southerners who feared the British would not stop until they had destroyed slavery per se, made such cooperation impossible. In the end Webster and Ashburton finessed the issue with yet another exchange of letters, this time agreeing that the two countries would, acting separately, keep naval units off the African coast to intercept the slavers. Twenty years later Washington actually undertook to fulfill that promise.

Four months of painstaking, often nit-picking negotiations finally produced the Webster-Ashburton Treaty of 1842. From the American point of view it was not anything to write home about. There is no doubt that on the most pressing issue dividing the two countries—the northeastern boundary—Webster had gone more than halfway to achieve a settlement. That part of the agreement might well have been drafted in the British Foreign Office. Still, Webster was pleased, for like Aberdeen he believed it would have been absurd to go on quarreling over the issues that divided America and England at the time. There was little to be gained and, considering the vital economic relationship that existed between the two countries, much to be lost by carrying things to extremes.

That may have been Webster's view, but Senator Thomas Hart Benton of Missouri most emphatically did not agree. When the treaty came before the Senate he denounced the boundary compromise, pointed out that the administration had done nothing to settle the Oregon question, and attempted to arouse southern anger by pointing out that there had been no satisfactory settlement to the *Creole* affair. But the national economy was in such a state that even the most rabid proslavery advocates could not be goaded into opposing the treaty. John C. Calhoun, speaking for the South and the cotton interest, agreed that the *Creole* issue remained unresolved. But given the state of the economy and the importance of the British market, he thought war should be avoided. "Peace is the first of our wants in the present condition of our country," he said. "If we have not gained all that could be desired, we have gained much that is desirable, and if all has not been settled, much has been—and that not of little importance."[5] The Senate agreed with the senator from South Carolina, voting 39–9 for the treaty and peace.

THE LONE STAR REPUBLIC

American frontiersmen began crossing illegally into Texas at the beginning of the nineteenth century. But it was only in the 1820s that significant numbers of Americans settled there. At the beginning of that decade Moses

Austin, a transplanted Yankee living in Potosi, Missouri, visited Texas, hoping to create a commercial link with that part of Mexico. On arriving in Bexar, however, he sensed other possibilities. Claiming that he spoke for three hundred families interested in establishing a colony in Texas, he talked the Spanish provincial governor into making him a large land grant. Under the terms of the grant, settlers had to be Catholics and swear an oath of allegiance to Spain, nothing more.

Moses Austin died before he could begin the colonization project. But his twenty-seven-year-old son Stephen picked up where he left off. In 1824 the revolutionary government in Mexico City approved the transfer of the grant from father to son and sought to encourage American settlement through a generous colonization law. At the same time the new Mexican constitution made it more attractive for Americans to settle in Texas by granting the state of Coahuila Y Texas an unusual degree of local autonomy. By 1830, as a result of the work of Austin and other impresarios there were perhaps twenty thousand Americans, including one thousand slaves, living in Texas.

As the American population swelled, the Mexican government began to wonder whether it had created a monster. The first indication that the American settlers were restive under Mexican rule came in December 1826, when about twenty settlers seized the fort at Nacogdoches and declared the independent republic of Fredonia. Austin and the great majority of the settlers remained loyal to Mexico, even helping the authorities quell the revolt. Still, in Mexico City the Fredonia uprising was viewed as a dangerous portent of things to come. In 1829, when President Andrew Jackson made a rash attempt to buy Texas, the Mexicans became even more worried. Jackson's proposal left an indelible imprint, deepening already grave suspicions about American intentions.

By the year 1830 many in the Mexican government were convinced that if something was not done Texas would be lost. Lucas Alamán, secretary of foreign relations, warned the Mexican Congress that an American conspiracy was afoot in Texas. He believed that American imperialism often developed in stages. First came the settlers promising loyalty to a neighboring government. Next, when enough settlers were in place, there was a revolution. Then Washington would swoop down and annex the territory. It had happened in West Florida, and Alamán believed it would happen in Texas unless Mexico acted to prevent it.

Mexico's answer to the American threat was the Colonization Law of 1830, which prohibited further American immigration and was intended to create closer ties between Texas and Mexico City by developing a more sophisticated commercial relationship. The law also authorized the stationing of military forces in Texas to secure the region against illegal immigrants and potential rebels.

It was one thing to enact such legislation and another to enforce it. In fact, the Colonization Law worked to Mexico's disadvantage in two ways. First, it tended to keep out solid propertied Americans who, if caught violating the law by squatting on land in Texas, had something to lose. On the other hand, since the Mexican authorities couldn't effectively seal the long border, poor squatters and lawless adventurers—those who would be most ready to seize the main chance in a rebellion—continued to enter Texas in large numbers. The stationing of Mexican troops in Texas also turned out to be a mistake, for they came in numbers insufficient to control the area. At the same time their presence was provocative, leading to clashes between the soldiers and the settlers.

The growing tension between the Texans and Mexico City came to a climax in October 1835, when the pompous, vainglorious Mexican dictator, Antonio López de Santa Anna, issued a decree claiming all power for the central government. State legislatures were dissolved, and local officials were made agents of the government in Mexico City. For the Texans this decree was very nearly the last straw. They had struggled for years to separate Texas from the state of Coahuila in order to develop greater local autonomy. Now the government was denying any form of local self-rule whatsoever. Before the end of November a convention of Texans meeting at San Felipe established a provisional government. Though the delegates stopped short of declaring Texas independent, Santa Anna took this as the beginning of a revolt and marched north at the head of an army of four thousand.

After the advancing Mexicans massacred the garrisons at Golidad and the Alamo, another Texan convention declared independence, organized a government, and made Sam Houston commander in chief of the army. Houston's task was to fashion and discipline an army while at the same time fighting a war. To accomplish these goals he gave ground before Santa Anna's advancing force until on April 21, 1836, he turned to fight on the banks of the San Jacinto River. There his force of eight hundred surprised the virtually unguarded Mexican encampment and won a decisive victory, killing 630 Mexicans and taking prisoner 730 more, including Santa Anna himself.

Santa Anna was set free only after he signed two treaties ending hostilities; agreeing to the Mexican evacuation of Texas, and recognizing a Texas boundary on the Rio Grande River. These agreements were quickly repudiated by the Mexican government, which continued to insist that Texas remained part of Mexico. Nevertheless, the battle of San Jacinto did establish the de facto independence of the Lone Star Republic. Occasional raids into Texas by small bands of Mexican troops kept the Texans on edge thereafter. But Mexico was in a state of internal chaos and in such deplorable economic condition that it was never again able to mount even the threat of an invasion.

For nearly ten years after San Jacinto, Texas remained an independent republic—not because its leaders necessarily wanted it that way. On the contrary, as early as 1836 a Texan representative was in Washington proposing annexation to President Jackson, who seven years before had attempted to buy Texas. But Jackson was forced to defer to certain political realities. First, the Mexicans had made it clear that annexation would mean war. More important, the sectional controversy, which cut across party lines,

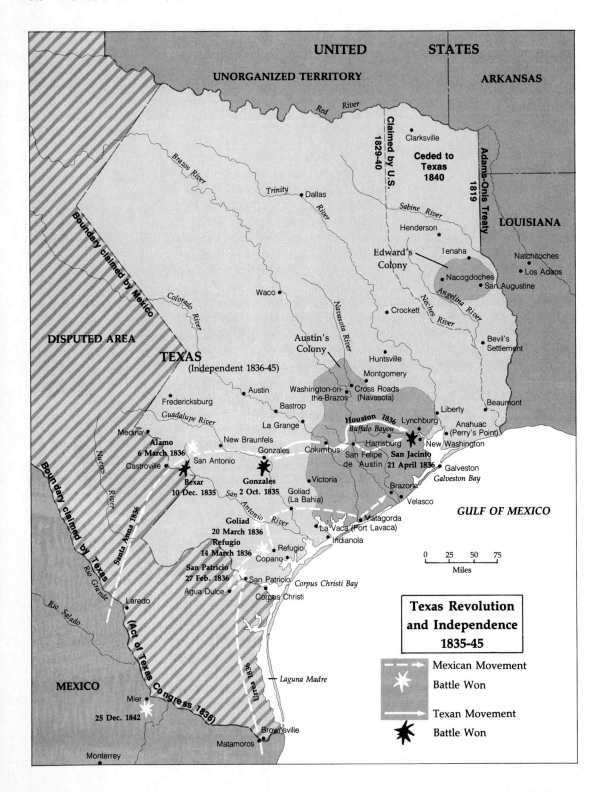

UNITED STATES

UNORGANIZED TERRITORY

ARKANSAS

Red River

Clarksville

Claimed by U.S. 1829-40

Ceded to Texas 1840

Adams-Onis Treaty 1819

Sabine River

LOUISIANA

Henderson

Brazos River

Trinity River

Dallas

Waco

Tenaha

Natchitoches

Edward's Colony

Nacogdoches

San Augustine

Los Adaos

Angelina River

Colorado River

Crockett

Neches River

Bevil's Settlement

DISPUTED AREA

Boundary claimed by Mexico

Huntsville

Austin's Colony

TEXAS
(Independent 1836-45)

Montgomery

Washington-on-the-Brazos

Cross Roads (Navasota)

Liberty

Beaumont

Austin

Fredericksburg

Guadalupe River

Bastrop

La Grange

Houston 1836

Buffalo Bayou

Lynchburg

Anahuac (Perry's Point)

Medina

New Braunfels

Columbus

Harrisburg

New Washington

Alamo 6 March 1836

Gonzales

San Felipe de Austin

San Jacinto 21 April 1836

Castroville

San Antonio

Nueces River

Bexar 10 Dec. 1835

Gonzales 2 Oct. 1835

Victoria

Galveston

Galveston Bay

San Antonio River

Goliad (La Bahia)

Brazoria

Velasco

Goliad 20 March 1836

Refugio 14 March 1836

Refugio

Copano

La Vaca (Port Lavaca)

Indianola

Matagorda

GULF OF MEXICO

Boundary claimed by Texas

Santa Anna 1836

San Patricio 27 Feb. 1836

San Patricio

Corpus Christi Bay

Agua Dulce

Corpus Christi

Laredo

Rio Grande

(Act of Texas Congress 1836)

Rio Salado

Urrea 1836

0   25   50   75
Miles

MEXICO

Mier

25 Dec. 1842

Laguna Madre

┌─────────────────────────┐
│ **Texas Revolution**   │
│ **and Independence**   │
│   **1835-45**   │
└─────────────────────────┘

- - ▶ Mexican Movement

✶ Battle Won

──▶ Texan Movement

✹ Battle Won

Brownsville

Matamoros

Monterrey

had become so intense that the president could not risk incorporating new slave territory into the Union. He was especially sensitive to that danger because 1836 was a presidential election year. Annexation would have fractured the Democratic party and thrown the election to the Whigs. The president was so attuned to this danger that he even refused to extend diplomatic recognition to Texas until December 1836, after the Democrat, Martin Van Buren, had been safely elected.

This situation remained unchanged until 1843, when President John Tyler turned his gaze toward the Southwest. A Virginia planter and slaveholder, Tyler had spent most of his adult life as a member of the Democratic party. But he broke with President Jackson during the struggle over the recharter of the Bank of the United States, resigned his Senate seat, and joined the Whigs. In 1840, hoping to make their presidential ticket more appealing in the South, the Whigs chose Tyler to be William Henry Harrison's running mate. Tyler inherited the presidency only a month after Harrison's inauguration, when the old man suddenly died. Tyler was a Whig in name only; his states rights philosophy and opposition to key elements of the Whig party's domestic program soon made him persona non grata to Whigs as well as Democrats.

By 1843, Tyler was a man without a party who was nevertheless anxious to remain in the White House. And he thought it could be done. Neither political party was particularly strong at this time. Though the Whigs were the weaker of the two, either might collapse under the weight of sectional animosities. Tyler hoped to create a new majority based on an alliance between the South and the West. The leaven that was to hold this new majority together was a national commitment to territorial expansion, a popular idea in those sections as well as with many in the Northeast.

Expansionism's appeal differed in each section of the country. In the South, the annexation of Texas meant the addition of new slave states to the Union and at least a temporary resolution to the South's most terrifying fear—that it would become a helpless minority section exploited by the more powerful northern states and vulnerable to abolitionist demands. Business-oriented expansionists as well as many in the Middle West, meanwhile, focused on the importance of acquiring more western lands and seaports along the Oregon and California coast. Their minds filled with visions of transcontinental railroads, they viewed Pacific ports as essential to the penetration of Asia's beckoning markets and the development of the vast interior of North America.

As expansionism gained in popularity, it developed an ideological component that tended to mask the real ambitions that actually motivated expansionists in these years. An increasing number of romantically inclined nationalists began to argue in the late 1830s and more vehemently in the following decade that it was America's Manifest Destiny to dominate the hemisphere. Among the most prolific of those purveying this view was John L. O'Sullivan, the editor of the *United States Magazine and Democratic Review*. In fact, it was O'Sullivan who first coined the phrase "Manifest Destiny" in an article written in 1844. But this New York newspaperman knew what destiny intended for the republic long before that. In an essay entitled "The Great Nation of Futurity," published in 1840, O'Sullivan described America's future in this way: "Its floor shall be a hemisphere—its roof the firmament of the star-studded heavens, and its congregation an Union of many Republics . . . governed by God's natural and moral law of equality."[6]

America's hemispheric preeminence was not to be achieved through conquest, at least in the conventional sense. It was an article of faith with O'Sullivan, as with others who idealized America's republican values, that wherever its citizens migrated they made deserts bloom and brought with them free institutions. Thus, in an editorial supporting the annexation of Texas, O'Sullivan denied that Americans would conquer the continent to despoil it. As an enlightened people they were "above and beyond the influence of such views. . . . We take from no man; the reverse rather—we give to man. This national policy, necessity or destiny, we know to be just and beneficent."[7] When Americans brought civilization, culture, and freedom, where once there existed only savagery and superstition, who could call that wrong?

FOREIGN DEVILS IN TEXAS

Though Tyler believed it possible to ride the expansionist issue back into the White House in 1844, he made no move to annex Texas until after having been warned that the British were plotting to establish a satellite antislavery republic there. His concern seems to have been triggered by a letter from Duff Green, a Maryland politician and speculator with a penchant for gossip and rumor mongering. Writing to Tyler from London, Green claimed that the British, leaders in the world antislavery movement, were involved in a plot to abolish slavery in Texas and then use it as a base of operations to achieve the same end in the United States. Green also alleged that "Lord Aberdeen has agreed that the British Government will guarantee the payment of the interest on the loan [Texas's national debt] upon condition that the Texan Government will abolish slavery." Though he knew better, Ashbel Smith, Texas's proslavery minister in London, sent a similar letter to South Carolina's John C. Calhoun in which he claimed to believe that London intended to transform Texas into "a negro nation, a sort of Hayti on the continent," and a British protectorate.[8]

Tyler and Secretary of State Abel P. Upshur, a Virginian who replaced Webster in 1843, either accepted these judgments or (and this is more likely) believed that focusing on the supposed danger of British interference in Texas could place the annexation question in a new, more acceptable light. They may have considered the threat of a foreign menace on America's southern border as a force potent enough to stifle the objections of those opposed to the expansion of slavery.

Was it true? Were the English plotting to abolish slavery in Texas and transform it into a protectorate? There is no doubt that British policy makers had reason to want an independent Texas. The republic's very existence was a check on southward American expansion. Its low tariff policy meant that as its population grew it would provide an expanding market for British manufactures. In time, Texas might also become an increasingly important source of cotton, making England less dependent on the United States. Finally, a weak but independent Texas would probably be anxious for an alliance. That would strengthen Britain's strategic position in the Gulf of Mexico and the Caribbean. Charles Elliot, the British chargé d'affaires in Texas, used all these arguments when trying to convince his superiors that an independent Texas was important to Britain.

Elliot's efforts notwithstanding, London showed little interest in transforming Texas into a British protectorate. Thus, although Palmerston once argued that the future of Anglo-Texan relations ought to "seriously engage the attention of the House and of the British Public," as prime minister he all but ignored the Lone Star Republic, even failing to extend recognition until 1840.[9] Palmerston's successor, Lord Aberdeen, went somewhat further. But he acted cautiously. His initiatives were limited and he never took risks. Texas was simply not that important to him.

But what of the allegation that the British were involved in an abolitionist plot in Texas? Edward Everett, the American minister in London in 1843, discussed this question at considerable length with Aberdeen and concluded that, far from representing the antislavery cause abroad, the "action of the present government has . . . been frankly of a restraining rather than a stimulating character." Britain's ministers were, he believed "disinclined to endanger the public peace, for the promotion of ends recommended by their opponents on liberal principles."[10] The British plot was Duff Green's fantasy. It was, however, a fantasy that had the power to move presidents.

NEGOTIATING ANNEXATION

Secretary of State Upshur, like Tyler, a Virginia slaveholder, was if anything more anxious than the president to bring Texas into the Union. Not even a warning from Mexico's foreign minister, José Maria Bocanegra, that his government would consider annexation "equivalent to a declaration of war" deterred him from informing Austin in 1843 that he was prepared to make an annexation proposal.[11]

But if Upshur thought that Sam Houston, now the president of Texas, would leap where opportunity knocked, he was in for a surprise. Houston's reply was three months in coming and was not at all what the administration had been hoping for. Houston agreed to negotiate. But he wanted military protection during the talks in the event that the Mexicans attacked Texas before annexation was completed. Aware of the power wielded in Congress by antislavery forces, he also wanted assurances that the Senate would approve a treaty of annexation. Perhaps sensing Washington's concern over the growing influence of Britain and France in Texas, Houston played on that fear, remarking that he was loath to sacrifice the excellent relationship Texas enjoyed with these countries by negotiating a treaty of annexation only to have it killed in the Senate.

In a long reply written in February 1844, Upshur rhapsodized over the advantages Texas would enjoy as a member of the Union, warned Houston of the dangers posed by a connection with Britain, and added that "at no time since the question was first presented . . . have there been so many circumstances combining to secure the favorable action of the Senate."[12] Houston probably took Upshur's assurances about Senate support with a grain of salt. But from the tone of the secretary's letter he was reasonably sure of one thing—the administration wanted to make a deal. When Tyler sent a naval force to protect the Texas coastline and stationed a contingent of regulars on the Sabine, where they would be ready to intervene if the Mexicans moved, he was certain of it.

In the spring of 1844 Upshur and a delegation from Texas began secret negotiations in Washington. But before the secretary could complete his work he was killed while on a visit to the USS *Princeton*, when a large naval cannon, nicknamed "the Peacemaker," exploded. South Carolina's John C. Calhoun replaced Upshur at the State Department and completed the negotiations.

On April 24, 1844, Calhoun forwarded the treaty of annexation together with a body of supporting documents to the Senate. Among these papers was a copy of a letter from Calhoun to Richard Pakenham, Her Majesty's minister in Washington. In it the secretary accused London of heading up an international conspiracy aimed at abolishing slavery the world over and explained that under the circumstances the United States had no choice but to annex Texas to protect itself against this nefarious plot. With one foolish stroke of the pen, Calhoun thus confirmed what antislavery forces had contended all along—that the administration's real motive for annexing Texas was to be of service to the "slave power." Lewis Tappan, a Free Soil senator from Ohio, leaked the Calhoun letter to the press, setting off a furious public outcry in the North.

If the publication of the secretary's letter did not seal the treaty's fate, what followed certainly did. Even as the Senate debated annexation, Henry Clay and Martin Van Buren, the leading candidates of the Whig and Democratic parties as the 1844 elections approached, agreed that with the slavery controversy at white heat and war with Mexico a possibility, it would be best to keep the Texas question in the background during the election campaign. On April 27, 1844, both men published letters opposing the annexation of Texas, at least for the time being. It is not surprising, then, that on June 8, when the treaty came to a vote in the Senate, it was soundly defeated.

Henry Clay won his party's nomination for the presidency in 1844. But Martin Van Buren wasn't so fortunate. At the Democratic national convention his forces and the supporters of Michigan's Lewis Cass, a more or less mindless expansionist, became hopelessly deadlocked. George Bancroft, a Massachusetts Jacksonian and a pioneer American historian who was a delegate to the convention, broke the deadlock when he proposed nominating James K. Polk, the first dark horse candidate in the history of presidential elections. Polk, a former Speaker of the House of Representatives, an old-line Jacksonian, and a committed expansionist, was nominated and ran on a platform that sought to balance sectional antagonisms by calling not only for "the re-annexation of Texas" but also for the reoccupation of all of Oregon to the 54' 40" line (54 degrees, 40 minutes north latitude).

John Tyler entered the race as a third-party candidate. But his support was limited to a few diehard southerners, and he soon withdrew. He had been right about one thing, though. Expansionism was an issue that could be ridden into the White House. There was just one problem. He was not the man in the saddle. It was Polk, who won a razor-thin victory that November.

Following Polk's victory, Tyler, a lame-duck president until March, renewed his call for the annexation of Texas. Doubtful that two-thirds of the Senate would approve the once-rejected treaty of annexation, he asked that Texas be annexed by a joint resolution of Congress, which would require only a simple majority of both the lower and upper houses. Claiming that the recent presidential election was a popular mandate for expansion, and supported behind the scenes by Polk's vast patronage power, Tyler at last triumphed. Late in February, Congress passed a joint resolution annexing Texas. On March 1, 1845, as one of his last official acts, the outgoing president had the pleasure of signing the resolution that, when accepted by the Texans, would finally mean annexation.

POLK AND OREGON

James K. Polk had none of the charisma that made his friend and patron Andrew Jackson a popular leader. Although he came to the presidency at a time when intellectual life in America was bursting into full flower, he hardly noticed the explosion of art and literature that was taking place around him. His horizons did not go beyond politics. Devoted to Jacksonian principles and the Democratic party, he distrusted all Whigs and had little use for those former Democrats who had broken with Jackson to join the opposition during Old Hickory's tempestuous presidency.

For all his narrow-mindedness, Polk had strengths, too. Skillful at manipulating people, he enjoyed having and using power. He was a tireless worker who fought tenaciously to achieve his ends. Moreover, he had a clearly defined expansionist agenda. Texas had been first on his list. He also sought Oregon and California, areas important to him not simply because they would add to the landed domain of the United States but because the

James K. Polk, an old-line Jacksonian and a dedicated expansionist, acquired Oregon from Britain, fought a war with Mexico for the purpose of acquiring California, and in the process exacerbated the sectional controversy that was to rend the Union in 1861.

ports at San Diego, San Francisco, and Puget Sound seemed the keys to internal development and an expanded Asiatic trade.

Polk's views on how to achieve his aims were predictably uncomplex. He distrusted all Europeans, but the British most of all. When dealing with such an inveterate foe—and he would have to in order to acquire Oregon— he believed it essential to first assume a position of strength. "Great Britain was never known to do justice to any country with which she had a controversy, when that country was in an attitude of supplication or on her knees before her," he once wrote.[13] Firmness seemed the answer, too, when dealing with the Mexicans, who then held California. But there was a difference. Polk didn't like the English but he respected their power. He had nothing but contempt for Mexico and was convinced that through a mixture of bullying and threats he could force the Mexicans to surrender California without a fight.

In his inaugural address Polk let the British know that there was rough sledding ahead when he asserted that the American claim to all of the Oregon country from the Rockies to the Pacific and extending northward to the 54″ 40′ line was "clear and unquestionable."[14] His bombastic assertion that all of this vast area belonged to the United States had no basis in fact, for England, too, had legitimate claims to the territory. Moreover, on three earlier occasions American administrations had offered to compromise the Oregon question by extending the 49th parallel boundary already in place

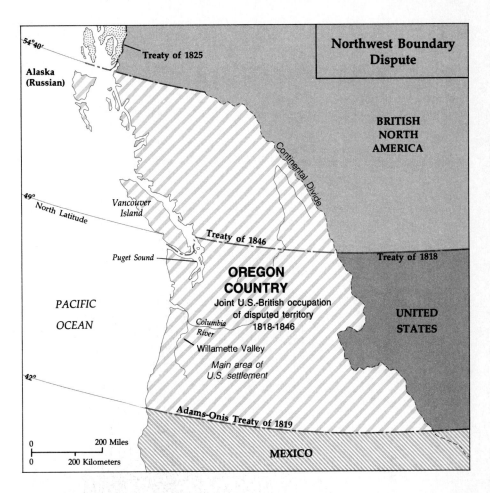

east of the mountains westward across the southern tip of Vancouver Island to the Pacific.

London had rejected these earlier compromise offers because the Hudson's Bay Company, which carried on a lucrative trade in the region, sought control of the mouth of the Columbia River and inland navigation in order to expand its interests there. In fact it was only a small rectangle of land bounded by the Columbia on the South, the Snake River to the East, the 49th parallel on the North, and the Pacific on the West that had been in dispute prior to Polk's presidency.

During the election campaign of 1844, London ignored Polk's extreme statements, passing them off as mere rhetoric. But his inaugural address was a different matter. Sir Robert Peel's ministry didn't want to fight but wouldn't be bullied either. Preparing for the possibility of war, the Admiralty sent an extra frigate to defend Britain's position on the Oregon coast, while the War Office began beefing up defenses in the region, especially at the mouth of the Columbia. At the same time, while speaking before the

House of Lords, Foreign Secretary Aberdeen reminded the president in somber tones, "We too . . . have rights which are 'clear and unquestionable,' and these rights we are ready to maintain." All of this was music to the ears of the editor of the *Times* of London, who warned that "Oregon will never be wrested from the British crown, to which it belongs, but by war."[15]

In fact, Polk had no intention of fighting for all of Oregon. He made the offending statement in his inaugural for two reasons. First, it satisfied the extreme expansionists who had helped elect him. Second, by taking this outrageous position early, he believed he was showing toughness and at the same time strengthening his bargaining position for the compromise settlement he actually sought. Polk would have happily accepted a boundary that ran along the 49th parallel to the Pacific with the right to use the Straits of Juan de Fuca. Such a settlement would have provided him with one of the ports on the Pacific that he craved. He had no great desire to acquire territory above this line or the southern tip of Vancouver Island, especially if it required a war to do it.

While Polk continued to insist publicly that America would settle for nothing less than all of Oregon, Secretary of State James Buchanan and Louis McLane, his envoy in London, worked with Lord Aberdeen to arrange a compromise. Negotiations had to be done carefully, since the administration had to take into account the negative domestic repercussions of such a settlement. British bellicosity over Polk's claim to all of Oregon had been the signal for an outpouring of extremist rhetoric from American expansionists, all of whom seemed willing to fight to the last drop of someone else's blood. Polk found this warlike enthusiasm useful in softening up the British. But the really rabid expansionists were in most instances Democrats, members of his own party. He would have to find a way to let them down easily when the time came.

Aberdeen had similar problems. The Whigs, led by Lord John Russell and the fiery Palmerston, could be depended upon to make the most of anything that smacked of a surrender. The foreign secretary also had his cabinet colleagues to contend with. To a man they insisted that England should continue in control of the mouth of the Columbia and Puget Sound.

During the spring and early summer of 1845, London and Washington negotiated in an informal and gingerly way, using unofficial intermediaries until satisfied that a compromise was within reach. At length, when he thought the basis for an acceptable settlement had been set in place, the president decided to make the first official move. On July 16, 1845, Secretary Buchanan proposed to Richard Pakenham, the British minister, that the Oregon dispute should be settled by extending the 49th parallel across the southern tip of Vancouver Island. Ports on that part of the island controlled by the United States would be open to both powers.

This proposal, which offered the British no concessions with regard to the fur trade or navigation on the Columbia River, was less generous than earlier American offers. Polk and Buchanan no doubt realized this. But they intended the proposal as an opening gambit in what both imagined would be a long and difficult negotiation. Concessions would come later. Imagine Polk's surprise then when, without consulting London, Pakenham rejected the proposal, ending the negotiation before it had begun. Evidently unaware of the private talks that had preceded Buchanan's July initiative, and unmindful of his government's desire to open talks, Pakenham had blundered badly.

Polk was furious. He had risked alienating the expansionists in his own party by offering to compromise. That seemed worthwhile only because he thought he had an arrangement with Aberdeen. Now he *knew* the British were not to be trusted. After Pakenham's peremptory and scarcely civil rebuff, he promptly withdrew the compromise proposal, reverting to his original extreme position. He would settle for nothing less than all of Oregon.

When Aberdeen learned how Pakenham had mishandled the American proposal, he was dumfounded, telling Louis McLane that if only Polk's offer had been forwarded he felt certain that a settlement could have been arranged. The foreign secretary reprimanded Pakenham and sent him hat in hand back to the State Department to see if he could undo his error. Buchanan and McLane both urged the president to give ground. But Polk seemed adamant, giving no hint that he would even consider compromising.

In fact, Pakenham's visit to the State Department told Polk something he very much needed to know. The British genuinely wanted a peaceful settlement. Armed with this valuable piece of information, he decided that his best strategy was to put increasing pressure on the British by demanding all of Oregon while appearing disinterested in compromise. Polk was bluffing. He knew that the only way he could have all of Oregon was to fight for it. And he never intended to let things get that far out of hand.

For the next several months Polk was content to hold his ground. Then, in his December 1845 annual message he intensified the pressure by asking Congress to pass a resolution giving the required twelve-month notice that the United States was withdrawing from the 1827 agreement which renewed the 1818 accord for the joint occupancy of Oregon. At the end of that period the United States would presumably organize a territorial government there, an act the British were bound to resist.

LONDON FINDS A WAY

Polk's policy of bluff seemed to be moving England and America closer to the flash point of war. But the president was convinced that by adding to the pressure he was in fact driving toward a compromise.

Lord Aberdeen, who was surprisingly undisturbed by the president's bellicosity, agreed. Aware that the United States would never accept a settlement that denied it a port on Puget Sound, he had failed to convince Prime Minister Peel and others in the government to abandon their insistence on continued control of the mouth of the Columbia River. He failed because the cabinet was too concerned about how the British public and the Whig opposition would react to such a concession, especially in the face of so much arrogant Yankee posturing. Under the circumstances, Aberdeen may have believed that the more it appeared that England and America were drifting toward war, the more reasonable Peel and the others would become.

Toward the end of 1845, before Aberdeen had a chance to test his theory, the political situation in England changed dramatically. Agitation against the hated corn laws (tariffs that kept cheap foreign produce out of England and the price of food high) peaked after the failure of Ireland's potato crop. The Anti-Corn Law League, a pressure group committed to free trade, insisted that with people starving repeal was essential. Both political parties were driven into confusion by the crisis, and Peel resigned. His resignation opened the way for Lord John Russell, the Whig leader, to form a new government. But prominent Whigs refused to support Russell because, if he moved in at Downing Street, Palmerston, who opposed any concessions to the United States on the Oregon question, would take over the Foreign Office. The Whigs feared that Palmerston would take the nation to war over Oregon at a time when England had more than it could handle at home.

Deeply embarrassed, Russell allowed Peel to organize a new government. In the interest of political stability, the two leaders agreed on certain fundamentals. First the Tories would support the repeal of the corn laws, which was more a Whig than a Tory measure. Second, to avoid a clash with the Americans, they agreed to offer a compromise on the Oregon question that would give the United States a boundary to the Pacific along the 49th parallel line, thus abandoning Britain's claim to control the mouth of the Columbia. In the bargain, Russell agreed to silence Palmerston. This he did by publicly expressing his support for a compromise at the 49th parallel. With the leader of his party supporting Tory policy, Palmerston had no choice but to go along. The way was now open for renewed talks.

With all sides in Britain now willing to cooperate, Aberdeen once again took the diplomatic initiative, renewing his offer to arbitrate the Oregon dispute. But Polk wasn't interested. The extreme position he had taken regarding Oregon made him very popular with the jingoes in his own party. He could not then suddenly agree to an arbitration that was certain to result in the division of Oregon without seeming to have cynically abandoned his own followers. Moreover, it wasn't clear that arbitration would produce the one thing the president absolutely required—a port on the Pacific.

Polk needed a concession from London, and a good one. Minister McLane was instructed to inform Aberdeen that time was running out and that if the ministry truly wanted peace a new proposal would have to be forthcoming. Nor would Polk enter into any more negotiations. McLane told the foreign secretary that the president was personally committed to acquiring all of Oregon and would not back away from that position. However, Aberdeen was also told that he would not oppose a compromise if "the senate should otherwise determine."[16]

This was Polk's way out of an embarrassing situation. The Constitution requires the president to submit treaties to the Senate for its "advice and consent." Polk was now preparing to use the advice and consent provision of the Constitution "creatively." If Britain proposed an agreement that was in the president's judgment worthy of consideration, he would submit it to the upper house (where he and Aberdeen both knew peace sentiment was strong). If the Senate approved the British compromise plan, Polk would go along. An arcane interpretation of the Constitution, not to say a devious ploy, it was the best Polk could do if he was to accept a compromise and at the same time retain the loyalty of at least some of his expansionist followers.

The British proposal for a settlement to the Oregon question included a boundary at the 49th parallel that stretched across the Rockies to Puget Sound and then ran southwest through the Straits of Juan de Fuca, leaving all of Vancouver Island in British hands. It also called for the free navigation of the Columbia River by representatives of the Hudson's Bay Company.

Under other circumstances, Polk might have rejected the British proposal, for he was strongly opposed to the second of these terms. But conditions were not normal. The Mexican War had begun the month before. Because of this Polk was persuaded to submit the proposal to the Senate, where it was approved by an overwhelming vote of 37–12.

The diplomatic history of the Oregon settlement is a study in bungled diplomacy. Polk and Aberdeen both wanted a compromise from the very beginning. But jingoes on both sides of the Atlantic made a settlement difficult to come by. Minister Pakenham's miscue made things even more difficult. Nevertheless, in the end Polk got what he wanted most—a boundary settlement that gave the United States a port on Puget Sound.

First Texas and then Oregon—the president was certainly getting on. Now it was time for California.

ENDNOTES

1. Lord Palmerston, quoted in Kenneth Bourne, *Britain and the Balance of Power in North America* (University of California Press, Berkeley, Cal., 1964), p. 86.

2. William H. Seward, quoted in Norma L. Peterson, *The Presidencies of William Henry Harrison and John Tyler* (University of Kansas Press, Lawrence, Kans., 1989), p. 116. The best treatment of the Mcleod affair is Howard Jones, *To the Webster-Ashburten Treaty, A Study in Anglo-American Relations, 1783–1843* (University of North Carolina Press, Chapel Hill, N.C., 1977) pp. 48–69.

3. Lord Aberdeen, quoted in Wilbur Devereux Jones, *Lord Aberdeen and the Americas* (University of Georgia Press, Athens, Ga., 1958), p. 11.

4. John C. Calhoun, quoted in Peterson, *The Presidencies of Harrison and Tyler*, p. 123.

5. Calhoun, quoted in *ibid.*, p. 130.

6. John L. O'Sullivan, "The Great Nation of Futurity," quoted in Albert K. Weinberg, *Manifest Destiny, A Study of Nationalist Expansion in American History* (Quadrangle Books, Chicago, 1963), p. 107.

7. *New York Morning News*, Oct. 13, 1845, quoted in Frederick Merk, *Manifest Destiny and Mission in American History* (Alfred A. Knopf, N.Y., 1963) p. 25n.

8. Duff Green to John Tyler, July 3, 1843, in Frederick Merk, *Slavery and the Annexation of Texas* (Alfred A. Knopf, N.Y., 1972), p. 22; Ashbel Smith, quoted in David M. Pletcher, *The Diplomacy of Annexation, Texas, Oregon, and the Mexican War* (University of Missouri Press, Columbia, Mo., 1973), pp. 122–23.

9. Palmerston, quoted in Kenneth Bourne, *Britain and the Balance of Power in North America*, p. 77.

10. Edward Everett, quoted in Pletcher, *The Diplomacy of Annexation*, pp. 122–23.

11. José Maria Bocanegra, quoted in *ibid.*, p. 126.

12. Abel Upshur, quoted in M.K. Wisehart, *Sam Houston, American Giant* (Robert B. Luce and Co., Washington, D.C., 1962), p. 457.

13. James K. Polk, quoted in Charles G. Sellers, *James K. Polk, Continentalist* (Princeton University Press, Princeton, N.J., 1966), p. 358.

14. *Messages and Papers of the Presidents*, ed. James D. Richardson (Washington, 1900), IV, p. 381.

15. Aberdeen, quoted in Pletcher, *The Diplomacy of Annexation*, pp. 238–39; *London Times*, quoted in Sellers, *James K. Polk*, p. 235.

16. Louis McLane, quoted in Sellers, *James K. Polk*, p. 412.

VOLUNTEERS !

Men of the Granite State!

Men of Old Rockingham!! the

strawberry-bed of patriotism, renowned for bravery and devotion to Country, rally at this call. Santa Anna, reeking with the generous confidence and magnanimity of your countrymen, is in arms, eager to plunge his traitor-dagger in their bosoms. To arms, then, and rush to the standard of the fearless and gallant CUSHING---put to the blush the dastardly meanness and rank toryism of Massachusetts. Let the half civilized Mexicans hear the crack of the unerring New Hampshire rifleman, and illustrate on the plains of San Luis Potosi, the fierce, determined, and undaunted bravery that has always characterized her sons.

Col. THEODORE F. ROWE, at No. 31 Daniel-street, is authorized and will enlist men this week for the Massachusetts Regiment of Volunteers. The compensation is $10 per month---$30 in advance. Congress will grant a handsome bounty in money and ONE HUNDRED AND SIXTY ACRES OF LAND.

Portsmouth, Feb. 2. 1847.

A recruiting poster urging New Hampshire's sons to join in the war against "the half civilized Mexicans."

9

WAR WITH MEXICO, 1846–1848

American political leaders developed an interest in California long before James K. Polk entered the White House. Part of John Quincy Adams's concern over the extension of Russian claims on the Northwest Coast in 1821 had to do with the future of the area. In 1835, President Andrew Jackson attempted to buy California, authorizing his minister in Mexico City, Colonel William Butler, to offer $5.5 million for a Texas "stretched" from the Rio Grande to the Pacific. Jackson wasn't particularly fussy about the southern boundary of this purchase. He was willing to leave that to the Mexicans so long as one valuable piece of real estate fell on the American side of the line. "The main object," he wrote, "is to secure within our limits the whole Bay of San Francisco."[1] During the Tyler administration, Daniel Webster, who thought San Francisco Bay worth far more than Texas, told Lord Ashburton that he would accept an Oregon boundary at the mouth of the Columbia River if London could convince Mexico to sell California to the United States.

During the 1840s, enthusiasm for the acquisition of the golden land quickened for two reasons. First, after its 1842 defeat in the Opium War, China opened five treaty ports to foreign merchants, making an expanded Asian trade seem increasingly attractive. Second, Americans were becoming aware of the possibilities stemming from the construction of a transcontinental railroad linking the East with ports on the Pacific. Asa Whitney was among the best known of those advocating this vast undertaking. A New Englander by birth but a New Yorker by choice, Whitney traveled to China as a commercial agent in the late 1830s. He returned a few years later a rich man with a mission—to convince his countrymen that a transcontinental railroad would allow the United States to develop Asian markets while at the same time stimulating the rapid economic development of the vast and largely unpopulated interior of North America.

Whitney saw the transcontinental link as transforming the United States into what publicists at the time saw as "the great middle kingdom" able to dominate the trade of Europe and Asia alike. The wealth of the Orient, Whitney argued, had been the foundation of every great western empire and, so it would be with the United States. "Here we stand forever," he told an audience of Pennsylvania legislators in 1848. "We reach out one hand to all Asia and the other to all Europe, willing for all to enjoy the great blessings we possess, claiming free intercourse and exchange of commodities with all." America, Whitney continued, would not seek "to subjugate any" nation. But because of the economic power it would wield, "all" would be "tributary, and at our will subject to us."[2]

President Polk viewed California as the third jewel in the expansionist crown he was fashioning, the diadem of an expanding American empire. If all else failed, he was prepared to fight for the territory, as eventually he did. But early in his administration he didn't think it would come to that. Mexico, virtually bankrupt and in a state of near-anarchy, was in no position to defend itself. Moreover, it was clear that it was going to lose California one way or another and very soon. Mexican authority in the province had already broken down to such an extent that many Mexican settlers there, including General José Castro, the prefect for much of northern California, and Mariano Vallejo, the wealthiest man in the province, were already toying with the idea of annexation to the United States. There were strong differences of opinion among California's many foreign residents about which power to turn to. But the prevailing sentiment was in favor of joining the United States. The Mexicans, Polk no doubt thought, would be insane to fight over what they were destined to lose in any event, especially since he was willing to pay handsomely for it.

As Polk saw it, four issues divided Mexico and the United States. First, American citizens had unpaid claims against the Mexican government for losses sustained during the Mexican Revolution totaling more than $2 million. The second and third issues had to do with Texas. The Mexicans had not yet accepted the fact that Texas was now part of the United States. Nor did they agree that Texas's southern boundary lay along the Rio Grande, since as a province of Mexico that line lay to the east along the Nueces River. Finally, there was California. Polk was determined to have a Texas boundary at the Rio Grande and, though he kept this part of his thinking a profound secret, New Mexico and California as well. In return he was prepared to pay

Mexico a large sum of money and assume the claims American citizens had lodged against the Mexican government.

Polk adopted a characteristically aggressive posture in preparing for the coming diplomatic encounter with Mexico. Thus, even before a Texas convention approved entering the Union he had a military force under the command of General Zachary Taylor poised at Corpus Christi, near the disputed area between the Nueces and the Rio Grande. He also sent a flotilla of warships to patrol the Gulf of Mexico. Polk was certain that the best way to avoid conflict and achieve his aims was to brandish naked American power.

SLIDELL IN MEXICO

In the spring of 1845, Polk learned through private sources that President José Juaquin Herrera of Mexico might be interested in settling outstanding disagreements with the United States. Acting on these incomplete though promising rumors, Polk sent William S. Parrott to Mexico to learn more. Parrott confirmed early reports, informing the president that the Herrera government seemed inclined to receive a commissioner from Washington empowered to negotiate.

Parrott and later the Mexican foreign minister, Manuel de la Peña y Peña, made it a point to distinguish between a commissioner and a minister plenipotentiary, which the government would not receive. Mexico City believed that to receive an official minister would in effect be to accept de facto the loss of Texas to the United States. Since this was a point that they wished to negotiate, they were not prepared to undercut their position by accepting the loss of Texas as a fait accompli. Moreover, anti-American passions were running high in Mexico, and the government was unstable. Herrera believed that if he received an American minister, those who opposed negotiations of any sort would stage a coup. Obviously he had to be cautious.

In spite of these warnings, Polk appointed the Louisiana Democrat, John Slidell, minister plenipotentiary to Mexico. Moreover, though Peña y Peña had warned him that Parrott was persona non grata in Mexico City, the president made him Slidell's secretary of legation. Polk's behavior in these matters will seem curious only to those who don't understand the man. He despised the Mexicans and intended to deliberately insult and humiliate them. With the country in a state of virtual anarchy and incapable of resisting American power, Polk decided to show no quarter. Ignoring the possibility that the Mexicans might prefer war to humiliation, he used a bludgeon to achieve his aims, confident that Mexico had no option but to give in.

John Slidell arrived in the Mexican capital on December 6, 1845. But news of his mission preceded him. The superpatriotic Mexican press, suspecting that the government was about to sell out to the Americans, denounced the "vile and hypocritical philosophers" in the presidential palace and charged that Slidell came bearing a substantial bribe for the president.[3]

Meanwhile at San Luis Potosí, General Mariano Paredes y Arillaga watched and waited, calculating the best moment for a coup.

President Herrera, a well-intentioned but ineffectual leader, wanted to settle the dispute with the United States. But he couldn't receive Slidell without risking a revolution. On the other hand, he couldn't reject him without infuriating Polk. He therefore put Slidell off, refusing to receive him for technical reasons but leaving open the possibility that in a few weeks or months the obstacles to accrediting him might be overcome. The main obstacle, of course, was General Paredes, who looked on menacingly from San Luis Potosí.

In January, after learning that Slidell had not been received, the president ordered General Taylor to advance from his post at Corpus Christi into the disputed territory between the Nueces and the Rio Grande. At the same time he strengthened American naval forces in the Gulf of Mexico. Lieutenant Colonel Ethan Allen Hitchcock, an officer in Taylor's command, believed that Polk was attempting to provoke a Mexican attack. "Our force is altogether too small for the accomplishment of its errand," he wrote. "It looks as if the government sent a small force on purpose to bring on a war, so as to have a pretext for taking California and as much of this country as possible."[4]

Until recently, most historians agreed with Hitchcock's on-the-spot analysis. New research, however, suggests that in January 1846, when Polk ordered Taylor forward, he still entertained the hope that he could get what he wanted short of war. These latest military gestures were designed to make it clear to the Mexicans that he was serious and that their situation was hopeless.

Three weeks after Slidell arrived in Mexico, General Paredes did overthrow Herrera. Polk then instructed Slidell to make another attempt at opening negotiations. He was to warn Mexico City that a refusal to negotiate would mean war. If these efforts came to nothing Slidell was to find some way to "throw the whole odium of the failure of the negotiation upon the Mexican Government," demand his passports, and leave.[5]

Slidell followed his instructions to the letter, playing his last cards during March 1846. Paredes must have known that he couldn't win a war with the United States. His government, like Herrera's, was unstable, threatened by domestic enemies, and insolvent. But after having come to power alleging that Herrera was about to make a humiliating surrender to the United States, he was in no position to negotiate. He therefore sought refuge in strong rhetoric, charging in a note to Slidell that if war came responsibility would rest on the shoulders of James K. Polk. At that the American envoy promptly collected his passports and headed for the United States. "Depend upon it," the frustrated Slidell wrote in his last dispatch before leaving Mexico, "We can never get along well with them until we have given them a good drubbing."[6]

THE CALIFORNIA CONSPIRACY

During the autumn of 1845, at the same time that he was planning the Slidell mission, Polk received news of a most disturbing nature. Thomas O. Larkin, the American consul living in Monterey, California, reported that the British government was financing an army to be raised in Mexico and officered by Europeans for the purpose of reimposing Mexican authority in California. Larkin's warning was completely inaccurate. But it threw a scare into Polk and Secretary of State James Buchanan, who now feared that Britain might beat them to the control of California. A week later Buchanan had completed new instructions for Larkin. He was to do everything in his power to thwart attempts by any European power to take California. He was also to warn the residents there about the disadvantages of being ruled by a monarchy while hinting at the bright future California might enjoy as part of the American Union.

Buchanan was explicit on one important point. The United States would not involve itself in support of a revolution undertaken by the settlers. However, if after the revolution had been completed "the people should desire to unite their destiny with ours they would be received as brethren."[7] A Texas-type revolution to be followed by annexation was here clearly outlined. But it had to be done with great caution. The United States must not appear to be involved.

Consul Larkin had no code cypher at his post in Monterey. Therefore, the only safe way to convey these new instructions was by special courier. Chosen for the job was a Spanish-speaking marine, Lieutenant Archibald H. Gillespie, who was to travel across Mexico disguised as a merchant. Gillespie also carried instructions for Commodore John D. Sloat, who commanded America's Pacific Squadron. Polk did not expect war with either England or Mexico at this time. But to be on the safe side, he instructed Sloat to seize the harbors of Monterey and San Francisco if war did break out. Later, San Diego was added to the list.

Before Gillespie could leave on this secret mission, Polk revealed his plans to Missouri's Senator Thomas Hart Benton, who reminded the president that his son-in-law, the ambitious adventurer, Captain John Charles Frémont, was even then on his way to California at the head of a sixty-man scientific expedition. Benton thought and Polk agreed that it would be wise to have Gillespie make contact with Frémont and inform him of Larkin's instructions.

Gillespie, who encountered serious delays along his route, arrived in Monterey on April 17, 1846, and gave a delighted Thomas Larkin his new instructions. He then rode north in search of Captain Frémont. He found this restless wanderer and his party camped near Klamath Lake in Oregon and revealed Larkin's instructions to him. Frémont, who had earlier been ordered out of California by Mexican authorities, immediately broke camp and headed south down the Sacramento Valley.

Captain John Charles Frémont led a ragged group of "Bear Flaggers" in a rebellion against Mexican authority in California in 1846.

Though the president hoped for a California revolution, he wanted the United States government to stay well in the background. He did not want to present his enemies either at home or abroad with the opportunity to claim that he had provoked it. But Frémont now dashed the president's hopes. He rode south into a land filled with dark rumors that the Mexican authorities in California were inciting the Indians to burn the homes and fields of the settlers and to massacre those who refused to leave. Extremists among the settlers, encouraged by Frémont, started a rebellion. They seized the town of Sonoma a few miles above San Francisco, raised a crude flag with the image of a bear emblazoned upon it, and proclaimed California independent. Frémont, perhaps recalling Sam Houston's role in Texas, took command of an "army" of 134 rebels and headed south in search of a Mexican force that was rumored to be heading toward Sonoma. Encountering no resistance, this ragtag army of Bear Flaggers reached Monterey on July 19, 1846. There Frémont found the American flag flying from the customs house and seven ships of Sloat's command in the harbor. War had broken out between the United States and Mexico in May. The would-be conqueror of California now joined forces with Sloat and Colonel Stephen W. Kearny's force to complete the job.

WAR WITH MEXICO

News that John Slidell's mission to Mexico had ended in failure arrived in Washington on April 6, 1846. Though he now saw no other method of acquiring California but war, Polk hesitated. The Oregon question remained unsettled, and he wanted to nail down an agreement with the English before taking any action. But there were limits to how long Polk could wait. The longer he delayed, the more his domestic critics, still unaware that his real objective was California, argued for a compromise settlement to the Texas boundary dispute, which they believed was the major issue dividing Mexico City and Washington.

Polk hoped that the Mexicans would help him out of this embarrassing situation by attacking Taylor's forces in the disputed area between the Nueces and the Rio Grande. But the Mexicans, who didn't want to negotiate, didn't seem to want to fight either. Taylor had marched unopposed to the Rio Grande and established artillery positions that commanded the center of the city of Matamoros on the Mexican side of the river. And the Mexicans had done nothing about it.

On Saturday, May 9, with the Oregon question still up in the air and no really convincing justification for war at hand, Polk nevertheless decided he was through waiting. He prepared to send a war message to Congress on the following Tuesday, justifying war on the altogether flimsy ground that the Mexicans had refused to settle either the Texas boundary or the claims questions. That evening, as he pondered how Congress would react, the news that he longed for arrived. A large Mexican force had ambushed a smaller body of Taylor's infantry north of the Rio Grande, killing eleven, wounding five, and capturing the rest.

Even though his argument was strengthened by recent events along the Rio Grande and wildly erroneous press reports that General Taylor's army was in danger of being wiped out, Polk believed that any direct call for a declaration of war was bound to stir up a hornet's nest of opposition from Whigs, Free Soil Democrats, and some southern Democrats as well. He therefore worked craftily, developing a proposal that congressional opponents of war would find difficult to reject. On the appointed day Polk's congressional supporters introduced a bill to raise $10 million and fifty thousand volunteers for the purpose of supplying and reinforcing General Taylor's outnumbered and supposedly endangered army on the Mexican border. The preamble to the bill explained that this was necessary because "notwithstanding our efforts to avoid it," war "exists by the act of Mexico herself."[8]

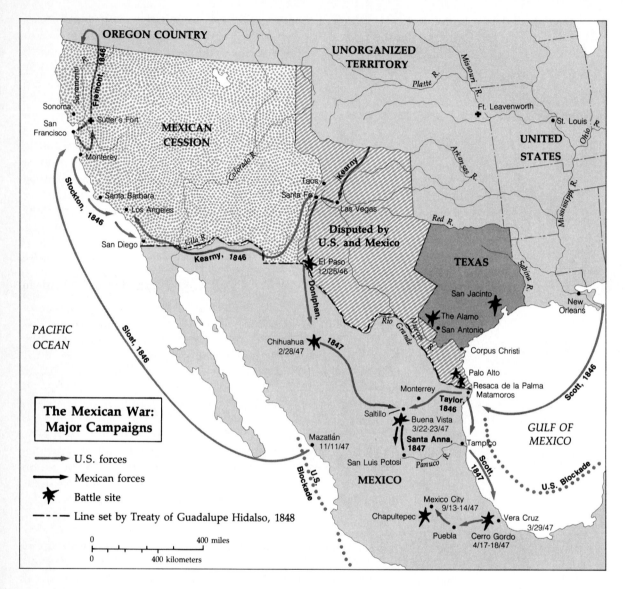

The Mexican War:
Major Campaigns

→ U.S. forces

→ Mexican forces

★ Battle site

----- Line set by Treaty of Guadalupe Hidalso, 1848

0 —— 400 miles

0 —— 400 kilometers

Even those in Congress who were opposed to war found it next to impossible to vote against reinforcements and supplies for an army that was reportedly in danger, threatened by a larger and more powerful enemy. Yet to vote for the bill was to endorse the premise that war already existed. Polk's clever maneuver produced fierce skirmishing in Congress. But in the end he won out, as both houses voted overwhelmingly for the bill.

It is doubtful that President Polk had ever heard of, let alone read, the writings of Karl von Clausewitz. Yet he was a firm believer in the Prussian strategist's dictum that war is the extension of diplomacy by other means. The threatened use of force having failed to produce a Mexican surrender,

Polk now took the next step, a measured use of force. But he had no intention of fighting an all-out war. Nor did he intend that it should last very long. For one thing, he was sensitive to the fact that wars create military heroes and that military heroes make nearly unbeatable presidential candidates. Since both General Taylor and his superior, Winfield Scott, were Whigs, a long war that gave these gentlemen maximum public visibility might prove disastrous for the Democrats in 1848. Polk would fight this war with one eye on the Mexicans and the other fixed firmly on his own general officers.

Polk told his friend, Senator Thomas Hart Benton, that the war would be over inside of four months. By that time the Mexicans, having been sufficiently chastised, would certainly sue for peace. Benton was not so certain. He sensed in Polk a man who did not fully comprehend the power of the forces he had set in motion:

> It is impossible to conceive of an administration less warlike, or more intriguing, than that of Mr. Polk. They were men of peace, with objects to be accomplished by means of war; so that war was a necessity and an indispensability to their purpose; but they wanted no more of it than would answer their purposes. They wanted a small war, just large enough to require a treaty of peace, and not large enough to make military reputations, dangerous for the presidency. Never were men at the head of a government less imbued with military spirit, or more addicted to intrigue.[9]

Polk's policy was, as Benton suspected, terribly flawed, for it assumed that the Mexicans could be made to see how hopeless their situation was by the direct application of force. In fact it had the opposite effect. The Mexicans, angry at being victimized by the United States, refused to behave "reasonably." The more force Polk applied, the more determined the men and governments who ruled Mexico during this chaotic period became not to surrender. Polk was, in fact, about to learn a sad lesson. It is often easier to start a war than to end one.

Polk was ready to make peace two months after the fighting had begun. General Taylor had won important victories at Palo Alto and in the battle of Resaca de la Palma. California's ports were in Sloat's hands, and Colonel Stephen Kearny was at the head of a large force that was heading cross-country from Missouri to complete the conquest. Surely now, the president thought, the Mexicans would agree to settle.

Polk used every artifice at his command to make Mexico City see reason. He ordered General Taylor to seek out local political and military leaders in Mexico's northern provinces and urge them to declare their independence and join the United States as allies. He sent secret agents into Mexico to make contact with high officials there in hopes of laying the groundwork for a settlement. For the same reason, he became involved in a conspiracy to bring the exiled Mexican leader, Santa Anna, back to power.

The Santa Anna conspiracy began with a secret mission to Havana undertaken by John Slidell's nephew, Navy Commander Alexander Slidell

Mackenzie. On July 6, 1846, Mackenzie and Santa Anna held a three-hour conference, during which the young naval officer informed the opportunistic Mexican leader that the president endorsed his return to power and that he had ordered Commodore David Conner, whose Gulf squadron was blockading the Mexican Coast, to let him pass. Mackenzie returned to Washington with the news that he and Santa Anna had struck a bargain. Once back in power Santa Anna promised to end the war and grant the United States the territories it demanded in return for a substantial sum of money.

Unhappily for Polk, his plans for making peace through political conspiracy came to nothing. Taylor, a bluff soldier with little taste or talent for political intrigue, made no headway with the secessionist scheme. The secret missions inside Mexico ended in failure, too. And Santa Anna, who did return to power later in 1846, took command of the Mexican army and led the resistance to the American invaders. The war had become a quagmire for Polk. What began as a brief display of American might was transformed into an ongoing and increasingly costly struggle.

GROWING DOMESTIC TROUBLES

As the war continued, opposition groups in the United States grew more vocal. The Whigs always insisted that they had voted to supply the troops but did not endorse what one of them described as "this unjust and unconstitutional war."[10] They fumed, sniped, and nit-picked, occasionally winning a victory, as when they blocked the appointment of Thomas Hart Benton to be a lieutenant general in the army. Their most significant political victory, no doubt discouraging to Polk, came in the November congressional elections, when they won control of the lower house.

Antislavery Whigs in Congress, of whom the aged John Quincy Adams was perhaps the most outspoken, were vehement in denouncing the war, which they charged was being fought to bring new slave territories into the Union. Adams insisted that since Congress had never officially declared war Polk was acting outside the Constitution. To fight an unconstitutional war was bad enough; but to fight one in the interests of the "slaveocracy" was almost more than the old man could bear. Adams charged that the war was the outcome of a conspiracy to expand slavery and that its true territorial objects had not yet been revealed to the country. He thought that Polk's purpose was to "dismember Mexico, and to annex to the United States not only Texas, but several of her adjoining Provinces on this side of the Continent," including "the Californias." Another outspoken antislavery Whig, Senator Thomas Corwin of Ohio, thundered this warning from the floor of the upper house: "If I were a Mexican I would tell you, 'have you not room in your own country to bury your dead men? If you come into mine we will greet you with bloody hands, and welcome you to hospitable graves.'"[11]

Outside the Congress other powerful voices spoke in opposition to the war. Henry David Thoreau's essay on "Civil Disobedience" (1849) was more than literature. A prescription for peaceful resistance to immoral government actions, it had a powerful impact not only on members of his own generation but also on Mahatma Gandhi, Martin Luther King, Jr., and the many peace activists who advocated nonviolent resistance during the Vietnam years. William Ellery Channing, Ralph Waldo Emerson, Reverend Theodore Parker all spoke eloquently against slavery and war. But it was James Russell Lowell, just twenty-seven and at the height of his powers when the war broke out, who best expressed the antislavery opposition to the war in his famous *Biglow Papers* (1848).

Confronted by an increasingly powerful opposition, Polk was unable to bring his own fractious Democratic party into line behind him. He had sacrificed the allegiance of many of his expansionist followers by compromising on the Oregon question. Others had become alienated by differences with the president over a variety of domestic issues. Still others, like the Whigs, felt that Polk had manipulated Congress once too often in pushing through what passed for a declaration of war. Finally, many Northern Democrats, like their Whig colleagues, recognized that opposition to the expansion of slavery was becoming increasingly popular, even among those in the North who were not abolitionists.

Democratic disenchantment with Polk's leadership came suddenly into focus on August 8, 1846, when the president submitted a request for $2 million, which he hoped to use to buy peace with Mexico. Polk justified this by suggesting that in "the adjustment of a boundary, we ought to pay a fair equivalent for any concessions which may be made by Mexico."[12] Here for the first time Polk publicly admitted that he sought more than a Rio Grande boundary with Mexico, that he might, as some of his critics contended, be seeking territory for the expansion of slavery.

After hurried consultations with some of his northern friends, David Wilmot, a Pennsylvania "free soil" Democrat, added a proviso to the appropriations bill Polk sought, stipulating that slavery should be prohibited from any territory added to the Union as a result of the war. The bill along with the Wilmot Proviso failed. But the issue had been raised and would remain at the center of national politics until finally decided by the Civil War. Polk, who obviously paid far less attention to the growing slavery controversy than it deserved, had sewn the whirlwind.

TRIST IN MEXICO

General Winfield Scott's army took Veracruz before the end of March 1847. No sooner had Polk learned of Scott's easy victory than he appointed the chief clerk in the Department of State, Nicholas Trist, to be his peace emissary and accompany Scott on the march toward Mexico City. Trist was instructed to seek a Rio Grande boundary, New Mexico to the 32d parallel and both upper and lower California, though he was authorized to give up lower California if necessary. In return the United States was prepared to

General John A. Quitman, pictured here leading American marines into Mexico City, was an ardent expansionist who wanted to keep all of Mexico after the war and acquire Cuba to boot.

assume all claims by American citizens against the Mexican government, and in addition to pay Mexico as much as $30 million, depending on how much territory actually changed hands.

Trist seemed an ideal choice. His political credentials as a reliable Democrat were impeccable. He had married one of Thomas Jefferson's granddaughters and had for a time served as Andrew Jackson's private secretary. Moreover, he was a polished and experienced diplomat with a good legal background.

Before Trist left for Mexico his superiors had convinced him that General Scott, a potential Whig candidate for the presidency, could not be trusted and was using his position to advance his own and the Whig party's interests. It is not surprising, then, that Trist and Scott fell to bickering almost immediately. Trist kept Scott completely in the dark about his mission and treated him in a peremptory and condescending way. Naturally Scott, with an ego to match his massive frame, quickly grew angry, on one occasion describing Trist as "a combination of Danton, Marat, and St. Just—all in one."[13] It wasn't long before all communication had ceased between these two men, whose cooperation was so important to peace.

This hopelessly unworkable situation continued for some time, until at length Trist fell ill. At this point, and for reasons that remain obscure, he decided to make the first move toward reconciliation, informing Scott as to the purpose and details of his mission. Scott responded in a friendly way, sending Trist a case of guava preserves as a sort of peace offering. Rather belatedly Trist concluded that his superiors in Washington were wrong about Scott. He was just a good soldier trying to do his duty. A cordial relationship soon developed between Trist and Scott, who worked closely together for the rest of the war.

Utilizing the good offices of Edward Thornton, the British chargé d'affaires in Mexico City, Trist opened talks with the Mexican government on June 6, 1847. But these early discussions proved futile. The Mexicans continued to insist on a Texas boundary on the Nueces River and were unwilling to cede as much of upper California as Polk thought indispensable. But as American forces won a succession of victories, finally taking Mexico City itself, the Mexicans grew more flexible. By mid-October, the latest in the series of Mexican governments, this one headed by Peña Y Peña, appeared ready to cede the territory that Polk most desired.

It was precisely at this moment in time that Polk, who was not well informed as to the changing political situation inside Mexico, decided to break off the talks. In making this decision the president was moved by a variety of considerations. First, Trist's early dispatches indicated that the Mexicans remained intractable. One method of convincing them that he meant to have his way was to abandon the negotiations while continuing to pursue a military solution. Second, as Scott's army advanced Polk began to reconsider his own earlier thinking. Influenced by Secretary of the Treasury Robert Walker, a southern expansionist, and Secretary of State Buchanan, he now wondered whether it might not be wise to take all of Northern Mexico down to the 26th parallel instead of stopping just below San Diego. Third, the cordiality that existed between Scott and Trist worried Polk, who, a frequent conspirator himself, forever worried about political conspiracies.

Trist received his letter of recall on November 19, 1847, at a moment when it seemed that a successful negotiation was in the offing. Nevertheless, he prepared to leave and would have done so but for the importunings of Scott, the British chargé, and other foreign as well Mexican observers, who thought he might be throwing away the only chance for peace. These people feared that if Trist left, the war would continue, and the extremists who wanted to carry on the war at all costs would take power. The United States would then be tied down in Mexico indefinitely, winning battles but unable to secure a settlement. Persuaded by these arguments and his own firsthand experience, Trist violated his instructions, entering into negotiations with the Mexican government.

After weeks of dickering, the two sides signed a peace treaty at Guadalupe Hidalgo, just north of Mexico City. The treaty established the Rio Grande as the boundary between Texas and Mexico and ceded New Mexico and upper California to a point just below San Diego to the United States. Mexico received $15 million in compensation for the cession and the United States assumed the outstanding American claims against Mexico.

Polk was furious when he learned that Trist had disobeyed his instructions. Nevertheless, he decided even before seeing the terms of the treaty that if it conformed with his minimum demands he would submit it to the Senate. The only other option was to resume the war. And that would no doubt have triggered violent domestic opposition. The opponents of the war had long since accused Polk of seeking to annex all of Mexico. If he now rejected a treaty that offered so much, it would appear to many that the charge was true. And if the strength of the opposition grew, Congress might refuse to continue financing the war, leaving the army with no choice but to go over to the defensive. The Mexicans would take heart, and what Trist had gained might finally be lost.

Polk also realized that there were grave political risks in continuing the war. The Whigs had already won the House of Representatives. Continuing the war might cost the Democrats the presidency in 1848. Therefore, though Polk thought Trist "an impudent and unqualified scoundrel,"[14] he felt he had no choice but to submit the treaty to the Senate where it was ratified by a vote of 38–14.

As for poor Nicholas Trist, he suffered the agonies of the damned for having disobeyed the president. He was arrested and forced to remain in Mexico for months following the end of the fighting to testify before a court of inquiry formed to investigate the conduct of the war. Later Polk dismissed from his post in the State Department and refused to pay his salary for the period he served in Mexico. It took Congress twenty-five years to correct this injustice, later granting Trist $14,599.20 in back salary. Shoddy treatment all around for the man who ended the Mexican War!

The war cost the United States thirteen thousand dead and just short of $100 million. In return the country gained more than a half-million square miles of territory and an expanded Pacific shoreline. At the same time the acquisition of this territory let loose a terrible genie that a generation of cautious American politicians had kept more or less bottled up since the days of the Missouri Compromise. The question of whether slavery should be allowed into these new territories fed the flames of sectional conflict that resulted in Civil War.

ENDNOTES

1. Andrew Jackson, quoted in Frederick Merk, *The Monroe Doctrine and American Expansionism, 1843–1849* (Alfred A. Knopf, N.Y., 1966), p. 106.

2. Asa Whitney, quoted in Henry Nash Smith, *Virgin Land, The American West as Symbol and Myth* (Harvard University Press, Cambridge, Mass., 1970), p. 33.

3. Quoted in David M. Pletcher, *The Diplomacy of Annexation: Texas, Oregon, and the Mexican War* (University of Missouri Press, Columbia, Mo., 1973), p. 354.

4. Ethan Allen Hitchcock, quoted in Bernard DeVoto, *Year of Decision, 1846* (Riverside Press, Cambridge, Mass., 1960), p. 110.

5. Polk, quoted in Pletcher, *The Diplomacy of Annexation*, p. 365.

6. John Slidell, quoted in Charles G. Sellers, *James K. Polk, Continentalist: 1843–1846* (Princeton University Press, Princeton, N.J., 1966), p. 404.

7. James Buchanan, quoted in *ibid.*, p. 334.

8. *Messages and Papers of the Presidents*, ed. James D. Richardson (Washington, 1900), IV, p. 442.
9. Thomas Hart Benton, *A Thirty Years View* (D. Appleton and Co., N.Y., 1854–1856), II, p. 680.
10. Quoted in Frederick Merk, *Manifest Destiny and Mission in American History* (Alfred A. Knopf, N.Y., 1963), p. 99.
11. John Quincy Adams, quoted in Samuel Flagg Bemis, *John Quincy Adams and the Union* (Alfred A. Knopf, N.Y., 1949), II, p. 499; Thomas Corwin, quoted in the *Congressional Globe*, 29th Congress, 2nd session, appendix, p. 217.
12. Polk, quoted in David M. Potter, *The Impending Crisis* (Harper and Row, N.Y., 1976), p. 19.
13. Winfield Scott, quoted in Pletcher, *The Diplomacy of Annexation*, p. 504.
14. Milo M. Quaife, *The Diary of James K. Polk* (A.C. McClurg and Co., Chicago, Ill. 1910), III, p. 358; see also Glyndon van Deusen, *The Jacksonian Era* (Harper and Row, N.Y., 1958), pp. 244–45.

10

NEW WORLDS TO CONQUER, 1848–1861

Senator Thomas Hart Benton of Missouri envisioned a network of railroads and roads that would consolidate the nation. A sophisticated transportation system and the Pacific trade, he felt certain, would stimulate economic growth, transforming the Middle West into the "garden of the world."

Oregon and California together formed the centerpiece of Polk's expansionist policies. He sought these regions, as the historian Norman Graebner has pointed out, not because he was driven by some ideological conviction relating to America's Manifest Destiny but for a specific purpose—the acquisition of deep sea ports on the Pacific.[1] Clearly Polk believed that America's future was somehow conjoined with the Pacific. But it was his friend and sometime political ally, Thomas Hart Benton of Missouri, who best articulated the idea that moved them both. Benton saw the development of a "passage to India" and the internal economic development of the United States as closely linked. For this reason he advocated a transportation network that would connect the East Coast with the Pacific and lay the foundation for the penetration of Asia. Benton predicted that not only American but European merchants, too, would ship their goods across the midsection of the United States to the Far East and that the "rich commerce of Asia will flow through our center." This trade would make agriculture burgeon until America became "the garden of the world." And where trade flowed, vast cities rivaling any that had yet appeared would grow up. "An American road to India through the heart of our country," he explained, "will revive upon its line all the wonders of which we have read—and eclipse them. The Western wilderness, from the Pacific to the Mississippi, will start into life under its touch."[2]

Toward this end President James K. Polk became involved in plans to control at least one of the three transit routes that might one day connect the Atlantic with the Pacific—Mexico's Isthmus of Tehuantepec, the San Juan River route across Nicaragua, or the Isthmus of Panama. This search put the United States in direct competition with Great Britain, the dominant power in Central America, and set off a new round of conflict in what by this time had become a seemingly endless cycle of confrontations.

It was the Tehuantepec route, farther to the north than either Nicaragua or Panama, that first attracted Polk's attention. He hoped to extract it from the Mexicans along with New Mexico and California as the price of peace. Polk was thwarted, however, when José de Garay, the Mexican national who held the transit rights, transferred his lease to a group of London capitalists, who were at that time planning a British-owned canal there.

While these British investors closed the door on one opportunity, the British government inadvertently opened another further to the south. In 1846, Sir Robert Peel's government gave way to a new Whig ministry headed by Lord John Russell. Lord Palmerston returned to the Foreign Office and quickly adopted a more energetic approach to Central American affairs. Palmerston had been forced to accept the Oregon settlement as part of the 1845 arrangement between Russell and Peel. But now, with California in American hands and American forces operating in Mexico, he worried about Britain's interests in Central America. London had footholds in Belize (British Honduras) and the Bay Islands and claimed a protectorate over the Mosquito Indians, who inhabited the Atlantic Coast of Nicaragua. To strengthen Britain's position in the region, Palmerston authorized a search for a naval base there and strengthened British ties to the Mosquito Indians.

These developments did not go unnoticed in Bogotá, capital of New Granada (Colombia), where Benjamin A. Bidlack, the American chargé d'affaires, was negotiating a new commercial treaty. Fearing that the British intended to extend their Mosquito protectorate down the entire Atlantic Coast of Central America including Panama, Bogotá offered Bidlack a proposition he found it impossible to refuse. The Bidlack Treaty of 1846 granted the United States the commercial concessions it sought as well as transit rights across the Isthmus of Panama. In return, Bidlack agreed that the United States would guarantee the security and neutrality of the isthmus as well as New Granada's sovereignty in the area.

Polk, who had the Bidlack Treaty on his desk from early 1847 onward, was at first reluctant to submit it to the Senate. He was at the time still attempting to conceal his expansionist purposes. And in any event, the treaty ran so directly contrary to the traditional American unwillingness to form alliances that it stood a good chance of being defeated.

While Polk weighed the possibilities, the British acted. In January 1848 a force of Mosquito Indians, led by a British officer, entered Greytown at the mouth of the San Juan River in Nicaragua. They expelled the Nicaraguan authorities there, claiming that Greytown was part of Britain's

Mosquito protectorate. Had England been able to sustain this claim, it would have won control of what then appeared to be the best of the three possible transit routes.

Polk reacted in two ways. First, he submitted the Bidlack Treaty to the Senate, where, probably because of Britain's recent aggressive Nicaraguan policy, it was promptly approved. Next, he responded to a frantic appeal for help from Nicaragua by sending a special agent, Elijah Hise, to study the situation there. Convinced that the entire region was in danger of falling to the British, Hise signed a treaty with Managua that gave the United States exclusive rights to build and fortify a canal using the San Juan River route. This agreement also committed the United States to the defense of Nicaragua in the event that it was attacked or its sovereignty encroached upon by some other power.

The Hise Treaty touched off a fierce competition between local British and American representatives in Central America for control of transit routes and strategic locations near those routes. Fortunately, by the time this crisis came to a head, Polk had left the White House to be replaced by the more peacefully inclined Whig, Zachary Taylor.

The Taylor administration was, like its predecessor, interested in transit routes and anxious to make certain that, if a canal was constructed, it did not fall under the sole control of the English. But neither Taylor nor Secretary of State John M. Clayton was willing to fight for exclusive control over a canal. Since Palmerston's major purpose was to check the advance of American expansionism in Central America and to prevent the construction of a canal controlled exclusively by the United States, it isn't surprising that the two governments were able to reach an understanding.

The Clayton-Bulwer Treaty, signed on April 19, 1850, stipulated that neither Britain nor the United States would seek sole control over any canal in the region. Nor would they colonize or attempt to control in any other way any part of Central America. Each side also agreed to encourage the construction of a canal and to guarantee its neutrality when it was finished.

Though the vague wording of the treaty gave rise to disputes as to its precise meaning almost from the beginning, it did more or less serve the purpose that was intended. The canal controversy was temporarily set to rest.

FIRST CONTACTS WITH ASIA

The American interest in developing a Far Eastern connection, reflected so clearly in Polk's expansionist policies, is virtually as old as the republic itself. On February 22, 1784, the 360-ton ship, the *Empress of China*, owned by a consortium headed by the New York financier Robert Morris, sailed for Guangzhou (Canton) carrying ginseng and other products of the North American continent. Two years later it dropped anchor at an East River pier carrying a cargo of silk, tea, nankeens (trousers of a rough cloth), and porcelain dinnerware. The 30 percent profit that Morris and his partners realized on the voyage was more than sufficient to encourage others to undertake similar enterprises. Soon a small but thriving Far Eastern trade grew up.

American merchants journeyed to China, where along with the merchants of other lands they settled in a kind of commercial ghetto called a "factory" or "hong" outside the city walls of Guangzhou, the only port in China open to foreign trade. Forbidden from visiting the city or traveling in the countryside, they became in effect prisoners, free to leave but restricted so long as they remained.

Business conditions were just as curious as daily life in the "factory" at Guangzhou (Canton). For one thing, Chinese tariff schedules were neither regularized nor published, making it possible for corrupt customs officials to charge what the traffic would bear. Rates might be high or not so high depending on who did the collecting. Moreover, all business had to be conducted through the Co-Hong Merchants, a state-authorized monopoly that set prices and controlled all aspects of the trade carried on between China and the foreigners. Still, even given the extraordinary disadvantages, trade proved profitable.

These unusual conditions persisted through the decade of the 1830s. But in 1838 trouble developed between the foreign merchants at Guangzhou and the Chinese authorities that was to change things forever. All foreign merchants, but especially the British, sold Turkish and Indian opium in China, where it found a ready market. The drug, which was widely used, had a dreadful effect on the Chinese population. Moreover, opium purchases were draining the country of specie, contributing to a grave economic crisis.

The Chinese authorities demanded that the foreigners stop importing opium into China. When the merchants refused, workmen walled up the "factory" in which the foreign colony lived. Troops surrounded them on the land side, while war junks took up menacing positions in Whampoa Harbor. At length the American merchants, whose interest in opium had been minimal to begin with, agreed to the Chinese demand. The British, however, refused and then left Guangzhou (Canton). Shortly after this British naval forces bombarded several Chinese coastal cities. It was the beginning of the Opium War, a conflict China had no chance of winning.

The trade in opium was only the given reason for the war. Out of patience with the unpredictable behavior of Chinese officialdom, irritated by tariffs that changed as if by magic depending on who was collecting them, and annoyed by the generally inhospitable circumstances surrounding trade with the Celestial Empire, Britain had decided that it was time to open China more completely. At the same time Britain was determined to have all of the rules governing trade clearly spelled out in a commercial treaty between London and Beijing (Peking).

The Americans who stayed in Guangzhou (Canton) during the war profited hugely, picking up much of the trade formerly handled by their

British competitors. At the same time they became increasingly concerned, especially because the British seemed certain to force important trade concessions from the Chinese. America's Guangzhou merchants therefore petitioned Congress to send an envoy to Beijing for the purpose of negotiating a commercial treaty. At the same time they urged Washington to station a permanent naval squadron in Far Eastern waters to protect American interests in the region.

Congress promptly buried the merchants' petition in committee, where it remained for the next two years. Then came news of the Anglo-Chinese Treaty of Nanjing (Nanking) (1842). The British had won a large indemnity, taken Hong Kong, opened four additional Chinese ports to trade, abolished the hated Co-Hong monopolies, required Beijing to publish a uniform tariff, and established the principle of extraterritoriality, which exempted British citizens from the jurisdiction of local Chinese laws. From this time forth Britons accused of crimes in China were tried in their own special courts.

On reading the terms of the Nanjing agreement, Secretary of State Daniel Webster grew mightily disturbed. Were these privileges extended only to the British, or would the United States also benefit from them? The China trade had never been a vital aspect of the overall American foreign trade. But the prospect for growth was very real, and he believed the United States ought to do something to secure its position in Asia. Webster drafted a message that President John Tyler signed and sent to Congress on December 30, 1842. Because "the commercial interests of the United States connected with China require at the present time a degree of vigilance such as there is no agent of this government on the spot to bestow," Tyler urged Congress to appoint a resident commissioner in China to handle all commercial and diplomatic affairs there.[3] The appointment went to Caleb Cushing, a forty-four-year-old Whig Congressman from Newburyport, Massachusetts.

In fact there was little for Cushing to accomplish on his mission. While the Treaty of Nanjing (Nanking) and the Treaty of the Bogue (1843) were purely bilateral agreements between London and Beijing, all of the privileges that the British obtained by these agreements were granted freely by the Chinese to all other foreign nations trading in China. Nevertheless, Cushing, who for the benefit of the Chinese had dressed himself in an elaborate major general's uniform, pushed aggressively for a separate Sino-American agreement and got one.

The Treaty of Wanghia signed by Cushing and Kiying, the imperial commissioner and governor general of Guangdong (Kwang-tung) and Guangxi (Kwangsi), granted the United States the same trade concessions Britain had won. The American claim to the right of extraterritoriality was more carefully defined than in the British treaties. And the Chinese granted the United States most-favored-nation status, meaning that if in the future the Chinese extended more concessions to any other power they would automatically accrue to the United States as well. Together the British and

American treaties signaled a new era in the history of the Celestial Empire. The way was now open for the foreign domination of China.

COMMODORE PERRY OPENS JAPAN

Early in the age of discovery, Japan had been open to Western penetration. But the cupidity of Western traders and the religious turmoil created by unwelcome Christian missionaries caused the shogun to issue a series of decrees which by 1639 closed the country to foreign influence. Only a Dutch-run "factory" on the island of De-Jima, in Nagasaki's harbor, was left open as Japan's window to the West. Under the circumstances it is not surprising that contact between the United States and Japan was sporadic and usually confined to the rescue and return of shipwrecked sailors.

It was only after the War of 1812 that Americans began to show an interest in developing a commercial relationship with Japan. And it wasn't until the 1840s that the movement became serious. Several developments account for this. First, the Opium War opened Shanghai to trade and in effect moved China a thousand miles closer to the West Coast of North America. Second, as steamers replaced sailing ships in the transoceanic trade, a need for coaling stations developed. Japan, on the road to the China market, was rumored to have large quantities of coal and was ideally located as a refueling stop. Finally, and by no means incidentally, there was the prospect of developing a commercial relationship with a nation that the *North American Review* described as a country with "an immense population" as well as "great wealth and industry."[4]

Not surprisingly, the first effort at opening Japan came in 1846 during the Polk administration. Alexander Everett of Massachusetts, who had been appointed to serve as the American commissioner in China, also had instructions to negotiate a commercial treaty with Japan. When Everett fell ill, he turned responsibility for the negotiations over to Commodore James Biddle, who sailed the ninety-gun USS *Columbus* into Tokyo Bay in July 1846. The visit was a disaster from first to last. Biddle had no interpreters with him, a fact that made communication next to impossible. As for the Japanese, they were no more interested in negotiating a trade treaty than they had been over the past two hundred years. The official reply to Biddle's request to open talks was an unsigned order to leave. After ten frustrating days during which Biddle was not even allowed to set foot on Japanese soil, he did so.

The end of the Mexican war and the acquisition of California quickened American interest in opening Japan. Polk's secretary of the treasury, the expansionist Robert Walker, observed that "Asia has suddenly become our neighbor and a placid, intervening ocean invites our steamships upon the track of a commerce greater than that of all Europe combined." Advocates of a transcontinental railroad fairly drooled at the prospects. "This sir is the road to India! This is the great western passage for which contending nations have struggled for centuries."[5]

Pressed hard by missionaries and merchants alike, President Millard Fillmore authorized a naval expedition to visit Japan for the purpose of establishing a coaling station and opening a commercial relationship with that country. The assignment went to Commodore Matthew Calbraith Perry. At sixty, "Matt" Perry had none of the dash and swagger sometimes associated with naval officers of the era. He was a stocky man of medium height, with dark wavy hair, a prominent nose, and fierce, determined looking eyes. In all he had the look of a man who was used to being obeyed. A tough, nearly humorless disciplinarian, he managed, nevertheless, to secure the respect of the men who served in his command.

Matthew Perry was in important ways a man well ahead of his time. He was a navalist who envisioned a major role for the United States in the Pacific that involved both trade expansion and the establishment of bases from which fleet units could operate to protect that trade.

In 1852 before leaving for his own personal rendezvous with destiny in Tokyo Bay, Perry was given an unusual opportunity to advance that vision. Secretary of State Daniel Webster fell seriously ill before he had time to do a final draft of Perry's instructions. The acting secretary, C. M. Conrad, allowed Perry to play a major role in drafting his own instructions.

Where Webster had originally instructed his envoy to be cautious and polite in seeking a commercial treaty, Perry and Conrad changed the tone of his orders entirely, recommending an aggressive posture in dealing with the Japanese. But perhaps more significantly, the Japanese mission was placed in the context of a more broadly based Pacific policy. Perry's instructions noted the many technological and political changes that had taken place during the Polk administration and remarked that these had "brought the countries of the East in closer proximity to our own." While all of the consequences of these changes were not yet in focus, the instructions continued, it was clear that the Pacific trade, which had already expanded greatly, would continue to grow, that "no limits can be assigned to its future extension."[6]

Rumors that the Japanese had badly mistreated shipwrecked American sailors and that they were a "vindictive" and "deceitful" people determined the approach that Perry took toward them. Convinced that he was dealing with "a weak and semi-barbarous people," he sailed for Japan determined to impose his will upon the Shogunate.[7]

When Perry agreed to undertake the mission, he had expected to command a squadron of eleven vessels. But the navy was able to provide him with only two of the new steam frigates and two sloops for his first foray into Japanese waters. Still, when he sailed into Tokyo Bay with his frigates belching black smoke, the effect was to throw the city into a panic:

> In all directions were seen mothers flying with their children in their arms, and men with mothers on their backs. . . . The tramp of war-horses, the

clatter of armed warriors, the noise of carts, the parade of firemen, the incessant tolling of bells, the shrieks of women, the cries of children, dinning all the streets of a city of more than a million souls, made confusion worse confounded.[8]

The Japanese knew of the Opium War and the fate that had befallen China. They imagined that much the same might be in store for them. Soldiers took up positions in makeshift forts, while samurai warriors prepared to do battle with swords against modern naval cannon.

The local authorities in Tokyo, showing a bold front, ordered Perry to remove his squadron to Nagasaki. Perry refused, insisting he had a letter from the president of the United States that he had been instructed to deliver personally to the emperor. After a week of fencing, the Japanese agreed to allow Perry to come ashore and deliver his letter to a representative of the emperor. An impressive ceremony ensued. Perry landed to martial music provided by not one but two bands. He was escorted by a contingent of one hundred marines in dress uniform and flanked by two tall, muscular, heavily armed blacks. In the background the American squadron rode easily at anchor, its guns run out and decks cleared for action.

The Japanese greeted Perry with at least equal pomp. They constructed a special building for the historic meeting of East and West and surrounded it with thousands of troops. As Perry approached, the sun glinted on the swords and spears of the warriors and flashed off their helms, while overhead, pennants in a rainbow of colors fluttered in the breeze.

Perry delivered his letter, which requested the establishment of commercial relations and a coaling station, and then informed his discomfited hosts that he would return in the spring with a larger fleet to receive their reply. Perhaps to make it clear to the Japanese that he would come and go at his own pleasure and not theirs, Perry did not leave Tokyo Bay immediately. Instead, for the next several days he sent boat crews out to chart the harbor and even travel partway up some of the rivers that fed into the bay. Then, having made his point, he sailed south to Okinawa, where he cowed the local authorities into allowing him to establish a coal depot. Though Japan claimed the island, there is little doubt that had he been left to his own devices Perry would have seized Okinawa for the United States. He had already laid claim to Peel Island (later renamed Chichi) in the Bonin group and sent Washington a plan for its colonization.

Perry's appearance in Tokyo Bay touched off a major debate in Japan. The isolationist policy that had been in place for two centuries had worked well. But it now seemed questionable whether it would be wise to hold to that course. The Russians were expanding into the Kuril islands to the north, and the British, having forced China open, were expanding their commercial and whaling enterprises throughout the entire Far East. All factions agreed that it was imperative for Japan to begin an immediate program of military modernization. But there were sharp differences of opinion over what to do in the period before Japan was able to meet the

In 1860 Japan sent its first treaty commission to the United States.

Western nations on their own terms. Some insisted on holding firm, while others advocated opening Japan's doors wide to foreign trade and Western influences. The policy finally decided upon was a compromise. Japan would give ground slowly, opening the door a crack while developing modern military capabilities. The lesson of the Opium War was too obvious to be ignored.

Perry's return to Japan in February 1854 marked the beginning of real negotiations, in which Perry settled for much less than he wanted. The Japanese refused to establish a regular commercial relationship but did agree to open the ports of Shimoda and Hakodate for the provisioning of American ships. An American consul would also be allowed to reside at one of the treaty ports.

Perry had made only a modest beginning at breaking down the wall of isolation that separated Japan from the rest of the world. Nevertheless, on his return to the United States he was greeted as a conquering hero. Congress voted him a $20,000 bonus, and the New York Chamber of Commerce presented him with an elegant silver service as a token of thanks for bringing "this secluded Empire into the intercourse of nations."[9]

Townsend Harris, the first American consul in Japan, arrived at Shimoda on board the USS *San Jacinto* in August 1856. Harris had traveled widely in Asia before going to Japan and during that time had developed a curiously ambivalent attitude toward the people there. On the one hand, he thought all Orientals were duplicitous and untrustworthy. Yet at the same time, like so many Americans who visited Asia in these years, he was outraged by the treatment meted out to the Chinese and other Asians by European imperialists. A remarkable man, Harris wanted Japan to be "the one spot in the Eastern world [where] the advent of Christian civilization did not bring with it its usual attendants of rapine and bloodshed."[10]

In Japan, Harris practiced patience and understanding. After fourteen months alone in Shimoda with only his Dutch-born secretary for company, patience was rewarded. He journeyed to Tokyo and there negotiated a treaty that opened six Japanese ports to trade, established the right of Americans to live in Japan, and set a uniform system of low tariffs. Japan's wall of isolation was in a shambles. It was the beginning of a new era in its relations with the West.

SLAVERY AND FOREIGN POLICY

Ralph Waldo Emerson, the essayist and philosopher, once warned that the conquest of Mexico would be a disaster for the United States. "It will be as the man swallows the arsenic which brings him down in turn. Mexico will poison us."[11] Postwar political developments confirmed Emerson's prediction. The ratification of the Treaty of Guadalupe Hidalgo brought the people of the United States face to face with a domestic crisis of unprecedented intensity.

North and South had never lived comfortably under the same political roof. From the time of the Constitutional Convention, national unity had been repeatedly challenged by differences over slavery. Each time the issue reemerged, it proved more difficult to resolve. In 1819 an aging Thomas Jefferson described the Missouri controversy as "a fire bell in the night," warning of perilous times ahead.[12] During the next three decades national political leaders struggled to keep the smoldering sectional controversy under control and the Union intact. But as political and economic power accumulated in the free states, the South became increasingly cognizant of its minority status and fearful of what that might mean.

After the Mexican War, the flames of sectional discord threatened to engulf the Union. The specific issue that divided slave from free states was whether slavery would be allowed to expand into the territories. The battle was joined even before the Mexican War was over when David Wilmot, a young Democratic congressman from Pennsylvania, added a proviso to an appropriations bill stating that "neither slavery nor involuntary servitude shall exist" in any territory acquired from Mexico.

The Wilmot Proviso was defeated. But the issue it raised would not disappear. In the North the voices raised in defiance of the slave power grew increasingly strident. Southern leaders, meanwhile, driven by the fear that the North was bent upon abolishing their "peculiar institution" and

Narciso López led two filibustering expeditions against Cuba. On the second try his luck ran out. He was captured and garroted in Havana's central square.

keenly aware of their section's declining political power, struggled against the noose they saw tightening around them.

In 1850 Congress enacted a patchwork compromise to the sectional controversy that its sponsors hoped would remove slavery from the arena of political debate. But this latest compromise proved to be nothing more than a truce between contending forces. During the decade that followed virtually every aspect of political life in the republic, including foreign policy, was subordinated to this divisive issue.

Few could have been more aware of the threat of disunion than Millard Fillmore's secretary of state. Daniel Webster had been a major figure in American political life for more than thirty years when he returned to the State Department in July 1850. During all of that time he had adhered fixedly to the view that while slavery was morally wrong, disunion was an even greater evil that should be avoided at all costs. Now in the twilight of his career, Webster understood that this once-formidable argument had lost much of its persuasive power. With the prospect of disunion staring him in the face, Webster looked to the foreign arena for a distraction, something that might reunite a nation that seemed on the verge of tearing itself apart.

Recent European developments seemed promising. When in January 1848, the people of Palermo took to the streets in rebellion against the despotic rule of Ferdinand II of Naples, they touched off a rebellion that

UBA DEFIES THE LAW OF POLITICAL GRAVITATION

Thomas Jefferson was the first but by no means the last sitting president to cast a covetous eye in the direction of Cuba. With the coming of Latin America's revolutions, it seemed inevitable that Spain would lose control of the Pearl of the Antilles and that the island, so valuable from a commercial point of view, would become part of the growing American empire. John Quincy Adams, who, as the reader will recall, equated these projected developments with a sort of natural law of politics, argued that if

> an apple severed by the tempest from its native tree cannot choose but fall to the ground, Cuba, forcibly disjoined from its own unnatural connection with Spain, and incapable of self-support, can gravitate only towards the North American Union, which by the same law of nature cannot cast her off from its bosom.[16]

Adams penned these words at a time when sectional differences were not so important to him as national priorities. Later in his career he had second thoughts about the immutability of his law of political gravitation. As the slavery controversy heated up and it became apparent that Cuba would enter the Union as one or more slave states, like others opposed to slavery expansion, Adams opposed annexation.

Southern expansionists, on the other hand, came to view Cuba with its thriving economy and its population of 418,000 whites and 619,000 slaves as one solution to the South's minority status in the Union. Cuba might be divided into two or perhaps even three new slave states. These same Southerners were moved by another consideration as well. Since 1833, Britain had been a leader in the struggle for the worldwide abolition of slavery. Southerners feared that under British pressure Spain, too, might abolish slavery in its empire. This fear of the "Africanization" of Cuba grew to nightmarish proportions after France abolished slavery in its West Indian holdings in 1848. Many Southerners believed that one way, indeed the only way, to make certain that Cuban slavery was never abolished was to annex the island.

Pressure from Southern congressmen, the expansionist press, and Cuban exiles living in the United States prompted the Polk administration to offer Spain $100 million for the island. But the negotiations never got beyond the point of vague propositions. Pedro Pidal, the Spanish minister of state, told the American envoy that "sooner than see the island transferred to *any power*" he "would prefer seeing it sunk in the Ocean."[17]

Following Polk's abortive attempt to purchase Cuba, southern expansionists formed an alliance with a group of Cubans who likewise supported annexation to the United States. The leader of this group was General Narciso López. A Venezuelan, López had fought on the Spanish side during the wars for Latin American independence. In 1823 he left South America and, after a short stay in Cuba, traveled to Spain, where he spent many years before relocating in Cuba.

swept across Europe. Within a month the contagion had spread t
where King Louis Philippe was forced to abdicate. Metternich w
from power in Austria, and soon all Europe was caught up in tl
revolutions of 1848.

The American people watched with great interest and er
as the Old World was enveloped in revolutionary fire. No part o
attracted more attention, however, than Hungary, where the la
journalist Louis Kossuth led a Magyar uprising against Austrian
Hungarian uprising attracted such support in the United State
State Department sent its chargé d'affaires in Paris, A. Dudley M
secret mission to Budapest. If it was warranted, Mann was t
diplomatic recognition to the new Hungarian government.

Before Mann's arrival, Austrian and Russian troops cri
Hungarian uprising, forcing Kossuth to flee to Turkey, wher
imprisoned. Then an embarrassing development took place.
Mann's instructions fell into the hands of the Austrian author
issued a strong protest over America's interference in their intern

By no means unhappy to receive the Austrian protest, W
real advantages to a pseudocrisis with Austria over Kossuth. The
real danger of war. Yet, he thought, the Austrians had presented
an opportunity to distract the country from its obsession wit
Webster's published reply to the Austrian note offered no apo
instead affirmed Washington's sympathy for all Europe's liberals,
Kossuth. In case they had forgotten, Webster reminded the Aus
"the source and center" of the world liberal movement "has doub
and now is these United States." Nor would the secretary be intin
warnings from a puny central European despotism. He noted
comparison" to America, "the possessions of the House of Hapsbu
as a patch on the earth's surface."[13]

Some critics objected to the "boastful and rough" tone of
note. But the secretary explained that he wanted to "write a pa
would touch the national pride and make a man feel *sheepish* an
who should speak of disunion."[14]

Webster fed the national enthusiasm for liberal revolution b
the release of Louis Kossuth from his Turkish prison and bringi
the United States, where he dined at the White House and was h
Congress. But his request that America and England join in h
Magyar people secure their independence fell on deaf ears. Web
drink a toast to "Hungarian Independence, Hungarian self-go
Hungarian control of Hungarian destinies." But, as he told one
if anyone spoke to him of intervention he would "have ears more
adders."[15] It took Kossuth only a short while to realize that the Un
had no intention of intervening on Hungary's behalf. In a few
Kossuth enthusiasm had passed, and Americans were left to ref
attention on the continuing domestic crisis.

López was a curious mixture of romanticism, liberalism, and racism. He admired the United States as a politically and economically progressive nation and deplored Cuba's connection with backward Spain. At the same time he was a staunch defender of slavery who, like many in the American South, feared that Spain might one day abolish the institution on the island. López concluded, therefore, that it was in Cuba's interest to separate itself from Spain and seek annexation to the United States.

Together with a few like-minded Cubans, López first began plotting revolution in 1848. But the Spanish nipped the scheme in the bud, whereupon López and a few co-conspirators fled to the United States. This setback, which nearly cost the general his life, didn't deter him, however. From his headquarters in New York, where he found enthusiastic supporters in Moses Y. Beach, the publisher of the *New York Sun*, John L. O'Sullivan, and a bevy of southern expansionists, he planned his return to Cuba.

In 1849, López collected a force described by one observer as the "most desperate creatures as ever were seen," men who "would murder a man for ten dollars." The general lured these men to his banner with promises of "plunder, women, drink, and tobacco" as well as a $1,000 bonus and 160 acres of land if they succeeded in driving the Spanish from Cuba.[18]

Unhappily for the general, the Taylor administration smashed the expedition before it could sail. Whatever feelings Zachary Taylor had about Cuba (he was a southern slaveholder), he could not have done otherwise, for he was then deeply involved in the fierce sectional struggle over the expansion of slavery into the territories. Had he allowed a southern-supported Texas-style revolution to take place in Cuba, it would have destroyed not only his credibility as a national political leader but all hope of a compromise to the sectional controversy as well.

López, disappointed but not discouraged, transferred his activities to New Orleans, where he developed even closer relations with a number of southern expansionists—especially Governor John A. Quitman of Mississippi. One of the South's most fervid proslavery advocates, Quitman had once advocated taking all of Mexico. Now he wanted Cuba.

Convinced that once he had established a foothold on the island the people there would rush to his support, López organized another descent on Cuba. This time, leading a force of more than six hundred, only five of whom were actually Cubans, he evaded the navy's efforts to stop him and landed on the island. But again he was disappointed. At Cárdenas the townspeople fled into the hills instead of joining in the revolt. Attacked and nearly captured by Spanish forces, López and his men were lucky to make it back to their ship for the flight to Key West.

López appears to have been suffering from a bad case of cognitive dissonance. He was unwilling to accept the facts that there was no popular support inside Cuba for his revolution and that without that support he could not hope to overthrow Spanish rule there. Instead he persisted in his fantasies, plotting still another Cuban expedition. In mid-summer 1851 he led a force of 435, including William Crittenden, the nephew of the U.S.

attorney general, in another descent on Cuba. At last the odds caught up with López and his men. Crittenden and about fifty other members of the expedition were quickly captured, tried, and shot in Havana's public square. López, captured shortly thereafter, was publicly garroted. Of the 160 survivors of the expedition, only four were set free. The remainder were sentenced to a life of slavery in Spain's quicksilver mines. Ultimately, however, after long and difficult negotiations between Spain and the United States, these men were released.

The election of Franklin Pierce in 1852 gave southern expansionists reason to believe that their dreams of empire might yet come true. This "doughface" Democrat from the Granite State was every bit as much an expansionist as Polk. Moreover, in the bitter aftermath of the Compromise of 1850, he was especially anxious to preserve his party's unity by placating its militant southern wing.

Pierce wasted no time making his views known, remarking in his inaugural address that he would "not be controlled by any timid forebodings of evil from expansion" and that "our attitude as a nation and our position on the globe render the acquisition of certain possessions not within our jurisdiction [Cuba] eminently important for our protection."[19]

The new president chose William L. Marcy, a moderate New York expansionist, to be his secretary of state, and larded his administration with southerners who were anxious to drive southward into the Caribbean. The key ministries in London and Paris went to James Buchanan, former secretary of state to Polk, and John Y. Mason, a Virginian. Both men supported the acquisition of Cuba. Pierre Soulé, a fiery proslavery Louisianian who had once held the Senate entranced with a speech on the importance of taking Cuba, was sent to Spain. And General James Gadsden, a South Carolina railroad promoter who entertained visions of a southern empire that included half of Mexico, was named minister to Mexico.

Gadsden set out on his assignment with $50 million to spend and instructions to purchase as much of northern Mexico as proved possible. At the very minimum he was to acquire a right of way for a transcontinental railroad that would run from the American South through the Southwest to the Pacific.

When the South Carolinian arrived in Mexico City, he found Santa Anna once again in power and, as usual, short of cash. Still, opportunist though he was, the aging dictator recognized some limits. Hard bargaining produced a treaty, but not such a one as Pierce and Gadsden had envisioned. In return for $10 million, Mexico ceded about 20 million acres of desert land just south of the Gila River. Gadsden got the railroad right-of-way he wanted but no more. That was perhaps just as well, since even this innocuous agreement ran into stiff opposition from "free-state" senators, who opposed the acquisition of any territory to the south, even when as in this case the land in question seemed virtually uninhabitable. After fierce skirmishing the treaty passed the Senate, but only on reconsideration and only by the barest majority.

TROUBLE IN NICARAGUA

The Clayton-Bulwer Treaty of 1850 had been useful in helping England and America resolve, at least temporarily, their quarrel over transit rights and canal routes across Central America. In a very short while, however, London and Washington were exchanging brickbats over the actual meaning of the ambiguous agreement. Secretary Marcy complained in 1853 that "the more it is studied, the more enigmatical it seems to be. It resembles more than anything of the kind I ever read a response of the Delphic oracle."[20]

The United States believed that by signing the treaty the British had abandoned their so-called Mosquito protectorate. London, on the other hand, insisted that the treaty did not apply to political arrangements made prior to the agreement. The British added more fuel to the flames of Anglo-American discord when, subsequent to signing the treaty, they annexed the Bay Islands in the Gulf of Honduras.

While London and Washington squabbled over the meaning of the Clayton-Bulwer Treaty, the situation inside Nicaragua grew threatening. Under license from the Nicaraguan government, Cornelius Vanderbilt led a consortium of capitalists in establishing the Accessory Transit Company, which transported passengers and freight between the Atlantic and Pacific coasts. The company established a small settlement at the mouth of the San Juan River across from Greytown, which was, recall, part of Britain's Mosquito protectorate. Friction soon developed between company employees and the inhabitants of Greytown. The situation culminated in a nasty riot and the destruction of some company property after an American sea captain shot and killed a native boatman.

Transit Company officials demanded that the Pierce administration do something. The president responded by sending the frigate *Cyane*, Captain George Hollins commanding, to Greytown. Hollins was instructed to demand an apology and compensation for the damage done by the rioters. When local officials refused, Hollins leveled the town with gunfire and put marines ashore to burn what remained.

The Greytown incident, a direct challenge to Britain's protectorate over the Mosquito Indians, produced a predictable response from London. George William Frederick Villiers, Lord Clarendon, the foreign secretary, denounced Hollins's act as an "outrage without parallel in the annals of modern times." And Lord Palmerston, who in this ministry ran the Home Office, advised taking immediate military action.

> In dealing with Vulgar minded Bullies, and such unfortunately the people of the United States are, nothing is gained by submission to Insult & wrong: on the contrary the submission to an Outrage only encourages the commission of another and a greater one—such People are always trying how far they can venture to go; and they generally pull up when they find they can go no further without encountering resistance of a formidable character.[21]

For a time it appeared that Palmerston might have his way. But before the end of the year London gave up all thought of a quarrel with the United States. In March 1854, England and France entered the Crimean War against the Russians, hoping for a quick victory. By the autumn of that year it was clear that the war would last for at least another year and that the Anglo-French army would have to face the rigors of a Russian winter unprepared.

Under the circumstances, Lord John Russell, also a member of this coalition government, urged negotiations and a peaceful settlement with the United States. But the prime minister, Lord Aberdeen, rejected that proposal, perhaps because he feared that negotiations with the rambunctious Pierce administration would do more harm than good. Instead, he did something quite remarkable, initiating Britain's unilateral withdrawal from Central America. The prime minister had recognized a fundamental truth—that Britain's position in Central America was untenable. There was little to be gained by persisting in the struggle for control of the region and much to be lost. The United States was too important as a source of cotton and foodstuffs and as a market to quarrel with over trifles.

The British press was surprisingly supportive of Aberdeen's policy. The usually Yankeephobic London *Times* reminded its readers that while the United States envisioned all of North America as coming under its control, in this instance there was "no reason . . . to resist the process." The *Economist* agreed, arguing that England hadn't the power to stop the United States from taking all of Central America even if it wanted to. But more to the point, the *Economist* continued, England had no reason for doing so.

> Our interest lies all the other way. We wish ourselves for no extension of territory on that continent. We are half inclined to regret that we hold any possession at all there south of the Union. Desiring no territory, we desire only prosperous industrious, civilized and wealthy customers. . . . Central America peopled and exploited by Anglo-Saxons will be worth to us tenfold its present value.[22]

Britain's abandonment of its Mosquito protectorate by no means ended Nicaragua's travails. They simply entered a new and more colorful phase with the activities of the filibustering adventurer, William Walker.

By the time Walker arrived in California in 1850, he had already tried careers in medicine and the law. He went west planning to pursue a career in journalism. But nothing so staid could long contain the energies of this "grey eyed man of destiny," who soon hatched a scheme for the conquest of Central America and Cuba.[23]

Walker's first filibustering escapade, a foray into lower California, ended in failure. But the romantic Tennessean refused to abandon his plan to create a Central American empire. In 1855, aided by Cornelius Vanderbilt's Accessory Transit Company, Walker led a force of adventurers into Nicaragua and succeeded in establishing a dictatorship there

Walker does not seem to have been a proslavery fanatic. But southern expansionists claimed him as their own and he recognized that support from North American sources could be invaluable. It is not surprising, then, that following a visit to Managua by the rabid proslavery expansionist Pierre Soulé, Walker announced the reintroduction of slavery and the slave trade in Nicaragua. The Pierce administration, which had looked the other way when Walker launched his invasion of that unfortunate land, obviously approved, for in 1855 it extended diplomatic recognition to the Walker government.

Walker might have remained the dictator of Nicaragua for some time had he not overestimated his own strength. His original success had been largely due to the support he received from the Vanderbilt interests. But in 1857 Walker infuriated Vanderbilt by canceling the Accessory Transit Company's charter for control of the transit rights across Nicaragua and granting a new charter to Byron Cole, publisher of the newspaper Walker had worked for before he took to filibustering. Vanderbilt, not a man to be trifled with, sent agents to Central America, who successfully encouraged Costa Rica, Honduras, and other Central American states to launch the military offensive that drove Walker from power and back to the United States. With him went slavery's toehold in Nicaragua and the fond hopes of southern expansionists.

Walker tried twice more to establish a personal empire in Central America. When his last expedition, this time aimed at Honduras, was broken up by the Royal Navy, he hoped to save his skin by surrendering to a British naval officer. But the English handed him over to the Honduran authorities, who executed him on September 12, 1860.

THE OSTEND MANIFESTO

Cuba had from the beginning been the centerpiece of Franklin Pierce's expansionist plans. At first he seemed willing to acquire the island as Tyler had won Texas, through a revolution that would pave the way for annexation. In 1853 the instrument for achieving this end appeared to be at hand in the person of John A. Quitman, the former Governor of Mississippi now a would-be filibuster. Quitman, who had been designated the "Civil and Military Chief of the Revolution" by a Cuban exile group, was at the time planning yet another invasion of the island.[24]

Unlike Narciso López, who had to contend with an unsympathetic Whig administration, Quitman seems at first to have been assured by members of the Pierce cabinet that the government would not stand in his way. But Quitman waited too long. By the spring of 1854 the administration had changed its attitude. In May the president issued a proclamation warning against any attempt to take Cuba by force. Quitman himself was subsequently arrested and charged with conspiracy.

This sudden decision to squelch the Quitman expedition was the result of domestic political developments and did not mean that the administration had abandoned its Cuban ambitions. By this time it had become clear as a result of the fierce sectional battle over the future of Kansas and

Nebraska that to acquire Cuba by unethical means would so infuriate the opponents of slavery expansion that the Democratic party and perhaps the Union would not survive. Another more legitimate method of acquiring the island would have to be found.

After abandoning Quitman, Secretary of State Marcy instructed Pierre Soulé in Madrid to offer the Spanish $130 million for the island. In one unfortunately ambiguous section of Soulé's instructions the secretary, anticipating the possibility of a rejection, remarked that "the next most desirable object" would be "to detach that island from the Spanish Domination and from all dependence on any European power."[25] Marcy probably meant by this that if annexation proved impossible an independent Cuba would be better for the United States than one that remained under Spanish control. But Soulé interpreted this phrase to mean that if the United States couldn't acquire the island one way she would have to try another.

By temperament Soulé was clearly the wrong man to undertake the delicate task of convincing proud Spain to cede Cuba. During his short and tempestuous career as a diplomat he had repeatedly embarrassed his government. Within weeks of his arrival he fought a duel with the French ambassador that scandalized the diplomatic community and left poor M. Turgot with a permanent limp. The ostensible reason for the duel was that at a party given at the French embassy someone—not the ambassador— made an off-color remark about Mrs. Soulé's plunging neckline, which evidently plunged too far. Later, when instructed to protest the seizure by Cuban customs officials of the *Black Warrior*, an American steamship, Soulé exceeded his instructions by insisting on the dismissal of the officials responsible and a $300,000 indemnity. To make matters worse, he gave the Spanish foreign minister only forty-eight hours to comply. The Spanish, of course, ignored Soulé, thus leaving not only the envoy but his government humiliated. Later, during his exciting fifteen-month tenure in Spain, Soulé even plotted with Spanish revolutionaries for the overthrow of the monarchy.

Considering Soulé's penchant for doing the wrong thing, it is not surprising that Marcy wanted to replace him with someone more responsible. But the Louisianian, the darling of southern expansionists, could not be dismissed so easily. And so, instead, the secretary tried another method of establishing some control over his often-errant envoy before sending him to negotiate for the purchase of Cuba.

Marcy instructed the three most important American representatives in Europe to meet prior to the opening of talks to plan strategy. He no doubt assumed that James Buchanan in London and John Y. Mason in Paris would impress upon Soulé the importance of moderation. If so he erred, for it was the fiery Soulé who dominated this gathering.

The three diplomats met at Ostend in October 1854, but quickly moved on to Aix-la-Chapelle for three days of conferences. The major outcome of their efforts was a memorandum, largely Soulé's work, that came to be known as the Ostend Manifesto. The document was dressed in the high-flown, romantic rhetoric of the age of Manifest Destiny. But stripped of the window dressing, it advocated first an attempt to purchase Cuba for $130 million. Soulé, who had not forgotten what Marcy himself had written about "detaching" Cuba from Spain, also incorporated into the document a second point. If purchase proved impossible, the report advocated taking the island by force.

The manifesto was an internal State Department memorandum not intended for public exposure. But within weeks of its arrival in Washington, the document's substance had been leaked to the *New York Herald*. There followed a furious public outcry punctuated by congressional demands that the administration produce the document. At first Pierce and Marcy held back, hoping to ride out the storm. Finally, however, in March 1855 the president sent the manifesto to Congress. The public outcry in the North was deafening.

The publication of the Ostend Manifesto wrote "finis" to the hopes of all expansionists. The sectional controversy, revolving as it did around the central issue of the expansion of slavery, made further growth impossible. Not until after the Civil War would Americans again be able to think seriously about expanding their frontiers.

ENDNOTES

1. Norman Graebner, *Empire on the Pacific* (Ronald Press, N.Y., 1955).

2. Thomas Hart Benton, quoted Henry Nash Smith, *Virgin Land, The American West in Myth and Symbol* (Harvard University Press, Cambridge, Mass., 1970), pp. 22–23.

3. John Tyler, quoted in Norma L. Peterson, *The Presidencies of William Henry Harrison and John Tyler* (University of Kansas Press, Lawrence, Ks., 1989), p. 19.

4. *North American Review*, quoted in Foster Rhea Dulles, *Yankees and Samurai* (Harper and Row, N.Y., 1965), p. 17.

5. Robert Walker, quoted in William L. Neumann, *America Encounters Japan: From Perry to MacArthur* (Johns Hopkins University Press, Baltimore, 1963), p. 24.

6. Perry's instructions, quoted in Samuel Eliot Morison, *"Old Bruin," Commodore Matthew Calbraith Perry*, (Little, Brown and Co., Boston, 1967) pp. 282–87.

7. Matthew Perry, quoted in Neumann, *America Encounters Japan*, p. 31.

8. Quoted in *ibid.*, p. 24.

9. New York Chamber of Commerce testimonial, quoted in Morison, *"Old Bruin,"* p. 417.

10. Townshend Harris, quoted in Dulles, *Yankees and Samurai*, p. 83.

11. Ralph Waldo Emerson, quoted in Bernard DeVoto, *Year of Decision, 1846* (Houghton Mifflin and Co., Boston, 1960), p. 214.

12. Thomas Jefferson to John Holmes, April 22, 1820, *The Works of Thomas Jefferson*, ed. Paul L. Ford (G. P. Putnam's Sons, 1892–1899), XII, pp. 158–60.

13. Daniel Webster, quoted in C.A. Duniway, "Daniel Webster," in Samuel Flagg Bemis, ed. *American Secretaries of State and Their Diplomacy* (Alfred A. Knopf, N.Y., 1927), V, pp. 85–87.

14. Webster, quoted in Robert F. Dalzell Jr., *Daniel Webster and the Trial of American Nationalism* (Houghton Mifflin and Co., Boston, 1973), p. 227.

15. Webster, quoted in Donald S. Spencer, *Louis Kossuth and Young America: A Study in Sectionalism and Foreign Policy, 1848–1852* (University of Missouri Press, Columbia, Mo., 1977), p. 87.

16. John Quincy Adams to Hugh Nelson, *The Writings of John Quincy Adams*, ed. Worthington C. Ford (Macmillan Co., N.Y., 1913–1917), VII, p. 373.

17. Pedro Pidal, quoted in Philip Foner, *A History of Cuba and its Relations with the United States* (International Publishers, N.Y., 1962), II, pp. 27–28.

18. Quoted in *ibid.*, p. 43.

19. *Messages and Papers of the Presidents*, ed. James D. Richardson (Washington, 1900), V, pp. 198–99.

20. William L. Marcy, quoted in Ivor D. Spencer, *The Victor and the Spoils: A Life of William L. Marcy* (Brown University Press, Providence, R.I., 1959), p. 243.

21. Lord Palmerston, quoted in Kenneth Bourne, *Britain and the Balance of Power in North America* (University of California Press, Berkeley, Cal., 1967), pp. 182–83.

22. The *London Times* and the *Economist*, both quoted in *ibid.*, pp. 200–201.

23. Quoted in Robert E. May, *The Southern Dream of a Caribbean Empire* (Louisiana State University Press, Baton Rouge, La., 1973), p. 77.

24. Quoted in Foner, *A History of Cuba*, II, pp. 71–72; see also Robert E. May, *John A. Quitman, Old South Crusader* (Louisiana State University Press, Baton Rouge, La., 1985), pp. 270–95.

25. Soulé's instructions, quoted in Spencer, *The Victor and the Spoils*, pp. 324–29.

COTTON IN THE STOCKS.

M. *Mercier*:—"HOW MUCH LONGER IS THIS TO LAST? OR ARE YOU WAITING
UNTIL WE INTERFERE?"

It was commonly understood during the Civil War that the Confederacy was
withholding cotton supplies from England and France hoping to force them to
intervene in the war. In this cartoon the French minister in Washington puts the
question directly to an evil-looking, whip-wielding slavemaster.

11

THE DIPLOMACY OF WAR, 1861–1865

On April 12, 1861, Confederate shore batteries opened fire on federal forces
occupying Fort Sumter in Charleston Harbor, signaling the beginning of the
Civil War. In Richmond, the Confederate capital, and in Washington as well,
policy makers believed that the outcome of the fighting might depend on
the behavior of three great European powers—Britain, France, and to a
lesser extent Russia. Had one or more of these nations extended full
diplomatic recognition to the Confederacy or actively intervened on its
behalf, the South might have won its independence.

Of the three nations thought capable of influencing the outcome of
the war, only Britain posed a real threat. From first to last the Russians were
unwavering in their support of the Lincoln administration. Still smarting
from his defeat in the Crimean War and contemplating the possibility of
another contest with the British Lion in the future, the czar wanted a strong
United States as a threat to Britain on its exposed North American flank.
France, on the other hand, had ambitions in the Western Hemisphere that
might have been advanced by the destruction of the Union. But Emperor
Louis Napoleon had European ambitions of even greater moment and was
therefore wary of becoming entangled in a war in North America. Although
openly sympathetic to the South, he was never willing to risk involvement

unless joined by the British. And so the crucial question was how London would behave.

KING COTTON

Like the majority of southerners, President Jefferson Davis and his secretary of state, the Georgia fire-eater Robert Toombs, were convinced that England would quickly intervene to support the Confederacy. First, it appeared to be in England's interest to have two North American republics each threatening the other instead of one constantly menacing Canada. There would be economic advantage in a divided United States, too. The North, which was then rapidly industrializing, had become Britain's competitor in world trade. Moreover, the Morrill Tariff of 1861, which was intended to encourage the growth of American industrial power while reducing Britain's share of the American marketplace, challenged Britain economically. The South, in contrast, was prepared to play the economic game by British rules. As an independent agrarian nation, it would provide a large and expanding market for British manufactures at a moment when protectionism had become an economic byword in the North.

Finally, it was an article of faith among most southerners that Britain and France, too, would intervene in support of the South because in the last analysis they had no choice. In France more than 700,000 workers depended for their livelihoods on access to southern cotton. In the north of England at least three times as many jobs were at stake. Southern theorists believed that if the Confederacy denied these European powers access to its cotton, they would suffer economic and social crisis. To avoid such a crisis, these two great nations would be forced to do the South's bidding.

In 1858, South Carolina's Senator M. B. Hammond asked, "What would happen if no cotton were furnished for three years?" His conclusion was that "England would topple headlong and carry the whole civilized world with her save the South. No, you dare not make war on cotton. No power on earth dares make war on it. Cotton is King." The editor of the *Richmond Whig* who seems to have been just as deluded, remarked, "the Confederacy has its hand on the mane of the British lion and that beast, so formidable to all the rest of the world, must crouch at her bidding."[1]

This extraordinarily arrogant and mistaken view was held not only by a majority of the Confederacy's leaders but by rank-and-file southerners as well. William Russell, who covered the Civil War for the London *Times*, explained to his readers that, even as they prepared for combat, soldiers in the Confederate ranks doubted that the fighting would last very long. And if it did, they fully expected England to come to their aid. "The Yankees aint such a cussed fools as to think they can come here and whip us, let alone the British," one young soldier told Russell. When asked what the British had to do with this war, the young volunteer explained that they were "bound to take our part: if they don't we'll just give them a hint about cotton, and that will set matters right."[2]

At the beginning of the war the Confederate government tested its "King Cotton" doctrine by burning 2.5 million bales of cotton and calling for a voluntary embargo on cotton exports. But Southern economic pressure notwithstanding, London proved maddeningly difficult to influence. It is true that by late 1861 the mill towns of Lancashire were experiencing widespread unemployment. Government statistics indicated that 27,000 operatives had been thrown entirely out of work, while another 161,000 were working reduced hours.

But Lord Palmerston's government was also aware that the depression in the cotton districts was not the result of a lack of raw material. The South had produced bumper cotton crops in 1859 and 1860. England's warehouses were overflowing with unwanted raw cotton when the Civil War began. Even as late as early 1862, at a time when the depression in the cotton industry was already quite serious, British warehouses contained a larger supply of raw cotton than they had at the beginning of 1860, the last year of peace. Britain's cotton industry was suffering not from a lack of raw material but from inadequate and glutted markets. Thus, at least until mid-1862 cotton wholesalers and manufacturers wanted no new supplies of cotton. The South's embargo, which kept much of the 1861 cotton crop off the market, actually benefited England's cotton manufacturers, enabling them to sell finished products already on hand and avoid the more serious depression that might have developed had the South added to the international cotton glut. It is also worth noting that during the four years of the war approximately three-quarters of a normal year's shipment of southern cotton reached British shores. These resources plus cotton produced in India and Egypt allowed the industry to begin a recovery by 1863.

The South's economic policies, which had little to do with the depression in England's cotton districts, had even less effect on the overall British economy. The long moribund wool and linen industries began a revival at this time. War industries grew, too, as British manufacturers sold prodigious amounts of war material to both North and South. Finally, as Confederate raiders drove American shipping from the seas, the British merchant fleet expanded to produce more jobs and income for the island empire.

The war did cause some dislocations in British economic life. But these were mere annoyances. Throughout the war the national unemployment rate remained in the normal range as the British economy hummed prosperously along. On at least one occasion during this period Chancellor of the Exchequer William Gladstone was even able to announce a balanced budget and a tax cut simultaneously.

Southern leaders not only miscalculated the economic power of cotton, they failed to take British national pride into account, foolishly assuming that London would quickly surrender to their blatant form of international blackmail. England was at the height of its power, the arbiter of the destiny of a substantial portion of the world. It is inconceivable that it should have allowed its foreign policy to be dictated by the upstart Confederacy. Lord John Russell, Palmerston's foreign secretary, made just this point when he remarked that to "recognize the South simply because they keep cotton from us would be ignominious beyond measure," and "no English Parliament could do so base a thing."[3]

SEWARD'S DIPLOMACY

While the South pinned its hopes on being able to force European intervention on its behalf, the basic objective of northern diplomacy was to make certain that Europe remained uninvolved. That was the responsibility of William H. Seward, chosen by Abraham Lincoln to take over the State Department. Henry Adams, who served as his father's private secretary in the London legation during the war, described his friend Seward as "a slouching, slender figure" with "a head like a wise macaw; a beaked nose; shaggy eyebrows; unruly hair and clothes; hoarse voice; offhand manner, free talk and perpetual cigar."[4] He was, to put it another way, a cartoonist's dream.

By the time the charming and loquacious Seward moved into the State Department, he had a long and successful political career already behind him. He had served as the governor of New York and in the Senate, where his always colorful and sometimes extreme rhetoric earned him an undeserved reputation as a radical. But it was as a diplomat that this disciple of John Quincy Adams earned his greatest laurels, first for his handling of Anglo-American relations during the war and later as the first in a new breed of postwar expansionists.

Seward's first foray into the field of diplomacy in no way foretold the greatness that was to come. He felt certain that a wellspring of national patriotism remained among the South's people. The problem was to reach it. In late March 1861, before the cannonading of Fort Sumter announced an end to talk, Seward thought he had found a way. At this time northern newspapers were filled with rumors of foreign intervention in the Western Hemisphere. An Anglo-French fleet was reported to be sailing for the Caribbean, and the Spanish seemed about to seize Santo Domingo. Napoleon III was supposed to be eyeing Haiti and preparing for a military adventure in Mexico, where a bloody civil war was then in progress.

When news arrived in Washington that the Spanish had in fact landed forces on Santo Domingo, Seward urged Lincoln to "demand explanations" of Spain as well as France. If these proved inadequate, he proposed asking Congress for a declaration of war.[5] This step would allow the United States to take Cuba from Spain while disabusing the French of any notions they might have of intervening in the Western Hemisphere. Such a war, the secretary believed, would cause a resurgence of national patriotism in the South, causing its people to rush to the colors while abandoning thoughts of secession. Keenly aware that the South longed to acquire Cuba, he thought it impossible that southerners could refuse to support a war for that purpose or that they would be willing to see the North conquer the island and perhaps abolish slavery there.

In one of his very few major foreign policy decisions, President Lincoln rejected Seward's recommendation. The secretary assumed that the South was not serious about secession and that there was a vast reservoir of national patriotism there just waiting to be tapped. But what if the South was serious? In that case a war with France and Spain would provide the Confederacy with two important allies. If this happened, could Britain be restrained from recognizing southern independence? The risk, the president clearly saw, was not worth the gamble.

Once the war had begun, Seward quickly settled down. He carefully defined his purpose, which was to isolate the South, denying it all hope of foreign support in order to break its will to resist. Toward this end he left no doubt that the administration viewed the war as a conflict between the legitimate government of the United States and a group of insurgents and that Washington would consider the recognition of the Confederacy by any European state an extremely unfriendly act. On all lesser subjects Seward showed great flexibility, hoping to avoid any action that might provoke the Europeans into intervening in support of the South.

BRITAIN DECLARES NEUTRALITY

Britain's prime minister, Lord Palmerston, didn't like Americans; he never had. Moreover, as William Gladstone later wrote, Palmerston "personally desired the severance" between North and South "as a diminution of a dangerous power."[6] But the prime minister also had an almost endless list of reasons for wanting to stay out of the American war. Had England come to the South's aid, it would have lost a valued market in the northern states, jeopardized huge investments recently made in that rapidly industrializing part of the country, and run the risk of having its merchant fleet mauled by rapacious Yankee privateers. If the economic implications of a war with the North were less than appealing, Palmerston found little to his liking when considering the military possibilities. It is true that the Royal Navy might have bombarded America's seaboard cities at the beginning of a war. But this was an era of revolutionary change in naval armament. Only ironclad vessels truly counted in the calculus of modern naval warfare, and Britain had few of these. Industrial America was capable of building a modern fleet that could challenge Britain's control of the sea. All it needed was an incentive. Palmerston saw no reason to provide one. Another military fact of life not lost on the prime minister was that, in any war with the United States, Canada would surely be lost.

Nor could Palmerston afford to ignore the moral and domestic political issues raised by the American war. Even though President Lincoln made it clear that the war was being fought to preserve the Union and not to abolish slavery, the British, leaders in the world antislavery movement, had difficulty envisioning themselves as aiding in the creation of a large, expansionist slave state in the Western Hemisphere. Finally, as Palmerston clearly realized, the shaky coalition government he headed lacked a consensus on the American question and would probably have collapsed had he deliberately adopted a prosouthern policy.

It is by no means surprising, then, that Palmerston tried to steer clear of the American war or that his foreign secretary, Lord John Russell, should have told Parliament that "nothing but the imperative duty of protecting British interests if they should be attacked justifies the Government in at all interfering." He then added, "For God's sake, let us if possible keep out of it."[7]

But could England stay unentangled? Its problem was not entirely dissimilar from that faced by James Madison before the War of 1812. Britain traded with both belligerents. And that trade was an interest that had to be protected.

Early in April 1861, President Jefferson Davis announced that the South would soon begin privateering activities; Confederate warships would stop and search British vessels for contraband. A few days later, on April 19, the Lincoln administration established a naval blockade along the entire 3,100 miles of southern coastline, thus placing British ships trading with southern ports in similar straits.

On learning of these developments, London declared its neutrality and in so doing recognized the belligerent status of the South. France quickly followed suit. This action, which seemed to presage full diplomatic recognition, boosted southern morale, gave semiofficial status to Confederate envoys then fanning out to various foreign capitals, recognized the right of Confederate warships to visit and search neutral merchantmen on the high seas, and made it very likely that southern agents would be able to float loans in support of the war effort.

London did not wish to provoke a war with the North by extending full diplomatic recognition to the South. Yet since virtually all British policy makers assumed that the South would succeed in its bid for independence, it seemed in Britain's interest to lay the foundation for future good relations with the Confederacy, Britain's principal supplier of raw cotton and an important trading partner. The decision also had immediate benefits for the English. Their merchant ships would not be harassed by Confederate privateers unless they were found to be carrying contraband to the North, and they could profit from a large and expanding war trade with the South.

The ministry, even including several members who were friendly to the Union, thought a declaration of neutrality the only appropriate policy for a nation that was trying to steer clear of the conflict while at the same time protecting its real interests. And after all, as the government pointed out, Lincoln himself had already recognized the belligerent status of the South by declaring the area under blockade. In international law, as Washington certainly understood, a blockade could only be declared by one sovereign nation against another.

THE CRITICAL YEAR, 1861

If London thought its neutral policy entirely reasonable, Seward viewed it as a bold and hostile act. When he subsequently learned that Lord Russell had held conversations with three Confederate envoys at the Foreign Office, he quickly concluded that London was on the verge of recognizing the South. In a letter to his wife he explained that Britain and France were about "to try to save cotton at the cost of the Union" and that Britain was "in great danger of sympathizing so much with the South, for the sake of peace and cotton, as to drive us to make war against her as the ally of the traitors." "God damn 'em," he told Charles Sumner, chair of the Senate Foreign Relations Committee, "I'll give 'em hell."[8]

Seward tried to do just that, dashing off a set of threatening instructions for Charles Francis Adams, the American minister in London. Adams was to inform the foreign secretary that diplomatic relations would be suspended if Russell established an official relationship with the Confederacy's representatives and that British recognition of the South would probably mean war.

The harsh and threatening tone of this dispatch was softened by President Lincoln, who deleted the angriest portions of the message before it was forwarded to Adams. And where Seward had instructed his envoy to read the dispatch in its entirety to Lord Russell, no doubt with appropriate flourishes, Lincoln stipulated that the dispatch should remain confidential. It would be up to the minister to convey in his own terms the government's meaning. Even with Lincoln's changes, Seward's instructions and his overall strategy remained intact. Toughness and threats would be used to forewarn the British against going too far.

Charles Francis Adams, son and grandson of presidents, arrived in London only a few days after the Foreign Office had recognized the South's belligerent status. According to his son Henry, the new envoy "naturally looked on all British Ministers as enemies." After all, he quipped, "The only public occupation of all Adamses for a hundred and fifty years at least . . . had been to quarrel with Downing Street."[9] It is not surprising, then, that like Seward, Charles Francis Adams should have concluded that the British would do everything in their power to aid the Confederacy. But in the several weeks that elapsed before he received the secretary's provocative instructions, Adams noted what he took to be a more correct attitude on the part of Lord Russell, who, after that first meeting, kept the southern envoys at arm's length and prohibited southern privateers from using British ports either to sell their prizes or to refit.

By the time Seward's instructions arrived, Adams was more or less satisfied that the British were not quite so hostile as he had at first suspected.

Charles Francis Adams served with distinction as America's minister to the Court of St. James's during the Civil War.

He feared war if he followed his instructions to the letter. Rather than throw "the game into the hands of the enemy," he therefore adopted a more conciliatory approach than his instructions called for.[10] At his June 12 meeting with the foreign secretary, Adams accepted Russell's explanation that his first meeting with the three southern agents was of no official importance and that "he had no expectation of seeing" them in the future. Adams made no threats, deciding instead to await developments. In this instance Adams and not Seward was correct. The secretary had been too brash.

Just what sort of game were the British playing? That was a question neither Seward nor Jefferson Davis, for that matter, was able to answer during that critical first year of the war. London's decision to recognize southern belligerency was hailed in Richmond as the precursor to full diplomatic recognition and denounced in Washington for the same reason. But the British reaction to the Union's naval blockade of the South was of an entirely different nature.

At the beginning of the war the United States Navy consisted of ninety ships, only forty of which were steam powered. This tiny force had the gargantuan responsibility of blockading more than three thousand miles of southern coastline. Inevitably, especially in the early years of the war, the blockading squadrons were unable to perform the prescribed task. The British consul in Charleston, Robert Bunch, was correct in describing the Union blockade as "a laughing stock" and "totally ineffective."[11] By 1864 the navy had vastly expanded. Even so, the blockade was not entirely proof against blockade runners. Since in international law only an effective blockade is considered legal, and since the South did enjoy belligerent rights, the British government had cause to protest northern interference with its trade with the Confederacy. And in the early stages of the war that seemed to be precisely the course Britain would follow.

Hardly had Washington announced plans for a blockade before Richard Bickerton Pemell, Lord Lyons, the British minister, entered a strong protest. He warned Seward that any attempt to interfere with British access to southern ports would probably prove a "fatal step . . . bringing the powers of Europe into the quarrel." But Lyons was quickly reversed by higher authorities in London. To the South's utter dismay, Palmerston and Russell decided to acquiesce in Washington's ineffective blockade. As Russell explained, so long as there were enough ships in the blockading squadron "to create an evident danger of entering or leaving" a blockaded port, "the fact that various ships may have successfully escaped through it . . . will not of itself prevent the blockade from being an effective one by international law."[12]

It was a rocky road that Britain and the United States traveled in 1861, but never more pitted and dangerous than in the month of November, when the *Trent* affair brought the two nations to the very brink of war. John Slidell of Louisiana and James M. Mason of Virginia had been appointed envoys from the Confederacy to France and England respectively. Basking in the glow of the victory at the first battle of Bull Run and still optimistic about prospects that the cotton embargo would bring intense pressure on London and Paris, the Davis administration sent these envoys off with high hopes that they would be received and the Confederacy recognized as a sovereign nation.

Sailing from Charleston on board a swift, side-wheeling steamer, Mason and Slidell ran the blockade, arriving in Havana on October 16. They booked passage on the British mail steamer *Trent* for St. Thomas in the Danish West Indies, where they expected to catch a packet for England. But they never got that far. A week after Mason and Slidell arrived in Havana, the USS *San Jacinto*, commanded by Captain Charles Wilkes, put in at Cienfuegos. There Wilkes learned that the two Confederate diplomats would be on board the *Trent* when it sailed for the Danish West Indies. Stationing his ship in the Old Bahama Channel, the impulsive, not to say vainglorious, Wilkes stopped the *Trent*, kidnapped Mason and Slidell from under the protection of the Union Jack, and sailed for Boston, where the two southerners were imprisoned in Fort Warren.

From the very beginning opinion in the North was divided over what Wilkes had done. There was jubilation because these were grim times for a people thirsting for any sort of a victory after the humiliations suffered at Bull Run and Ball's Bluff. The northern press was lavish in its praise of Wilkes, Secretary of the Navy Gideon Welles sent him a letter of commendation, and Congress awarded him a gold medal. But there was concern, too, over how London would respond. Thus Wall Street reacted to the news nervously, while many on both sides believed that Mason and Slidell would do more for the South's cause in a northern prison than ever they could in London and Paris.

Aware that the British would not take this insult lying down, Seward quickly informed the Foreign Office that Wilkes's action was unauthorized and expressed the hope "that the British Government will consider this subject in a friendly temper." He assured Lord Russell that he could "expect the best disposition on the part of this Government."[13]

News of the *Trent* affair came like a thunderclap to the American legation in London. Henry Adams wrote, "How in the name of all that's conceivable could you suppose England would sit quiet under such an insult? *We* should have jumped out of our boots at such a one."[14] The minister himself fell into a state of utter despair. He had feared all along that Britain might end up joining the South. But to have it come about over the foolish escapade of a glory-seeking naval commander was too much for him to bear. Even before the British had time to react, Charles Francis Adams advised Seward to release the prisoners. So, too, did Seward's friend Thurlow Weed, then in England on a diplomatic mission.

A few days after news of the *Trent* affair reached London, the ministry hurled its thunderbolt. Lord Lyons was instructed to demand an apology along with the release of the prisoners and appropriate reparations. If the Lincoln administration did not concede these points within seven days, Lyons was to collect his passports and leave immediately.

Seward needed no prompting, arguing doggedly in favor of surrendering to the British demands. It was the president who hung back, no doubt because he feared a public backlash if Mason and Slidell went free. But when Senator Charles Sumner came to the White House with letters from friends in London indicating that England and the Union would soon be at war unless Mason and Slidell were released, he gave in. Early in January the two Confederate envoys were quietly removed from Fort Warren and put aboard a British warship, which had been sent to retrieve them

The relief was palpable not only in Washington but in London as well. The ministry had been momentarily carried away by the public's as well as its own emotional response to Captain Wilkes's behavior. But on sober second thought, Russell and Palmerston realized that they had perhaps bitten off more than they could or at least wanted to chew. The foreign secretary regretted his instructions to Lyons almost as soon as they had been sent. He did not question Lord Lyons's decision to give the Lincoln administration more than the allotted seven days to make its surrender. He also interpreted Secretary Seward's explanation that Wilkes had not acted on the authority of the government as equivalent to an apology and abandoned all talk of reparations. At the height of the crisis he even suggested that, if the United States would agree to return Mason and Slidell, Britain would renounce the right to impress seamen. Thus Britain would win the immediate point while the United States could claim victory on an issue that had been a cause of irritation for generations.

BRITAIN SQUINTS AT MEDIATION

The year 1861 had seen repeated crises in Anglo-American relations. But it was in the summer of the following year that key members of the British government, including Palmerston, Russell, and Chancellor of the Exchequer William Gladstone considered intervening in the war by offering to mediate a settlement on the basis of southern independence. If the Lincoln administration refused, the plan called for London to recognize the Confederacy, an act that might well have resulted in a war with the United States.

The Palmerston government had a number of reasons for considering such an extraordinary move. First, British trade was suffering a variety of inconveniences as a result of the northern blockade. Moreover, in the North of England, where it was widely though mistakenly *believed* that unemployment was a result of the war, there was a growing demand that the government gain access to southern cotton. And while the government realized that the current depression in the cotton districts was not the result of a "cotton famine," it also felt that it could not go on without American cotton indefinitely. There also existed a deeply rooted conviction among the educated classes in England that the Lincoln administration could never achieve the gargantuan goal it had set for itself. Even those who sympathized with the North thought that in the end the South could never be reintegrated into the Union. After a year of bloody warfare fought on a scale never before seen, many in England thought it was time for the North to face reality. As Gladstone himself remarked in a now-famous speech, it seemed that Jefferson Davis had "made a revolution and was about to make a nation." The world could, he thought, "anticipate with certainty the success of the Southern states as far as regards their separation from the North."[15]

Still, all of these considerations would not have moved the ministry to consider mediation had it not been for the fact that the South seemed on the verge of winning its independence on the battlefield. The failure of General George B. McClellan's Peninsular Campaign, the South's victories at Murfreesboro and later at the second battle of Manassas, and General Robert E. Lee's advance into Maryland marked the high point of the southern war effort and gave the ministry reason to believe that the time was not far off when the Lincoln administration would have to face facts.

In 1862 the Palmerston government toyed with the idea of intervening in the war in support of the South. The British decided to wait, however, because of the drawn battle of Antietam. The North's victory at Gettysburg, which came at such a high price—a portion of the battlefield is pictured here—ended any possibility that the British might intervene.

With the military situation in North America clearly favoring the South, Russell and Palmerston began planning an Anglo-French offer of mediation. But before this plan was even partially matured, things began to go awry. First the French, who had long advocated joint intervention, hesitated. Deeply involved in a war in Mexico, where he had deployed twenty-eight thousand troops, and fishing in Italy's troubled waters, Napoleon III had doubts about becoming embroiled elsewhere. Then Gladstone created problems when he agreed to support mediation only if Russia was added to the group of nations making the offer. Palmerston and Russell could not propose mediation to the cabinet without the support of the powerful chancellor of the exchequer. Yet it was most unlikely that the Russians would cooperate. Finally, even with Gladstone's endorsement, the cabinet remained badly divided on the question. To press the issue would have been to risk the collapse of the government.

In spite of the many obstacles, Lord Russell wanted to pursue the scheme. But Palmerston drew back. When, early in October, London learned that the southern advance into Maryland had been checked at the battle of Antietam, he lost interest in proposing mediation, at least for the moment. The "pugilists must fight a few more rounds," he told Russell, "before the bystanders can decide that the state should be divided between them."[16] The mediation proposal, postponed in October, 1862, died in infancy. As the military situation in America shifted in favor of the North, London became correspondingly less inclined to risk the ire of the Lincoln administration.

BRITAIN AND THE CONFEDERATE RAIDERS

The fact that England wanted to avoid war was no guarantee that it would be able to do so. Northern opinion had grown distinctly hostile toward the British for a variety of understandable reasons. Their early decision to recognize southern belligerency, their continued trade with the Confederacy, the *Trent* affair and the rumors that regularly surfaced indicating that London was preparing to recognize the South all contributed to rising trans-Atlantic tensions. From Washington's perspective it seemed clear that the Palmerston government had, from the moment it recognized the belligerent status of the Confederacy, skewed its neutrality to serve southern interests. Nothing demonstrated this more clearly or aroused more fury in the North than the British government's willingness to allow the construction of Confederate warships in British shipyards.

At the beginning of the war the Confederacy had no navy and no means of building one. To compensate, Richmond sent Captain James D. Bulloch to England to acquire the ships and naval armaments that would make the Confederacy a sea power. On his arrival, Bulloch sought legal advice regarding the precise meaning of Britain's neutrality law, the Foreign Enlistment Act of 1819. This statute, which seemed straightforward enough, stipulated that it was illegal to "equip, fit out, or arm in British jurisdiction a ship whose intent is to cruise against the commerce of a friendly power."[17] But Bulloch soon learned that it was possible to build warships in British yards and even purchase their armaments from English manufacturers. The law required only that ships thus built should not be armed while within British jurisdiction. Once he became aware of this huge loophole in the law, the resourceful Bulloch quickly signed contracts with the Laird Brothers of Liverpool for the construction of several swift-sailing steamers.

Thomas Dudley, the sharp-eyed American consul in Liverpool, soon learned of a mysterious vessel being constructed in the Laird Brothers's yard. He hired private detectives to keep the ship, called the *Oreto*, under surveillance. He collected testimony from workmen and others familiar with the *Oreto* tending to prove that it was being built for the Confederacy and that its sailing would therefore be a violation of the Foreign Enlistment Act.

Armed with Dudley's evidence, Charles Francis Adams demanded that the Foreign Office detain the vessel, which was nearly ready for sea trials. That was on February 18, 1862. A month passed, during which the government took no action. Adams renewed his demand, but too late. Before the end of March the *Oreto* sailed for Nassau. Renamed the *Florida* and armed with naval cannon shipped separately from England, it set out on a twenty-one-month rampage against American shipping. It took forty prizes before being sunk by the USS *Wachusett* off the coast of Brazil.

Adams had little time to fret over the *Florida*'s escape. At that very moment a sister ship called the "290" was nearing completion in the Laird shipyards. Again Dudley turned up a mass of information tending to prove that the "290" was a Confederate raider. And again Adams protested to the Foreign Office. This time the American demand became the occasion for a bureaucratic scuffle among the Law Officers of the Crown, the Board of Customs, and the Foreign Office. Finally Russell, who hoped to avoid further problems with the Americans over the Confederate raiders, ordered the "290" detained. But it was too late; the ship had escaped. Named the *Alabama*, it proved to be the most feared of the Confederate raiders, taking more than seventy prizes before it, too, was sunk by an American warship.

When Adams again appealed to the government, this time for the detention of the *Alexandra*, another ship under construction in the Laird yards, Russell acted with greater dispatch. Even in the face of serious doubts that the Foreign Enlistment Act could be used to condemn it, he ordered the ship detained. The legal owners sued, and the case was tried in the Court of Exchequer before the octogenarian judge, Jonathan Frederick Pollock. In his instructions to the jury, Pollock, a Confederate sympathizer, interpreted the law in the narrowest way conceivable and offered his opinion that the *Alabama* had not been in violation of the law when it put to sea. The jury, taking its cue from the judge, freed the *Alexandra*, which, once outside British jurisdiction was armed and renamed the *Shenandoah*.

Adams was by turns furious and depressed over these developments. Russell and Palmerston could not hide behind an inadequate neutrality law. If the law had a loophole, the remedy was simple—change it. As for the British, they seem to have been of two minds about these developments. On the one hand their official position remained consistent. If weapons makers had a right to sell munitions to the North, they had an equal right to build ships for the South. At the same time, however, the extensive damage done to northern shipping by these commerce destroyers was difficult to ignore. Whatever the legalities of the situation, the prime minister and the foreign secretary both admitted privately that the Lincoln administration had cause to complain.

Though it may not have appeared so to Adams, the ministry's action in the case of the *Alexandra* reflected an increasing desire to pacify Washington. There were a number of reasons for this shift. First, the South had lost the initiative on the battlefield. Then, too, the kaleidoscopically changing European political situation had to be taken into account. Late in 1862 Greek insurrectionists overthrew King Otto and left the British, who were among the guarantors of Greek independence, the problem of intervening to create a new Greek government that would be acceptable to the Greeks and other interested powers as well. Next came a Polish rebellion against Poland's Russian rulers and even greater instability in Eastern Europe. When the Prussians and the Russians joined forces to put down the rebellion, France was drawn into the political infighting that soon gripped most of Europe. L.Q.C. Lamar, a southern diplomat who was passing through London at this time, noted sadly that Palmerston was so engrossed with "conferences, jealousies, and rivalries between the leading powers of Europe" that he had no time to worry about "the fate of constitutional government in America."[18]

At the beginning of the Civil War the Confederacy had neither ships nor seamen to man them. The British provided both. The willingness of the British government to allow the construction of Confederate warships in British yards was a major issue between London and Washington.

By the summer of 1863 the dispute between England and the United States over the construction of Confederate warships had reached a critical stage. Laird Brothers was then building two large armored rams so powerful it was alleged that if they ever put to sea they could shatter the northern blockading squadron and hold the entire eastern seaboard under their thrall. The potential power of these rams may have been exaggerated. Certainly the Royal Navy thought so. But Charles Francis Adams believed the rams could do incalculable damage to the Union's war effort and warned the Foreign Office that if they sailed it would certainly mean war.

By the time Adams issued his ultimatum, Russell and Palmerston had both decided that it was absolutely vital to stay out of the American war. The European political situation had grown more volatile as the Russians mobilized their military forces; the cabinet remained hopelessly divided on the American question; and the depression in the cotton districts, which in 1862 had produced some demands from the North of England for intervention, had clearly abated. The ministry would probably have seized the rams in an instant to avoid difficulties with the North, but now it had the court decision in the case of the *Alexandra* to contend with. Making matters worse, Captain Bulloch, who contracted for the construction of the rams, was careful

Confederate ironclads like the *Merrimac,* pictured here sinking the USS *Cumberland,* might have destroyed all of the wooden-hulled ships of the Union navy but for the fact that the North countered with its own flotilla of *Monitor*s.

to stay inside the law. To be absolutely certain that the ships could not legally be touched, he transferred ownership of the vessels to François Bravay, a French businessman, who fronted for him. Bravay claimed that the rams were being built for the pasha of Egypt and challenged the Law Officers of the Crown to prove otherwise.

Faced with the *Alexandra* decision on the one hand and a series of increasingly strident notes from Adams on the other, Lord Russell vacillated. He didn't want another *Alabama* to put to sea. Yet the law was the law. He therefore informed Adams that he had no legal grounds to hold the vessels. Then, in a complete turnabout he ordered the rams detained until it could be ascertained whether they were in fact destined for the Egyptians.

Adams, who knew nothing of Russell's sudden change of heart, but assumed he was playing the same old game, fired off an angry letter to the foreign secretary denouncing his irresponsible policy while remarking that it "would be superfluous in me to point out to your Lordship that this is war." For many years it was assumed that Adams's threat of war caused the British to reconsider their policy toward the Laird rams. Recent scholarship has demonstrated, however, that four days before his letter reached Russell the cabinet had decided to detain the rams.[19] A month later, after the pasha of Egypt had renounced all interest in them, the ships were seized and the Law Officers of the Crown began lengthy preparations for a court test that they had little hope of winning, since the *Alexandra* decision stood as solid precedent. Finally, a deal was struck between Bravay and the British government. The legal case against the rams was dropped and Bravay was allowed to sell the rams to the Royal Navy.

THE SOUTH IN CRISIS

Britain's decision to detain and then seize the Laird rams came as a shattering blow to southern hopes and had a devastating effect on relations between the Confederacy and London. Southern leaders had never been able to shake the Anglophobia that was part of their cultural heritage. In the beginning they had assumed that London would intervene on their behalf because of Britain's dependence on cotton. And when the Palmerston government acted quickly to recognize the South's status as a belligerent, it seemed they were right. But Britain's decision to acquiesce in the North's blockade, its refusal to extend full diplomatic recognition, its strong objections to the Confederacy's practice of drafting British citizens living in the South into military service, and finally its seizure of the rams led to a total break.

James M. Mason, who for more than two years remained in London waiting to be recognized as the minister from the Confederate States of America, was ordered to terminate his mission there and join John Slidell in Paris. At the same time all British consular officials in the South were ordered to leave. Before the end of 1863, Richmond had abandoned all hope of British aid and was pinning its remaining hopes on Louis Napoleon. But the emperor of the French was less inclined than ever to intervene unilaterally. His involvement in Mexico had proven more costly than he had at first imagined. Moreover, the European situation continued unstable and threatening.

By 1864 it was clear that the South's sun was at last beginning to set. This fact led both Britain and France to think in terms of improving their relationship with the Lincoln administration, possessor of the world's most powerful war machine. Napoleon cracked down on Captain Bulloch, who had transferred his operation to France and was at the time contracting for the construction of ironclad ships in French yards. Meanwhile, across the channel in London, Lord Russell demonstrated his own increasing interest in preserving peace and harmony with the North by putting a stop to the activities of Confederate guerrillas using Canadian territory for raids into the North.

In the waning days of the war the South made one last desperate effort to avoid a humiliating surrender. Throughout the entire period of the fighting the South had been at a serious disadvantage in Europe because of its commitment to the perpetuation and expansion of the institution of slavery. Now Duncan Kenner, a Louisiana congressman, was sent to Europe to offer a bargain. The South would abolish slavery in exchange for British and French recognition. A futile effort, the Kenner mission revealed only the desperation of the leaders of a failed rebellion. The South was finished, and both Britain and France knew it.

None of the great states of Europe had ever been prepared to intervene in the American Civil War unless Britain led the way. And the Palmerston government had no compelling reason to take such a gamble. "King Cotton" turned out to be sheer fantasy. On the political front it is important to note that Lord Palmerston headed a shaky government that might well have fallen had he pressed for the recognition of the South and war with the United States. Finally, the unstable European political situation was a positive disincentive to intervention. With Greece in rebellion, Poland in flames, and Austria and Prussia struggling to decide who would unite Germany, the last thing in the world London needed was an American war.

Frequently in the past the United States had taken advantage of Europe's political difficulties to advance its own interests. Now these same distractions served to keep Britain and all of Europe neutral while the outcome of the war was decided on North American battlefields.

ENDNOTES

1. M. B. Hammond, quoted in Frank L. and Harriet Chappell Owsley, *King Cotton Diplomacy* (rev. ed., University of Chicago Press, Chicago, 1959), p. 16; The *Richmond Whig*, quoted in H. C. Allen, *Great Britain and the United States* (St. Martin's Press, N.Y., 1955), p. 476.

2. Confederate soldier, quoted in David P. Crook, *The North, the South, and the Powers, 1861–1865* (John Wiley and Sons, N.Y., 1974), p. 21.

3. Lord John Russell, quoted in Brian Jenkins, *Britain and the War for the Union* (Queens University Press, Montreal, 1974), I, p. 170.

4. Henry Adams, *The Education of Henry Adams* (Random House, Modern Library ed., N.Y., 1946), p. 104.

5. William H. Seward, quoted in Glyndon Van Deusen, *William Henry Seward* (Oxford University Press, N.Y., 1967), p. 282.

6. William Gladstone, quoted in H.C. Allen, *Great Britain and the United States*, p. 456.

7. Lord John Russell, quoted in Norman B. Ferris, *Desperate Diplomacy, William H. Seward's Foreign Policy, 1861* (University of Tennessee Press, Knoxville, Tenn., 1976), p. 37.

8. Seward, quoted in David Donald, *Charles Sumner and the Rights of Man* (Alfred A. Knopf, N.Y., 1970) p. 23; see also Brian Jenkins, *Britain and the War for the Union*, I, pp. 103–4.

9. Henry Adams, *Education*, p. 116; Henry Adams, quoted in H. C. Allen, *Great Britain and the United States*, p. 456.

10. Charles Francis Adams diary entry for June 10, 1861, quoted in Charles Francis Adams, "Seward and the Declaration of Paris," Massachusetts Historical Society, *Proceedings*, XLVI, p. 41.

11. Robert Bunch, quoted in Frank L. and Harriett Chappell Owsley, *King Cotton Diplomacy*, pp. 233–34.

12. Lord Lyons and Lord Russell, both quoted in Crook, *The North, the South and the Powers*, pp. 49, 177.

13. Seward to Adams, Nov. 30, 1861, quoted in Van Deusen, *Seward*, p. 313.
14. Henry Adams, quoted in H. C. Allen, *Great Britain and the United States*, p. 470.
15. Gladstone, quoted in Frank and Harriet Owsley, *King Cotton Diplomacy*, pp. 348–49.
16. Palmerston, quoted in Jenkins, *Britain and the War for the Union*, I, p. 176.
17. Interpretation of Britain's Foreign Enlistment Act, quoted in Frank J. Merli, *Great Britain and the Confederate Navy* (Indiana University Press, Bloomington, Ind., 1970), p. 60.
18. L.Q.C. Lamar, quoted in Jenkins, *Britain and the War for the Union*, II, p. 240.
19. E. D. Adams, *Great Britain and the American Civil War* (2 vols, London, 1925; Russell and Russell reprint, N.Y. no date) II, pp. 141–44; see also Crook, *The North, the South and the Powers*, pp. 324–27.

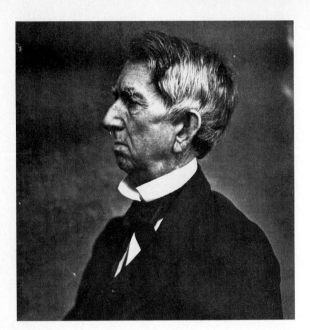

During the Civil War, Secretary of State William H. Seward managed the Union's foreign relations expertly. Following the conflict he became an outspoken exponent of both trade and territorial expansion.

12

KEEPERS OF THE FLAME:
Seward and Grant, 1865–1876

The Civil War ended anticlimactically. Wars sometimes do. Surrounded and with no hope of escape, Robert E. Lee surrendered his army to General Ulysses S. Grant at Appomattox Courthouse on April 9, 1865. That night Confederate and Union veterans sat together around communal campfires spinning yarns and exchanging war stories. Nearby, General Grant spotted his old friend, the Confederate corps commander General James Longstreet, and called out, "Come on, Pete, let's play another game of brag." It was all very mundane.[1]

Though most of the 800,000 men who shed their uniforms over the next few months were glad to be free from the fear of violent death and the privations of war, the transition to peacetime life was not always easy. For many the war had been a consuming reality. Its passing left a great void. This emptiness of purpose was no doubt more true for the warrior-commander Grant than for most others. It is perhaps not surprising, then, that like great military leaders before and since, Grant, who had been lionized by the nation for his achievements, imagined he could dispel the emptiness he felt by finding another war to fight. He didn't have far to look.

Even before the South's final defeat, Grant began to pay close attention to developments south of the Rio Grande. In 1864 the Emperor Louis Napoleon of France culminated a three-year intervention in Mexico

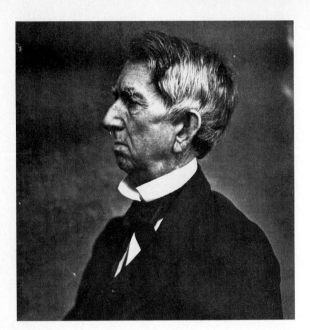

by offering the Archduke Maximilian of Austria the throne there. Ignoring State Department protests, he also placed an army of twenty-eight thousand regulars in Mexico. The army's mission was to crush the guerrilla forces of President Benito Juárez, who opposed Napoleon's imperial ambition.

With Appomattox behind him, General Grant prepared to give the French his complete attention. At the end of the war he ordered General Philip Sheridan to take command of a 52,000-troop force on the Rio Grande and laid plans to send General John Schofield into Mexico itself at the head of an army of former Confederate and Union soldiers. But the general's plans for this war after the war came to nothing. Secretary of State Seward found other means of ending Napoleon's Mexican adventure. As for Grant, his future lay elsewhere.

Seward, an admirer of John Quincy Adams and a committed expansionist, felt certain that Mexico was destined to become part of the United States. Even in 1864, with French troops stationed there, he thought that soon Mexico would be "opening herself as cheerfully to American immigration as Montana and Idaho are now."[2] But first, of course, the French had to go.

Not long after the first French troops set foot on Mexican soil, Seward warned Paris that any attempt to establish a monarchy in Mexico would be "injurious and practically hostile" to the United States. But with the Civil War to be won and an alliance between the Confederacy and France a real possibility, he behaved cautiously. He refused to invoke the Monroe Doctrine and adopted a strict hands-off policy toward the fighting between French and Mexican forces. The press, lacking similar constraints, was often more direct. Thus the *New York Herald* warned old Europe against "ruffling the pinions of the American Eagle." "We cannot brook the interference of any European power on this continent," the *Herald* maintained, "and those who take advantage of our present troubles to intrude will someday reap the whirlwind they are surely sowing."[3]

At the end of the war Seward did not immediately harden his position toward the French, preferring instead to tighten the diplomatic screws slowly. Thus, instead of sending General Schofield into Mexico at the head of an army as Grant proposed, he sent him to France with instructions "to get your legs under Napoleon's mahogany and tell him he must get out of Mexico." During the summer of 1865, Seward increased the pressure, finally warning Napoleon that his continued presence in Mexico was "in direct antagonism to the policy of this government and the principles on which it was founded."[4]

Seward was pushing on an open door. Napoleon had never intended to become bogged down in a major war in Mexico. He had imagined that the Mexican people would welcome Maximilian and the promise of a stable government under French protection. The war had caused economic as well as political problems for him at home. Moreover, he was increasingly concerned over the threatening European political situation and the growth of Prussian power. Thus, at the first sign of serious American pressure, he gave in.

Napoleon first offered to withdraw his forces from Mexico if the United States would recognize Maximilian's government. But when Seward refused, warning that the continued presence of French troops in Mexico would jeopardize Franco-American relations, Napoleon decided to call it quits, ordering the staged withdrawal of all French forces from Mexico. Maximilian, no less a romantic than his patron, remained to fight it out with Juárez. But without French support, his government quickly collapsed. He surrendered to Juárez on May 14, 1867, and in spite of widespread appeals for clemency, met his fate before a firing squad a month later.

THE ALABAMA CLAIMS CONTROVERSY

Seward was effective in handling the Mexican question. His attempts to settle outstanding issues with Great Britain were far less successful, however. The most serious cause of friction between Washington and London had to do with the vast losses Americans sustained during the Civil War at the hands of the CSS *Alabama* and other Confederate raiders. The secretary contended that because these ships had been built in British yards and had been allowed to sail over American protests, London should pay damages for the losses they inflicted on American shipping. But Lord John Russell, still the foreign secretary, refused to acknowledge any violation of international law.

London's refusal to admit the legitimacy of the *Alabama* claims did not sit well in the United States, where the ordinarily intense level of Anglophobia had been raised to new highs as a result of Britain's wartime policies. In July 1866, the House of Representatives emphasized that point when, with a general European war seemingly near at hand, it enacted legislation authorizing American citizens to sell ships of war and munitions to nations at peace with the United States. England was on notice. It could expect America to be a distinctly unfriendly neutral if war came.

In mid-1866 a new government came to power in London and Edward Henry, Lord Stanley, took over at the Foreign Office. With Russell and the Whigs at last out of power, the time seemed right for a settlement to the claims question. Lord Stanley quickly agreed to settle the *Alabama* claims through arbitration. But there remained one sticking point. Seward contended that by recognizing southern belligerency in 1861 Britain had unnecessarily prolonged the war and should pay for losses stemming from that action. Seward was not thinking of a money payment. Anxious to establish a naval base and coaling station in the Caribbean, he had in mind all or part of the British West Indies as appropriate compensation. Not surprisingly, Lord Stanley thought otherwise. When Stanley refused to include America's indirect claims in the arbitration, the negotiations broke down.

In 1868 the American minister in London, the Maryland Democrat

Reverdy Johnson, made another attempt to resolve the claims question. From an objective standpoint, the agreement he and Lord Stanley initialed late in the year was reasonably sound. As amended by Secretary Seward it called for a commission to be made up of two members selected by each side, with a fifth umpire to be selected by the commissioners themselves. Claims that could not be settled by the four would be referred to the fifth member for a decision.

It was a simple, neat, and clean solution to a festering problem. But it suffered on a number of counts. First Johnson, anxious to establish better relations between Washington and London, ignored the all-important issue of indirect claims. Second, the jovial and easy-going envoy was selling a product—Anglo-American friendship—that few in the United States were ready to buy. Finally, Johnson made a number of serious political errors while in England that raised questions about his credibility. He spent too much time with former Confederates who had chosen exile in England over life in the postwar United States. He shook hands in public with one of the infamous Laird brothers, shipbuilders to the Confederacy, and he dined at the same table with J. A. Roebuck, a staunch supporter of Confederate interests in Parliament during the war.

When the treaty Johnson helped fashion was submitted to the Senate in January 1869, the opposition successfully branded it the work of an untrustworthy "toady." President-elect Grant opposed the agreement, and the powerful chair of the Senate Foreign Relations Committee, Charles Sumner, shredded it in a speech that ranks as one of his most impressive oratorical performances. In that speech, Sumner, like Seward earlier, demanded that the British compensate the United States for the indirect damages resulting from its recognition of southern belligerency. The senator claimed that the war had been prolonged by two years as a result of Britain's prosouthern policies and calculated that this error ought to be worth in excess of $2 billion in damages.

Though Sumner made no mention of Canada in his speech, it was generally understood that he was suggesting a trade—Canada in lieu of a cash payment. Britons and Canadians alike were infuriated. Wrote Charles Dickens: "If the Americans don't embroil us in a war before long it will not be their fault. What with their swagger and bombast, what with their claims for indemnification . . . and what with Canada, I have strong apprehensions." And the young Henry Adams wrote: "If war was his object, and Canada were worth it, Sumner's scheme showed genius . . . but if he thought he could obtain Canada from England as a voluntary set-off to the *Alabama* Claims, he drivelled."[5]

It is often the case that a new president can accomplish things that would have been politically impossible for his predecessor. This was certainly true in the case of Ulysses S. Grant. Yet even this new and popular president was chary about spending any of his political capital on a question as highly charged as the claims controversy. Grant and his very capable Secretary of State, the New York attorney Hamilton Fish, tried to avoid the issue since anything short of a clear-cut diplomatic victory would disappoint the public. As the president explained to his wartime confidant, Adam Badeau, "It is not half so important that the *Alabama* claims should be settled as it is that when they are settled it should be on terms credible to this nation. I do not see that any harm is to arise from the matter standing in an unsettled state."[6]

Grant was correct to a point. But during 1869 and 1870, Anglo-American relations continued to deteriorate, not only because of the unresolved claims controversy but also because of an intensifying dispute between Canada and the United States over fishing rights and the activities of the Fenians, Irish-Americans who provided financial support for Irish revolutionaries and who carried out armed forays across the Canadian border. At length Fish concluded that the talks with London would have to be reopened. It seemed so to the British, too. The Franco-Prussian War as well as threatening Russian moves in the area of the Black Sea were harbingers of dangers ahead.

Unofficial talks between Fish and John Rose, the Canadian minister of finance, set the stage for a negotiation. Secretary Fish abandoned talk of acquiring Canada, agreeing instead to an arbitration that would guarantee the United States an indemnity for losses suffered at the hands of the *Alabama* and other southern cruisers and would also contain an expression of regret from London. Neither Rose nor Fish made any mention of America's indirect claims.

In February 1871, an Anglo-American commission met in Washington to hammer out the details. The Treaty of Washington of 1871 was in many ways favorable to the United States. Over Canadian objections, the United States won major concessions on the fisheries question. The treaty also stipulated that the future of the San Juan Islands in Puget Sound would be settled by arbitration and that the *Alabama* claims would be decided by an arbitral board that would meet in Geneva later in the year. That commission handed down a judgment in favor of the United States in the sum of $15.5 million. The *Alabama* claims had at last been settled. The issue of indirect claims was never again raised.

After the Grant administration cashed Britain's check for the claims and the canceled voucher had been returned, Britain's foreign secretary had it framed and hung on a wall in the Foreign Office. For the British, beset by growing European problems, the settlement had been a bargain. American policy makers were just as pleased to be free of this politically explosive question.

REKINDLING THE SPIRIT OF EXPANSION

To describe William H. Seward as an expansionist and leave it at that is truly to have mastered the art of understatement. His vision of the American future amounted to nothing less than a magnificent obsession. Like Thomas Hart Benton, John Quincy Adams, and others of the preceding generation, he believed that America was to become the last and greatest of the world's empires. It was, he thought, a "higher law, a law of Providence— that empire has for the last three thousand years . . . made its way constantly westward, and that it must continue to move on westward, until the tides of the renewed and of decaying civilizations of the world meet on the shores of the Pacific Ocean."[7]

But what sort of empire did Seward envision? Was there inherent in the secretary's often grandiloquent rhetoric some carefully conceived plan? Perhaps the best way to answer that question is to suggest that there was much that was traditional about the secretary's brand of expansionism. Yet at the same time there were elements that smacked of something rather different. Like his mentor, John Quincy Adams, Seward imagined that the republic would expand territorially, carrying republican institutions with it, to the far reaches of the Western Hemisphere and beyond. Thus as early as 1853 he wrote that the "borders of the federal republic . . . shall be extended so that it shall greet the sun when he touches the tropics, and when he sends his gleaming rays towards the polar circle, and shall include even distant islands in either ocean."[8]

But to achieve this magnificent future, Seward realized that certain conditions would have to be met. First, the United States would have to become the world's dominant economic power, for, as he once pointed out to his Senate colleagues, "The nation that draws the most materials and provisions from the earth, fabricates the most, and sells the most of productions and fabrics to foreign nations, must be and will be the great power of the earth."[9]

On the domestic scene, Seward supported the development of transcontinental railroads to tie California and the West more securely to the rest of the nation and to create a vast and expanding national market for the food and manufactured goods Americans were producing. Aware of the vital importance of communications to economic development, he also became an early sponsor of a transcontinental telegraphic system. He supported high tariffs to protect domestic industries from foreign competition. Because America needed farmers to populate its undeveloped areas and cheap labor for its factories and mines, he also endorsed an open immigration policy and homesteads for settlers in the West.

Seward's program for domestic economic growth was complemented by an equally ambitious expansionist foreign policy. He envisioned the United States expanding to include Mexico and Canada as well as Russian America (Alaska). He even saw the possibility of adding Greenland and Iceland to this enormous empire. Because he recognized the importance of seaborne commerce and foreign trade to a maturing economy, he also sought a canal to provide industries located on the Atlantic seaboard with easy access to the West Coast of the United States and South America as well as to the as yet undeveloped markets of Asia.

A canal, Seward believed, would make America "the great middle kingdom" of the modern age. The United States would trade with both

Europe and Asia and would attract Europe's trade with the Orient westward, profiting enormously while developing economically. Finally, Seward sought coaling stations in the Caribbean and the Pacific. These were important as refueling stops for merchantmen trading with Latin America and the Orient and for their strategic value as naval bases, too.

ISLAND OUTPOSTS AND A CANAL

Early in 1866, on a trip to the Caribbean, Seward began planning the acquisition of bases there. These would, he asserted, "constitute a half-way station for our national commerce with South America and the Pacific Coast, an entrepôt for our trade with tropical regions and a relay for our squadrons of war." After a visit to the Island of Santo Domingo, he sent Admiral David Porter there to see Samaná Bay in the Dominican Republic for himself. An enthusiastic Porter reported that the bay "occupies a most important position in reference to the trade of the Gulf of Mexico and the interoceanic routes across Central America." That was all the encouragement Seward needed. In December 1866 he sent his son Frederick, a professional diplomat, to Santo Domingo to purchase Samaná Bay for the United States. These initial negotiations failed. But Seward kept talks going with the Dominican government while allowing his eye to stray to Haiti on the other half of the island, where the port at Môle Saint Nicolas seemed to beckon.[10]

When both countries were swept by rioting and near-anarchy in 1868, the secretary thought he heard opportunity knocking. Why not make Haiti and the Dominican Republic protectorates, restore order on the island, and in the process acquire the bases he sought? It was an ambitious scheme, too ambitious for a nation clinging to a continentalist tradition and caught up in the turmoil of Reconstruction.

At the same time that Seward vainly pursued the possibility of acquiring a base on Santo Domingo, he was involved in on-again, off-again negotiations with the Danish government for the purchase of the Danish West Indies (the Virgin Islands). At length the Danes agreed to sell two of the islands, St. Thomas and St. John, for $7.5 million. Seward was optimistic that his Danish treaty would pass the Senate. But this time he had to contend not only with the knee-jerk inclination of many in the Senate to oppose anything the Johnson administration proposed but with the forces of nature, too. With the Senate already disinclined to endorse any administration initiatives and grumbling at the cost, an earthquake rocked St. John, and a huge tidal wave swept over St. Thomas. Needless to say the treaty was never ratified.

Central to Seward's hopes for the expansion of American trade with Latin America and the Far East was his dream of an interoceanic canal. This was, of course, not a new idea. Beginning in the Polk administration and continuing until the sectional controversy brought expansionism to a temporary halt in the 1850s, a succession of American planners had shown an interest in transit rights and a canal. But no one gave the question more serious attention than Seward, who, in spite of the Clayton-Bulwer Treaty, was determined that an all-American canal would span the Isthmus of Panama.

Developments on the other side of the world convinced the secretary that it was imperative for the United States to move quickly. In Egypt, Ferdinand de Lessep's Suez Canal was coming close to completion. When that route to the Far East opened, European and even American trade might, he feared, move eastward through the Mediterranean. In that case, American interests would be subordinated "to ancient and effete Egypt."[11]

At Seward's urging, a group of New York capitalists organized the Isthmus Canal Company in 1868. Seward then went to work on the Colombians, sending the able Caleb Cushing to negotiate for the rights to build an American-controlled canal across Panama. Cushing's mission was a spectacular success. In a few days he had negotiated a treaty granting either the United States or an American company the rights Seward sought. Colombia would be paid 10 percent of the canal's net earnings until the costs of construction had been paid. Then its share of the profits would increase to 25 percent. For a brief moment Seward and his New York friends were jubilant. Then the agreement fell apart. The Colombian Senate, evidently convinced that the government had sold out too cheaply, rejected the treaty.

Seward's attempts to expand American interests in the Pacific were hardly more successful. In 1867 an American naval officer claimed Midway Island, a tiny speck of Pacific real estate. In the same year, Seward edged toward a far more important acquisition, the Hawaiian kingdom itself. After rejecting a British proposal that the two Anglo-Saxon nations guarantee the independence of the islands, the secretary negotiated a trade reciprocity treaty with the Hawaiian government. Seward's hope was that closer economic relations would pave the way for annexation. Again, however, his plans were thwarted by the Senate, where the treaty was defeated.

THE ALASKA PURCHASE

Only one of Seward's many expansionist moves actually came to fruition. In 1867 he succeeded in purchasing Alaska from the Russians. From St. Petersburg's point of view, Russian America was no longer an asset. The Russian government itself was more interested in developing the Amur River Valley than the territory it controlled across the Bering Sea. The Russian-American Trading Company, the primary economic interest in the area, had been running in the red for some years. Moreover, it was clear that the area was indefensible in war, that Russia could only hold it at a certain cost to Russian-American relations, and finally that the future of North America was for Britain and America to decide. Why not, then, turn an asset of marginal utility into cash to be used for development elsewhere? In December

1866 these considerations prevailed. The czar decided to sell Alaska to the Americans.

Early in 1867, Edouard, Baron de Stoeckl, onetime Russian Minister to the United States, arrived in New York empowered to sell Russian America. He had come at the right time. American enthusiasm for the acquisition of Canada was then very great, and Seward believed that possibilities of actually annexing that vast territory would be enhanced if it was "sandwiched" between American holdings.

Russian-American negotiations moved swiftly, with the major sticking point the price. Stoeckl had been authorized to sell for as little as $5 million but was holding out for more. When Seward offered $7.2 million the Russian was satisfied. On the evening of March 29, or so the story goes, Stoeckl appeared unannounced at Seward's Washington, home, where he found the secretary playing whist. The Russian broke the good news; he was ready to sign the papers and would be at the State Department early the next morning. Seward rose from the card table saying, "Why wait till tomorrow, Mr. Stoeckl?" The ebullient secretary of state rousted members of his staff from their homes. The surprised Russian envoy did the same. And together they worked until about four o'clock the next morning to prepare a treaty for the Senate.[12]

Some parts of the press howled their opposition to the purchase of "Seward's Icebox," attacking the secretary for what they viewed as his propensity to pick up any loose piece of real estate that happened to be available. Seward fought back, this time successfully. His greatest accomplishment was winning the support of the powerful head of the Senate Foreign Relations Committee, Charles Sumner, who, like Seward, believed that the Alaska purchase would improve chances for the annexation of Canada. With Sumner leading the way, opposition withered. The final count was 37–2 in favor. Alaska with its vast resources became an American preserve.

Though Seward left office with most of his ambitions unfulfilled, he was able to count more than his share of successes as well. Transcontinental railroad and telegraph systems tied the nation together, creating the basis for an expanding national market. He had successfully fostered a liberal immigration policy to provide American industry with a supply of cheap labor. A high tariff was in place to protect developing industries from foreign competition. And, of course, there was his crowning achievement—Alaska.

GRANT'S DOMINICAN FIASCO

If William H. Seward kept the spirit of expansionism alive in the postbellum period, President Ulysses Simpson Grant nurtured it through his eight years in office. There, however, the similarity between Seward and Grant ended. Seward had a vision that connected expansion abroad to republican ideology and the needs of a developing domestic economy. Grant, on the other hand,

President Ulysses S. Grant, who came to office in 1869, kept the spirit of expansionism alive at a time when the country was fixated on domestic considerations.

was an instinctive expansionist who gave little thought but all of his enormous energy to the idea of growth.

In 1869, Grant learned of an opportunity to acquire an outpost in the Caribbean. The president of the Dominican Republic, Buenaventura Baez, had in effect decided to sell his country to the United States. Baez felt he had no alternative, for no sooner had he taken power in 1868 than Dominican military leaders, supported by the Haitians, moved to overthrow him. Baez realized that his days were numbered unless he could find support from abroad. The best, really the only, option open to him seemed to be annexation.

The Dominican leader did not come to this conclusion on his own. Two American speculators with substantial interests on the island, "General" William L. Cazneau and "Colonel" J. W. Fabens, were instrumental in bringing Baez into what became an annexationist conspiracy. Cazneau and Fabens together with a group of New York capitalists stood to make millions if the Dominican Republic became part of the United States. They held vast landholdings as well as mining and timber concessions on the island and had a monopoly on steamship travel to and from the Dominican Republic as well.

In 1868 Cazneau and Fabens came to the United States to lobby for Dominican annexation. They found natural allies in the expansionist New York press. Thus the *New York Herald* urged annexation while describing the island as "the garden of the Antilles" sparsely populated with fertile soil and "extremely rich in gold deposits."[13] They also worked on congressmen and senators, offering bribes where necessary to win support. One man Cazneau and Fabens could not reach was Secretary of State Hamilton Fish. A former congressman, senator, and governor of New York, Fish was a gentleman of the old school who lived by principles that were fast going out of fashion in Gilded Age America. Fish wanted no part of the annexationist schemes of Cazneau and Fabens. In the first place, there was a serious risk involved. The Spanish had sent troops to pacify the Dominican Republic in 1861, imagining they could reestablish control over the island. But after four years of bloody guerrilla war, they pulled out. Fish did not want to be drawn into a similar quagmire. More to the point, Fish was both offended by the corrupt methods Colonel Fabens was using to sell the idea of annexation to the press and Congress and alive to the fact that Cazneau and Fabens stood to make millions if they succeeded.

The fact that Fish was cool to his annexationist scheme in no way deterred Colonel Fabens, who had direct access to the White House. Powerful businessmen, among them Ben Holliday of Pony Express fame, lobbied Grant in favor of annexation. Fabens also had the support of high-ranking naval officers, including Admirals David Porter and Daniel Ammen, both of whom were anxious to establish a naval base in the Caribbean. Secretary of War John Rawlins also favored annexation. But perhaps most important, Fabens had the support of the president's private secretary, General Orville E. Babcock, a personable young man on the make who sought wealth and position and wasn't particularly concerned about how he got them. Babcock, who went on to immortality by defrauding the country of millions in revenues as a member of the "Whiskey Ring," became Fabens's chief co-conspirator in an effort to convince the president to annex the Dominican Republic.

Fabens didn't realize it, but he was practicing a form of political overkill. Grant needed little persuading. Early in July 1869, the president announced more or less offhandedly to his cabinet that, because "the navy people seemed . . . anxious to have the Bay of Samaná as a coaling station," he was sending Babcock to the island on a fact-finding mission.[14] A stunned Hamilton Fish sat silent, aware that when this very stubborn president had made up his mind there was no point in arguing.

During his visit to Santo Domingo, Babcock seldom strayed far from the presidential residence, allowing himself to be wined and dined by Baez, Fabens, and others interested in annexation. He returned to the United States in December bearing not only stories of the island's fabulous wealth but a protocol calling for the annexation of Santo Domingo by the United States in exchange for a $1.5 million payment to the Baez government.

Fish wanted the president to ignore the protocol. But the delighted Grant instructed him to rework the agreement in appropriate diplomatic language. He then had President Baez and the American consular agent on the island, R. H. Perry, sign this more formal document. After the signing, Grant transferred $50,000 in arms and another $100,000 in cash from his secret service funds to the Baez government. At the same time he ordered fleet units into Dominican waters to protect the Dominican Republic from "foreign aggression or machination." Baez would not be allowed to fall before the Senate acted on the treaty.[15]

Throughout the Christmas holidays, though speculation flew thick and fast, the president managed to keep the treaty under wraps. Then, early in January, he belatedly thought about marshaling legislative support. On the evening of January 2, 1870, Grant strolled across Lafayette Square to the home of the powerful chair of the Senate Foreign Relations Committee, Charles Sumner. When the president of the United States appears unannounced at one's front door, it causes quite a stir. It certainly did with Sumner, who was entertaining two friends that night.

Grant came hoping to convince the senator to support the treaty. But he hadn't bothered to bring a copy with him, and his description of its content was very unclear. Flustered and ill at ease, he soon rose to leave. Sumner saw him to the door, remarking as he did that he would "give the subject my best thought and will do all I can rightly and considerately to aid you."[16] Grant took this as a promise of support. The senator believed he was committed only to studying the matter.

On January 10, the State Department sent the Treaty of Annexation to the Senate Foreign Relations Committee, where it remained under study for the next two months. Finally, in March, the committee reported it to the full Senate with an unfavorable recommendation. Sumner spoke for the majority in opposing the agreement.

Believing that the Massachusetts senator had violated his earlier promise of support, Grant fell into a fury, resolving then and there that if he could he would destroy Sumner politically. At the same time he began a belated but aggressive lobbying campaign on behalf of his treaty. But even as Grant lobbied, press and public opinion were turning against the agreement. Newspaper reports revealed the role that Cazneau, Fabens, and other speculators had played in Dominican affairs, emphasizing the fortunes they stood to make after annexation. The public learned, too, that a plebiscite held in the Dominican Republic, which ostensibly showed widespread support for annexation, was a fraud. At the same time, editorial pages in many metropolitan newspapers rang with warnings that once the United States had taken the Dominican Republic it would have to annex Haiti and that a long and bloody guerrilla war would be the result.

In the final analysis, it was the race issue that killed most of the public and senatorial enthusiasm for the treaty. With the question of the freedmens' future in the United States still unresolved and the whole race question a burning national issue, few were enthusiastic about annexing a large population of uneducated blacks. Sumner made the point on the Senate floor, telling his colleagues that Santo Domingo had been set apart "by a higher statute" for "the colored race. It is theirs by right of possession, by their sweat and blood mingling with the soil; by tropical position; by its burning sun and by unalterable laws of climate."[17]

President Grant had no chance against the powerful forces arrayed against him. On June 30, the Senate divided 28–28; the treaty was defeated for lack of a two-thirds majority.

GRANT'S PACIFIC QUEST

In 1869, the same year that the president became involved in his ill-fated Dominican adventure, events that took place half a world away in the ancient land of Egypt rekindled the American interest in a Central American canal. The grand opening of the Suez Canal, which provided Europe with its own passage to the Orient, was an event of such international consequence that it attracted numerous crowned heads, among them the Empress Eugénie of France, the Austrian Emperor Franz Joseph, and a Prussian crown prince. All came to pay homage to Ferdinand de Lesseps, the hero of all Europe, who for his great engineering achievement was granted, among many other

Hamilton Fish, who served as Ulysses S. Grant's secretary of state, proved to be an able if often frustrated advocate of overseas expansion.

honors, France's Legion of Honor and Britain's Grand Cross of the Star of India.

The American press was, of course, filled with descriptions of this gala opening. But for thoughtful Americans, de Lesseps's achievement was more than just the occasion for a marvelous celebration. They understood that Suez posed a direct threat to the long-standing American dream that European trade with the Orient would travel west through the United States or by way of an American-controlled canal. To a generation caught up in the throes of the industrial revolution and just beginning to look outward for markets, it also seemed clear that the Suez Canal gave European businessmen an advantage in the competition for Asian markets. An earlier generation had, of course, seen the importance of an Isthmian canal to America's future. But with the opening of the Suez route to the Indian Ocean, a Central American canal became for many a matter of necessity. Grant's secretary of the navy wrote that with "the Suez Canal . . . opened for navigation, we are doubly stimulated to such efforts as will lead to the success of our own great enterprise . . . The time has come for action."[18]

Grant, a man of few words but boundless energy, threw himself headlong into the effort to acquire canal rights across the Isthmus of Panama. Ignoring the Clayton-Bulwer Treaty, he appointed an old army friend, General Stephen A. Hurlbut, to negotiate an agreement with Colombia. Grant was, as usual, none too careful in selecting his emissary. Hurlbut was a drunk and a military incompetent who, while commanding occupation forces in Louisiana during the Civil War, had been tried and convicted on charges of taking a bribe. In this case, however, Grant's confidence was not entirely misplaced. Hurlbut managed in relatively short order to negotiate a canal treaty with Bogotá. But again the Colombian Senate balked, this time by attaching amendments to the agreement that proved unacceptable in Washington.

The indefatigable Grant refused to give up. An 1867 treaty gave the United States transit rights across Nicaragua. Grant now hoped to improve on that by winning the right to build and control a canal there. But the Nicaraguans proved no more cooperative than the Colombians.

Having more or less run out of options, Grant finally abandoned the attempt to negotiate a canal treaty. But he never lost interest in the project, either during his presidency or later. In 1872, probably at the suggestion of his good friend Admiral Daniel Ammen, he created the Interoceanic Canal Commission, authorizing it to do scientific studies and make a recommendation as to the best route for a canal. Four years later the commission recommended the Nicaraguan passage. This commission's work not only dominated American thinking on canal construction for the next quarter century, it resulted in the organization of three private American canal companies whose efforts kept the idea of a canal alive for years to come.

In the short run, it is clear that Grant, like Seward before him, had failed to solve the knotty problem of negotiating a treaty that was acceptable to the Senate, the Central Americans, and the British—the partners of the United States under the terms of the Clayton-Bulwer Treaty. But his efforts kept the idea of a canal very much alive, to be acted upon by a later generation.

President Grant was just as interested in the Pacific as he had been in the Caribbean. But whereas Secretary of State Fish had been distinctly cool to the Dominican adventure, he was if anything more enthusiastic than his chief about acquiring the Hawaiian Islands. Together the secretary and the president made a formidable team.

The Hawaiian group was discovered in 1778 by the British explorer, Captain James Cook. The first Americans to stop there were seafarers on their way to China. Then came the whalers, who made Hawaii a base of operations for the dangerous and bloody business they carried on in the North Pacific. American missionaries first arrived in Hawaii in 1820 and soon came to have an important influence on the material as well as the spiritual development of the islands.

In spite of the growing American presence there, prior to the mid-1850s American policy makers never seriously considered annexing the islands. The acquisition of colonies was contrary to America's political values and to its continentalist tradition. Moreover, bringing a large population of nonwhites under American control at a moment when the slavery question had not yet been resolved raised political and moral issues that most national political leaders wanted to avoid.

All things considered, a succession of American presidents preferred to see the islands remain independent but open to economic exploitation. Thus in 1842, when it was feared that certain European nations were showing too much interest in Hawaii, secretary of state Daniel Webster warned them off. And in 1849, after a French naval officer claimed Honolulu, Secretary John M. Clayton informed Paris that although the United States did not "covet sovereignty over" the islands, it could not "allow them to pass under the dominion or exclusive control of any other power."[19] The French, perhaps influenced by this warning, quickly abandoned their claim to the islands.

During the 1850s the American attitude toward Hawaii began to change. The acquisition of California and the establishment of a large population there created a heightened interest in the Asian trade. The development of steamships, which brought Yokohama and Canton within three weeks of American ports on the Pacific, quickened that interest while at the same time creating new needs. Hawaii, two thousand miles from San Francisco on the route to Asia, was an ideal location for a coaling station. It is not surprising, then, that in 1854, the same year in which Admiral Matthew C. Perry paid his famous visit to Japan, another American envoy should have been in Hawaii negotiating a treaty of annexation with the Hawaiian king.

Though President Franklin Pierce was an enthusiastic expansionist, the treaty, which called for Hawaiian statehood, went too far even for him.

It would certainly have added fuel to the fires of sectional discord by exacerbating the race question. He therefore refused to submit the agreement to the Senate.

By the time President Grant entered the White House, two further attempts to create a binding relationship between the islands and the United States had failed. But if the diplomats had not been able to bring Hawaii into the American orbit, economic development on the islands, specifically the growing importance of the sugar industry, made integration essential. The Hawaiian sugar industry was in fact so utterly dependent upon the American market that in the early 1870s the Hawaiian king offered the United States a naval base at Pearl Harbor in exchange for guarantees that Hawaiian sugar would receive favorable treatment in the American market.

Negotiations between the Grant administration and the Hawaiian government, which took place in 1875, produced a reciprocal trade treaty that eliminated duties on most American goods marketed in Hawaii and on Hawaiian products, including sugar, sold in the United States. Because of unexpected native opposition to the alienation of territory, the treaty did not, however, provide the naval base at Pearl Harbor that American policy makers wanted.

The treaty ran into unexpectedly strong opposition at home. American sugar producers and a group of California sugar refiners led by Claus Spreckels feared Hawaiian competition would drive prices down. They were joined by a number of Republicans who, devoted to the party's traditional high tariff policies, feared that the administration might use the precedent established by this reciprocity agreement to press for the elimination or reduction of tariff barriers elsewhere, especially in relation to Canada. The treaty finally passed, however, but only after the Hawaiians accepted a Senate amendment under which they agreed not to provide a naval base or similar economic concessions to any other nation.

Grant and Fish had failed in their basic objective, the annexation of the islands. But the treaty they negotiated created a situation that led inexorably toward that end. Once it became clear that Hawaiian sugar and other products would have a privileged place in the American market, American capital flowed into the islands. Investments, especially in sugar production, boomed, while American political as well as economic influence proliferated. Before the end of the century the Hawaiian islands had become an economic appendage of the United States. As modern naval armaments made Hawaii's strategic location increasingly important, the pressure for annexation grew until finally the combination of economic and strategic considerations could no longer be resisted.

During the years immediately following the Civil War, a succession of American policy makers managed to keep the idea of expansionism very much alive. They struggled against a continentalist tradition to focus on a form of insular aggrandizement reaching beyond the "great natural boundary of the seas." They fought the inclinations of a majority that had turned inward, more concerned with the great question of Reconstruction and a myriad of domestic issues raised by the industrializing process. Their immediate successes were few. But they left an indelible legacy for those who followed and would achieve in the last two decades of the nineteenth century what the leadership of the immediate post–Civil War era had sought.

ENDNOTES

1. Ulysses S. Grant, quoted in William B. Hesseltine, *Ulysses S. Grant, Politician* (Dodd Mead and Co., N.Y., 1935), pp. 52–53.

2. William H. Seward, quoted in Glyndon Van Deusen, *William Henry Seward* (Oxford University Press, N.Y., 1967) p. 488.

3. *New York Herald*, quoted in David P. Crook, *The North, the South and the Powers 1861–1865*, (John Wiley and Sons, N.Y., 1974), p. 282.

4. Seward, quoted in Van Deusen, *Seward*, pp. 489–90.

5. Charles Dickens, quoted in H. C. Allen, *Great Britain and the United States* (St. Martin's Press, N.Y., 1955), 506; Henry Adams, *The Education of Henry Adams* (Random House, Modern Library ed., N.Y., 1946), p. 275.

6. Ulysses S. Grant, quoted in Hesseltine, *Ulysses S. Grant, Politician*, p. 229.

7. Seward, quoted in Walter LaFeber, *The New Empire, An Interpretation of American Expansion 1860–1898* (Cornell University Press, Ithaca, N.Y., 1963), p. 26.

8. Seward, quoted in Ernest N. Paolino, *The Foundations of American Empire: William H. Seward and U.S. Foreign Policy* (Cornell University Press, Ithaca, N.Y., 1973), p. 7.

9. Seward, quoted in LaFeber, *The New Empire*, pp. 26–27.

10. Seward, quoted in Paolino, *The Foundations of American Empire*, p. 127; David Porter, quoted in *ibid.*, p. 122.

11. Seward, quoted in *ibid.*, p. 142.

12. Frederick W. Seward, *Reminiscences of a War-Time Statesman and Diplomat, 1830–1915* (G. P. Putnam's Sons, N.Y., 1916), p. 362.

13. The *New York Herald*, quoted in Allan Nevins, *Hamilton Fish* (Dodd Mead and Co., N.Y., 2nd. ed., 1957), p. 267.

14. Grant, quoted in *ibid.*, pp. 264–65.

15. Grant, quoted in *ibid.*, p. 310.

16. Charles Sumner, quoted in David Donald, *Charles Sumner and the Rights of Man* (Alfred A. Knopf, N.Y., 1970), p. 437.

17. *Congressional Globe*, 41st Congress, 3rd sess., December 21, 1870, pp. 226–27, 231; see also Donald, *Charles Sumner and the Rights of Man*, pp. 442–43.

18. George M. Robeson, quoted in Charles S. Campbell, *The Transformation of American Foreign Relations 1865–1900* (Harper and Row, N.Y., 1976), p. 61.

19. John M. Clayton, quoted in Mary Williams, "John Middleton Clayton" in *The American Secretaries of State and their Diplomacy*, ed. Samuel Flagg Bemis (Alfred A. Knopf, N.Y., 1927), VI, p. 14.

Benjamin Harrison's administration developed a coherent strategy for expansion that placed an emphasis on foreign markets, the development of a modern navy, and overseas bases to service that navy.

13

SLOUCHING TOWARD EMPIRE, 1877–1895

For more than a decade first Secretary of State William H. Seward and then President Ulysses S. Grant struggled in the face of popular disinterest and a variety of domestic political and economic preoccupations to keep the spirit of expansionism alive in the United States. They were largely unsuccessful. But beginning in the 1880s new forces came into play that strengthened expansionism's appeal among policy makers, opinion leaders, and the public at large. The change was not immediate or even particularly dramatic. Nevertheless, one may find in the foreign policy of the early 1880s the germ of what would later develop into a headlong rush toward empire.

There were a variety of reasons for this change. First, in the post–Civil War era the United States emerged as a nation not to be trifled with. It was only natural, then, that at least some members of the postwar generation should have found themselves in rebellion against a foreign policy tradition that denied America a place among the world's great powers. Looking back on those days, Henry Adams wrote that by 1867 "the revolution since 1861 was nearly complete, and for the first time in History the American felt himself almost as strong as an Englishman. He had thirty years to wait before he should feel himself stronger."[1] Certainly then, one of the forces at work moving the country toward a more assertive foreign policy was a developing sense of national greatness.

Others, not necessarily concerned with prestige, believed that America's domestic economic problems might best be resolved by an aggressive search for overseas economic outlets. In the decade prior to the Civil War, America began its rapid rise toward economic maturity. The war put a temporary stop to this development, damming up the creative impulses that drove the industrial revolution. But with the coming of peace, the latent tendencies of the prewar era quickly reasserted themselves. The economic growth rate of the United States during the last third of the nineteenth century was astonishing. Between 1869 and 1901 the gross national product skyrocketed from about $9 billion to just a bit beyond $37 billion. Farm production tripled in this period, but it was industrial growth that was truly phenomenal, increasing by nearly six times.

Unhappily, economic growth was not accompanied by stability and general prosperity. On the contrary, this period was marked by repeated economic depressions, the first lasting from 1873 to 1878 and the last beginning in 1893 and continuing for four long and painful years. Even in the 1880s, a decade unmarked by a major depression, economic instability was the rule. The unemployment and general human distress that characterized the period were constant reminders of the yawning chasm that had developed between the rich and the middle class on the one hand and a growing population of poor people on the other. The once nearly homogeneous republic was developing distinct classes and, some thought, the potential for class conflict.

A number of contemporary observers believed that social instability was directly related to the enormous burst of productivity the American economy was experiencing. America had, it seemed, become too productive. The surpluses it produced glutted the marketplace, driving price levels down and triggering depression, unemployment, and social disorder. A more aggressive foreign policy that placed a premium on the development of foreign markets to absorb domestic surpluses, these same observers believed, was the solution to this problem. Thus the Republican expansionist John A. Kasson explained that if America did not look outward for markets, "our surplus will soon roll back from the Atlantic coast upon the interior, and the wheels of prosperity will be clogged by the very richness of the burden which they carry, but cannot deliver."[2]

Nor could the United States afford to wait very long before asserting itself. The great European powers, having begun a new round in the old game of empire building, were already busy in Asia and Africa. The United States would have to act decisively or it would miss its chance. Thus it was with a certain sense of urgency that the *Boston Sunday Herald* called South America "the great market for our manufactures . . . [which] lies at our door neglected." Other expansionist journals pointed to the Near East and Asia as likely areas for trade expansion. The *American Protectionist*, for example, described "China and Japan . . . [as] one of the largest outlets that we may ever be able to secure for our products of all kinds."[3]

The decade of the 1880s does not represent a revolution in American foreign policy. Most Americans remained preoccupied with domestic problems and wedded to a foreign policy tradition that placed a priority on restraint and noninvolvement in the affairs of other nations. Still, there was a restiveness on the part of some, a dissatisfaction that led a few to want to test the waters of international affairs in ways never before attempted. American diplomacy in the early part of the decade was a compendium of contradictions, aggressive and yet built on the shifting sands of self-doubt, assertive yet lacking in confidence. The fledgling was testing its wings. A few years more and it would be ready to soar.

BLAINE'S SPIRITED DIPLOMACY

When the Republican "Half-Breed" James A. Garfield moved into the White House, he selected an old friend, James G. Blaine, to be his secretary of state. Blaine, the incarnation of Gilded Age politics, was a man of enormous charm and wit, the most popular politician of the era, and unblushingly corrupt. His foreign policy was intended to appeal both to those who sought to establish America as a great power and those interested in trade expansion. Leading America toward greatness, Blaine believed, would also lead him to a prize that had thus far eluded him, the presidency.

Blaine focused his attention on Latin America—an area of obvious geographical importance, a place where the United States might reasonably expect to assert itself successfully, and one where American businessmen would have a better than average chance of developing expanded markets. His strategy was simple—to establish the United States's credentials as politically preeminent in the hemisphere while at the same time reducing European influence there. Once these goals had been accomplished, he felt certain that economic opportunities would follow.

At the time that Blaine took over the State Department, the War of the Pacific between Chile and Peru had not yet been settled. A bit closer to home a boundary dispute between Mexico and Guatemala threatened to flare into violence at any moment. By intervening to resolve these disputes, Blaine sought to further his ambitions. As Stephen A. Hurlbut, his minister to Peru put it, the policy of the United States was to intervene between Chile and Peru "in such a way as to compel an honorable peace, thus securing lasting national prestige and commercial superiority for us."[4]

If Blaine's approach was more or less theoretically sound, his policy broke down in practice. Blaine lacked subtlety, made poor appointments to key positions in Latin America, and failed to control the behavior of his representatives once they had gone abroad. Most important, he failed to appreciate the fact he could not safely adopt an aggressive Latin American policy when he lacked support for that policy at home

Blaine's approach to the War of the Pacific is a case in point. The war had been a mismatch from the start. By the time Blaine came on the scene, the Chilean army had overrun the rich guano and nitrate-bearing territory of Tarapaća and occupied the provinces of Tacna and Arica further to the north. The Peruvian army had collapsed as had the government. The only representative body left in the country was an ad hoc government headquartered in Lima, one the Chileans refused to recognize because it would not agree to cede Tarapaća as part of a settlement.

Without giving any consideration to what he would do if the Chileans rejected his proposals, Blaine urged them to surrender their conquests and make peace without demanding territorial concessions. At the same time, unbeknown to the secretary, who should have been paying closer attention, his blundering minister in Lima gave the government there a clear signal that the United States was prepared to intervene rather than see Tarapaća change hands. Encouraged by this remarkable news, Peru quite naturally showed no interest in making peace.

The Chileans, meanwhile, who saw Blaine's diplomacy as a naked attempt to steal the fruits of their military victory, were furious and in no mood to give in to his pressure. They clung to Tarapaća, Tacna, and Arica and tried to organize their own Peruvian government, one willing to cede the territory they wanted. As for Blaine, since neither Congress nor the public would support a military option, he was left helpless and humiliated. His first effort at establishing American preeminence in the Americas had been a complete failure.

Blaine's initial intervention in the dispute between Guatemala and Mexico over the province of Chiapas had about the same result. The dictator of Guatemala at this time, Rufino Barrios, was more talented and ambitious than most Central American leaders in terms of both his ability and vision. It was his ambition to unite the many weak Central American states into a single stable national state ruled from Guatemala City. He also seems to have accepted the necessity of American predominance in the region. Since Barrios's ambition coincided with Blaine's purposes, the secretary took Guatemala's side in her quarrel with Mexico—but to no effect, save to irritate the Mexicans.

When Blaine took over the State Department, he assumed that he would serve for a rather long period during which he would set American foreign policy on a new course. But fate cut short his tenure at State. On July 2, 1881, just four months after taking office, President Garfield was felled by an assassin's bullet. He died two months later.

Vice-President Chester A. Arthur followed Garfield into the White House. A member of the opposing "Stalwart" faction of the badly divided Republican party, Arthur wanted Blaine out. The secretary, however, clung to office for several months after Garfield's death. During this period he took a number of important foreign policy initiatives in Central and South America as well as in the Pacific. He seems to have had two purposes in doing this. First, he wanted to bind the Arthur administration to the new trail he was blazing. Second, he was still counting on his record as secretary of state to help carry him into the White House.

By no means was Blaine the first American diplomat to concern himself with Isthmian questions, nor would he be the last. But in 1881 the situation in Panama did seem more than ordinarily threatening to American interests there. Two years before, in 1879, the Colombians granted a canal concession to a group of French capitalists headed by Ferdinand de Lesseps. The presence of important French economic interests in Panama naturally raised fears in Washington that European political penetration would follow. Thus when Blaine received a report indicating that Bogotá had invited a consortium of five European governments to join in a treaty guaranteeing Colombia's sovereignty over the isthmus as well as the neutrality of the projected canal, he became extremely aggitated.

The State Department had no objection to foreign investment in a canal project. But in a warning to the powers, Blaine asserted that the strategic and economic importance of Panama to the United States was so great that he insisted upon political predominance there. And while Washington would not oppose the peacetime use of the canal by all nations, a waterway would be too important from a strategic point of view for the United States to allow foreign military forces to use it in time of war. Blaine didn't mention the Monroe Doctrine in his warning—he didn't have to.

In the months between Garfield's death and his own resignation in December, Blaine moved to further assert America's Central American claims. The Clayton-Bulwer Treaty had long been an obstacle to American ambitions in the region. In a note to the British foreign secretary, Blaine demanded that the treaty be revised to allow the United States to build, fortify, and control a canal across Nicaragua. Describing the Nicaraguan route as a "purely American waterway to be treated as part of our own coastline," he explained that it was "the fixed purpose of the United States to confine it strictly and solely as an American question, to be dealt with and decided by the American governments."[5]

Blaine could hardly have been surprised when London rejected his almost impertinent demand. He probably wasn't even disappointed. His object had not been to resolve this long-standing problem but to set the United States firmly on a course toward its resolution along lines that would assure both American control of a Nicaraguan canal and political preeminence in Central America.

The secretary of state matched his bold stand on the question of the canal with an assertion of predominance over the Hawaiian Islands. In the years following the enactment of the 1875 reciprocity treaty, Hawaii's plantation economy grew beyond anyone's wildest imaginings. One result was a chronic labor shortage on the islands. The problem remained unresolved when in 1881 the British consul there suggested to King Kalakaua that large numbers of coolie laborers from Britain's Asian empire be recruited to solve the problem.

Blaine viewed the prospect of a large group of British subjects migrating to the islands as another threat to American hegemony in Hawaii, since they might one day come to outnumber the native Hawaiians and Americans on the islands. In a warning to the Foreign Office, Blaine contended that Hawaii was "a part of the American system of states," and the "key to the North Pacific trade." As such the United States could not "permit any changes" that might tend to "cut it adrift from the American system" to which it clearly belonged.[6] Blaine never actually used the word "protectorate" in describing the relationship that existed between the islands and the United States. He came very close to it, however, and in so doing took a major step in the direction of annexation.

Blaine's most ambitious initiative in those last frantic weeks before he finally resigned focused on the whole of Latin America. As part of this strategy he developed a more assertive policy regarding the war between Chile and Peru. He instructed William H. Trescot, his special emissary to the two warring states, to warn Santiago that the United States would not sit idly by if it persisted in its demand that Peru cede Tarapaća as the price of peace. In instructions which one historian has described as coming "dangerously near to the language of an ultimatum" he threatened to organize a Joint *démarche* (diplomatic countermove) of western hemispheric republics in opposition to Chilean aggression.[7]

Blaine next issued invitations to most of the governments of the Americas to meet in Washington in what would have been the first Pan-American congress. The stated object of the gathering was to find methods of eliminating war from the Americas. Its unstated purposes were to make it clear to the Chileans that Blaine meant what he said and to establish the United States's claim to leadership, perhaps even hegemony, throughout the Western Hemisphere.

ARTHUR AND FRELINGHUYSEN

Blaine retired from the State Department on December 19, 1881, before any of his policies could come to fruition. He was replaced by the Republican "Stalwart," Frederick T. Frelinghuysen. Cautious by nature, and no doubt also motivated by political considerations, the new secretary of state moved quickly to undo most of what Blaine had set in motion during his last weeks in office. He retreated from the extreme position his predecessor had taken with regard to the boundary dispute between Guatamala and Mexico, canceled the planned Pan-American conference, and softened the American position with regard to the continuing War of the Pacific.

Clearly Blaine had gone too far and too fast for Arthur and Frelinghuysen. Yet for them, too, expansionism was an appealing idea. This is nowhere better illustrated than in Central America, where Frelinghuysen's course was no less assertive than Blaine's. Not only did the new secretary of state aggressively pursue the vision of an American-controlled canal across Central America; he made a decision that was of vital importance for any future canal project. Frustrated by the inability of private companies to come up with the capital necessary to build a canal, he and President Arthur agreed that it should be built, owned, operated, and defended by the government of the United States.

The Clayton-Bulwer Treaty remained an obstacle to the achievement of American hopes for a canal. Though less truculent about it, Frelinghuysen picked up where Blaine had left off, urging the British to agree that the treaty should be abrogated by mutual consent. Two years of frustrating diplomacy followed, until finally the secretary decided simply to disregard American commitments to Britain. Early in 1884 he plunged into negotiations with the Nicaraguans. In December, he and Joaquin Zavala, a former president of Nicaragua, signed a convention granting the United States the right to build a canal across that Central American country.

In submitting this agreement to the Senate, President Arthur used the by then traditional argument that this "path between the seas" would open Asia and the West Coast of South America to American trade. He lobbied vigorously on behalf of the treaty, as did the secretary of state. But this was early 1885, and Arthur was a lame-duck president with little influence over the Senate, where the treaty became a partisan issue. Democrats opposed ratifying the agreement, arguing that the United States could not ignore the Clayton-Bulwer Treaty without running grave risks. They also charged that Nicaraguan officials had been bribed to agree to the canal convention. When the vote finally came, the treaty failed for lack of the necessary two-thirds majority. The Senate agreed to reconsider the question in the next session. But when the Democrat Grover Cleveland took office in March 1885, he withdrew the treaty.

There was never any doubt in Frelinghuysen's mind that, once completed, the Nicaraguan canal he envisioned would have to be defended and that for this purpose the United States would require Caribbean naval bases guarding its approaches. During his three years in the State Department not one but two opportunities to acquire such bases materialized.

The first of these came about as a result of foreign threats to the Venezuelan dictator, Antonio Guzmán Blanco, who sat uneasily in his presidential palace. In the early 1880s Guzmán Blanco was feeling pressure from both London and Paris. For almost forty years the British government and Caracas had engaged in an on-again, off-again quarrel over the boundary dividing British Guiana from Venezuela. Now the British seemed determined to occupy the territory they claimed. Serious as this situation was, it paled in significance compared to the troubles the Venezuelan dictator was having with the French, who were pressing Caracas for payment of long-standing debts to French creditors.

Convinced that the British and French both intended to move against him, Guzmán Blanco turned in panic to the Arthur administration. In the autumn of 1883 he offered his country as a virtual protectorate of the United States in return for an alliance. Guzmán Blanco was not in a bargaining mood. There is no doubt that had the administration been interested it could have obtained a naval base as part of the deal.

At about the same time, a similar opportunity arose in Haiti, where the resident dictator, Lysius Salomon, was attempting without much success to crush a revolt. Salomon, who was also engaged in a dispute with the British over log-cutting rights on the island of Tortuga, was convinced that the rebels were being supported from London. He seems to have concluded that his days were numbered when, in September 1883, British, French, and Spanish troops went ashore at Port-au-Prince to put down a riot there. Though Salomon had earlier taken a strong anti-American line, he now appealed to Washington for support, offering in return to cede a naval base on Tortuga or at Molê Saint Nicolas.

Frelinghuysen considered these proposals and was evidently tempted by the Haitian offer. At least he sent a naval vessel to Port-au-Prince to survey the port. Finally, however, and in spite of the fact that Caribbean naval bases did seem vital to the security of the projected canal, he refused to become politically entangled with either Caribbean nation. Frelinghuysen reasoned that no matter how tempting the prize, the political guarantees that these two dictators demanded would have gone far beyond anything the United States had ever undertaken before. Even if he had been willing to extend the sort of guarantees required, Congress would certainly have repudiated his actions, just as it had repudiated earlier initiatives undertaken by Seward and Grant.

The power of expansionism was growing, but it had not yet reached its zenith. The nation was not yet supportive enough of an expansionist policy to accept such political obligations, and the secretary knew it. Thus he ruefully explained in rejecting the Haitian offer of a naval base that the United States had "never deemed it needful to their national life to maintain impregnable fortresses along the world's highways of commerce."[8]

The fact that neither Congress nor the public was as yet prepared to agree to political or military commitments even for the purpose of securing a canal and its approaches did not entirely discourage Frelinghuysen, who attempted to achieve certain of his purposes by other means. Like Blaine, he hoped to be able to reduce the European influence in the Caribbean region while at the same time extending the Monroe Doctrine and American economic opportunities there. He chose as the instrument to achieve these aims the bilaterally negotiated trade reciprocity treaty. The effectiveness of this device in developing a close and profitable economic relationship while simultaneously building political influence had already been demonstrated in Hawaii. The secretary reasoned that the same result could be achieved through the negotiation of similar treaties with nations closer to home.

Before he was through, Frelinghuysen had negotiated reciprocity treaties with the Dominican Republic and Mexico. He also sent Ambassador John W. Foster to Madrid to negotiate a similar agreement with Spain that would open Cuba and Puerto Rico to American economic penetration. Foster, who succeeded where statesmen of an earlier generation had failed, described his treaty as "annexing Cuba in the most desirable way."[9] He meant, of course, that the United States could have the economic advantage of almost uninhibited trade with the island while avoiding the nasty political implications of either governing a subject people or incorporating large numbers of people viewed as racially inferior into the Union.

Like the canal treaty, all of the reciprocity agreements so painstakingly negotiated were defeated in the Senate by a phalanx of Democrats and high tariff Republicans. Arthur and Frelinghuysen had failed. But it was not for lack of trying. Their defeat suggests very clearly that partisanship and traditionalist attitudes toward foreign policy could still combine to command a congressional majority. But their commitment to the development of an American interoceanic canal even at the risk of serious difficulties with Britain and their attempted use of reciprocity treaties to expand American economic opportunities and political influence in the Caribbean speak volumes for the growing power of the idea of expansionism.

HARRISON AND BLAINE

During the first Cleveland administration (1885–89) America's expansionist tendencies remained latent. The president himself was primarily responsible. Though he endorsed the idea of trade expansion, he was not prepared to do anything about it. Cleveland's first administration was characterized by an extreme unwillingness to risk foreign entanglements. He took a minimalist approach to foreign policy, reacting only to those issues that demanded his attention, such as a dispute with London over the perennial fisheries question.

Benjamin Harrison, the Republican who replaced Cleveland in the White House in 1889, showed none of his predecessor's lack of interest in international affairs. On the contrary, during his administration "the annexation of trade" and overseas expansion became important ingredients in America's developing foreign policy.

Harrison had next to nothing in common with his warm and affable secretary of state, James G. Blaine, who now returned to the State Department. The historian Walter LaFeber recalls that a contemporary once described Harrison, a cold and distant Hoosier lawyer, as the sort of fellow who could keep ice cubes in his pockets on a hot July day "and never lose a drop." Yet Harrison and Blaine were in complete accord on America's foreign policy objectives. Blaine spoke for the administration when he remarked that the country's "great demand is expansion. I mean expansion of trade with countries where we can find profitable exchanges."[10]

Blaine's first opportunity to begin the conquest of new markets came almost immediately. In 1888, President Cleveland, reacting to a growing demand for closer economic ties with Latin America, organized Washington's first Pan-American conference. Seventeen nations attended. But when the conference convened the next year Cleveland wasn't there to greet them.

For Blaine, who had sponsored a similar conference eight years earlier only to have his initiative repudiated by Secretary Frelinghuysen, the conference came as a heaven-sent opportunity. He hoped the delegates would endorse the creation of a regional customs union that would reduce or eliminate tariff barriers on the products of western hemispheric nations while maintaining higher tariffs on the products of all non-American states. Such a two-tiered system would have created vast opportunities for trade expansion throughout the hemisphere. He also sponsored the creation of an intercontinental railroad network and hoped to stimulate the growth of steamship connections for the same purpose. Finally, to encourage the political stability that was so vital to foreign investment and general economic growth, he championed the idea of a regional agreement to resolve disputes among western hemispheric nations by arbitration.

The secretary's best efforts notwithstanding, he achieved few tangible results. Latin Americans feared that a customs union would lead to the domination of their economies by their powerful northern neighbor. Some also believed that since the United States competed with them in the production of food stuffs and raw materials, it was not a natural trading partner. They concluded that it would continue to be in their interest to focus on Europe, where raw materials and foodstuffs found a better market. Nor were the delegates ready to consider Blaine's planned arbitration agreement.

This first Pan-American conference was not a complete failure, however. The delegates established a special railroad commission to work on plans for a hemispheric rail system and recommended the creation of an inter-American bank. More tangibly, they created the International Bureau of the American Republics. Housed in Washington in an elegant building provided by the steel mogul Andrew Carnegie, this organization evolved into the Union of American Republics and since 1948 has been known as the Organization of American States.

Blaine did an enormous amount of good for United States–Latin American relations during the conference. Had he been free to continue the wooing uninterrupted, who knows what he might have achieved? Unhappily, however, in 1891 a crisis boiled up in Chilean-American relations that revealed the mailed fist beneath the gloved hand Blaine had extended at the conference.

The British, with a large colony of their own nationals in Chile, had not only dominated the market for foreign goods there but had wielded considerable influence over a succession of Chilean governments. That was the case until 1886, when a pro-American president, José Balmaceda, took power. From that time until 1891, when civil war broke out, American influence in Chile grew steadily, while Britain's position there deteriorated.

The Chilean Civil War was replete with significant international overtones. President Balmaceda looked to the United States for support, while his opponents, the Congressionalists, cultivated the British and to a lesser extent the Germans. All sides clearly understood what was at stake. If Balmaceda won, the United States could look forward to continued good relations with his government and in all likelihood an increased share of the Chilean market. British interests would best be served by a Congressional victory.

During the war the United States supported Balmaceda by illegally seizing a shipment of arms intended for the Chilean rebels, stationing a naval force off the Chilean coast as a symbol of American support for the government, and, much to the annoyance of the Congressionalists, offering its good offices in an attempt to arrange a compromise settlement when it became clear that the Balmacedists were about to be defeated. The English played a similar game, rendering valuable services to Congressional forces during the war. It is not surprising, then, that after the rebels had triumphed the English found themselves in a most advantageous position. "We may now dismiss our fears . . . in regard to the United States influence in Chile," John G. Kennedy, the British Minister in Santiago, reported. He was also pleased to note that Patrick Egan, the American envoy, was "in very bad odour."[11]

The new government in Santiago was, not unnaturally, bitter toward the United States for the role it had played during the war. That bitterness was only exacerbated when Patrick Egan, the American minister in Santiago, offered sanctuary to some eighty Balmacedists fleeing revolutionary justice. When Egan refused a demand from the Chilean government to surrender these refugees, police surrounded the American ministry. There was even some talk of setting fire to the building to force an exodus.

It was at this point, with a full-fledged international crisis brewing, that Captain Winfield S. Schley of the USS *Baltimore*, which was then anchored in Valparaíso harbor, made a serious error in judgment. He gave shore leave to 117 members of his crew. The sailors did what sailors ashore traditionally do. They got drunk and in a variety of ways made themselves unappreciated. At the True Blue Saloon, a waterfront dive, a riot broke out in which two sailors were killed and seventeen others were injured. In his report to Washington, Schley, who didn't even bother with an investigation, laid complete responsibility for this unhappy occurrence on the Chileans. The sailors, Schley charged, were the victims of an unprovoked, premeditated attack in which the police participated.

The battle of the True Blue Saloon was not an isolated incident but the culmination of a rapidly developing estrangement between Santiago and Washington. If Schley asked no questions, taking the word of his men as gospel, Harrison did the same. He ordered the navy readied for sea and after a brief delay sent an ultimatum to the Chilean government. It would apologize and make reparations for the attack on men wearing the American uniform or face the consequences. Without waiting for the Chilean reply, Harrison delivered a special message to Congress. Describing the affair at the True Blue Saloon as an unprovoked attack on the national honor, he left it to Congress to take "such action as may be deemed appropriate."[12] Only a speedy surrender by the Chileans kept the situation from becoming very ugly.

Harrison's jingoistic response to events in Chile was, of course, popular at home. But at the same time it confirmed old Latin American fears and suspicions of American purposes, erasing the good that had been done by the Pan-American conference. This business of conquering trade was turning out to be more difficult than the government had at first imagined

MAHAN ON SEA POWER

One important manifestation of this administration's determination to compete more aggressively in the international arena was its adoption of Captain Alfred Thayer Mahan's views on the relationship between naval policy and trade expansion. Although the captain's first major work, *The Influence of Sea Power upon History* (1890), had not yet been published when Harrison took office, his lectures and articles had been common fare for the country's business, intellectual, and political leaders since the middle of the preceding decade.

Mahan, president of the Naval War College from 1886 to 1889 and again from 1892 to 1893, wasn't well thought of by the old salts who ran the United States Navy. He was too much the intellectual, not at home striding the quarterdeck, shouting commands over the roar of a storm-tossed sea. But his thinking was extraordinarily influential throughout the industrialized world. Kaiser Wilhelm II of Germany, for example, was so impressed that it is said he made Mahan's works required reading for the officers of the German navy.

Like many others, Mahan was distressed by America's almost frightening ability to produce more than it was able to consume. He noted that since the Civil War the United States had concentrated on protecting the home market through high protective tariffs. But, he argued, such a policy had been made obsolete by the fact that the home market could no longer absorb even domestic production. America would have to look outward to solve the problem of the surplus. Since the same situation was developing in all modernizing countries, he believed that the inevitable outcome would be an increasingly tense struggle for access to cheap raw materials and overseas markets. Given these assumptions, Mahan concluded that to compete successfully the United States would need a large merchant fleet to carry on its foreign trade, a large navy capable of defending trade routes and lines of communications, and a network of coaling stations as well as naval bases to serve merchantmen and warships alike. Of course, too, America would need an Isthmian canal to bring the markets of the Orient and the West Coast of South America closer to the sources of American production.

Mahan's influence, which was profound, rested not only on the timeliness and seeming merit of his economic argument but also on the fact that he was able to integrate into his theories the then popular quasi-Darwinian view that the Anglo-Saxon and Teutonic peoples were in a struggle for survival with other races. Those who accepted this view, and they were many, believed that nothing less than the domination of the world was at issue. Europe and America, Mahan argued, constituted an "oasis set in the midst of a desert of barbarism." His message was clear. The struggle would be decided, Western culture would triumph or collapse, depending on whether it could resolve the problem of the surplus. The United States, Mahan insisted, could no longer settle for a policy of passive self-defense. "All around us now is strife," he wrote. "'the struggle for life,' 'the race of life' are phrases so familiar that we do not feel their significance till we stop to think about them. Everywhere nation is arrayed against nation; our own no less than others."[13]

President Harrison and other key members of the administration appear to have accepted Captain Mahan's views unquestioningly. We know beyond any doubt that Secretary of the Navy Benjamin F. Tracy used them as his guide in developing a new and revolutionary naval policy for the United States. And that was no easy task, for much needed to be changed.

During the Civil War, under the stewardship of Secretary of the Navy Gideon Welles, the United States had become a large naval power. The blockade and the necessity of protecting American shipping while tracking down the *Alabama* and other Confederate raiders demanded nothing less. But in the postwar era the navy fell quickly into decline, a victim of congressional and popular indifference, Gilded Age corruption, a small-navy tradition, and a leadership that spurned the many technological innovations that were revolutionizing naval warfare at this time.

Throughout its history the United States Navy had suffered from one problem above all others: few thought it was important. The peacetime navy was viewed as a pointless extravagance. And in wartime Americans had characteristically relied on swarms of privateers supplemented by a few fast commerce destroyers to carry the war at sea to the enemy. The militia tradition left no room for a large professional navy.

It might have been possible to maintain a small yet up-to-date navy but for two other considerations. First, after Secretary Welles retired, the Navy Department fell into the hands of a succession of Republican boodlers. Corruption and pork-barrel politics ate at the fabric of the institution. Second, the officer corps itself was badly divided between older officers, who controlled the service bureaucracy and who had grown up in the days of sail, and younger men, who believed that no matter how beautiful a fully rigged ship was when running before the wind, the future belonged to coal and steam.

The younger officers stood no chance in the battle for control of policy, especially with Admiral David D. Porter as the navy's ranking officer. A fierce enemy of technological innovation, he purged the department of all its engineering officers. One historian explains that he even went so far as to require ship commanders to "log in red ink every ton of coal consumed and to pay fines for unauthorized fuel bills."[14] Largely as a result of the efforts of Porter and like-minded officers, during a period when the world's navies were acquiring modern ironclad steam-driven vessels mounting large rifled cannon that could fire heavy explosive shells accurately over long distances, the American navy was in what might be described as a technological time warp. In 1881 the United States ranked twelfth among the nations of the world in ironclad naval strength—behind even Brazil, Chile, and China.

Early indications that change was on the way came during the Arthur administration and continued at an accelerated pace during the first Cleveland administration. But still the Navy Department had no strategic plan. Ships were built because money was available, but the navy's mission remained undefined. That all changed during the Harrison administration when Secretary of the Navy Benjamin Tracy, aided by Captain Mahan and other navalists, developed a modern strategic doctrine and then set out to build a navy capable of carrying it out.

A New York attorney and Civil War hero—he was one of a select few to win the Congressional Medal of Honor and live to tell the tale—Tracy came to the Navy Department with no background in naval affairs. But he was a superior administrator who, aware of his own inadequacies, let the experts, especially Captain Mahan, guide his thinking. He quickly committed himself to the development of a modern battleship navy capable of protecting and nurturing America's expanding foreign trade. This decision led to what Professor Walter Herrick has described as "the most revolutionary change in doctrine ever experienced by the Navy Department."[15]

Tracy amassed an enviable record during his term of office. He reorganized the Navy Department for greater efficiency, did much to take naval construction out of the hands of Republican spoilsmen, and rescued the Naval War College from those inside the navy who wanted to kill it. Most important, he was the guiding spirit behind the Naval Act of 1890. Tracy and the president had hoped for more than they got in that epochal piece of legislation. But the three *Oregon* class battleships laid down that year were as large, fast, and powerful as anything afloat. The old Jeffersonian naval tradition that depended on privateersmen and fast commerce destroyers had been replaced by a new doctrine. America would have a navy capable of standing up to the world's most powerful battle fleets. Its officers, trained in strategy and tactics at the Naval War College, would be completely professional. The country could afford nothing less.

THE SAMOAN STORY

Benjamin Harrison deplored the international scramble for empire then going on in what the young Theodore Roosevelt described as "the waste places of the earth." He was, he explained to his secretary of state, "not much of an annexationist." But Harrison did believe that "in some directions, as to naval stations and points of influence, we must look forward to a departure from the too conservative opinions which have been held heretofore."[16] He therefore approved an effort to acquire Molê Saint Nicolas as a naval base. Failing in that endeavor he tried to acquire Samaná Bay but was again frustrated. He sought Senate approval to begin the construction of a canal across Nicaragua, only to be thwarted for a third time.

If Harrison failed to achieve much in the Caribbean and Central America, his record was not so bleak in the Southwest Pacific, where he had better luck defending American interests. The Samoan Islands lie along the 14th parallel about halfway between Hawaii and Australia. British missionaries had settled there before the middle of the ninteenth century. They were soon followed by German traders and American whalers who used the magnificent harbor of Pago Pago on Tutuila Island as a base of operations from which to hunt the great sea mammals of those southerly climes.

The first political connection between the United States and the Samoans came in 1872, when an American naval officer, Commander R. W. Meade, signed a treaty with native leaders on Tutuila that granted the United States a naval base at Pago Pago. In return, Meade agreed that the island should become a protectorate of the United States.

Meade, acting without instructions, had clearly taken an extraordinary step. But his action was by no means out of keeping with the expansionist spirit that prevailed inside the Grant White House. Still smarting from the defeat over the annexation of Santo Domingo, Grant sent Meade's treaty to the Senate. But when it became clear that the treaty would not pass, he decided not to force a vote. Instead he used executive power to encourage the development of a special relationship with Samoa.

The next crucial step in the development of the Samoan-American relationship came in 1878, when the Senate agreed to a treaty with the Samoans by which the United States gained a naval base at Pago Pago. In exchange the Hayes administration agreed that if the Samoans should find themselves in difficulties with another government (the natives feared German encroachment) the United States would use its good offices to resolve the dispute. This agreement, coming at a time when the European powers were scrambling for colonies in Africa and the Pacific, evidently caused some concern in Berlin and London. Within a year first Germany and then Great Britain signed similar agreements with the Samoans. For the next five years the United States, Britain, and Germany cooperated in what amounted to a joint protectorate over the islands while recognizing King Malietoa as the legitimate local ruler.

Cooperation was the rule in Samoa because none of the powers was interested enough in the islands to seek unilateral control at the risk of a serious international incident. All of that changed, however, when Prince Otto von Bismarck, very much against his own inclinations, gave in to commercial pressures at home and propelled Germany into the scramble for overseas colonies.

Bismarck made no move in Samoa until after he had made certain that he would not encounter British opposition. In 1884, at a general European conference on the governance of the Belgian Congo, British and German representatives made an agreement that was to change fundamentally the situation in the southwestern Pacific. The British gained German approval for their continued occupation of Egypt. In return they gave

Germany a more or less free hand with regard to its ambitions in equitorial Africa and the Pacific.

Having secured his flank against British interference, Bismarck made his move to acquire control of Samoa. King Malietoa reacted to growing German pressure by offering Samoa to New Zealand as a protectorate. The New Zealanders were interested but could not act without London's approval and, of course, London was bound by its commitment to Bismarck.

When the Germans learned of Malietoa's appeal to New Zealand, they acted quickly. The German consul general in Apia raised the German flag there and laid claim to the nearby Milinuu Penninsula as well. He also sponsored a local coup against the king. A new Samoan government headed by another chief, Tamasese, and backed by German power was established at Apia.

This naked grab for control of Samoa enfuriated both President Grover Cleveland and his secretary of state, Thomas Bayard. The United States had been perfectly served by the old tripartite protectorate, which guaranteed the United States the naval base and coaling station it wanted in the southwestern Pacific with a minimum of political involvement. Berlin's move threatened that position. Thus, when the German minister in Washington informed the State Department that Germany intended to take over the administration of Samoa but would be careful not to infringe on American interests there, Secretary Bayard made it clear that the United States would never agree to such an arrangement.

Bayard made an attempt to resolve the crisis through diplomacy. But a tripartite conference held in Washington in June 1887 settled nothing. Tensions mounted two months later, when a flotilla of German warships and a complement of marines arrived in Samoan waters. Germany declared war on Malietoa, recognized Tamasese's government, and then deported the deposed island king.

That, the Germans no doubt thought, should have been that. But they hadn't counted on the emergence of a band of native partisan fighters led by a popular leader named Mataafa. When Mataafa and his men ambushed a force of German marines, killing twenty and wounding another thirty, the German commanders on the scene fell into a frenzy. Their indiscriminate retaliations, threatening to American lives and property, prompted Berthold Greenebaum, the American consul, to send a frantic telegram to Washington calling for immediate naval support. Cleveland reacted immediately dispatching a flotilla of four warships to Samoa and sending a special message to Congress in which he warned that all of their assurances to the contrary notwithstanding, the Germans were not to be trusted and that their real purpose was to turn Samoa into a German colony.

Cleveland's message had the anticipated effect. There was a good deal of emotional rhetoric in Congress about protecting American rights. There was even some real action. Just before its January adjournment, Congress voted special funds for the defense of American interests in the archipelago.

The Harrison administration, then, took power in the midst of what appeared to be a full-blown crisis. But in this case there was more smoke than fire. Bismarck, never an enthusiastic supporter of overseas expansion, wanted no part of a dispute with the United States over Samoa. Enough was enough. He called for a second tripartite conference, this one to meet in Berlin.

At this point, with the Germans already beginning to backtrack, a hurricane struck Samoa. At the time seven foreign vessels (three German, three American, and one British) were anchored there. Only the British ship survived the storm. All told, 150 seamen including 49 Americans, lost their lives. The disaster at Apia, a chastening blow, seems to have cooled tempers all around.

The Berlin Conference, which convened in late April 1889, produced an agreement in six weeks. Malietoa was restored as the native king, and Samoa was granted what amounted to quasi-independence under terms not dissimilar from those that had prevailed before. Ten years later Britain withdrew from Samoa, while Germany and the United States agreed to divide the islands between themselves. Germany took control of the two largest islands, but the United States got what it wanted, Tutuila Island and the harbor at Pago Pago. Later John Hay, William McKinley's secretary of state, would write an epitaph to this affair when he explained: "Our interests in the Archipelago were very meager, always excepting our interest in Pago Pago, which was of the most vital importance. It is the finest harbor in the Pacific and absolutely indispensable to us."[17]

THE HAWAIIAN PEAR: PLUCKED AND DROPPED

John Hay's estimate of the importance of Pago Pago was most certainly an exaggeration. But no one questioned the importance of another island group that lay several thousand miles to the north and east of Samoa. The Hawaiian Islands were recognized as the strategic gateway to the Pacific Coast of North America and a vital way station on the route from San Francisco to the Orient.

The first Americans to settle in the islands were missionaries who arrived there during the Jacksonian era. The children and grandchildren of these first settlers, about two thousand in all, went into business and in the post–Civil War era came to control Hawaii's one-crop sugar economy. The preferential treatment that Hawaiian sugar received in the American market after the enactment of the 1875 reciprocity treaty made this new white aristocracy rich and powerful while at the same time creating an indissoluble bond between the islands and the United States.

It was never entirely clear when annexation would take place, but the strategic location of the islands and the economic relationship that grew in the last quarter of the century left little doubt that a wedding there would be. In 1881, during his first go-round in the State Department, Secretary of

State Blaine remarked quite pointedly that the "situation of the Hawaiian Islands, giving them the strategic control of the North Pacific, brings their possession within the range of questions of purely American policy." Like Cuba in the Caribbean, which Blaine also coveted, Hawaii was part of an "American system." Eight years later and back in the State Department, Blaine had not changed his mind. On the contrary, he insisted in a letter to the president that there were only three places outside the continental limits of the United States that were worth taking as colonies. He did not know when Puerto Rico and Cuba would fall from the Spanish tree, but Hawaii, he thought, might "come up for a decision at any unexpected hour and I hope we shall be prepared to decide it in the affirmative."[18] President Harrison and, of course, Navy Secretary Tracy were in complete agreement.

By the time Blaine wrote that letter, the economic and political connection between Hawaii and the United States had been further strengthened by the renewal of the 1875 reciprocity treaty. Under terms of this agreement Hawaiian sugar continued to receive preferential treatment in the American market and the United States held a naval base at Pearl Harbor.

Until 1890, the white planters who dominated the Hawaiian economy were satisfied with the arrangement as it stood. Some, in fact, opposed the next logical step—annexation—on the ground that under United States law they would be forbidden from bringing contract laborers (read "slaves") from the Orient to work on their plantations. But in that year the planters were dealt a harsh economic blow when Congress enacted the McKinley Tariff, which placed all foreign sugar on the free list while granting a subsidy of two cents a pound to domestic sugar growers. The value of Hawaii's sugar crop dropped by 40 percent as a result of this change, and many white planters, anxious to cash in on the new bounty, became annexationists almost overnight.

In 1891 the political situation on the islands changed, too, when King Kalakaua died and was succeeded by his sister, Liliuokalani. The new queen and her advisers deplored the growth of foreign influence on the islands and hoped to restore native rule. For more than a year tension mounted between the queen and the white aristocracy. Then, on January 14, 1893, she prorogued the Hawaiian legislature, the seat of white power, and proclaimed a new constitution that went far toward restoring native supremacy in Hawaii. Three days later, in a near-bloodless coup the white elite deposed the queen and proclaimed a new provisional government for Hawaii.

The American minister in Honolulu, John Stevens, played a major role in the coup that overthrew "Queen Lil." On his instructions Captain G. C. Wiltse, commander of the cruiser *Boston*, then anchored in the Pearl River, sent a contingent of sailors and marines ashore. Before taking up positions around the government buildings on the island, this polyglot force marched through the streets of the town intimidating natives who might otherwise have resisted the white rebels. On the day that the sailors and marines went ashore, Stevens wrote to the State Department, "The Hawaiian pear is now fully ripe, and this is the golden hour for the United States to pluck it."[19] To make that task easier Stevens extended de facto recognition to the provisional government. Shortly afterward he declared Hawaii an American protectorate and raised the Stars and Stripes on government buildings in Honolulu.

While all of this was going on, Sanford B. Dole, president of the new Hawaiian provisional government, sent a delegation to Washington seeking annexation. Not surprisingly, the Hawaiian delegates, who arrived in Washington on February 3, had the enthusiastic support of Stevens, who described them in one of his dispatches as representing "a large preponderating proportion of the property holders and commercial interests of these islands."[20]

By this time Blaine lay near death at his Bar Harbor home. And President Harrison, having been denied renomination by his party, had little enthusiasm or political capital left for even one more battle. The burden of decision making, therefore, fell to the new secretary of state, John W. Foster. A committed annexationist (he had made an attempt to purchase Hawaii from the queen in 1892), Foster was not at all interested in looking too deeply into Minister Stevens's activities during the Hawaiian coup. He did think the envoy had gone a bit far in declaring the islands a protectorate and repudiated that decision. But he went no further. Like Stevens, he wanted the islands and was not particularly concerned about how he got them.

Foster was aware that it might be difficult for a lame-duck administration to convince the Senate to approve a treaty of annexation. But the auguries were so positive that he decided to make the attempt. In the first place, there was absolutely no foreign opposition to annexation. The Germans even claimed that they "had always considered . . . Hawaii . . . a *quasi* protectorate" of the United States.[21]

At home apathy prevailed. There were of course isolated pockets of domestic opposition. Thus Carl Schurz, a leader among German-Americans and an important Republican reformer, denounced annexation as a repudiation of democratic principles and urged President-elect Grover Cleveland, about to enter the White House for his second term, to block annexation. And the *Minneapolis Times*, revealing that racism cut two ways, opposed annexation on the ground that it would certainly one day result in conferring citizenship "upon the leprous descendants of the Sandwich Island cannibals." On the other hand, imperialists agreed with the *New York Independent*, whose editor wrote: "The ripe apple falls into our hands, and we should be very foolish to throw it away." The islands would provide the United States with "perfect control of the ocean route across the Pacific. . . . We need its tropical products, and we need its harbors. . . . This will give us a dominating influence among all the islands of Oceanica."[22]

Foster sent a completed treaty of annexation to the Senate a week after the Hawaiian delegates arrived in Washington. With the general public in a more or less indifferent mood and expansionists calling for immediate ratification, the upper house would probably have approved the treaty had it not been for the intervention of President-elect Cleveland, who asked the senators for the opportunity to study the question. Since without bipartisan support the treaty would not have passed, the Senate agreed. But the annexationists were not particularly concerned by Cleveland's intervention. The president-elect had given no indication that he opposed the treaty, only that he wanted to consider it. It wasn't until a few days after his inauguration, when Cleveland withdrew the treaty from the Senate, that the annexationists began to suspect that the treaty was in trouble.

Treaty supporters failed to realize that although Cleveland was no less interested in trade expansion than they were themselves, he saw it as coming about through general reductions in the tariff and not as a result of empire building. On the contrary, he recoiled at the idea of annexing colonies and ruling over subject, non–Anglo-Saxon peoples. Moreover, Cleveland believed the United States already had what it needed in Hawaii—domination of the economy and a secure naval station. Nor would he take seriously the danger of foreign intervention in the islands. The reaction of the powers to recent events demonstrated that although the islands did not enjoy the official status of a protectorate, they were viewed in that light. Beyond these practical considerations, Cleveland was offended by the unsavory, not to say unethical, behavior of Minister Stevens and John W. Foster, both of whom seemed determined to have the islands no matter what it took.

THE BLOUNT INVESTIGATION

After withdrawing the treaty from Senate consideration, Cleveland appointed a special commissioner who was instructed to study the circumstances surrounding the Hawaiian Revolution. Georgia's James H. Blount was a twenty-year veteran of the House of Representatives who, while serving as the chair of the House Foreign Affairs Committee, had opposed both the creation of a modern navy and the construction of an isthmian canal. Since there can be no doubt that Cleveland knew of Blount's antiexpansionist sentiments, there can also be no doubt that he expected a report critical of recent American actions in Hawaii and was looking for a reason to refuse to resubmit the treaty to the Senate.

It was only after Blount's appointment that the annexationists realized Cleveland's real purposes. Reacting furiously, the *New York Commercial Advertiser* screamed:

> In ordering Old Glory pulled down at Honolulu, President Cleveland turned back the hands on the dial of civilization. Native rule, ignorant, naked, heathen, is reestablished; and the dream of an American republic at the crossroads of the Pacific—a dream which Seward and Marcy and Blaine indulged, and the fulfillment of which the more enlightened of our

65,000,000 people awaited with glad anticipation—had been shattered by Grover Cleveland, the Buffalo lilliputian![23]

The annexationists could rant to their heart's content. But the facts that Blount uncovered were irrefutable. First it was beyond doubt that John L. Stevens had been up to his neck in the revolutionary conspiracy. Blount also demonstrated that the revolution had no popular roots and was motivated primarily by the planters' desire to take advantage of the bounty the American government paid to domestic sugar growers.

Blount's report settled one point. As far as Cleveland was concerned, the treaty was dead. He refused to resubmit it to the Senate. But was that enough? An American representative had used American military power to overthrow a popular government and help establish an unpopular one. Shouldn't the United States do something to redress this wrong? Secretary of State Walter Q. Gresham thought so and recommended that the president should consider forcing the restoration of Queen Liliuokalani. But Cleveland was well aware that no matter what had taken place in the recent past, toppling a government controlled by whites to restore native rule in Hawaii would not go over well in the United States. He was, however, willing to exert a certain amount of diplomatic pressure toward this end. He therefore urged President Dole, head of the new Hawaiian government, to restore the queen to her throne. Not surprisingly, Dole demurred. In fact, through the new American minister in Honolulu, he told Cleveland to "go to Halifax."[24] The United States had recognized his government, and that, at least for the time being, was that.

In spite of his opposition to annexation, then, Cleveland was unable to reverse everything the Harrison administration had accomplished in Hawaii. The native government had been overthrown and the white elite remained in power waiting for the proper moment to press once again for annexation. That moment came five years later, when another Republican administration with trans-Pacific ambitions succeeded where Harrison had failed.

The Harrison administration had not achieved all or even most of what it had hoped for. Yet it had something that its predecessors lacked—a clearly defined policy of expansion and a sophisticated amalgam of strategies for achieving that end in the Caribbean, Central America, and the Pacific. Expansionism had come a long way since 1881.

ENDNOTES

1. Henry Adams, quoted in H. C. Allen, *Great Britain and the United States* (St. Martin's Press, N.Y., 1955), p. 518.
2. John A. Kasson, quoted in Charles S. Campbell, *The Transformation of American Foreign Policy, 1865–1900* (Harper and Row, N.Y., 1976), p. 85.
3. The *Boston Sunday Herald* and the *American Protectionist*, quoted in David M. Pletcher, *The*

Awkward Years: American Foreign Policy Under Garfield and Arthur (University of Missouri Press, Columbia, Mo., 1962), p. 181.

4. Stephen Hurlbut, quoted in *ibid.*, p. 45.

5. James G. Blaine, quoted in *ibid.*, p. 65.

6. Blaine to James Comly, December 1, 1881, *Foreign Relations of the United States, 1881* (Washington D.C., 1882), pp. 636, 638.

7. Blaine, quoted in David S. Muzzey, *James G. Blaine, A Political Idol of Other Days* (Dodd Mead and Co., N.Y., 1934), p. 75.

8. Frederick T. Frelinghuysen, quoted in Pletcher, *The Awkward Years*, p. 135.

9. John W. Foster, quoted in Michael J. Devine, *John W. Foster: Politics and Diplomacy in the Imperial Era 1873–1917* (Ohio University Press, Athens, Ohio, 1981), p. 31.

10. Blaine, quoted in Walter LaFeber, *The New Empire: An Interpretation of American Expansion, 1860–1898* (Cornell University Press, Ithaca, N.Y., 1963), pp. 105–6.

11. John G. Kennedy, quoted in Campbell, *The Transformation of American Foreign Relations*, p. 170.

12. *Messages and Papers of the Presidents*, ed. James D. Richardson (Washington, 1900), IX, p. 186.

13. Alfred Thayer Mahan, quoted in Richard Hofstadter, *Social Darwinism in American Thought* (Beacon Press, Boston, 1955), p. 188.

14. Walter R. Herrick, *The American Naval Revolution* (Louisiana State University Press, Baton Rouge, La., 1966), p. 17.

15. *Ibid.*, p. 43.

16. Benjamin Harrison to James G. Blaine, October 1, 1891, in Albert T. Volwiler, "Harrison, Blaine and American Foreign Policy, 1889–1893," *Proceedings of the American Philosophical Society*, LXXIX (1938), pp. 638–39.

17. John Hay, quoted in Howard K. Beale, *Theodore Roosevelt and the Rise of America to World Power* (Johns Hopkins University Press, Baltimore, Md., 1956), p. 59.

18. Blaine to Comly, November 19, 1881; Blaine to Lowell, December 10, 1881, *Foreign Relations of the United States, 1881* (Washington, 1882), pp. 569–70, 633–35; see also Blaine to Harrison, August 10, 1891, in *Correspondence of Benjamin Harrison and James G. Blaine, 1882–1893*, ed. Albert T. Volweiler (American Philosophical Society, Philadelphia, 1940), p. 174.

19. John Stevens, quoted in Michael J. Devine, *John W. Foster: Politics and Diplomacy in the Imperial Era*, p. 65.

20. Stevens, quoted in *ibid.*, p. 64.

21. John W. Foster, quoted in *ibid.*, p. 65.

22. The *Minneapolis Times* and *The Independent*, quoted in Ernest R. May, *Imperial Democracy, the Emergence of America as a Great Power* (Harcourt Brace and World, N.Y., 1961), pp. 15–16.

23. The *New York Commercial Advertiser*, quoted in Allan Nevins, *Grover Cleveland, A Study in Courage* (Dodd Mead and Co., N.Y., 1932), p. 553.

24. Sanford B. Dole to Albert S. Willis, *Foreign Relations of the United States, 1894*, Appendix II, (Washington, 1895), pp. 1276–82; see also Nevins, *Cleveland*, p. 559.

14

WAR AND EMPIRE:
America in World Affairs, 1895–1900

William McKinley didn't want war with Spain. But when it became unavoidable, he used the struggle to expand into the Caribbean and the Pacific. Before his assassination in 1901 he was also well on the way to establishing the canal across Central America that had been on the minds of presidents dating back to James K. Polk.

If any period in the history of American foreign policy deserves to be considered a watershed, certainly the years from 1895 to 1900 qualify. In this short span of time the United States asserted its predominance in the Western Hemisphere and fought a war with Spain that netted it imperial holdings in the Caribbean and the Pacific. By tradition a continentalist power and a reluctant participant in international political affairs, after 1898 the United States became more assertive, especially in the Far East. In the face of opposition from many of the powers already entrenched there, particularly Russia and Germany, it developed an aggressive policy designed to secure complete equality of commercial opportunity for American businessmen seeking trade and investment opportunities.

The crisis that gripped Anglo-American relations in the year 1895 came and went like a desert thunderstorm. It appeared for a moment that America and Britain were headed toward war over a question of no great consequence—the exact location of an obscure boundary dividing Venezuela from British Guiana. But war didn't come. Instead, policy makers scrambled to put out the fire. Before the end of 1896 the dispute had been resolved. On the surface it may seem that the entire affair was much ado about very little. But there was more to this crisis than met the eye. The Venezuelan boundary controversy marked the first in a series of developments that established the United States as preeminent throughout Latin America.

Britain acquired its South American colony from the Dutch in 1814. But for decades thereafter the boundary between British Guiana and Venezuela remained unknown, hidden in the Guiana Highlands, an area of tropical rain forests, vast plateaus punctuated by sheer escarpments, rushing rivers, deep gorges, and magnificent waterfalls.

In 1841 a British engineer, Sir Robert Schomburgk, braved this magnificent wilderness to draw the first boundary. But neither Caracas nor London accepted the Schomburgk line. For several decades thereafter, the boundary dispute remained unresolved, a matter of little consequence to either country. In the 1880s, however, after rich gold deposits were uncovered in the area (a 509-ounce nugget, the largest ever found, came from this region), the boundary dispute heated up.

The question might have been settled by direct talks between Caracas and London. But the Venezuelans were unwilling to negotiate. The long and corrupt rule of Antonio Guzmán Blanco, which ended in a coup in 1888, had left the country bankrupt and heavily in debt to British and other foreign creditors. The new Venezuelan leaders, who had no intention of honoring these debts, nevertheless hoped to acquire most of the gold-bearing lands of the Guiana Highlands by extending their boundary eastward beyond the Schomburgk line into areas that the British had already settled. Since direct negotiations would allow London to raise the debt question, the Venezuelans insisted that the boundary line be established through arbitration. Toward this end they appealed to Washington to intercede with London on their behalf.

President Grover Cleveland never seems to have asked himself why the Venezuelans rejected direct talks in favor of arbitration. Nor was he aware that they would only accept as arbitrators the United States or Spain, countries they believed were prejudiced in their favor. To the bluff, slow-thinking Cleveland, Caracas was just being reasonable. And so during his first administration he urged London to settle the boundary dispute through arbitration. The British agreed, but only if territory east of the Schomburgk line was excluded. Not surprisingly, Caracas was not interested.

Cleveland returned to the White House in 1893, but at first he paid no attention to renewed Venezuelan requests that the United States again intercede with London on its behalf. The economic crisis and social unrest associated with the depression which struck in that year, the battle to uphold the gold standard against the attacks of silverites and bimetalists, and the effort to lower the tariff left him little time for anything else.

The congressional elections of 1894, however, led Cleveland to reconsider his earlier indifference to the Venezuelan question. In that election the Democrats lost control of both houses of Congress to the Republicans. The main reason for this shift was, of course, the state of the economy. But superpatriotic jingoes like Theodore Roosevelt had also attacked Cleveland for refusing to annex the Hawaiian Islands, for failing to do anything about a British military incursion in Nicaragua, and more generally for conducting a weak and ineffective foreign policy.

There wasn't much the conservative Cleveland could do about the economy. He no doubt realized, however, that a more aggressive foreign policy—especially if it involved twisting the British Lion's tail—would serve his and his party's political ends very well indeed. He was also aware that his critics had a point. The Europeans had been showing a disquieting tendency to interfere in western hemispheric affairs.

It was, then, for a variety of reasons, some domestic and political but others having to do with America's future role in the Western Hemisphere, that in his December 1894 message Cleveland asked Congress to take cognizance of the Venezuelan boundary dispute. Congress responded with a resolution calling upon London to arbitrate its differences with Venezuela. At the same time the president instructed Thomas A. Bayard, minister to the Court of St. James's, to raise the issue with the Foreign Office.

Bayard's discussions with the Foreign Secretary, John Wodehouse, Lord Kimberley, revealed some disquieting facts. First, the British again refused to include any land east of the Schomburgk line in an arbitration. Moreover, as the two diplomats pored over a map of British Guiana, Kimberley laid claim to an extra thirty-three thousand square miles of territory, including the mouth of the Orinoco River, a vast waterway that offered access to the interior of the upper third of South America. Bayard and Cleveland were deeply concerned by this, for, as the historian Allan Nevins long ago pointed out, "If Great Britain perched on that huge waterway, she would be in a position to control much of the internal trade of a vast region."[1]

It is now difficult to imagine just how important control of the Orinoco seemed at the time. Yet there is substantial evidence to support Nevins's view. The feeling was so widespread in fact that Sir Julian Pauncefote, the British ambassador in Washington, informed London "that the desire of the United States to prevent Great Britain from gaining a permanent foothold at the mouth of the Orinoco, is likely to warp the judgment of all Americans."[2]

Still, to focus exclusively on the Orinoco question would be to miss the forest for a single tree. The decade of the 1890s was the heyday of European imperialism. And if to that point the Near East, Asia, and Africa had been the focus of imperialist endeavor, there were disturbing signs that Latin America might be next. For example, in April 1895, after President José Santos Zelaya of Nicaragua claimed sovereignty over the Mosquito Coast and expelled the British consul at Bluefields, a British force landed in the Nicaraguan town of Corinto, seized the customs house there, and remained until Zelaya offered an apology and paid an indemnity of £ 75,000. A month after the British landing in Nicaragua, the French, who laid claim to a 155,000-square-mile parcel of land in Brazil, landed troops there. And after a French citizen was killed in the Dominican Republic, Paris demanded reparations and threatened to seize that country's customs houses to secure payment. Add to these developments Britain's refusal to establish a boundary with Venezuela through arbitration unless territory east of the Schomburgk line was excepted, as well as its new claim to the Orinoco, and it is not difficult to understand the Cleveland administration's fear that European imperialism had come to the Western Hemisphere with potentially serious consequences for United States interests in the region.

The mood in Congress and the White House was perfectly captured by Senator Henry Cabot Lodge, who denounced London's Venezuelan policy while pointing out that it wasn't an obscure piece of territory but a major principle that was at stake. As he put it, "if England can set up a territorial claim and then refuse to arbitrate about it, there is nothing to prevent her taking any amount of territory." The administration had to take action, for, if "Great Britain can extend her territory in South America without remonstrance from us, every other European power can do the same and in a short time you will see South America parcelled out as Africa has been." The Monroe Doctrine and America's "rightful supremacy in the Western Hemisphere" were the real issues.[3]

It was at this time that Cleveland had a well-publicized conference with his friend Congressman Don Dickinson, a Michigan Democrat. Shortly afterward, Dickinson returned to his home district, where he gave a speech urging America's "watchmen" to "keep an eye upon our good friends across the Atlantic" lest "they begin to take an interest, not altogether born of curiosity or of a purely Christianizing spirit, in this hemisphere." In this speech, which was widely viewed as reflecting Cleveland's thinking, Dickinson linked his concern for the future of the Monroe Doctrine to American economic interests when he said: "We are a great nation of producers; we need and must have open markets throughout the world to maintain and increase our prosperity."[4]

OLNEY'S TWENTY-INCH GUN

Late in April, even before Dickinson gave his speech, the president instructed Secretary of State Walter Q. Gresham to prepare a note protesting London's Venezuelan policy. Before he could complete the task, however, the secretary became ill, contracted pneumonia, and died. Thirteen days later Attorney General Richard Olney, an aggressive and strong-willed former railroad lawyer, succeeded Gresham.

No less determined than Cleveland to beard the British Lion in his den, Olney began work on a note that would drastically expand the meaning of the Monroe Doctrine. On July 2, 1895, his task completed, Olney left the sweltering heat of Washington for Gray Gables, Cleveland's summer place at Buzzards Bay, Massachusetts. After leaving the message with the president, he went on to his own summer hideaway at nearby Falmouth to await the president's reaction.

Cleveland, who had just become the father of a "plump" and "loud-voiced" baby girl, thought Olney's note "the best thing of the kind I ever read." He was particularly delighted because in his judgment the note placed the Monroe Doctrine "on better and more defensible ground than any of your predecessors—or *mine*."[5]

Olney's "twenty-inch gun" as Cleveland described it, redefined the Monroe Doctrine, which he claimed had only one purpose—to make certain that "no European power or combination of powers shall forcibly deprive an American state of the right and power of self-government and of shaping for itself its own political fortunes and destinies." British policy toward Venezuela, the secretary claimed, was just such a threat since in refusing to include in the proposed arbitration any territory east of the Schomburgk line London was saying to Caracas, "You can take your chance of getting a portion by arbitration, only if you first agree to abandon to me such other portion as I may designate." This, Olney asserted, was naked aggression, since territory so acquired would have been "wrested from" the Venezuelans as surely as if it had been taken by force.[6]

In one part of his note Olney clearly stated that the United States was not acting from narrow self-interest and that his only purpose in applying the Monroe Doctrine to the current situation was to protect the freedom and independence of the Latin American states. But he contradicted himself somewhat later, when he remarked with greater candor that the governments of Latin America were "friends and allies, commercially and politically, of the United States" and that the administration had a "vital interest" in preserving the established order. He went further, focusing on the dangerous precedent Britain was setting, when he remarked:

> "What one power was permitted to do could not be denied to another, and it is not inconceivable that the struggle now going on for the acquisition of Africa might be the partition of all South America. The disastrous consequences to the United States of such a condition of things are obvious . . . Our only real rivals in peace as well as enemies in war would be found located at our very doors."[7]

Olney argued that since the Latin American republics were incapable of defending their independence against an imperialist threat, the United States would assume that responsibility. He even went so far as to make the bold claim that "the United States is practically sovereign on this continent, and its fiat is law upon the subjects to which it confines its interposition." From this lofty position he explained to the Foreign Secretary of an empire upon which the sun literally never set that "distance and three thousand miles of intervening ocean make any permanent political union between an European and an American state unnatural and inexpedient."[8]

Only after having claimed the right to dictate how the Western Hemisphere would develop did Olney get down to essentials, warning the Foreign Office that he regarded Britain's Venezuelan policy "as injurious to the interests of the people of the United States" and a violation of an "established policy [the Monroe Doctrine] with which the honor and welfare of this country are closely identified." The secretary demanded that London agree to submit the boundary dispute to an arbitrator. He also asked for a reply to his note before December 2, when the president would address the opening of Congress.[9]

CRISIS AND COMPROMISE

On August 7, 1895, the American ambassador in London, Thomas Bayard, left a copy of Olney's bombastic note with Britain's prime minister, Robert Arthur Talbot, Lord Salisbury, who was at the time handling the affairs of the Foreign Office. Salisbury, who had a well-earned reputation as one of Europe's ablest diplomatists, expressed surprise that the United States should have chosen to make an issue out of a matter of such little consequence. He then sent the note to the Law Officers of the Crown, whose job it was to frame a reply.

At that point Salisbury, who also had a well-earned reputation for absentmindedness, seems to have forgotten about the American problem. It may be that he was distracted by other, more threatening situations, for during the next few months England was rocked by two major crises. The first developed in the eastern Mediterranean after the Turks massacred some fifty thousand Armenian Christians. There followed a period of war hysteria in England, with elements of the British press and public demanding that the government take action. Then came news that the Russians were on the move in the Far East, where they had extracted major concessions from the Chinese in Manchuria, including a naval base at Port Arthur and the right to build a railroad across Manchuria to Vladivostok. This Russian action, which threatened British interests in China, touched off another scare in the Foreign Office, further overshadowing the Venezuelan question.

With top policy makers otherwise occupied, the Crown's law officers took their time drafting a reply to Olney's "twenty-inch gun." At length, however, on November 26, the note, signed by Salisbury, was delivered to the American embassy. There was still time for a cable to reach Washington before the opening of Congress. But due to a mixup at the embassy, no cable was sent. A furious Cleveland was forced to admit in his address to the opening session of Congress that the British had not even bothered to reply to his demands of the preceding summer.

Lord Salisbury's note, when last it did arrive, was in no way calculated to reduce Cleveland's anger, for in it he mercilessly shredded Olney's arguments. He rejected the secretary's claim that the Monroe Doctrine was accepted international law and denied, in any case, that it applied to the situation. Britain was not seeking to impose a foreign "system" on Venezuela. Nor was it attempting to colonize any part of that country. Venezuela and Britain were neighbors involved in a boundary dispute, nothing more.

Salisbury went further, questioning Olney's understanding of the Monroe Doctrine. In his 1823 message Monroe had specifically denied that his purpose was to interfere with established European holdings in the Western Hemisphere. But Olney now claimed that distance as well as an intervening ocean made "any permanent political union between an European and an American state unnatural and inexpedient." This Salisbury fervently rejected, just as he denied the United States's right to intervene in the Venezuelan boundary dispute. The United States, like any other nation, had the right to intervene where its real interests were involved. But it was absurd to claim that American questions were for Americans and only Americans to decide. On the contrary, he wrote, the "Government of the United States is not entitled to affirm, with reference to a number of independent states for whose conduct it assumes no responsibility, that its interests are necessarily concerned in whatever may befall those states simply because they are situated in the Western Hemisphere."[10] Having thoroughly dissected Olney's argument, Salisbury reaffirmed his government's long-standing willingness to arbitrate the dispute but rejected Olney's demand that areas east of the Schomburgk line be included in the arbitration.

Cleveland was duck hunting in North Carolina when Salisbury's note arrived. When he returned and read it, he became "mad clean through." Quickly he and Olney drafted a special message to Congress. In it the president reasserted his claim that the Monroe Doctrine applied to the Anglo-Venezuelan controversy and informed Congress that since Britain would not agree to fair arbitration the United States would unilaterally draw a proper boundary. He announced the creation of a commission to establish the line, asked Congress for money to support its work, and announced that once the boundary had been drawn the United States would "resist by every means in its power" British attempts to take territory on the Venezuelan side of that line.[11]

For a brief moment it actually appeared that war was a real possibility. Extremists were, of course, gratified. Henry Cabot Lodge crowed, "I first alone in the wilderness cried out about Venezuela last June and was called a Jingo for my pains." But, he continued, "Jingoes are plenty enough now." Theodore Roosevelt, too, seems to have looked forward to a fight. "If there is a muss I shall try to have a hand in it myself! They'll have to employ a lot of men just as green as I am even for the conquest of Canada."[12]

Sir Julian Pauncefote reported to the Foreign Office that America was in the grip of a war hysteria. But the British ambassador had misread the signs. The jingoes were up in arms, to be sure. But there was no war talk in Congress. On the contrary, shortly after voting to provide the money for Cleveland's commission, the Senate offered up a prayer for peace. Businessmen, fearing that a war scare would interrupt the economic recovery that was then just gaining momentum, were sharply critical of the president and the jingoes. Firmness with the British was one thing, wrote the Massachusetts banker Henry Higginson, "well chosen language is quite another." And as for Theodore Roosevelt, Higginson was appalled "that a man of his influence and position should talk of war with Great Britain in what I could not but feel was a very juvenile fashion."[13]

Peace sentiment was strong in England, too, where a war between the two Anglo-Saxon countries was considered unthinkable. Lord Salisbury himself viewed the situation as serious but shrewdly guessed that this crisis had a long fuse on it since there could be no direct confrontation until after the American boundary commission had arrived at its conclusions. In the interim he hoped that good sense would prevail on both sides of the Atlantic.

Whatever tendencies might have existed in England to stand on principle in the face of American meddling in the Anglo- Venezuelan dispute vanished early in 1896 in the aftermath of the famous Jameson raid. In the early 1880s Dutch settlers—Boers—in southern Africa declared the Transvaal an independent republic. Then in 1895 Dr. Leander Jameson led a group of Cecil Rhodes's irregulars into the area, hoping to precipitate a rebellion against Boer rule there. Jameson's failure prompted Germany's Kaiser Wilhelm II to send a congratulatory telegram to President Paul Kruger of the Transvaal. This gratuitous intervention in the internal affairs of the British empire served to focus English hostility on Germany. After this, all interest in a war with the United States vanished. In fact, the threatening European political situation made a policy of "hands across the sea" almost a necessity.

Lord Salisbury set the stage for a settlement to the boundary controversy when he agreed to arbitration and announced that he would allow an arbitral board to consider Venezuelan claims to territory east of the Schomburgk line when establishing the new boundary. He excepted only those areas that had previously been settled by British subjects. After several more months of dickering, Cleveland and Olney accepted these terms. The final agreement between Washington and London, signed on November 12, 1896, laid the groundwork for a treaty between Britain and Venezuela. This agreement established a five-member arbitral board (two to be appointed by each side and a fifth member to be chosen by the original four) to determine the boundary between British Guiana and Venezuela.

Britain and America had found a solution to their problem. But what about the Venezuelans? A contemptuous Olney refused to include them in the negotiations that produced the Anglo-American settlement. As far as he was concerned, they could read about them in the newspapers. Moreover, he at first refused to allow Venezuela to have any role in the selection of members of the arbitral board. When at last he relented, allowing Caracas to select one of the arbitrators, he made it clear that no Venezuelan national would be acceptable. Faced with a great power fait accompli, Caracas put the best face possible on a humiliating situation and selected Melville Fuller, chief justice of the United States Supreme Court, to serve on the board.

Nor was this the last of Venezuela's disappointments. The commission granted almost all of the disputed territory save for control of the mouth of the Orinoco to British Guiana. With only minor deviations, the Schomburgk line became the official boundary between Venezuela and the British colony.

As Olney's treatment of the Venezuelans makes clear, the dispute between Britain and America was not about an obscure boundary line in the South American wilderness. Henry Cabot Lodge had been correct when he observed that the real issue was far more important. Cleveland and Olney had successfully revised and expanded the meaning of the Monroe Doctrine in support of the assertion that the United States was predominant in the region.

AMERICA AND THE CUBAN REVOLUTION

In February 1895, a rebellion broke out on the island of Cuba. Reacting to deteriorating economic conditions and Spain's repressive political regime, rebel guerrilla bands roamed the countryside looting and burning. This uprising, like earlier Cuban attempts to win independence, found considerable support in the United States. The New York based Cuban Revolutionary Junta, representing some twenty thousand Cuban exiles, supported the

The Cuban Revolutionary Junta had the American press on its side from the start. This souvenir lithograph is from a five-day fair held by the junta in New York in May 1896 to popularize the Cuban cause.

rebellion financially, sponsored filibustering expeditions, and sought to influence public opinion in the United States.

The Cubans had considerable success influencing American opinion because important elements of the American press took up the Cuban cause. This was especially true of William Randolph Hearst, the publisher of the *New York Journal*, and Joseph Pulitzer, who controlled the *New York World*. Engaged in a no-holds-barred circulation war, these two press moguls fed their readers a constant diet of sensational Cuban atrocity stories. Sometimes the reports reflected the facts, and sometimes they didn't. But all were aimed at creating sympathy for the rebel cause.

Take, for example, the case of Evangelina Cisneros. According to the New York papers, this young girl was facing a twenty-year prison sentence though her only crime had been to defend her chastity against the lustful advances of a brutal Spaniard. The *Journal's* stories about the young Evangelina produced a tidal wave of sympathy for the girl resulting in appeals for clemency to Maria Christina, Queen Regent of Spain, and the pope. When these failed, the *Journal* dispatched a reporter to Cuba who, according to the story he later filed, took a house near the prison, drugged the guards, sawed open the bars to Evangelina's cell, and escaped with the beautiful señorita in tow.

At one time historians placed heavy emphasis on the role of the "yellow press" in bringing about American intervention in the Cuban Civil War. And why not? William Randolph Hearst himself is said to have bragged that it cost him $3 million to bring on the Spanish-American War. Nor can there be much doubt that the sensational news stories printed at the time helped keep national attention focused on the Cuban situation. But it should be remembered that between 1895 and the spring of 1898, when the United States declared war on Spain, a variety of forces were at work moving the United States toward intervention. Not least among these were real conditions in Cuba.

The war in Cuba was a horrific bloodletting made worse by the ruthless tactics of the Spanish commander there in 1896, General Valeriano Weyler. Frustrated by his inability to distinguish friend from foe in a war in which peaceful peasants by day became guerrilla fighters by night, Weyler adopted a policy called "reconcentration." Peasants in the countryside were herded into concentration camps near the Spanish-controlled cities. Those who refused to move to the camps were considered rebels to be shot on sight.

This policy solved Weyler's immediate problem. By a simple act of definition he had identified the enemy. Unhappily, however, the Spanish bureaucracy in Cuba hadn't the resources to provide even basic sanitation facilities, let alone food, water, and medical attention, for those crowded into the camps. As a result, hundreds of thousands died from disease and malnutrition.

Reconcentration turned out to be a disaster for Spain. In the first place, it did not resolve Weyler's military problem, for the war remained stalemated. At the same time, many in the general population, aware of the fate that awaited them in the camps, preferred to take their chances by remaining on the land. Others swelled rebel ranks. In 1898, General Ramón Marqués de Peña Plata Blanco estimated that more than three hundred thousand *concentrados* were, at that very moment, perishing "from hunger and misery around the cities." No one knows how many had died over the preceding two years. But as early as 1896 the situation was so desperate that the Cuban correspondent for the *Times* of London wrote: "I see no way out of this terrible mess in Cuba, unless the United States intervenes. The Spaniards seems [sic] unable to do anything towards crushing the rebellion."[14]

The people of the United States didn't need Hearst and Pulitzer to manipulate them into intervening in Cuba. Simple humanitarianism seemed to require that America put an end to a contest that neither side could win or was willing to lose.

Nor should it be forgotten how long the United States had been forced to tolerate continued chaos on its southern flank. Between 1869 and 1878 Cuba was racked by a rebellion that finally subsided only after the Spanish government promised fundamental economic and political reforms on the island. But the reforms never materialized, and Cuba remained a bubbling cauldron, an explosion waiting to happen. In the years that followed, Washington was forced to deal with a whole variety of Cuban problems, including sporadic uprisings threatening to American property on the island, filibustering attempts undertaken by Cuban Americans, and a rumored attempt by Germany to purchase the island. Three decades of instability culminating in a barbaric, stalemated war was reason enough to intervene.

The 1895 uprising also had an immediate and deleterious effect on American economic interests. Rebel military strategy was designed to provoke American intervention on behalf of Cuban independence. Toward that end the leaders of the movement, Antonio Maceo, José Martí, and Máximo Gómez, adopted a scorched-earth policy that included the deliberate destruction of American holdings on the island. American investors were involved in Cuba's tobacco and sugar industries to the tune of some $50 millions. The war, which in its first year reduced the sugar crop by 80 percent and tobacco production by 90 percent was seriously damaging to these interests as well as to other businessmen with interests in the Caribbean region.

The Cubans counted on the pro-Cuban press in America to lay responsibility for American losses in Cuba at Spain's doorstep. But President Cleveland, aware of the attempted manipulation, denounced the "rascally Cubans." Yet if the rebels failed to convince Washington that Madrid was responsible for the destruction of American property in Cuba, they succeeded in the broader sense, convincing policy makers that the time had come to insist that order be restored on the island. Continued instability was unacceptable to an administration interested in protecting American interests in Cuba and developing Latin American markets.

CLEVELAND'S CAUTIOUS POLICY

The mounting pressure might have produced war sooner had someone other than Grover Cleveland occupied the White House in 1895. But this president was indifferent to Cuban aspirations and determined not to surrender to the jingoes and the yellow press, with its demands for intervention. Economic conditions in the United States were grim as the nation struggled through the second year of a major depression. Moreover, Cleveland already had one major foreign policy problem on his agenda, the Venezuelan boundary question.

Adopting a policy of strict neutrality toward the conflict, the president recognized the existence of an insurgency but refused to grant the rebels belligerent status, something interventionists were demanding. The administration also regularly intervened on behalf of American citizens of Cuban descent whose involvement in the rebellion landed them in Spanish prisons. But at the same time the president ordered the navy to intercept filibusters leaving American ports for Cuba.

Cleveland's neutral policies ran directly contrary to a rising tide of interventionist sentiment in the United States. The Cuban rebels won the support not only of the press but also of important elements of organized labor as well as dissident silverites in the Democratic party, who were disillusioned with Cleveland and entranced at the idea of a political campaign in 1896 that linked "free Cuba" and "free silver." Even some Gold Democrats jumped on the bandwagon, arguing that a war fought for Cuban independence by the fiscally conservative Cleveland administration would "do much towards directing the minds of the people away from imaginary ills, the relief of which, is erroneously supposed to be reached by 'Free Silver.' "[15] Before the end of the year mass demonstrations calling for military intervention in support of the Cubans had taken place in Chicago, Philadelphia, New York, and a number of other urban centers.

By early 1896 Congress had caught the jingo spirit. With the Senate leading the way, both houses quickly passed a concurrent resolution calling for the recognition of Cuban belligerency and urging the president to offer his good offices for the purpose of ending the war on the basis of Cuban independence.

Cleveland and Olney ignored this congressional advice. But they could not ignore the pressure that moved Congress in the first place. Secretary Olney, therefore, sent a strong but carefully phrased note to Madrid. Indifferent to the outcome of the stalemated contest, Olney urged Spain to implement the sort of economic and political reforms that would isolate the rebels, denying them popular support. If Madrid would agree to this move, the president would provide his good offices to end the war—no doubt on terms short of Cuban independence. A warning accompanied this good advice. Spain would have to understand that the United States could not tolerate the deadly stalemate indefinitely. American intervention was inevitable unless stability and order were restored in Cuba.

Washington's suggestion that by implementing reforms the Spanish government could undercut the rebels' popular support and end the Cuban insurrection, was seconded by France and other governments friendly to Madrid. But Antonio Cánovas, Spain's politically astute prime minister, was in no position to offer the necessary reforms. The queen regent, Maria Christina, was interested in one thing only—to preserve the monarchy until her twelve-year-old son came of age. This was Cánovas's primary concern as well. And that was the rub, for the enemies of the government and the monarchy, including powerful elements of the army, considered the implementation of reforms in Cuba as a dishonorable surrender and the justification for a coup.

Cánovas was caught in a treacherous political bind. Cuban reform might precipitate a coup that would destroy the government and the monarchy. Yet unless Spain could break the Cuban deadlock, it risked war with the United States and the loss of Cuba. It was a thin line the Spanish prime minister walked; somehow he had to hold Cuba and avoid war with the United States at the same time. The strategy he employed was to increase the military pressure on the Cuban rebels while at the same time promising them autonomy *after* they laid down their arms. That, of course, was a promise he never intended to keep.

Cánovas waited two months before rejecting Cleveland's mediation proposal. The delay served Spain's purposes well, for by the time the State Department received his reply the United States was in the grip of election fever. The nation rang with cries of "free silver," not "free Cuba." At the Democratic national convention of 1896 the president and his policies were repudiated. William Jennings Bryan won the Democratic nomination for president and began a months-long political crusade that temporarily drove Cuba from the thoughts of the people.

In the White House a lame-duck president fretted. Bryan's crusade against the gold standard was creating a hysteria in the country. Cuba had been temporarily forgotten. But Cleveland believed that the public's emotionalism was in itself a danger, that any sort of incident in Cuba or between the United States and Spain might result in a crisis. He told a friend visiting at Gray Gables that he would have to be "extremely careful; as the public mind seemed to be in an inflammable state, and a spark might kindle a conflagration. He said there seemed to be an epidemic of insanity in the country just at this time."[16]

As Cleveland prepared his last annual message to Congress, he knew that time was running out and that the United States would be forced to intervene if the dreadful, stalemated Cuban war was not soon ended. He therefore took the opportunity to warn once again that circumstances would "fix a limit to our patient waiting for Spain to end the contest, either alone in her own way, or with our friendly cooperation."[17]

MCKINLEY AND CUBA

On March 4, 1897, William McKinley took the oath of office as the twenty-fifth president of the United States. In some ways he was almost too good to be true. A Civil War hero and a family man who adored his invalid wife, he never swore and was, at least as far as anyone could tell, a devout Christian who never missed a Sunday in church.

If, however, McKinley was to all appearances virtue incarnate, he was also an ambitious politician. And that always seems to carry with it some sort of price. For McKinley it meant becoming beholden to powerful members of the business community who, during his tenure as governor of Ohio, saved him from public embarrassment and bankruptcy by paying his personal debts. It was at this point that Marcus A. Hanna, the powerful capitalist-politico who ran the Ohio Republican party, took charge of McKinley's career. And it was with Hanna and the Ohio machine behind him that McKinley made his successful run for the presidency in 1896.

Most historians believe that McKinley remained more or less independent of Hanna and his friends, making his own decisions. Still, it strains credulity to believe that the president's judgment was not influenced by the businessmen who saved him from personal humiliation, not to mention political oblivion.

The degree to which McKinley took his cues from Hanna and other business leaders can never be known with any certainty. One thing is clear, however. Until very late in the crisis that preceded the declaration of war in 1898, the consensus among businessmen was that the United States ought to avoid a war over Cuba since it might disrupt the economic recovery then under way. At the very least McKinley shared these views. He was literally dragged kicking and screaming into the war with Spain.

McKinley's anxiety to avoid war notwithstanding, like Cleveland before him he had no choice but to respond to the political pressures brought to bear on his administration. Congress and the public wanted the Cuban carnage ended. The Republican party was on the verge of a split as jingoes, including the powerful Henry Cabot Lodge and his own assistant secretary of the navy, Theodore Roosevelt (who described himself as "a quietly rampant 'Cuba Libre' man") called for intervention.[18] Moreover, the president was keenly aware that sooner or later, if he did not act to achieve a satisfactory settlement to the war, the Democrats would certainly steal the issue.

Bringing order and stability to the Caribbean was still another of the president's concerns. The war had undermined Cuban-American trade, destroyed American property, and threatened the safety of American citizens living in Cuba. Moreover, McKinley was committed to a policy of trade expansion in the Pacific and toward that end hoped to fulfill the dream of a succession of presidents by building an American-controlled interoceanic canal. Cuba stood athwart lines of communication between East Coast and Gulf Coast ports and the canal routes. For all of these reasons, it was vital that Cuba be pacified and politically stabilized.

During the early months of his administration, McKinley tried to buy time by throwing a few bones to the expansionists and jingoes in his party. He established a commission to recommend exactly where a Central American canal ought to be built, supported legislation to aid Americans caught in the cross-fire of the Cuban insurrection, and negotiated an annexation treaty with Hawaii. He also sent a personal emissary to Cuba to bring him a firsthand report on the situation there. But if he hoped that his special envoy would bring news of improved conditions, he was sadly disappointed. Cuba, William Calhoun explained in his twenty-two-page report, was "one of the most unhappy and most distressed places on earth."[19] The American consul general in Havana, Fitzhugh Lee, was equally discouraging. This former governor of Virginia and Confederate brigadier (who bore a striking resemblance to another southern gentleman of a later generation, a famous purveyor of fried chicken) had been advocating intervention for two years by the time McKinley took office. He was now more convinced than ever that intervention was the only way to bring peace to the strife-torn island.

Within three months of his taking office, the pressures on McKinley had become so intense that he could no longer delay taking action. He appointed, as his minister to Madrid, Stewart Woodford, a New York attorney and Republican politician who had held office in several preceding administrations. Woodford's instructions approximated an ultimatum. The minister was to demand an end to reconcentration, a program of political reform that would result in Cuban autonomy within the Spanish empire, a quick end to the fighting, and authorization for the United States to provide humanitarian aid to Cuba's starving population. McKinley gave Spain until November 1, 1897, to agree to these terms

By the time Woodford arrived in Spain in September 1897, the entire political situation there had changed. On August 8, Antonio Cánovas had been shot dead by a young anarchist. The queen Regent then called on the leader of Spain's Liberal party, Práxedes Mateo Sagasta, to form a new government. Even before Woodford could present McKinley's demands, Sagasta removed General Weyler from his command, promised an end to reconcentration, developed a plan for Cuban autonomy, and freed all American citizens held in Cuban prisons.

Madrid's changed policy provided McKinley with the strength he needed to continue his delaying tactics. It was, after all, difficult for the jingoes to quarrel with a president who appeared to have achieved so much through peaceful diplomacy. And so a sort of uneasy calm descended on the United States.

McKinley behaved as though a new era in Spanish-Cuban relations was dawning. Late in November 1897, an administration spokesperson told the press, "Thus far Spain has surrendered everything asked of her, and the policy of the Administration has been completely vindicated." A few days later, McKinley himself told Congress that Prime Minister Sagasta had committed himself to a policy of reform for Cuba from which he could not retreat. Spain, he said, deserved "a reasonable chance to realize her expectations and to prove the . . . efficacy of the new order of things to which she stands irrevocably committed."[20]

McKinley realized, of course, that the chances for a peaceful settlement to the Cuban crisis were slim at best. But by implying that peace was a reasonable expectation, he temporarily disarmed the interventionists. He used that time to exert continued diplomatic pressure on Madrid in the hope that he could force peaceful change before military action became necessary.

In fact, the Cuban autonomy scheme had no real chance of bringing peace to the island. The insurgents were opposed for obvious reasons. They wanted independence, not autonomy, and believed they were on the verge of achieving it through American intervention. Cubans loyal to Spain, most of whom were middle-class whites, were also opposed to the idea, fearing that in an autonomous Cuba they would have to share power with the poor, blacks, and people of mixed blood. Important elements in the Spanish military also opposed autonomy, viewing the plan and General Weyler's removal as elements of a dishonorable surrender.

THE CRISIS OF EARLY 1898

McKinley's hopes for peace notwithstanding, the events of early 1898 drove him toward intervention and war. On January 12, 1898, rioting broke out in Havana. As most riots go, this was an orderly affair. A number of Spanish officers and their men, along with some Cuban loyalists, attacked the offices of three newspapers that supported the autonomy scheme and had been critical of General Weyler. After the newspaper buildings had been sacked, Havana's streets returned to normal.

The Havana riots had a significant impact in the United States, however, where exaggerated reports of anarchy in Cuba led many in Congress to call for immediate intervention. The riots also had a powerful impact on the president, who seems to have feared that if anarchy did break out on the island he would be blamed for having done nothing to protect American citizens there

McKinley tried to deal with these problems and head off any congressional move to force intervention by ordering the battleship *Maine* to Havana on a "goodwill visit." He hoped that the presence of the ship would serve as a warning to Spanish authorities in Cuba that it was imperative for them to maintain order.

The *Maine* had hardly dropped anchor in Havana Harbor before another blow fell. Dupuy de Lôme, the Spanish minister in Washington, cared little for American society and less for McKinley. Shortly after the president's December message to Congress, to his eternal regret, de Lôme put some of these feelings on paper in a letter to a friend then visiting Cuba. The letter, which was intercepted by agents of the junta, was turned over to William Randolph Hearst, who published it on February 9 under the headline

"Worst Insult to the United States in Its History." In the letter de Lôme referred to McKinley as "weak and a bidder for the admiration of the crowd, . . . a would-be [read "third-rate"] politician who tries to leave a door open behind himself while keeping on good terms with the jingoes of his party."[21]

De Lôme, who of course realized that he was through in Washington, resigned. Madrid expressed regret, apologized, and appointed a new envoy. McKinley, still hoping to avoid war, was satisfied. Left to his own devices he would have forgotten the incident. But the damage was done. The public was outraged.

Not a week after the publication of de Lôme's indiscreet remarks, the heaviest blow of all fell on the president's hopes for peace. Early on the morning of February 16, he was awakened by aides who informed him that the *Maine* had blown up and sunk in Havana Harbor. Of the ship's 350-man crew, 266 had been killed.

No one has ever ascertained the true cause of the explosion that rocked the *Maine* that night. It might well have been an accident. Coal dust was thick in the ship's hold. A lighted lantern in the wrong place could have caused the explosion. Or Cuban insurgents may have planted a mine alongside the *Maine*, assuming that the Americans would conclude the Spanish were responsible. It might even have been angry Spanish loyalists or irate Spanish military officers who did the deed. One thing is certain. Of all the possible culprits, the Spanish government itself, desperately trying to hang on to Cuba while avoiding American intervention and war, had no motive whatsoever for sinking the *Maine*.

The destruction of the *Maine* set off a firestorm of indignation in the United States. The yellow press screamed for revenge, Hearst's *Journal* offering a $50,000 reward for information that would expose the identity of

The battleship *Maine* was sunk in Havana harbor by parties unknown. The ship may even have been the victim of an accident. But it made little difference in America, where it was assumed that the Spanish were behind the ship's destruction.

those who had destroyed the ship. Assistant Secretary of the Navy Theodore Roosevelt was less circumspect than Hearst, who at least implied that there was some doubt as to who was responsible. At a press conference TR stated categorically that the battleship had been the victim of "dirty treachery on the part of the Spaniards." Privately he said he would "give anything" if the president "would order the fleet to Havana tomorrow." When the president didn't, he remarked angrily that McKinley had "no more backbone than a chocolate eclair."[22]

As the historian Ernest May has observed, the war fever spawned by the destruction of the *Maine* raged furiously even in out-of-the-way places. Burning effigies of Spanish statesmen may well, at least temporarily, have replaced baseball as the national pastime. The *Carson City Appeal* explained that in Nevada, "the clamor for war is heard everywhere. Many people are for war . . . on general principles, without why or wherefore." Another observer, writing from central Missouri, explained that "everything is war talk up in our part of the country, and patriotism is oozing out of every boy who is old enough to pack feed to the pigs."[23]

This tidal wave of prowar sentiment notwithstanding, McKinley refused to be stampeded into war. He insisted instead on a thorough investigation into the sinking of the *Maine*. "I don't propose to be swept off my feet by the catastrophe," he said. "My duty is plain. We must learn the truth and endeavor if possible, to fix the responsibility. The country can afford to withhold its judgment and not strike an avenging blow until the truth is known."[24]

McKinley appointed a special naval board of inquiry to investigate the *Maine* disaster. At the same time the administration may have set a record for cable traffic between Washington and Madrid, as the president tried desperately to find a way to avoid war. He warned the Spanish that the situation was grave and that both sides would have to show "wisdom" and "prudence" if they were to avoid a crisis. Of course it is clear that, from McKinley's point of view, the most wise and prudent thing Spain could do was grant Cuba her independence.

Aware that actions always speak louder than words, McKinley also asked Congress for a special $50 million appropriation for the military. He could think of no better way to convince Madrid that the United States meant business. Fifty million dollars was an enormous sum in those years. But Congress voted the money almost immediately.

To some, at least, it appeared that this gesture might have the desired effect. From Madrid, Woodford explained that "to appropriate fifty millions out of money in the treasury, without borrowing a cent demonstrates wealth and power. Even Spain can see this. . . . The Ministry and press are simply stunned."[25]

Prime Minister Sagasta may, as Woodford believed, have been stunned. But he was also wrestling with the same set of unpalatable alternatives that had confronted Cánovas. To free Cuba at the insistence of the

United States would in all likelihood result in a military coup. But not to give up the island was to confront the distinct possibility of a war with the United States and the loss of Cuba, too. Since neither option was at all acceptable, the Spanish government stalled.

McKinley, too, hung on gamely. But he must have realized that unless something very unexpected happened, war was inevitable. By this time it wasn't just Theodore Roosevelt who was comparing his backbone to soft pastry. Much, therefore, depended on the report of the naval board investigating the explosion that sunk the *Maine*. On March 20, McKinley received the report, which, not surprisingly, turned out to be inconclusive. The investigators claimed that the *Maine*'s plates had been blown inward by the explosion of a mine. But who was actually responsible for the blast remained a mystery. Subsequently even the board's judgment that the explosion was caused by a mine came into question. Implosions caused by exploding munitions, boilers, or coal dust might also have pulled the plates of the ship inward.

After the Navy Board's report was made public, it was more or less expected that McKinley would ask for a declaration of war. But the harried chief executive continued to disappoint his critics. Counseling patience, he again approached the Spanish, this time demanding an immediate end to reconcentration, an armistice to be followed by peace talks, and large-scale humanitarian aid to the suffering Cuban population. McKinley's key demand was that, in the event direct negotiations failed, both sides would accept his good offices and binding arbitration. Though not clearly stated, Sagasta did not miss the point. If it came to arbitration, the president would certainly insist on Cuban independence.

Spain struggled against the tightening noose. The navy made preparations for war, and the government looked to other European nations for support. While the Spanish pursued that vain hope, they tried to buy time by agreeing to some of McKinley's demands—but not to the central one. They would not accept the president's good offices, and they had no intention of surrendering Cuba without a fight.

Sagasta did not deceive himself. Spain had no chance against a nation as powerful as the United States. Government leaders knew that one way or another Cuba would be lost, Minister Woodford explained. But they preferred to lose it as a result of defeat in combat. In that way the honor of the army would be preserved and the risk of a coup that would overthrow the government and the monarchy sharply reduced. The Russian foreign minister, Count Mikhail Nicolaevich Muraviev, remarked on how ironic the situation was, saying:

> "If the Queen is wise, moderate, and truly patriotic, she will fall and be thrown out; if, on the other hand, she puts herself at the head of the column and is neither wise nor patriotic, she can save her crown. This is cynical but so."[26]

LESLIE'S WEEKLY

YOUR
COUNTRY
CALLS YOU

R·M·WRIGHT
'98

Americans flocked to the recruiting offices after America declared war on Spain. There was an orgy of patriotism as the cry went up, "Remember the *Maine* and to hell with Spain."

WAR AT LAST

Even after he had exhausted all of the peaceful options and had no choice but to set the matter before Congress, McKinley continued to disappoint the war party. They wanted immediate recognition of the Cuban republic as well as an impassioned call to arms. They got neither. The president's war message, if it can be called that, reflected the weariness of a man who had exhausted himself seeking some way to preserve the peace but who could not reconcile himself to war. McKinley asked Congress for the power to intervene militarily to stop the fighting in Cuba and to force both sides to keep the peace. He neither asked for a declaration of war nor endorsed the idea of Cuban independence.

The president's message set off a furious debate in Congress, where many thought it a national disgrace. One angry senator raged, "That message does not mean the independence of Cuba. The message means, if it means anything, that the President asks Congress to authorize him to make the Cubans stop fighting for their liberty."[27]

The Senate passed resolutions, none of which were to the president's liking, recognizing Cuban independence, ordering the Spanish off the island, and *directing* the president to use force to achieve that end. Anti-imperialist elements in the upper house also pushed through the Teller Amendment, which stipulated that the United States would not seek to replace Spain as the colonizing power in Cuba.

In the House of Representatives the situation was somewhat different. There Thomas Reed, Speaker of the House, had long used his enormous power to thwart the prointerventionist party. But even "Czar" Reed found he could not stand against the tidal wave of support for war. He could and did, however, help fashion a compromise. Finally then, after days of wrangling, Congress enacted resolutions similar but not identical to those passed by the Senate. The first recognized Cuba's right to be independent but did not recognize the republic. The next two stipulated that Spain must leave Cuba and ordered the president to use force to achieve that end. Last came the Teller Amendment.

On April 23, President McKinley sent a final ultimatum to Madrid. When the Spanish government rejected Washington's demands, Congress officially declared war on April 25, 1898. The military phase of the long Spanish-American conflict had begun.

John Hay, who shortly after the fighting began left the embassy in London to become McKinley's secretary of state, called the Spanish-American conflict "a splendid little war." And perhaps from the diplomat's point of view it was. At any rate it was thankfully brief, ending with an armistice that went into effect on August 12, 1898.

American land forces had little opportunity to distinguish themselves during the war. An American army under the command of General William Shafter landed in Cuba and took the garrison at Santiago after only brief skirmishing. General Nelson Miles had even less trouble taking Puerto Rico. And in the Far East, an army commanded by General Wesley Merritt took Manila almost unopposed. Theodore Roosevelt's dash up Kettle Hill notwithstanding, the land war was not much to write home about.

The war at sea was just as one-sided. On July 3, 1898, Admiral William Sampson's Atlantic Squadron cornered and sunk a Spanish fleet attempting to escape from Santiago Harbor. More significant, however, was the May 1 victory of Admiral George Dewey over the Spanish at Manila Bay. If the truth be known, the battle of Manila Bay was no great achievement. The seven Spanish warships stationed there ranged in quality from obsolete to unseaworthy. None had armor plating and one, the *Reina Christina*, was made of wood. The six American ships in Dewey's squadron, all of which were modern armored vessels, outweighed the numerically larger Spanish force by more than seven thousand tons and carried heavier armaments as well.

But the mere fact that Admiral Dewey was in no position to lose the

Theodore Roosevelt, a jingo if there ever was one, resigned his position as assistant secretary of the navy and organized a company of mounted riflemen called the Rough Riders.

battle of Manila Bay was of little consequence to most Americans, who celebrated his triumph as though it were Saratoga and Yorktown rolled into one. The admiral became an instant legend. His face was to be found plastered across the front pages of newspapers, on shaving mugs, teacups, commemorative plates—anything that would sell. Dewey's victory at Manila Bay and the subsequent seizure of Manila itself did more than create a national hero, however. It set the stage for the rapid expansion of American territorial holdings across the Pacific.

A PACIFIC EMPIRE

Military victory, easily attained, created a national consensus in favor of acquiring an overseas empire. Expansionists including the likes of Captain Alfred Thayer Mahan and Henry Cabot Lodge had long advocated taking

The Spanish fleet in the Philippines hadn't a chance against Admiral George Dewey's modern warships. The wreck above is what remained of the *Reina Christina* after the battle.

the coaling stations and naval bases requisite for Pacific expansion. Now a substantial portion of the public at large, caught up in the enthusiasm of the moment, joined in the call for empire. Even business leaders who had opposed war until the last moment joined in the hunt, arguing that the country should strip Spain of its Pacific holdings and join in the competition for a piece of the China market.

McKinley had first moved in this direction a full year before the war provided him with the opportunity to seize Spain's Pacific holdings. The first item on his agenda had been Hawaii. In March 1897 he negotiated a treaty annexing the islands and then launched a full-scale lobbying campaign to win Senate support. McKinley fought hard, even raising the specter of a Japanese takeover of the islands if the Senate failed to approve the treaty. "If something be not done," he warned, "there will be before long another Revolution, and Japan will get control."[28] But McKinley's efforts fell short, as partisanship and racism combined to deny him the required two-thirds majority.

With the president's support the annexationists next tried to acquire Hawaii by joint resolution of Congress. But "Czar" Tom Reed opposed annexation, and he refused to let the Hawaiian question come to a vote. Not even Reed, however, could block annexation once the war had begun. When the Hawaiian treaty passed both houses in a burst of imperialist enthusiasm, a jubilant president remarked, "We need Hawaii just as much and a good deal more than we did California. . . . It is Manifest Destiny."[29]

Hawaii was only the first in a series of moves that the administration

America went to war to free Cuba. But it also fought to replace Spain as the colonial power in the Philippines. Here American soldiers are seen firing on Filipinos who, like the Cubans, also sought independence.

made in developing a Pacific empire. Almost immediately after learning of Dewey's victory in the Philippines, Secretary of the Navy John D. Long, acting on the advice of Captain Mahan and the Navy Board, ordered the seizure of the Spanish island of Guam, located between Hawaii and the Philippines. The Wake Islands were taken by the United States in January 1899.

But what to do about the Philippines? That was the crucial question. The economic significance of the islands was immediately apparent. Senator Henry Cabot Lodge had hardly learned of Dewey's victory before he remarked, "We must on no account let the islands go. . . . We hold the other side of the Pacific and the value to this country is almost beyond imagination." From Beijing (Peking) Minister Charles Denby, who viewed the islands as a stepping stone to the China market, urged their retention as "a grand thing for our trade." Mark Hanna, McKinley's closest political ally, wanted at least a base in the Philippines. From there, he thought, "We can and will take a large slice of the commerce of Asia. That is what we want. We are bound to share in the commerce of the Far East, and it is better to strike while the iron is hot."[30]

From the moment he learned of Dewey's victory there was never any doubt in McKinley's mind that the United States was in the Philippines to stay. The real question was, Should the United States occupy the entire archipelago, or keep only what it needed to maintain a naval base there?

The president's earliest inclination was to hold only the island of Luzon. In this way he hoped to secure the naval base that he, Mahan, and Hanna all wanted while at the same time limiting the role that the United States would have to play in governing the islands with their millions of dark-skinned people. McKinley told one wartime visitor to the White House that he supported "the general principle of holding on to what we get." But he also jotted this note to himself. "While we are conducting war and until its conclusion we must keep all we get; when the war is over we must keep what we want."[31]

Gradually, over several months, the few men in Washington with firsthand knowledge of the Philippines convinced the president that it would not be possible to take a naval base on the islands and cut the rest of the archipelago loose. They argued that Luzon alone was militarily indefensible, that the Filipino people were incapable of governing themselves, that chaos would follow an American withdrawal, and that other nations would quickly move in to seize parts of the archipelago. The danger of additional foreign intervention was felt keenly by McKinley, who knew that the Germans had ambitions in the area and that the Japanese would not tolerate a native government in the Philippines. Tokyo had made it abundantly clear that if the United States abandoned the islands Japan would establish "a suitable government for the territory," either singly or in concert with other interested powers.[32]

McKinley finally concluded that the wisest thing to do was to take all of the Philippines. He knew the business community, anxious to use the islands as a stepping stone to the China market, would support him and that the Christian missionary societies would, too. He wasn't quite certain, however, about how the American people in general would react to such a startling break with tradition. Determined to find out, he made a six-state whistle-stop tour through the American heartland. In speeches given along the way he spoke eloquently of America's new duties and responsibilities. While on this "swing around the circle," the president studied the public reaction to his remarks. At the end of the tour he was confident that he had the sort of grass-roots support he wanted.

On returning to Washington, McKinley issued new instructions to an American delegation that had for some time been in Paris negotiating a peace treaty with Spain. Cuba was to be independent. The United States would take Puerto Rico as well as Guam. Finally, whereas the envoy's earlier instructions had been indefinite on the subject, he now insisted that Spain must surrender the Philippines. Wrote John Hay, "Grave as are the responsibilities and unforeseen as are the difficulties which are before us, the President can see but one plain path of duty—the acceptance of the archipelago."[33]

The Spanish delegates in Paris fought a prolonged rearguard action against the inevitable. They objected to granting Cuba its independence, arguing that the United States should assume sovereignty over the island and responsibility for its very large debt. They also protested that since

Thousands of Filipinos, like those pictured here, died in the war for independence against the United States.

General Merritt's forces had taken Manila after a military truce had been signed, the United States had no claim to the Philippines. But Spanish objections notwithstanding, the administration stood firm. In the end Spain gave in but not until after the United States agreed to pay $20 million for the Philippines.

THE TREATY IN THE SENATE

The treaty that brought an end to the war and empire to the United States faced one major hurdle. The Senate had been the burial ground of more than a few treaties and even in those heady days of imperialist enthusiasm opposition was not hard to find.

Racism was endemic in the United States, and imperialists used it to justify assuming the "white man's burden." Thus Senator Albert Beveridge of Indiana rose from his place in the Senate to say:

> God has not been preparing the English-speaking and Teutonic peoples for a thousand years for nothing but vain and idle self-admiration. No! He has made us the master organizers of the world to establish system where chaos reigns. . . . He has made us adepts in government that we may administer government among savages and senile peoples.[34]

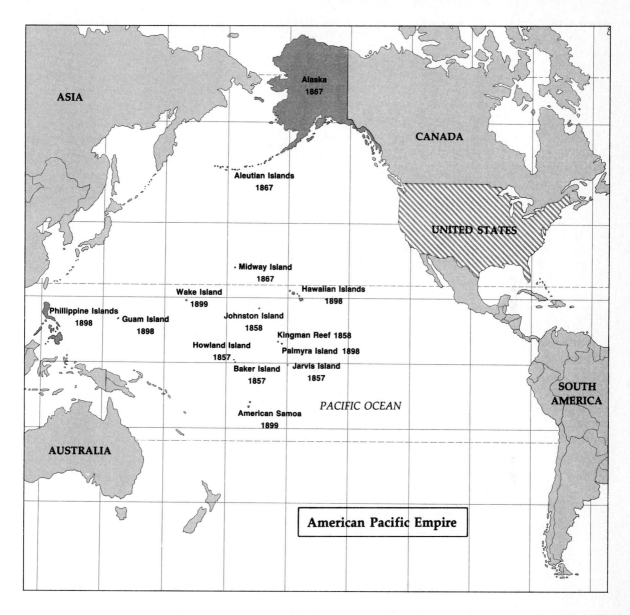

ASIA

Alaska
1867

CANADA

Aleutian Islands
1867

UNITED STATES

Midway Island
1867

Wake Island
1899

Hawaiian Islands
1898

Phillippine Islands
1898

Guam Island
1898

Johnston Island
1858

Kingman Reef 1858

Howland Island
1857

Palmyra Island 1898

Baker Island
1857

Jarvis Island
1857

SOUTH
AMERICA

PACIFIC OCEAN

American Samoa
1899

AUSTRALIA

American Pacific Empire

But racism was an argument that cut two ways. Not long before, many in Congress had opposed the annexation of Hawaii on the ground that it would lead to a mixing of the races that could only be detrimental to an Anglo-Saxon people. Thus Congressman James Beauchamp ("Champ") Clark of Missouri asked:

> How can we endure our shame when a Chinese senator from Hawaii, with his pigtail hanging down his back, with his pagan joss in his hand, shall rise from his curule chair and in pigeon English proceed to chop logic with

GEORGE FRISBIE HOAR or HENRY CABOT LODGE? O tempora, O mores![35]

No one went quite so far during the debate over the Philippines. But some Southern members did use the racial argument to suggest that the administration was on the brink of acquiring control over an inferior people who were clearly incapable of democratic self-rule and who would, therefore, hold America back in the struggle for survival then going on among the world's races. Senator John Daniel of Virginia thought there was a better chance of changing "the leopard's spots" than the "different qualities of the races which God has created in order that they may fulfill separate and distinct missions in the cultivation and civilization of the world."[36]

Opponents of the treaty did not rest their case solely on the danger posed by bringing an inferior race under the American flag. Andrew Carnegie, the steel mogul, warned that imperialism would raise taxes and be bad for business. "We shall be compelled to increase our navy. We must pay for a large standing army," and even so, he argued, there would be "neither rest nor security for us." "A false step now," he warned, "and the future of the republic will, in my opinion, be seriously impaired and its industrial career retarded." Others emphasized the dangers implicit in a break with the tradition of nonentanglement. Thus, the *Richmond Virginia Times* warned: "If ever we assume sovereignty over those islands, we will be at once and without help, plunged into the maelstrom of European politics and diplomacy, and will have wandered irretrievably away from the safe and firm foundations on which the wise fathers and founders of our republic planted its everlasting pillars and supports."[37]

The anti-imperialists also focused on what empire might mean for the future of American political institutions. Could America remain a republic at home while ruling over subject peoples abroad? Adlai E. Stevenson of Illinois thought not.

> Is it too much to say that the enforcement of the proposed policy of the expansionists in a large measure involves the question of a change in our form of government? It can hardly be contended that the measure proposed for the control or government of the Philippine Islands finds warrant in the Constitution. Shall the closing hours of the century witness the American people abandoning the pathway in which past generations have found prosperity and happiness, and embarking upon that of aggression and expansion, against which we are warned by the wrecks which lie along the entire pathway of history?[38]

The author and essayist Mark Twain, another outspoken opponent of imperialism, made a similar point in this toast, offered at one of those elegant dinners to which he was so frequently invited:

> I bring you the stately matron named Christendom, returning bedraggled, besmirched, and dishonored from pirate-raids in Kiao-Chow, Manchuria, South Africa, & the Philippines, with her soul full of meanness, her pocket

full of boodle and her mouth full of pious hypocrisies. Give her soap and a towel, but hide the looking glass.[39]

The opposition to the treaty was not only fierce but very nearly successful. Senate Republicans aided by some Democrats managed to pass the treaty with but a single vote to spare. William McKinley had created an empire that spanned the Pacific. The stepping stones were in place. America was ready to compete for economic preeminence in the China market.

ENDNOTES

1. Allan Nevins, *Grover Cleveland, A Portrait in Courage* (Dodd Mead and Co., N.Y., 1934), p. 553.

2. Sir Julian Pauncefote, quoted in Charles S. Campbell, *The Transformation of American Foreign Relations, 1865–1900* (Harper and Row, N.Y., 1976), p. 205.

3. Henry Cabot Lodge, quoted in Howard K. Beale, *Theodore Roosevelt and the Rise of America to World Power* (Johns Hopkins University Press, Baltimore, Md., 1956), pp. 50–51.

4. Don Dickinson, quoted in Walter LaFeber, *The New Empire, An Interpretation of American Expansion, 1860–1898* (Cornell University Press, Ithaca, N.Y., 1963), pp. 250–51.

5. Grover Cleveland, quoted in Gerald G. Eggert, *Richard Olney, Evolution of a Statesman* (Pennsylvania State University Press, University Park, Pa., 1974), p. 208.

6. Richard Olney to Thomas Bayard, July 20, 1895, *Foreign Relations of the United States, 1895* (Washington, 1896), I, p. 561.

7. *Ibid.*, p. 558.

8. *Ibid.*, p. 556.

9. *Ibid.*, p. 562.

10. Lord Salisbury to Sir Julian Pauncefote, November 26, 1895, in *ibid.*, p. 566.

11. Cleveland, quoted in Nevins, *Cleveland*, p. 640.

12. Henry Cabot Lodge, quoted in Beale, *Theodore Roosevelt*, p. 50; Theodore Roosevelt, quoted in *ibid.*, pp. 51–52.

13. Henry Higginson, quoted in *ibid.*

14. General de Peña Plata Blanco, quoted in Ernest May, *Imperial Democracy: The Emergence of America as a Great Power* (Harcourt Brace and World, N.Y., 1961), p. 163; *Times* correspondent, quoted in Campbell, *The Transformation of American Foreign Relations, 1865–1900*, p. 271.

15. Fitzhugh Lee, quoted in Ernest May, *Imperial Democracy*, p. 76.

16. Grover Cleveland, quoted in Nevins, *Cleveland*, p. 717.

17. *Messages and Papers of the Presidents*, ed. James D. Richardson (Washington, 1900), IX, p. 721.

18. Roosevelt, quoted in Howard K. Beale, *Theodore Roosevelt*, p. 59.

19. William Calhoun, quoted in Lewis Gould, *The Presidency of William McKinley*, (University of Kansas Press, Lawrence, Ks., 1980), p. 67.

20. McKinley, quoted in *ibid.*, p. 69; McKinley's Annual Message, December 6, 1897, *Foreign Relations of the United States, 1897* (Washington, 1898), p. xx.

21. Dupuy de Lôme, quoted in Walter Millis, *The Martial Spirit* (Riverside Press, Cambridge, Mass., 1931), pp. 97–100.

22. Roosevelt, quoted in Margaret Leech, *In the Days of McKinley*, (Harper and Bros., N.Y., 1959), p. 169.

23. The *Carson City Appeal* and Colonel Henry A. Newman, quoted in May, *Imperial Democracy*, p. 142.

24. McKinley, quoted in Leech, *In the Days of McKinley*, p. 168.

25. Stewart L. Woodford to McKinley, March 9, 1898, in *Foreign Relations of the United States, 1898* (Washington, 1901), p. 684.

26. Count Muraviev, quoted in May, *Imperial Democracy*, p. 132.

27. Senator Marion Butler, quoted in Charles S. Campbell, *The Transformation of American Foreign Relations*, pp. 272–73.

28. McKinley, quoted in Lewis L. Gould, *The Presidency of William McKinley*, p. 49.

29. McKinley, quoted in May, *Imperial Democracy*, p. 244.

30. Lodge, Charles Denby, and Mark Hanna, quoted in Campbell, *The Transformation of American Foreign Relations*, p. 286.

31. McKinley, quoted in H. Wayne Morgan, *America's Road to Empire*, (John Wiley and Sons, N.Y., 1965), p. 88.

32. Memorandum by John Bassett Moore, quoted in Gould, *The Presidency of William McKinley*, p. 133.

33. John Hay, quoted in *ibid.*, p. 140.

34. Albert Beveridge, quoted in Hofstadter, *Social Darwinism in American Thought* (Beacon Press, Boston, 1955), p. 180.

35. Beauchamp "Champ" Clark, quoted in H. Wayne Morgan, *America's Road to Empire*, p. 107.

36. John Daniel, quoted in Hofstadter, *Social Darwinism*, p. 192.

37. Andrew Carnegie, quoted in the *Literary Digest*, November 28, 1898, p. 567; the *Richmond Virginia Times*, quoted in *ibid.*, August 27, 1898, p. 224.

38. Adlai Stevenson, quoted in *American Diplomacy and the Sense of Destiny: The Initial Thrust*, ed. Perry E. Gianakos and Albert Karson (Wadsworth Publishing, Belmont, Cal., 1966), I, p. 92.

39. Mark Twain, quoted in Harold Larrabbee, "The Enemies of Empire," *American Heritage*, 1960, Vol. 11, Number IV, p. 77.

15

WORLD POWER,
1899–1913

In 1900, 140,000 Boxers, like the man pictured above, rose up
in a desperate attempt to drive foreign exploiters from China.

At the end of the Spanish-American War, the United States controlled a
Pacific empire as well as Cuba and Puerto Rico. But that was only the
beginning of a pattern of imperialism practiced first by President William
McKinley and after his assassination by President Theodore Roosevelt. Before
the new century was too far advanced the United States had fought a costly
war to quell a rebellion in the Philippines, asserted its claim to free access to
the China market, transformed Cuba into a protectorate, gained control of
the Isthmus of Panama, and begun construction of the canal that earlier
policy makers had only dreamed about. It was an extraordinary epoch in
the history of American expansion.

On July 25, 1894, a clash between Chinese and Japanese naval forces
signaled the beginning of a war in which Japan won not only major concessions
from her adversary but also the respect of many in the West, who realized
that it had, as Secretary of the Navy Hilary Herbert observed, "leaped, almost
at one bound, to a place among the great nations of the earth."[1] The Treaty
of Shimonoseki, signed on April 17, 1895, reflected the enormity of Japan's
victory. China was driven from Korea and forced to cede Formosa, the
Pescadores, and the Liaotung peninsula in southern Manchuria together
with the ports of Dalian (Dairen) and Lüshun (Port Arthur).

Japan had taken a giant step toward great power status. But in moving into Manchuria, it went too far for the Russians, who had their own ambitions in that part of the world. Supported by France and Germany, St. Petersburg forced Japan to return the Manchurian plumb to China. Even so, Japan had clearly emerged on the world stage, a power to be reckoned with in the Far East.

The end of the Sino-Japanese War marked only the beginning of China's difficulties. In the next few years the great European powers moved in on "the sick man of Asia," securing leaseholds and spheres of influence over large areas of the country. The Russians took a leasehold over Lüshun (Port Arthur) and Lüda (Dairen) on the Liaodong (Liaotung) Penninsula (the area they had only recently forced the Japanese to surrender) and expanded their influence throughout Manchuria. The Germans acquired a leasehold over the port city of Quingdao (Tsingtao) on Kiaochow Bay as well as economic privileges on the Shantung Peninsula. And Britain took the port of Weihaiwei while bolstering its sphere of influence in the vast Yanhzi (Yangtse) River Valley. By 1898, China seemed well on the way toward dismemberment, a victim of European colonialism.

These developments were viewed with alarm by a number of special interest groups in the United States, who urged the McKinley administration to adopt a more assertive China policy. The missionary societies that sent men and women to labor in God's Chinese vineyard demanded that the government protect their people from Chinese xenophobes and, just as important, that it save China from dismemberment.

Elements of the business community also called on the government to take a greater interest in China. American cotton manufacturers and the Standard Oil Company of New York, which had developed a large market for kerosene in China, led the fight. They were supported by the American China Development Company as well as other important bankers and capitalists interested in investment opportunities there. In 1898 concerned businessmen organized the American Asiatic Association and the Committee on American Interests in China to lobby for a more aggressive Far Eastern policy. Soon the periodical press began to feature articles on America's growing need for Asian markets, while Congress and the administration received an increasing volume of mail calling for action.

HAY'S OPEN DOOR NOTES

After the Spanish-American War, and in many ways because of it, President McKinley showed a new sensitivity to Far Eastern developments. The president was reacting to the growing domestic pressure, his own imperialistic ambitions, and the fact that other powers seemed on the verge of dismembering the Celestial Empire. He had not acquired Hawaii, Guam, and the Philippines only to be left on the outside looking in while other nations divided the China market among themselves. The president and Secretary of State John Hay both relied heavily on William W. Rockhill, chief of the

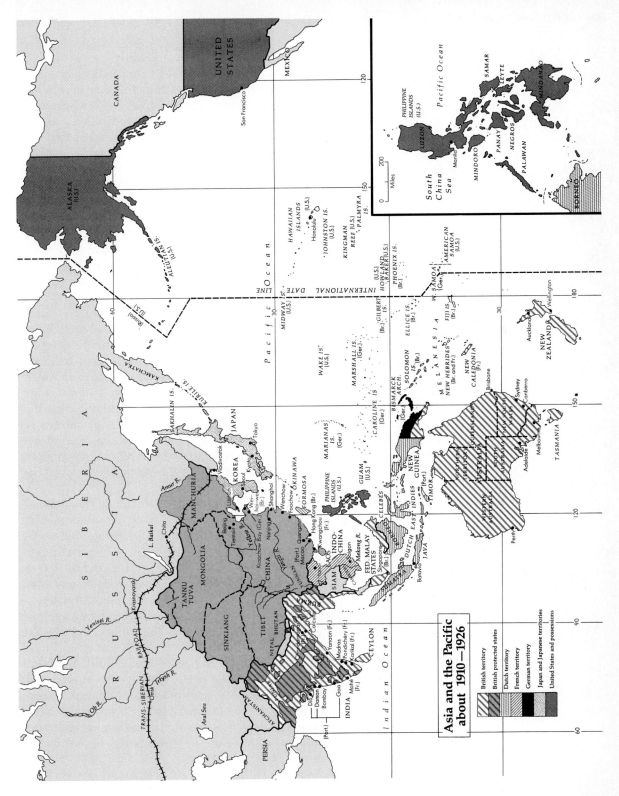

Asia and the Pacific about 1910–1926

British territory
British protected states
Dutch territory
French territory
German territory
Japan and Japanese territories
United States and possessions

CANADA

UNITED STATES

MEXICO

San Francisco

ALASKA (U.S.)

ALEUTIAN IS. (U.S.)

Pacific Ocean

INTERNATIONAL DATE LINE

HAWAIIAN ISLANDS (U.S.)

Honolulu

JOHNSTON IS. (U.S.)

KINGMAN REEF (U.S.)

PALMYRA

MIDWAY (U.S.)

WAKE IS. (U.S.)

MARSHALL IS. (Ger.)

GILBERT IS. (Br.)

PHOENIX IS. (U.S.)

HOWLAND (U.S.)

BAKER (U.S.)

W. SAMOA (Ger.)

AMERICAN SAMOA (U.S.)

ELLICE IS. (Br.)

FIJI IS. (Br.)

MELANESIA

SOLOMON IS. (Br.)

NEW HEBRIDES (Br. and Fr.)

NEW CALEDONIA (Fr.)

BISMARCK ARCH. (Ger.)

NEW ZEALAND

Auckland

Wellington

RUSSIA

SIBERIA

Yenisei R.

Ob. R.

Irtysh R.

Omsk

Krasnoyarsk

TRANS-SIBERIAN RAILROAD

Chita

L. Baikal

Aral Sea

PERSIA

AFGHANISTAN

TANNU TUVA

MONGOLIA

SINKIANG

TIBET

NEPAL

BHUTAN

BURMA

INDIA

CEYLON

SIAM

FED. MALAY STATES

Singapore (Br.)

LAOS

INDO-CHINA

Saigon

Mekong R.

Hong Kong (Br.)

Kwangchow (Fr.)

Macao (Port.)

Quangsi

CHINA

Yangtze R.

Nanjing

Shanghai

Wenchow

Foochow

FORMOSA

OKINAWA

KOREA

MANCHURIA

Amur R.

Vladivostok

Port Arthur

Seoul

Wei-hai-wei (Br.)

Kiaochow Bay (Ger.)

Yellow R.

Tientsin

Beijing

Kyoto

Tokyo

JAPAN

SAKHALIN IS.

KURILE IS.

KAMCHATKA

Yunnan R.

PHILIPPINE ISLANDS (U.S.)

GUAM (U.S.)

MARIANAS IS. (Ger.)

CAROLINE IS. (Ger.)

CELEBES

DUTCH EAST INDIES

JAVA

Batavia

TIMOR (Port.)

NEW GUINEA

NEW GUINEA (Br.)

AUSTRALIA

WESTERN AUSTRALIA

SOUTH AUSTRALIA

NORTHERN TERRITORY

QUEENSLAND

NEW SOUTH WALES

VICTORIA

Brisbane

Sydney

Canberra

Melbourne

Adelaide

Perth

TASMANIA

Indian Ocean

Goa [Port.]

Daman [Port.]

Diu [Port.]

Bombay

Yanaon (Fr.)

Madras

Pondichéry (Fr.)

Karikal (Fr.)

Mahé (Fr.)

Calcutta

South China Sea

Pacific Ocean

PHILIPPINE ISLANDS (U.S.)

LUZON

Manila

MINDORO

PANAY

NEGROS

PALAWAN

SAMAR

LEYTE

MINDANAO

BORNEO

Miles

0   200

State Department's Latin American Division and a leading expert on Far Eastern affairs, to develop a new China policy. As a dedicated Sinophile, Rockhill was naturally appalled at the prospect of China's destruction at the hands of the industrialized nations. But as a policy maker he was primarily concerned because he believed that the dismemberment of China would close the China market, undermine the balance of power in Asia, fuel the already intense competition among the imperialist powers operating there, and perhaps lead to a general war.

It seemed to Rockhill that the United States ought to take whatever steps were necessary to forestall these portentious developments by preserving an independent and sovereign China. He was so convinced that the breakup of China would prove catastrophic that he even believed Washington ought to intervene with force if necessary to preserve a sovereign China. But he realized that there was no domestic support for anything beyond peaceful interposition on China's behalf. Words unsupported by deeds would have to suffice.

Rockhill fashioned a statement that, slightly edited in the State Department and signed by Secretary Hay, was sent as a circular message to St. Petersburg, Rome, London, Paris, Berlin, and Tokyo. This first "open door" note, which was issued on September 6, 1899, did not directly challenge the legitimacy of foreign leaseholds or spheres of influence (an area in which a single power exercises near-exclusive influence) in China. To have done so would have been to invite a speedy rebuff. Instead it asked only that the powers agree to provide equality of commercial opportunity for citizens of all nations in leaseholds and spheres, that the Chinese tariff in treaty ports under foreign control should continue in force, that the Chinese government be allowed to collect these duties, and that they cooperate to support the open door principle.

The powers differed in their reaction to Hay's note. The Italians, who had no sphere of influence or leasehold in China at the time, quickly endorsed the open door policy. The British and Japanese responded ambivalently. And the Russians, Germans, and French were evasive, determined to keep competitors out of areas they controlled. One can hardly blame them. After all, a major reason for acquiring a privileged position in China was to lay the foundation for monopolistic trade and investment practices.

In spite of the fact that, aside from the clear and unqualified support for the open door offered by the Italians, the other interested powers responded evasively, Hay interpreted their replies positively, announcing in March 1900 that they had given his proposal "final and definitive" acceptance.[2] Even though this was clearly not the case, Hay felt certain that none of the nations with ambitions in China would admit publicly that they were unwilling to accept a set of principles so eminently fair. He was right. None of the nations involved ever did challenge his interpretation of what they had done. But that did not mean that they were prepared to live by the open door principle either.

Considering that he confined himself to mere note writing, Hay was

The Boxer uprising and the siege of Beijing led a number of foreign nations, including the United States, to send troops to quell the rebellion. Here members of the multi-national force are on parade inside the Forbidden City.

probably not too disappointed with what he had accomplished. He had quieted those business and missionary groups that were then calling for a more assertive China policy. He had also managed to make the American position regarding China clear while establishing the parameters for the international debate over China that was to follow. The open door policy did not protect China from international preditors. But it did serve to embarrass those who ignored it and to caution them, too, that their policy ran contrary to the stated interests of the United States, a nation to be reckoned with as the new century dawned.

Hay was aware that the status quo in China was fragile and that, open door or no, the more ambitious of the powers, Russia in particular, would seize any opportunity for further expansion at China's expense. Such an opportunity presented itself in June 1900, when the Boxer uprising broke out. The Boxers (in Chinese, I Ho Ch'uan, or Righteous, Harmonious Fists), 140,000 strong, were members of a secret society committed to the forceful expulsion of foreigners and foreign influences from China. Encouraged by the Dowager Empress Cixi (Tz'u-Hsi), and at first supported by elements of

A group of American cavalrymen, part of the multi-national force sent to put down the Boxer uprising, patrol along the Great Wall of China.

the Chinese army, the Boxers began their attacks on foreigners and Chinese Christian converts in 1898. This rising tide of officially sanctioned antiforeignism culminated in the summer of 1900, when the Boxers, supported by units of the Chinese army, besieged the diplomatic quarter in Beijing (Peking). The siege lasted for two months, until at length an international force of some twenty thousand, including British, French, German, Japanese, Russian, and American troops, marched into Beijing and rescued the besieged westerners.

At the time only a few prescient observers like Sir Robert Hart, head of the Chinese customs service, recognized the true significance of the Boxer uprising. Hart realized that the Boxers' purpose had been "to free China from the . . . corroding influence of a foreign cult and . . . from foreign troops, contamination, and humiliation." Though they had failed, Hart was convinced that the Boxers represented "today's hint to the future."[3]

Sensitive Western observers such as Hart were few and far between. Certainly Hay was not among them. Utterly contemptuous of the Chinese, he saw the Boxer uprising as significant only because it provided an opening for ambitious powers to make new encroachments on the already tottering Manchu dynasty, thus threatening America's interests in China as well as the Far Eastern balance of power.

Hay managed to block a proposal to use the international force assembled in Beijing to suppress the Boxers elsewhere in China. But he believed that further action was essential if the country was to be saved from partition. In July 1900, after a series of hurried consultations, he sent a second open door note to the powers, this time emphasizing the importance of preserving Chinese sovereignty and independence. Basing his argument on the fiction that the Beijing government had nothing to do with the Boxer uprising, the secretary of state insisted that the powers could have no legitimate objective in China beyond restoring order. China, he argued, should be preserved as a "territorial and administrative entity."[4]

Hay's second open door note had been a shot in the dark based on a desperate hope. And in fact it had no significant impact on the other nations involved in the China intervention. It is true that China was not partitioned, but other interested nations had recognized that taking control of large portions of China would be very costly. Moreover, they agreed with Hay's basic point, that a sovereign China was vital to the Far Eastern balance of power.

Although this second note had no real effect on the other interested powers, it is nevertheless important in that it broadened the meaning of the open door policy. At the beginning of the new century, Washington sought equality of commercial opportunity in China as well as the preservation of China as a sovereign entity. Still, the question remained, How would the United States go about achieving these aims? Hay himself was pessimistic, complaining that "not a single power" could be relied upon to support "our policy of abstention from plunder and the Open Door." The Russians, who were so obviously anxious to absorb Manchuria, were Hay's special concern. "Dealing with a government with whom mendacity was a science is an extremely difficult and delicate matter," he said.[5]

ROOSEVELT AND THE OPEN DOOR

After the siege of Beijing had been raised, the powers agreed to remove their forces from China proper. But St. Petersburg saw the vast province of Manchuria, an area rich in natural resources that had never been entirely under Chinese control, in a different light. The czar's government used the opportunity created by the Boxer uprising to station troops there and extend its influence throughout the region.

As the Russians tightened their control over Manchuria, American businessmen, especially cotton manufacturers who traded extensively there, urged Washington to do something. They feared, no doubt correctly, that once St. Petersburg had consolidated its position, American manufactured goods would be shut out of that growing market.

Theodore Roosevelt, who became president in 1901 after McKinley's assassination, responded with appropriate diplomatic protests but went no further. Even assuming that he was personally anxious to defend the open door against the Russians in Manchuria, he was in no position to do so. As the human and material costs of putting down the long and bloody Philippine insurrection grew, public enthusiasm for imperialism waned, making an aggressive Far Eastern policy impossible. And so Roosevelt interpreted the open door policy in a minimalist way. "All we ask," he told St. Petersburg, "is that our great and growing trade shall not be interrupted and that Russia shall keep its solemn promises. . . . We have always recognized the exceptional position of Russia in relation to Manchuria."[6] The Russians, however, were unwilling to concede even that much.

If Roosevelt felt constrained to allow St. Petersburg to close the door in Manchuria, the same was not true of Japan's leaders, who viewed Russian adventurism there as a great threat. As part of its quest for economic power and international respectability, Japan was committed to an expansionist policy. It set out first to expand its already established position in Korea. In 1910 the Hermit Kingdom was fully integrated into the Japanese empire. It is not surprising, then, that Japan viewed the Russian presence in neighboring Manchuria as a threat to its vital interests.

Aware that the United States was having no luck in securing equality of commercial opportunity in Russian-dominated Manchuria, Japan first turned to Washington, hoping for support in its efforts to check the Russian advance there. But Roosevelt was unable to help. Rebuffed by the United States, the Japanese turned to London, where they found a willing partner against a mutual adversary. The Anglo-Japanese Alliance of 1902 gave the Russians a temporary fright. Chastened by this threatening combination, they agreed to withdraw their military forces from Manchuria.

In Washington, Roosevelt and Secretary of State Hay tried to take advantage of the leverage provided by the Anglo-Japanese accord, increasing the diplomatic pressure on the Russians. A frustrated Roosevelt even told Hay, "I wish in Manchuria to go to the very limit the people will stand. If only we were sure neither France nor Germany would join in, I should not in the least mind going to 'extremes' with Russia."[7] But Roosevelt was blowing smoke. He knew there was insufficient domestic support for an aggressive China policy.

In 1903 the Russians reneged on their promise to withdraw their forces from Manchuria and rejected a Japanese proposal for a diplomatic resolution to the Manchurian question. Tokyo reacted on February 4, 1904, by breaking relations with St. Petersburg. Two days later the Japanese launched a surprise attack on Russian naval forces at Lüshun and then declared war. By May of the following year most of southern Manchuria was in Japanese hands. The final blow for the Russians fell on May 27–28, 1905, when, in the two-day battle of Tsushima Strait, a Japanese fleet sank thirty-two Russian war vessels in one of the most celebrated naval battles of all time.

When news of the Japanese attack on Port Arthur reached Washington, the president was delighted. He told his son, "I was thoroughly pleased with the Japanese victory, for Japan is playing our game." When Roosevelt made that remark he was only echoing the views of most informed Americans. Prior to the war Japan had shown no interest in China proper. It appeared that it would be satisfied with a secure sphere of interest in Korea and a guarantee for her "existing rights in Manchuria." But once the fighting began, Prime Minister Katsura Tarō later explained, Tokyo expanded its objectives to include a Manchurian "sphere of influence where our rights and interests could be maintained and expanded."[8]

As this change in Japanese policy became apparent, Roosevelt's thinking changed, too. Where once he saw Tokyo as a check on Russian expansionism and a champion of the open door, now he began to think in terms of using Russia to balance Japan's growing power in the region. He told his friend Senator Henry Cabot Lodge that while he believed a Russian victory in the war would have been "a blow to civilization," it was equally true that its "destruction as an eastern Asiatic power would also" have been "unfortunate." Russia, he thought, "should be left face to face with Japan so that each may have a moderating action on the other."[9]

In May 1905 a nearly bankrupt Japanese government asked Roosevelt to arrange a mediated settlement to the war. The president jumped at the chance, arranging a peace conference that met at Portsmouth, New Hampshire. Roosevelt relished the opportunity to be at the center of events, for he was by nature a performer. But he also had two very practical reasons for wanting to play the role of mediator. First, he could encourage the sort of balance of forces in the Far East that he had described to Lodge. But more important, Roosevelt knew that Japan had only two directions in which to expand. If it did not focus its energies on the Asian mainland, it would certainly move into the Pacific, where America had the Philippines and other territories to protect. Roosevelt used his position as peacemaker to direct Japanese energies toward Manchuria, where he hoped it would be occupied both by the economic opportunities the area offered and by the threat of a still-powerful Russia.

As a mediator Roosevelt had only limited influence over the outcome of the peace conference. Nevertheless, the Treaty of Portsmouth served his purposes very well indeed. Japan took over the Russian leasehold on the Liaodong (Liaotung) Peninsula, including Lüshun (Port Arthur) and Lüda (Dairen) and won control of the South Manchurian Railroad. The Russians also ceded the southern half of Sakhalin Island and recognized Japan's paramount interests in Korea. But Russia remained predominant in northern Manchuria, with control over the Chinese Eastern Railroad. It was still a power to be contended with in the Far East.

ROOSEVELT'S PACIFIC DIPLOMACY

The Russo-Japanese War left China in a worse position than before. Whereas once it had only to worry about Russian imperialism on its Manchurian frontier, now it had to concern itself with the Japanese as well. Unable to protect Manchuria from foreign imperialism, policy makers in Beijing, especially the very influencial Yüan Shikai (Shih-k'ai), tried to entice the United States into a large-scale economic involvement there. In this way they hoped to provide Washington with an incentive for defending not only American investments but China's sovereignty there as well. America seemed the logical choice for such a role, since it had no allies among the more rapacious imperialist powers, had shown no real interest in acquiring Chinese territory, advocated the commercial open door in China, and in its second open door note had publicly stated its concern for the preservation of Chinese sovereignty.

In 1906, at Yüan's urging, the Chinese government began a vigorous public relations campaign in the United States that was designed to reignite lagging American interest in the China market. At the same time Beijing tried to interest American capitalists in Manchuria as a field for investment. They attempted to convince E. H. Harriman, the railroad mogul, to build a railroad in southern Manchuria, an area then dominated by Japan's South Manchurian line. Later they tried to interest a number of influencial Americans, including Secretary of War William Howard Taft and the American consul in Shenyang (Mukden), Manchuria, Willard Straight, in using American capital to create a development bank for Manchuria. They even broached the subject of a Sino-American alliance that would "guarantee China against the ambitions of Japan, and at the same time safeguard American commercial interests."[10]

But all of China's efforts were to no avail, since they ran directly contrary to Roosevelt's purposes. In the aftermath of the Russo-Japanese War, the president became increasingly concerned over the possibility that Japan and the United States might come to blows in the Pacific. His fears may have been exaggerated, but they were not without foundation, for just as the Spanish-American War had stimulated popular support for imperialism in the United States, so the war with Russia had kindled the same sort of enthusiasm in the minds of many in Japan. Thus one Japanese expansionist, sounding for all the world like some nineteenth-century prophet of America's "Manifest Destiny," proclaimed:

> From the ice-bound northern Siberian plains to the continental expanses of China, Korea, and East Asia; farther south, to the Philippines, the Australian continent and other South Sea islands; then eastward to the western coasts of North and South America, washed by the waves of the Pacific Ocean- there is none in these regions which cannot be an object of our nation's expansion. If our people succeed in constructing new Japans everywhere in these areas and engage in vigorous activities throughout the Pacific, then our country's predominance over the Pacific will have been ensured.[11]

To discourage the eastward and southward tendency of Japan's expansionism, which would lead it into conflict with the United States, Roosevelt persisted in his efforts to use diplomacy to focus its expansive energies on Korea and Manchuria while securing the Philippines and America's other Pacific holdings against the possibility of Japanese aggression. Toward this end Roosevelt sent his affable secretary of war, William Howard Taft, to Tokyo for conversations with Japan's Prime Minister, Katsura Tarō.

By this time China, Russia, Britain, and France had all recognized that Korea had become part of the Japanese empire. Now, under terms of the Taft-Katsura agreement, Roosevelt, too, recognized Japan's suzerainty there. In return Japan "confirmed in the strongest terms" that it had no "aggressive designs" on the Philippines.[12] The president had what he wanted—a guarantee from the only real power the United States faced in the western Pacific that it did not covet the islands. And he had achieved this goal without surrendering anything tangible.

Roosevelt's attempt to secure America's Pacific holdings through diplomacy was almost immediately threatened by events over which he hadn't the least control. After 1870 perhaps as many as 100,000 Japanese immigrants settled in California and the other Pacific Coast states. Anti-Japanese sentiment in California grew in proportion to this population, but it became hysterical after Japan demonstrated its military strength during the Russo-Japanese War. This fear of the "yellow peril" first led to demands for the exclusion of all Japanese immigrants. Then, in October 1906, the San Francisco School Board carried Pacific Coast racism one step further, segregating some ninety-three Japanese children (twenty-five of whom were American citizens) in special schools.

Some Japanese reacted furiously to San Francisco's segregationist policy. Thus *Shinsekai*, a Japanese-language daily published in San Francisco, predicted that sooner or later Japan and the United States must fight. An editorial in the same paper urged those Japanese then living in California to resist white persecution.

> Japan is not China. Behind you stand the navy of five hundred thousand tons and the Army of one million men. Above all you have the support of forty-five million countrymen. Struggle, endeavor, and overwhelm the white race. Never use cunning means as the whites do. The struggle between races is not only a problem involving interests but is a problem of life and death.[13]

There was plenty of war talk in Japan, too. But the ruling elite there took a much different view of the matter. Convinced that the United States was fundamentally friendly and anxious to preserve the lucrative trade with America, Japan's leaders had no intention of allowing the immigration question to build to a crisis and were confident that the president would act expeditiously to correct the situation.

Tokyo may have been calm, but in Washington Roosevelt and Secretary of State Elihu Root, who had come to the Department after John Hay's death in 1905, were worried. Root thought the Japanese a "proud, sensitive, warlike" people who could take the Philippines, Hawaii and even the Pacific Coast from an unprepared United States. He believed that the anti-Japanese movement in California had created "an immediate and present danger to be considered and averted now, today."[14] Root's fears were no doubt exaggerated. But there can be no question that administration leaders believed that war over the immigration issue was a distinct possibility. Roosevelt even warned the governor general of the Philippines to prepare for an attack that, recalling Port Arthur, he thought might come with dramatic suddenness.

To extricate himself from what appeared to be a dangerous situation, Roosevelt brought the mayor of San Francisco and the entire city school board to Washington for some earnest persuasion. Out of this meeting came an agreement. If the president could secure an end to Japanese immigration, San Francisco would abandon its policy of school segregation.

Subsequent negotiations with Tokyo resulted in an exchange of notes, sometimes called the Gentlemen's Agreement that brought an immediate reduction in tension. Under terms of this unofficial accord, Japanese immigration from Hawaii to the mainland was halted, and Japan agreed to issue new passports only to relatives of those already in the United States or former residents of the United States. By mid-1908 the number of Japanese entering the United States had been reduced to a trickle.

THE GREAT WHITE FLEET

It was in June 1907, during this period of crisis in Japanese-American relations, that Roosevelt decided to send "the Great White Fleet"—sixteen battleships and auxiliaries all painted white—on a global cruise that included a three-day stop in Yokohama. At the time, the Japanese naval attaché in Washington informed his superiors that he had no doubt the sailing of the fleet was intended to impress Japan with America's naval might. It is likely the crisis with Japan did influence Roosevelt's thinking regarding the navy. But Roosevelt did not believe in making threats he could not carry out, and he knew that in the western and perhaps even the central Pacific the Imperial Japanese Navy ruled the waves.

In fact, Roosevelt's original motives for sponsoring this grand naval event had as much to do with domestic as with international affairs. By the summer of 1907 he had concluded that the long-range strategic interests of the United States required a larger navy—for two reasons. First, though negotiations which would lead to the Gentlemen's Agreement had reduced tensions, the president could not discount the possibility of a war with Japan at some time in the future. In such a war, he believed, America's Pacific holdings, even the Pacific Coast, would be hostage to Japanese naval power unless the United States had a much enlarged navy. Second, in 1906 the British commissioned the first of a new class of battleship, the HMS *Dreadnaught*, a ship destined to revolutionize naval warfare.

The development of this new *Dreadnaught* class of battleships and the naval armaments race that followed between England and Germany convinced Roosevelt that the United States would have to build four battleships a year to keep pace. The problem was how to win the support of an indifferent public and a downright hostile Congress to such a building program. The answer was "the Great White Fleet," a floating photo opportunity designed to attract media attention, arouse public support for American naval power, and thus influence Congress. It is true that before the fleet actually sailed Roosevelt came to believe that its presence in Pacific waters might have a calming effect on those in Japan who dreamed of Pacific conquest. But the real purpose of the scheme was to impress Americans, not the Japanese.

Roosevelt had a terrific knack for public relations, there is no getting around it. The fleet's sailing, and its visits to exotic ports of call around the world, had precisely the effect he hoped for. The public was entranced. And while Congress proved unwilling to fund the entire naval package Roosevelt proposed, it did agree to fund the construction of two battleships a year for an indefinite period.

When, on October 18, 1908, the American fleet dropped anchor in the harbor at Yokohama, the Japanese government viewed it not as a threat but as an opportunity, for they thought it of vital importance to establish a new basis for mutual understanding with Washington. Anxious to convince Roosevelt that the United States had nothing to fear from Japan in the Pacific, they treated the officers and men of the American fleet to a warm welcome.

Behind this fine reception for the American fleet lay the fact that during the summer of 1908 the Japanese government had at last developed some very clearly defined ideas about the course Japanese expansionism ought to take. Where once Japan's policy makers had debated the advantages of Asian expansion as opposed to expansion across the Pacific, Prime Minister Katsura Tarō turned Japan's complete attention toward Korea and Manchuria, areas where commercial and investment opportunities beckoned and where Japanese colonists were settling in increasing numbers. The Katsura ministry also decided that improved commercial relations with the United States should have a higher priority than the rights of overseas emigrants and clamped down hard on immigration to the United States, so that by the end of the year more Japanese were leaving American shores than were arriving.

Having thus set the stage, the Katsura government then opened negotiations in Washington, hoping to win Roosevelt's endorsement for an expanded Japanese presence in Manchuria. The result was the Root-Takahira Agreement of 1908. Under the terms of this accord, the two nations agreed to "respect the territorial possessions belonging to each other" in the Pacific, affirmed "the independence and integrity of China and the principle of equal opportunity for the commerce and industry of all nations in the Empire"; and agreed to maintain the status quo in the Pacific area.[15] In secret conversations the two sides clarified the vague understanding regarding Japan's interests on the Asian mainland. It was understood that Japan agreed to keep the door open for commerce in southern Manchuria but that because the area was vital, China should not exercise sovereignty there. For its part, Japan agreed to halt all emigration to the United States.

Root-Takahira was the capstone of Roosevelt's Pacific diplomacy. He had been convinced from the start that there was no genuine reason that Japan and the United States could not solve their differences peacefully. And between them he and Prime Minister Katsura had managed to do so. Roosevelt encouraged the Japanese to look to the continent of Asia and not to the Pacific as an area for expansion, thus securing America's Pacific possessions and blunting the threat of a contest for control of the Pacific basin. Toward that end he recognized Japan's suzerainty over Korea and its preeminent position in southern Manchuria. In return, the Japanese helped Roosevelt resolve the question of Japanese emigration into the United States and guaranteed continued United States control of the Philippines and her other Pacific holdings. Of course in the process Roosevelt had been forced to narrow (some have argued virtually abandon) the open door policy. But since the United States had neither the power nor the inclination to defend the open door, he felt he had lost very little.

CARIBBEAN ADVENTURE

At the same time that they were becoming increasingly involved in Asia, Washington's policy makers sought to transform the dream of an interoceanic canal into a reality. As President McKinley explained in his 1898 annual message to Congress, "The annexation of the Hawaiian islands and the prospective expansion of our influence and commerce in the Pacific" made an American-controlled canal indispensable. And even before he became president, Theodore Roosevelt, a "Mahonite" through and through, said:

> [I]f we are to hold our own in the struggle for naval and commercial supremacy ... we must build the Isthmian canal, and we must grasp the points of vantage which will enable us to have our say in the destiny of the oceans of the east and west.[16]

One major obstacle standing between Washington and the achievement of this goal remained, as before, the Clayton-Bulwer Treaty of 1850. The agreement had served a purpose at mid-century, but in 1898 the restraints it imposed on America's ambitions proved intolerable. Thus even before the Senate had ratified the treaty ending the war with Spain, Secretary of State Hay opened talks with the British minister in Washington, Sir Julian Pauncefote, aimed at abrogating the old treaty

The first Hay-Pauncefote Treaty, which was signed on February 5, 1900, was in some ways similar to the agreement it was designed to replace. The United States gained the right to build and control a canal. But it would still be bound to keep the waterway open to the commercial and naval vessels of all nations in war as well as in peacetime. Nor would Washington be allowed to fortify it against attack.

The agreement ran into stiff legislative opposition. Even Henry Cabot Lodge, a leading Senate Republican, refused to support it. Hay, who had little respect and less tolerance for most senators, was furious. To a friend he raged, "I have never seen such an exhibition of craven cowardice, ignorance, and prejudice." It had, he continued, "never entered into my mind that anyone out of a madhouse could have objected to the Canal

Convention." When a New York newspaper quoted Andrew Carnegie as saying that, if the treaty passed, it would be the death of the Republican party, Hay sneered, "the frantic little lunatic."[17]

But the last straw for Hay came when Theodore Roosevelt, then the Republican governor of New York, jumped into the fray, publicly criticizing the secretary's handiwork. "Et tu" Hay raged in what one historian has described as "a scorching" letter to his erstwhile friend. "Cannot you leave a few things to the President and the Senate, who are charged with them by the Constitution?"[18]

Hay's ranting notwithstanding, Lodge, Roosevelt, and the majority in the Senate had every right to be concerned. It is debatable whether the national interest would have been served by fortifying a canal. But there can be no doubt that a completely neutral canal open to America's enemies in wartime would have been enormously disadvantageous. After long debate, the Senate approved an amended version of the Hay-Pauncefote Treaty that would have allowed Washington to close the waterway to enemy shipping in the event of war.

When the British rejected the treaty as amended, a frustrated John Hay offered to resign. But McKinley would not hear of it. Instead he sent Hay back into the fray, no doubt with some sound advice on how important it was to keep in touch with Senate opinion when negotiating a treaty. On April 25, 1901, a new draft treaty, which authorized Washington to build, control, and fortify a canal, was forwarded to London. Though it was no more favorable to British interests than its predecessor, London reversed itself, approving the new pact. And so on November 18, Hay and Pauncefote met in the secretary's office in the old State, War, and Navy Building to sign the agreement. A few weeks later the Senate gave its assent.

PANAMA OR NICARAGUA?

At one time or another at least five different locations had been under consideration as possible sites for a canal. But by the early part of this century only two remained in contention. One, which crossed the Isthmus of Panama, had already been the scene of a failed attempt at canal construction by the defunct, De Lesseps Company. The other was the river and lake route that ran through Nicaragua.

The Nicaraguan route seemed an odds-on choice to be selected. The reports of various commissions dating back to President Ulysses S. Grant's time indicated that it was preferable from an engineering standpoint. Moreover, the Panama route was under lease to the New Panama Canal Company. This offspring of the De Lesseps Company was asking $109 million for its Panama holdings.

These considerations no doubt explain why, following the ratification of the Hay-Pauncefote Treaty, Secretary Hay undertook preliminary negotiations with Managua, and the House of Representatives passed a resolution by a vote of 308–2 calling for the construction of a Nicaraguan canal.

Critics of the New Panama Canal Company were right about many things, among them that the company's owners had no intention of actually building a canal. Their sole purpose was to sell the company's assets to the United States. To achieve this end they took into their employ one William N. Cromwell, partner in the New York law firm of Sullivan and Cromwell. A skilled lobbyist who reveled in his reputation as a mystery man about Washington—someone who brought people together and got things done— Cromwell worked for almost a decade to overcome official sentiment favoring the Nicaraguan route. He developed immense quantities of information to prove that Panama was the superior choice and spent lavishly to befriend and influence important political figures.

Cromwell's work paid off in a number of ways. He convinced Mark Hanna, the Ohio senator and confidant of President William McKinley, that the Panama route was the better of the two choices. And it was Hanna who turned out to be the most effective spokesperson for Panama during the Senate debate on the question. Cromwell was also instrumental in convincing President McKinley to appoint another commission of experts to report on the relative merits of each of the proposed canal routes. Moreover, it was Cromwell who convinced the commission members that they could learn most about the Panama route not in Central America's steaming, yellow fever–infested jungles, but in Paris, where the company had its records. And when the commission, headed by Admiral John G. Walker, arrived in the French capital, Cromwell was there to greet them. He remained with the commissioners throughout their long stay, providing information and of course lavish entertainment in that magnificent city.

While in Paris, the Walker Commission also came under the influence of Philippe Bunau-Varilla, the former chief engineer of the De Lesseps Company and once the director general of its successor. This charismatic Frenchman was driven by two parallel ambitions. First, he wanted to achieve the fulfillment of a dream he had entertained for two decades—the completion of a canal across the isthmus. Second, he wanted the New Panama Canal Company to net as much as was conceivable for its assets.

Between them, Cromwell and Bunau-Varilla put intense pressure on the Walker Commission, hoping for a report that would recommend building a Panama canal. Their best efforts notwithstanding, the commission's recommendation favored Nicaragua. The report did differ from earlier studies in one significant way, however. It made a strong case for the Panama route on engineering grounds. Only the fact that the New Panama Canal Company was asking $109 million for its assets made the Nicaraguan site more attractive. Admiral Walker explained to Bunau-Varilla that he believed the company's assets worth no more than $40 million and that at that price the Panama route would be more attractive.

On November 16, 1901, the commission made its recommendation public. With a bill authorizing the construction of a Nicaraguan canal already before Congress, all that remained, it seemed, was for Congress to return from its Christmas holiday and vote. At this point, however, the situation began to change. First, on January 4, 1902, following a stormy meeting of the stockholders, the New Panama Canal Company lowered the asking price for its lease and other assets to $40 million. Admiral Walker then told Congress that this change in the company's position changed things considerably. Finally, President Roosevelt jumped into the fray. After extensive discussions with the engineers on the Walker Commission, he became convinced that Panama was the superior route. At his suggestion the commission then issued a new report reversing its earlier recommendation. There ensued a battle royal in the Senate, where the Democrats, led by Senator John T. Morgan of Alabama, suspected that Roosevelt's sudden interest in the canal question had more to do with certain large political contributions made to the Republican party by Cromwell than with any engineering considerations.

All these developments notwithstanding, it still appeared that the Senate would endorse a Nicaraguan canal when the vote came. But that all changed just before eight in the morning on May 8, 1902, when a dormant volcano, Mount Pelée, on the island of Martinique exploded. In about two minutes the city of St. Pierre and its more than thirty thousand inhabitants perished.

The disaster came as wonderful news to Philippe Bunau-Varilla, who had come to the United States to lobby for the Panama site. For weeks he had been warning anyone interested in listening that Nicaragua, which was alive with volcanoes, was no place to put a canal. Now here was an example of what one could do. Aware that Nicaragua had issued a postage stamp with a picture of Mount Momotombo happily belching clouds of smoke, he rushed to a stamp dealer and purchased one of these little beauties for each senator. Bunau-Varilla's little gambit was hardly necessary. The catastrophe that had befallen Martinique was far too graphic a warning for the Senate to ignore. The Walker Commission's changed report, presidential pressure, and the explosion of Mount Pelée combined to change Senate opinion. By a vote of 42–34 the upper house voted in favor of a Panama site for the canal. A few days later the House fell into line, voting for Panama by the lopsided majority of 259–8.

REVOLUTION IN PANAMA

Bogotá had promised that, if Panama was selected as the site for the canal, there would be no trouble arranging an agreement transferring control of a canal zone to the United States. In fact, however, the negotiations turned into a nightmarish succession of frustrations for both sides. Two issues divided Washington and Colombia. The first was the question of sovereignty over the area in question. Washington wanted something akin to extraterritorial privileges, while President Marroquín, fighting for his political life, could ill-afford to make such a concession. The second issue had to do with the fact that the United States was prepared to pay $40 million to the New Panama Canal Company for its lease but only $10 million to Colombia for rights to the land.

After months of wrangling John Hay broke this deadlock by warning Dr. Tomás Herrán, the Colombian chargé in Washington, that if he refused to sign a treaty the administration would turn to the Nicaraguans. Hay was bluffing. Theodore Roosevelt was determined to have the Panama site. But the bluff worked. The Hay-Herrán Treaty signed early in 1903 authorized the United States to buy the French company's lease and granted Washington wide-ranging legal and administrative authority over a canal zone six miles wide. In return the United States agreed to pay Bogotá $10 million in cash and an annuity of $250 thousand. The agreement was to remain in effect for one hundred years and could be renewed at Washington's request.

Not long afterward rumors of Colombia's discontent began reverberating in Washington. When Roosevelt learned that the Colombian Senate might reject the treaty, he wrote that "those contemptible little creatures in Bogotá ought to understand how much they are jeopardizing things and imperiling their own future." As the moment of truth arrived, Hay, who had himself described the Colombians as "greedy little anthropoids," warned President Marroquín directly that if Colombia either rejected the treaty or delayed its ratification, the United States would take this as a breach of faith and that "action might be taken . . . which every friend of Colombia would regret."[19]

All of this bluster did no good. The Colombian Senate voted unanimously to reject the treaty. When Roosevelt learned of the rejection, he exploded in wrathful indignation. He was not going to allow "that Bogotá lot of jack rabbits . . . to bar one of the future highways of civilization." Hay agreed. The "poor creatures" in Colombia "had their spree," he wrote. "But now Blue Monday has come." Roosevelt and Hay now agreed that by hook or crook the United States would have the Panama route. Still, the secretary advised against moving too quickly. "Our intervention," he thought, "should not be haphazard."[20] Roosevelt, who agreed on the importance of moving carefully, ordered two army officers to Panama to assess the possibility of a revolution there. But before Roosevelt's agents could report, the president learned of a Panamanian revolutionary movement nearer at hand, one that promised to separate Panama from Colombia and provide the canal site the United States wanted with a minimum of direct American involvement.

This movement was headquartered in a very curious place, room 1162 of the Waldorf-Astoria Hotel, Philippe Bunau-Varilla's favorite haunt when in New York. Bunau-Varilla had come to New York for a meeting with Dr. Manuel Guerrero Amador, agent for a group of Panamanian revolutionaries. Almost from the moment of their meeting, Bunau-Varilla took charge of planning the revolution. With $40 million at stake, he wanted nothing to go wrong.

The Frenchman moved quickly, using a State Department go-between to arrange a meeting with the president. At this conference Roosevelt was careful to say nothing that could tie him directly to the revolutionaries. At the same time, however, he made his position clear. "I have no doubt," he later wrote, "that he was able to make a very accurate guess [as to how Roosevelt would react to a revolution] and to advise his people accordingly. In fact, he would have been a very dull man had he been unable to make such a guess."[21] A few days later, at a conference in the State Department, the Frenchman learned even more about what he might expect from the United States should Panama break from Colombia. When he remarked that Colombia's decision to reject the Hay-Herrán Treaty had made a Panamanian revolution more or less certain, John Hay said that the United States would not be caught napping in such an event. American naval forces, Hay pointedly explained, had already been ordered to sail for the isthmus.

Confident that he knew exactly what to expect from Washington, Bunau-Varilla provided Amador, who was to head Panama's provisional government, with the draft of a declaration of independence, a constitution, and a national flag that his wife and daughter had thoughtfully sewn for the revolutionaries. Most important he provided the $100,000 the revolutionaries needed to purchase the loyalty of the local Colombian garrison. On November 3, 1903, the day after the USS *Nashville* arrived in Colón on the Atlantic side of the isthmus, the conspirators in Panama City on the Pacific side declared Panamanian independence.

The revolution came off with only one hitch. Purely by chance a force of four hundred Colombian soldiers landed in Colón just before the rebels declared their intentions. Had this force been allowed to use the railroad that spanned the isthmus, it might have been able to crush the rebellion. But that possibility was blocked by Commander John Hubbard of the *Nashville*, who, acting on secret orders, forbade the use of the railroad to all military forces. There followed some tense negotiations involving Commander Hubbard, the officer in command of the Colombian force, and local railroad officials who were working in collusion with the revolutionaries. At length, however, with the *Nashville*, now close in shore, its decks cleared and its guns ready for action, the Colombians were persuaded to board a British steamer then docked at Colón and sail away. That was on November 5, the same day that the USS *Dixie*, the first of nine American warships to converge on Panama in the next several days, put four hundred marines ashore at Colón. On November 6, Washington extended de facto recognition to the republic of Panama.

The final stage in the rather tawdry story took place in Washington, where Bunau-Varilla had become Panama's first diplomatic representative. With the revolution an accomplished fact, he produced a revision of the Hay-Herrán Treaty that was so favorable to the United States there could be no doubt the Senate would give its blessings. Under terms of the revised agreement, sovereignty over the canal zone was transferred to Washington in everything but name. Second, the canal zone was to be controlled by

An American-controlled canal across Central America became a reality after Theodore Roosevelt and John Hay resorted to some blatant international skullduggery. Here the battleship USS *Utah* sails through the Gaillard Cut.

Washington "in perpetuity." Other articles of the treaty in fact turned Panama into a protectorate.

The first president to think seriously about constructing an interoceanic canal had been James K. Polk. Fifty years later the dream became a reality. And, although many criticized the president for this blatant act of international piracy, Roosevelt himself never doubted that he had acted correctly. In 1911, during a speech at the University of California's Greek Theater, he told eight thousand listeners, "I took the Isthmus, started the canal, and then left Congress not to debate the canal, but to debate me."[22] That was a view that never entirely lost its popularity. Seventy years later, when the Senate debated another Panama Treaty, this time one intended to return the Canal Zone to Panama, one senator who opposed the agreement remarked that the canal was ours, "we stole it fair and square."

CUBA, EVER ELUSIVE ISLE

Throughout the nineteenth century it had been a forgone conclusion among expansionists that one day the United States would annex Cuba. But when at last the opportunity came, the Teller Amendment—a pledge that the United States would not take the island—stood in the way.

The Spanish-American War left President McKinley in a dilemma. He was not prepared to violate the Teller Amendment. But neither was he willing to turn the island over to the insurgents, since no one of any stature in Washington believed the Cuban separatists were capable of creating a stable government. This judgment was founded on a set of interrelated considerations. First, the insurgents had thus far been unable to create anything resembling a functioning government. More important, American policy makers believed that to succeed, a government must have the support of its educated and propertied classes. But in Cuba this group had been almost solidly behind the Spanish during the war. Finally, there was the question of race. The Americans who went to Cuba were appalled by the character of the insurgent army. The guerrilla force that had fought the Spanish to a standstill was half-starved, poorly clothed, and undisciplined—and it was largely made up of illiterate Afro-Cuban peasants.

Many Americans who served in Cuba quickly concluded that civilization would not be served by turning Cuba over to the insurgents. "The Cubans are utterly irresponsible," one officer wrote. They are "partly savage, and have no idea of what good government means." Another thought that "Providence" had "reserved a fairer future for this noble country than to be possessed by this horde of tatterdemalions." Under American control Cuba would no doubt "blossom as the rose." And "in the course of three or four generations," he thought, "even the Cubans may be brought to appreciate the virtues of cleanliness, temperance, industry, and honesty." Welcomed by the Spanish and the propertied class of Cubans as though he had come to save the island from the insurgents, the American commander, General William Shafter wrote: "As I see it we have taken Spain's war upon ourselves."[23]

In a very short while such views came to dominate thinking in Washington, where policy makers agreed that the army should remain in Cuba until a stable, responsible, and friendly government had been established there. This arrangement, they believed, would prove mutually advantageous. For the United States it would mean increased trade, expanded investment opportunities, greater security for the canal that was soon to be built, and an end to European intervention in the region. For the indigenous population it would mean peace, prosperity, and a higher living standard. General Leonard Wood, who became governor general of Cuba in 1899, was quite specific in defining what he thought stability entailed: "When money can be borrowed at a reasonable rate of interest and when capital is willing to invest in the Island, a condition of stability will have been reached."[24]

As governor general, Wood worked to achieve two separate but related objectives—economic growth and the creation of a conservative, stable political order. His economic policies were a spectacular success. This growth, however, came at a price to the Cubans. The island was transformed into a virtual economic colony of the United States. Within three years American investments in Cuba had doubled. Over the next two decades Americans, who invested more than $1 billion in the island's economy, came to control a large share of the sugar and tobacco industries and were firmly entrenched in utilities, mining, banking, railroads, and communications.

As Roosevelt's secretary of war, Elihu Root drafted the Platt Amendment, which transformed Cuba into a protectorate of the United States and set the stage for American domination of the Caribbean region.

Unhappily for Wood, his efforts in the political realm did not work out nearly so well. He set out to create a Cuban-run administration for the island, recruiting upper-class Cubans to fill administrative positions wherever possible. By early 1900 the job was complete, and while he had been forced to employ some devoted Cuban nationalists who were less than enthusiastic about the American occupation, he still thought it "safe to say that eight out of ten people" in positions of authority "are our friends; by our friends I mean the friends of good government and of what we are doing."[25]

Creating a conservative administration for Cuba was one thing. But keeping it in power turned out to be quite another. Wood's instructions required him to hold an election to select delegates for a Constitutional Convention and to hold national elections as soon as possible. Aware that the great majority of the Cuban people had no use for those he was banking on to control Cuban political life, Wood disenfranchised about two-thirds of the Cuban electorate (males over the age of twenty-one) by establishing property and literacy requirements for voting.

These draconian measures notwithstanding, Wood's efforts to control the elections proved a dismal failure. The voting for delegates to the Constitutional Convention made it clear that Cuba's upper classes, too many of whom had supported Spain during the revolution, had no mandate to rule. "I am disappointed in the composition of the Convention," Wood explained to Secretary of War Elihu Root. It was controlled by the "worst agitators and political radicals in Cuba."[26] Under the circumstances, he warned, it would be a disastrous error for the United States to leave the island.

Satisfied that Cuba's future could not be left in the hands of the nationalists who controlled the convention, Secretary Root laid down harsh conditions that Cuba was required to meet before Washington would end the military occupation. The most important of Root's demands, which Congress enacted as the Platt Amendment to the Army Appropriations Act of 1901, gave the United States the right to intervene in Cuba to preserve the island's independence and to maintain a stable and responsible government on the island. It also guaranteed the United States rights to a naval base and stipulated that Cuba would not enter into arrangements with foreign powers tending to limit or impair the island's independence. Finally, it forbade the Cubans from leasing or in any other way alienating territory to a foreign government and required that they contract no debts that normal island revenues would be inadequate to repay.

The delegates to the convention at first resisted this obvious attempt to limit the new nation's sovereignty. But when it became clear that the alternative was continued military occupation, they very reluctantly incorporated the terms of the Platt Amendment in the new constitution. Cuba's leaders understood just how much they had surrendered, as did General Wood, who later observed, "There is, of course little or no independence left in Cuba under the Platt Amendment."[27] Cuba had become an American protectorate.

With the aid of General Wood, whose management of the election made the outcome a forgone conclusion, Tomás Estrada Palma was elected the first president of Cuba. The sixty-six-year-old patriot and former president of the Cuban Revolutionary party was, from the American point of view, a perfect choice. A naturalized American citizen who endorsed the Platt Amendment and advocated close economic ties with the United States, he viewed independence as a temporary condition, a way station on the road toward annexation to the United States. But the very same qualities that made him acceptable to the United States finally disqualified him to be president of a truly independent Cuba.

In 1906, following a corrupt election in which the opposition was systematically counted out at the polls by Estrada's Moderate party, a revolution broke out. This rebellion was in part a reaction to the crooked election. But it was also a reflection of the anger felt by Cuban nationalists who wanted more than the quasi-independence granted them by the United States.

President Estrada's government proved unable to put down the rebellion but was also unwilling to agree on a compromise that would have resulted in some sharing of power with the nationalist opposition. In fact

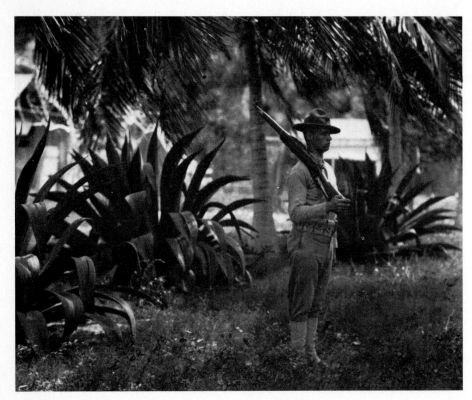

An American sentry stands guard at the Guantánamo naval base in Cuba, outpost of America's Caribbean empire.

the president and his supporters saw no reason to compromise. Instead they relied on the United States to crush the rebellion for them. Estrada resigned and informed Washington that he could no longer preserve order or protect life and property on the island. Under the terms of the Platt Amendment, this step should have triggered an American intervention to restore order and shore up the government.

Unhappily for Estrada's Moderates, things did not develop this way. Theodore Roosevelt, who had already gained an unsavory reputation in Latin America for earlier interventions, was furious. He had no desire to intervene in Cuba, especially to preserve a corrupt government. "I earnestly hope I can persuade the Cubans to act decently and go on governing themselves," he wrote. "I shall make every effort to this end and intervene only when it is evident that no other course is open."[28]

True to his word, Roosevelt sent not the marines but his premier troubleshooter, William Howard Taft, to look into the situation. Taft had hardly arrived in Cuba before he realized that the government Washington had so painstakingly created was "nothing but a house of cards."[29] That judgment was more accurate than even Taft guessed. Estrada Palma's government served Washington's interests very well indeed. But its pro-American policies meant that it could never claim the support of true Cuban nationalists. It had no mandate to rule save that conferred upon it by Washington.

Acting on Taft's advice and very much against his own inclinations, Roosevelt finally landed six thousand marines in Cuba and established a new provisional government for the island. Three years later, in 1909, a new Cuban government under General José Miguel Gomez took power. But the political realities remained unchanged. In years to come Cuban leaders often mouthed anti-American rhetoric when in search of political support at home. At the same time only a very few ever even considered throwing off the constraints imposed on Cuban independence by Washington. The Platt Amendment and Cuba's status as a virtual economic colony of the United States in a sense made real politics on the island impossible.

POLICING THE CARIBBEAN

When Theodore Roosevelt came to the presidency, he had no clear-cut policy for the Caribbean region. Within three years, however, a chain of events that began with a crisis in Venezuela and ended with another in the Dominican Republic led him to originate a new and revolutionary Caribbean policy that involved a major reinterpretation of the Monroe Doctrine.

Cipriano Castro, "the Lion of the Andes" and the dictator of Venezuela, provoked a crisis with England and Germany by refusing to repay debts owed to bondholders from those as well as certain other countries. After diplomatic efforts failed, Berlin and London agreed that, unless the United States objected, they would force Castro to pay up. The Roosevelt administration had no objections so long as no territory changed hands. On the contrary, as the president himself explained to a German acquaintance, "If any South American state misbehaves toward any European country, let the European country spank it."[30] In early December 1902, a joint Anglo-German naval force, taking TR at his word, destroyed or seized a number of Venezuelan gunboats, landed troops at La Guayra, and bombarded Puerto Cabello.

That was enough persuasion for Venezuela's Castro, who quickly suggested arbitration. Roosevelt, surprised by the strong negative reaction in the United States to the Anglo-German intervention, urged Berlin and London to agree, and they did so.

With Herbert Bowen, the American minister to Venezuela representing Castro, a settlement was hammered out that called for the repayment of Venezuela's debts to all bondholders regardless of their nationality. Only one issue remained unresolved. England and Germany insisted that their bondholders should be paid first since they had gone to the trouble and expense of forcing the Venezuelans to behave responsibly. This question was taken to the Permanent Court of International Justice at the Hague, where the justices upheld the claim of the blockading powers.

The court's decision, which placed a premium on the use of force, left Theodore Roosevelt in a quandary. Venezuela was not the only Caribbean nation to act irresponsibly toward foreign bondholders. On the contrary, such behavior was common practice in those southerly climes. It was unthinkable that the United States should protect Latin American countries attempting to repudiate their debts. But neither could the United States have the warships of foreign nations charging about an area as strategically and economically important as the Caribbean. Such thoughts led the president to only one conclusion. "If we are willing to let Germany or England act as the policemen of the Caribbean, then we can afford not to interfere when gross wrongdoing occurs. But if we intend to say 'Hands off' to the powers of Europe, then sooner or later we must keep order ourselves." In his December 1904 message to Congress, Roosevelt transformed that idea into a corollary to the Monroe Doctrine. Western hemispheric nations that behaved responsibly, he said, "need fear no interference from the United States." On the other hand,

> Chronic wrongdoing, or an impotence which results in a general loosening of the ties of civilized society, may in America, as elsewhere, ultimately require intervention by some civilized nation, and in the Western Hemisphere the adherence of the United States to the Monroe Doctrine may force the United States, however reluctantly, in flagrant cases of such wrongdoing or impotence, to the exercise of an international police power.[31]

In asserting America's role as the police of the Western Hemisphere, Roosevelt had a specific situation in mind. Between 1900 and 1903 the Dominican Republic had been under increasing pressure from European as well as American creditors. As if threats of foreign intervention to collect debts were not enough to trouble the government of President Carlos Morales, in 1903 civil war broke out on the island. To save himself, Morales proposed that the United States take the republic as a protectorate. But by this time Samaná Bay had lost its appeal. Roosevelt, who had enough foreign troubles without borrowing more, wanted no part of such an arrangement, telling a friend that he had "about the same desire to annex" the Dominican Republic "as a gorged boa constrictor might have to swallow a porcupine wrong-end-to."[32] Still, something had to be done to head off what appeared to be a carbon copy of the Venezuelan crisis. Though there was no immediate threat of European intervention, the situation inside the Dominican Republic was so chaotic, the chances that the Morales government would be able to pay its debts so remote, that Roosevelt felt compelled to head off that possibility.

The solution that Roosevelt settled upon was in effect a modified version of the Platt Amendment. President Morales agreed to negotiate a $20 million loan from American bankers to be used to refund the republic's debt and to allow Roosevelt to select a receiver general of customs. This official was to turn over 45 percent of the customs receipts to Morales for his country. The rest would go to pay the island nation's debts. To further ensure stability, order, and the continued rule of a cooperative government,

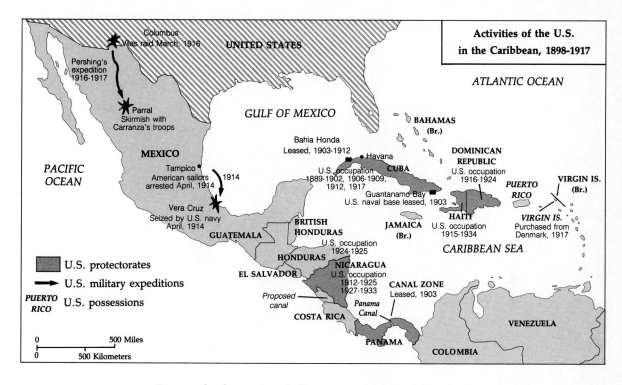

**Activities of the U.S.
in the Caribbean, 1898-1917**

ATLANTIC OCEAN

UNITED STATES

Columbus
Vilas raid March, 1916

Pershing's
expedition
1916-1917

GULF OF MEXICO

BAHAMAS
(Br.)

Parral
Skirmish with
Carranza's troops

Bahia Honda
Leased, 1903-1912

Havana

DOMINICAN
REPUBLIC

MEXICO

PACIFIC
OCEAN

Tampico
American sailors
arrested April, 1914   1914

CUBA

U.S. occupation
1889-1902, 1906-1909,
1912, 1917

U.S. occupation
1916-1924

PUERTO
RICO

VIRGIN IS.
(Br.)

Guantanamo Bay
U.S. naval base leased, 1903

Vera Cruz
Seized by U.S. navy
April, 1914

GUATEMALA

BRITISH
HONDURAS

JAMAICA
(Br.)

HAITI
U.S. occupation
1915-1934

VIRGIN IS.
Purchased from
Denmark, 1917

CARIBBEAN SEA

HONDURAS

U.S. occupation
1924-1925

EL SALVADOR

NICARAGUA
U.S. occupation
1912-1925
1927-1933

CANAL ZONE
Leased, 1903

Proposed
canal

Panama
Canal

VENEZUELA

COSTA RICA

PANAMA

COLOMBIA

◾ U.S. protectorates

➡ U.S. military expeditions

*PUERTO
RICO*   U.S. possessions

0   500 Miles
0   500 Kilometers

Roosevelt also ordered the navy to aid President Morales in his war against the rebels. Happy to oblige, the navy played a major role in bringing the war to a satisfactory conclusion. In fact the commander of the USS *Detroit* later claimed that he was "entirely responsible for the placing of Morales in power."[33]

Roosevelt, who was fond of the African proverb: "Speak softly and carry a big stick, you will go far," fundamentally altered the meaning of the Monroe Doctrine, transforming it into a justification for intervention in the internal affairs of nations throughout the hemisphere. Like those who succeeded him, he no doubt felt justified in taking this position. But repeated interventions have embittered Washington's relations with all of Latin America while making it abundantly clear that, so far as the United States is concerned, the sovereignty of almost all of the nations to the south has its limits. And those limits will be determined by policy makers on the Potomac.

TAFT, KNOX, AND DOLLAR DIPLOMACY

Theodore Roosevelt left the White House in 1909 satisfied that the country was in safe hands and that the policies he had established would be continued. But President William Howard Taft had very different ideas about a number of things, among them the sort of Far Eastern policy he hoped to pursue.

In the first place, Taft disagreed with Roosevelt's general assessment

When William Howard Taft entered the White House, he reversed Theodore Roosevelt's Far Eastern policy much to the disadvantage of the United States.

of both China and Japan. Roosevelt was disdainful of the Chinese, whom he viewed as a senile, untrustworthy, and despicable people. On the other hand, he had great admiration and respect for the Japanese, who had succeeded so well in superimposing a veneer of modernism over their traditional feudal culture. Taft, more sensitive than Roosevelt to the revolutionary stirrings then taking place in China, took a more sentimental position, arguing that the United States had a responsibility to guide and protect the Chinese as they went through the modernizing process.

Taft complemented his sympathy for China with an ingrained prejudice against Japan. In 1905 on a trip to the Far East he remarked, "A Jap is first of all a Jap and would be glad to aggrandize himself at the expense of anybody."[34] The anti-Japanese bias that Taft brought with him to the White House also had a powerful influence on his Far Eastern policies.

Taft chose as his secretary of state Philander Knox, a Wall Street attorney without previous diplomatic experience who shared his prejudices. Knox, who was given a free hand at the State Department, quickly abandoned Roosevelt's policy of accommodation with Japan in favor of one designed to challenge its position in Manchuria. The open door was once again in favor in Washington. But with a difference. John Hay had confined himself to note writing and what in those days passed for diplomatic finesse. Knox was short on finesse but determined to act on behalf of China and America's economic future there.

Where Roosevelt refused to be taken in by the delicious fantasy of the China market, both Knox and Taft spoke frequently of China's "almost boundless commercial possibilities" and saw their role at least in one sense as advance men for American commerce. "Today diplomacy works for trade," Knox said. "And the Foreign Offices of the world are powerful engines for the promotion of the commerce of each country."[35] If America was to achieve its commercial ends, China had to remain an independent and sovereign nation. Chinese integrity and America's commercial interests, therefore, were two sides of the same coin.

It was one thing to argue that the United States had a vital interest in defending the open door in China but quite another to develop a policy that had any chance of achieving that end. Russia and Japan were firmly entrenched in Manchuria, and the other imperialist powers continued to cling to their leaseholds and spheres of influence. Lacking domestic support for the forceful defense of the open door, how, then, was the United States to convince China's exploiters to change their ways?

The State Department's solution to this knotty problem was called "dollar diplomacy," a policy that aimed at creating an expanded American influence in China by economic means. This policy called for the government to take the lead in encouraging large-scale American investment in China's economic development with particular emphasis on railroad projects. Knox assumed that these investments would, as they had in the American West, begin a cycle of economic growth, creating vast new opportunities for further American investment. And just as the West had once formed an expanding market for eastern manufactured goods, so China would play a similar role for American producers in the decades to come. In this way the long-dreamed-of China market would become a reality, while China itself grew strong.

The political component of Knox's dream was as important as the economic side. As America's investment in China grew, Knox assumed that Washington's voice would necessarily carry more weight in deciding China's future. And the United States would exercise that influence to save China from dismemberment.

As a first step toward transforming dollar diplomacy from a theoretical possibility into a reality, Knox spearheaded a drive to organize the American Group, a consortium of powerful banking institutions. Members of the group, including representatives from Kuhn Loeb & Company, J. P. Morgan and Company, and National City Bank, agreed to work with the administration to develop investment opportunities in China. This partnership of government and business was never entirely cordial, however. The bankers were always interested in profits first, while the government often hoped to use the economic clout wielded through the American Group to achieve political aims regardless of profits.

Once the bankers had been organized, Knox pressed the Chinese, who were at first unenthusiastic, to allow American representation in a consortium of British, German, and French bankers then preparing to finance the construction of a railroad to run from Beijing (Peking) to Canton with a branch into Sichuan (Szechuan). At length, and much to the irritation of the European partners, Beijing granted the American Group a one-fourth share in the approximately £ 6 million loan.

In November 1909, encouraged by this early success, Knox undertook a much more ambitious initiative, this time trying for nothing less than the destruction of the Japanese sphere of influence in Manchuria. Knox advanced into the tangled thicket of Manchurian affairs ignorant and unprepared. The secretary's proposal was simplicity itself. He recommended that an international consortium of bankers purchase the Japanese and Russian railroads in Manchuria. In theory, once Manchuria's rail system had been internationalized, it was to be returned to China. In fact, however, the railroads would be supervised by the interested powers.

Had it succeeded, this "neutralization scheme" as it was called, would have destroyed the Russian and Japanese spheres of influence in Manchuria and opened the area to broadly based international investment that, Knox believed, would lead to rapid economic development, strengthen China's hold on the region, and create expanded opportunities for trade.

Knox seems to have assumed that the Russians would cooperate. He was just as convinced that the Japanese would not. But if Tokyo refused to sell, he proposed to build a railroad parallel to her South Manchurian line and engage in cutthroat competition to drive Japan from its sphere in southern Manchuria.

Seldom has a diplomatic initiative been more poorly conceived. Knox assumed, without consulting the Foreign Office, that he could count on British support for the plan. It is true that at this time London was trying to cultivate improved relations with the United States. But England could not afford to antagonize Russia or its ally Japan over Manchuria and so refused to support Knox. The secretary had also incorrectly assumed that the Russians were anxious to disentangle themselves from Manchuria and would happily sell the Chinese Eastern Railroad to an American-backed international consortium. Instead, the Russians categorically refused to play ball. As for the Japanese, they assumed, correctly, that Taft and Knox had aimed this initiative primarily at them. Their reaction was to draw closer to Russia. In January 1910, the two nations issued a joint statement denouncing the American plan. Six months later they announced a formal agreement recognizing each other's sphere of influence in Manchuria and agreeing to maintain the status quo there against the threat of foreign intervention.

Knox's scheme, designed to weaken the Russo-Japanese stranglehold over Manchuria, had instead strengthened it. China's control over the region had been further eroded, and the open door was less a reality than ever. Knox gained only one thing for his trouble—the enmity of Japan and Russia.

Criticism of administration blundering came from many quarters. But it was Roosevelt's personal criticism that stung Taft and Knox the most.

In attempting to put the administration back on the correct course, Roosevelt pointed out in a letter to Taft that "our vital interest" was to keep Japanese immigration at an absolute minimum while preserving Japan's "good will." On the other hand, the "vital interest of the Japanese is in Manchuria and Korea. It is therefore peculiarly our interest not to take any steps as regards Manchuria which will give the Japanese cause to feel, with or without reason, that we are hostile to them, or a menace—in however slight a degree—to their interests." Roosevelt thought the open door policy "an excellent thing," and he hoped that at some point in the future it could be "maintained by diplomatic agreement." But, he continued, "the whole history of Manchuria alike under Russia and . . . Japan" proves that the open door is closed "as soon as a powerful nation determines to disregard it, and is willing to run the risk of war rather than forgo its intention."[36]

Philander Knox defended his policies in a weakly argued reply to Roosevelt. But in the aftermath of the neutralization fiasco, he nevertheless changed his approach to Far Eastern affairs and moderated his hopes for what might be achieved in China. There would be no more spirited initiatives aimed at eliminating the Japanese and Russian spheres of influence in Manchuria. Instead, Knox tried to foster cooperation between the United States, Britain, Germany, and France. His hope was to work with these powers to moderate the more extreme behavior of Russia and Japan and win international support for the open door.

Toward that end Knox and Taft lent their support to the American Group, which was then negotiating an agreement under which American capitalists joined their European confreres in the Hukuang Railroad loan. Having failed to check the despoilers by direct action, Knox and Taft concluded that their only real choice was to join with them and to use the leverage created by economic cooperation to mitigate the worst aspects of imperialism in China. It was a forlorn hope based on the illogical assumption that one can be in league with a set of exploiters and yet not of them. The futility of this approach was brought home to American policy makers in 1911, when Japanese and Russian interests became part of the international consortium that Knox hoped to use to moderate their behavior.

Taft and Knox left office in March 1913, with their Far Eastern policy in a shambles. They had set out to establish the open door in China while at the same time protecting that unfortunate nation from exploitation and possible dismemberment. But they showed little understanding of international politics, adopting strategies that had no chance of succeeding. As a result of their efforts, Japan was transformed into a suspicious adversary commercial opportunities in Manchuria were further limited, and China' hold over that important province was further undermined.

DOLLARS AND BULLETS IN THE CARIBBEAN

Taft and Knox viewed the Roosevelt administration's Dominican experi as a great success. The country had a stable government; America's with the island republic was growing; and the country was paying its f debt promptly, thus reducing the danger of foreign intervention. Most important, all of this had been accomplished without a resort to force. Here, truly, it appeared that the United States had achieved its purposes by "substituting dollars for bullets." In the State Department, where dollar diplomacy was in vogue, they called it a "brilliant" achievement, a model for handling similar problems throughout the Caribbean and Central America.[37]

The Taft administration applied this remedy wherever instability reared its ugly head in Central America and the Caribbean, but always with disappointing results. The reason is clear. The premise that economic reforms alone could guarantee internal peace and stability in the region was a gross oversimplification based on an inadequate analysis of regional problems.

After 1905, for example, the Dominican Republic enjoyed a period of internal peace not because of the customs receivership but because it was ruled by President Ramón Cáceres, a strong and popular leader. Cáceres's assassination in November 1911 ushered in a long period of political unrest. A new government headed by General Alfredo Victoria quickly alienated other political leaders, who soon entered into armed opposition.

The Taft administration pressed the Victoria regime for economic and political reforms, hoping in this way to restore order. Failing that, Washington forced Victoria from power and arranged the election of a new government more completely under its control. But not even these efforts could end the chaos. When Taft left office in 1913, "the Dominican showcase" lay shattered, a monument to the illusion that dollars alone could bring stability to the region.

In 1907 the Roosevelt administration joined with Mexico in sponsoring a conference of Central American countries that met in Washington, D.C. Out of that conference came a treaty of peace and amity signed by all of the nations of the region. But Nicaragua's dictator, José Santos Zelaya, was more interested in consolidating Central America by conquest than in good relations with his neighbors. At the time Taft and Knox took power in Washington he was making threatening gestures toward Honduras and El Salvador. He was also encouraging revolutionary groups inside El Salvador and was interfering in Costa Rica's election. From Washington's perspective, he was the prime troublemaker in all of Central America and openly anti-American to boot.

In 1909, General Juan J. Estrada led a revolution against Zelaya. Though in fact Washington was delighted by this development, Taft and Knox, anxious to avoid arousing anti-American sentiment in Latin America, adopted a policy of strict neutrality in the early stages of the conflict. Then, however, Zelaya made a serious mistake, ordering the execution of Lee Roy Cannon and Leonard Groce, two American soldiers of fortune serving with the rebels. In Washington, where tears were seldom shed for the likes of Cannon and Groce, policy makers decided to make the most of the incident. The United States made a formal protest and demanded reparations. When Zelaya didn't move quickly enough, they gave serious consideration to military action but stopped short of that, breaking off diplomatic relations.

The purpose of this American pressure was to force Zelaya from power. And it succeeded. The dictator resigned and went into exile. But Washington was not pleased with José Madriz, who succeeded to the presidency. He had been too close to Zelaya, too much a part of the old governing elite. President Taft therefore decided to withhold recognition from the new regime, hoping that General Estrada's rebels would win the ongoing civil war. For a time that seemed unlikely. Early in 1910 government forces had Estrada's army pinned down in Bluefields, their last stronghold, and were preparing to deliver the decisive blow, when the United States Navy interceded to save him.

Once it became clear that the United States was prepared to use force on behalf of General Estrada, the Madriz government fell to pieces. Estrada became the provisional president on August 31, 1910.

With all of the pieces at last in place, Washington then attempted to apply the Dominican solution in Nicaragua. Secretary of State Knox withheld American recognition, something Estrada desperately needed, until Nicaragua agreed to negotiate a loan with American bankers for the purpose of reorganizing Nicaragua's finances. To secure the loan, Estrada was forced to appoint an American expert with control over Nicaragua's customs houses as well as the power to reorganize the country's finances. Only then did Washington extend recognition to his government.

Administration hopes notwithstanding, political instability continued in Nicaragua, and General Estrada was driven from power to be replaced by his vice-president, Adolfo Díaz. Still the instability continued.

In July 1912, the minister of war, General Luis Meña, led the army into open rebellion. Meña's rebellion posed an especially serious problem for Washington because it was accompanied by a virulent brand of anti-Americanism. With Nicaragua now heavily in debt to those American bankers who had only recently financed the refunding of the national debt, the American minister in Managua asked the Díaz regime to guarantee that it could protect American lives and property. The embattled Díaz, who saw this as an opportunity to save his tottering government, replied that such a guarantee was impossible and asked Washington to land troops not only to protect American lives and property but to protect "all the inhabitants of the republic."[38]

In the summer of 1912 the United States landed two thousand marines and bluejackets in Nicaragua. In earlier such ventures, troop landings had been enough to quell a rebellion. But in Nicaragua anti-Americanism was so strong that the American forces had to join in the fighting. By September the rebellion was virtually over and most of the marines had been withdrawn. But a large legation guard remained, a warning that the United States would not tolerate further revolutionary activity.

In Santo Domingo and Nicaragua, and in Honduras and Guatemala, too, dollar diplomacy failed. It failed because it was founded on the false assumption that the Caribbean and Central American elitists who struggled for power wanted one thing only—control of national revenues. In most instances this meant the customs houses. Policy makers concluded, therefore, that by establishing customs receiverships the United States could create a disincentive for revolution and encourage internal peace and stability. This hopelessly inadequate analysis failed to take into account the fact that political instability is often the result of cultural considerations, personal ambition, and other noneconomic factors. It also neglected the possibility that some governments provoked revolution simply by being needlessly repressive.

ENDNOTES

1. Hilary Herbert, quoted in Charles E. Neu, *The Troubled Encounter: The United States and Japan* (John Wiley and Sons, N.Y., 1975), p. 33.

2. John Hay, quoted in A. Whitney Griswold, *The Far Eastern Policy of the United States* (Harcourt Brace and Co., N.Y., 1938), p. 78.

3. Robert Hart, quoted in Michael Hunt, *The Making of a Special Relationship: The United States and China to 1914* (Columbia University Press, N.Y., 1983), p. 187.

4. John Hay, Circular Telegram, July 3, 1900, *Foreign Relations of the United States, 1900* (Washington, 1901), p. 299.

5. Hay, quoted in Howard K. Beale, *Theodore Roosevelt and the Rise of America to World Power* (Johns Hopkins University Press, Baltimore, Md., 1956) p. 195.

6. Theodore Roosevelt, quoted in Michael Hunt, *Frontier Defense and the Open Door: Manchuria in Chinese-American Relations, 1895–1911* (Yale University Press, New Haven, Ct., 1973), pp. 77–78.

7. Roosevelt to Hay, July 18, 1903, *The Letters of Theodore Roosevelt*, ed. Elting E. Morison (Harvard University Press, Cambridge, Mass., 1951), III, p. 638; see also Warren I. Cohen, *America's Response to China* (Columbia University Press, N.Y., 3rd ed., 1990) pp. 26–54.

8. Theodore Roosevelt to Theodore Roosevelt Jr., Feb. 10, 1904, *ibid.*, IV, p. 724; Prime Minister Katsura Tarō, quoted in Akira Iriye, *Pacific Estrangement, Japanese and American Expansion, 1897–1911* (Harvard University Press, Cambridge, Mass., 1972), p. 93.

9. Roosevelt, quoted in Beale, *Theodore Roosevelt*, p. 314.

10. Quoted in Hunt, *Frontier Defense*, p. 166.

11. Tōgō Minoru's *Nihon, Shokumin-ron*, translated and quoted in Akira Iriye, *Pacific Estrangement: Japanese and American Expansion, 1897–1911* (Harvard University Press, Cambridge, 1972), p. 132.

12. Taft Katsura Agreement, quoted in Tyler Dennett, *Roosevelt and the Russo-Japanese War*, (Doubleday and Page, N.Y., 1922), pp. 112–14.

13. *Shinsekai*, November 16, 28, 1906, translated and quoted in Iriye, *Pacific Estrangement*, pp. 140–41.

14. Elihu Root, quoted in Charles E. Neu, *The Troubled Encounter*, pp. 49–50.

15. Japanese Ambassador to the Secretary of State, November 30, 1908, *Foreign Relations of the United States, 1908*, (Washington, 1912), pp. 510–11; see also Raymond Esthus, *Theodore Roosevelt and Japan* (University of Washington Press, Seattle, Wash., 1967), pp. 266–87.

16. William McKinley, quoted in Lewis Gould, *The Presidency of William McKinley* (University of Kansas Press, Lawrence, Ks., 1980), p. 196; Roosevelt, quoted in David McCulloch, *The Path Between the Seas* (Simon and Schuster, N.Y., 1977), p. 254.

17. Hay, quoted in Beale, *Theodore Roosevelt*, pp. 102–3.

18. John Hay, quoted in *ibid.*, p. 103.

19. Hay, quoted in Henry F. Pringle, *Theodore Roosevelt, A Biography* (Harcourt Brace and Co., N.Y., 1931), pp. 311–12.

20. Hay, quoted in Kenton Clymer, *John Hay: The Gentleman as Diplomat* (Ann Arbor, 1975), pp. 205–7.

21. Roosevelt, quoted in Pringle, *Theodore Roosevelt*, p. 325.

22. Roosevelt, quoted *ibid.*, p. 330.

23. William Shafter and others, quoted in Louis A. Perez Jr., *Cuba Between Empires, 1878–1902* (University of Pittsburgh Press, Pittsburgh, Pa., 1983), pp. 215, 218.

24. Leonard Wood, quoted in David F. Healy, *The United States in Cuba, 1898–1902* (University of Wisconsin Press, Madison, Wis., 1963), p. 133.

25. Wood, quoted in Perez, *Cuba Between Empires*, p. 292.

26. Wood, quoted in *ibid.*, p. 310.

27. Wood, quoted in *ibid.*, p. 349.

28. Roosevelt, quoted in Dana G. Munro, *Intervention and Dollar Diplomacy in the Caribbean, 1900–1921* (Princeton University Press, Princeton, N.J., 1964), p. 129.

29. William Howard Taft, quoted in Henry F. Pringle, *The Life and Times of William Howard Taft* (Farrar and Rinehart, N.Y., 1939), II, p. 307.

30. Roosevelt, quoted in Dexter Perkins, *The Monroe Doctrine, 1869–1907* (Johns Hopkins University Press, Baltimore, Md., 1937), p. 333; see also Beale, *Theodore Roosevelt*, pp. 396–98, 406.

31. Roosevelt, quoted in Pringle, *Roosevelt*, p. 295; Roosevelt, quoted in Perkins, *A History of the Monroe Doctrine* (Little, Brown and Co., Boston, 1941), pp. 240–41.

32. Roosevelt, quoted in Dana G. Munro, *Intervention and Dollar Diplomacy in the Caribbean*, p. 91.

33. Quoted in *ibid.*, p. 94.

34. William Howard Taft, quoted in Hunt, *The Making of a Special Relationship*, p. 210.

35. Philander Knox, quoted in Michael Hunt, *The Making of a Special Relationship* (Columbia University Press, N.Y., 1983), p. 209.

36. Theodore Roosevelt, quoted in A. Whitney Griswold, *The Far Eastern Policy of the United States* (Yale University Press, New Haven, Conn., 1938), pp. 131–32.

37. Knox, quoted in Walter V. and Marie V. Scholes, *The Foreign Policies of the Taft Administration* (University of Missouri Press, Columbia, Mo., 1970), p. 40.

38. Alfredo Díaz, quoted in *ibid.*, p. 65.

Woodrow Wilson practiced a form of moral imperialism that led to repeated interventions in the internal affairs of America's Latin American neighbors.

16

WILSON AND MORAL DIPLOMACY, 1913–1917

In March 1913, Woodrow Wilson became the first Democrat since Cleveland and the first southerner since Zachary Taylor to take the oath of office as president of the United States. A Virginian and the son of a Presbyterian minister, Wilson was a true "scholar in politics." After receiving his Ph.D. in 1886, he taught history and political science at Bryn Mawr and then at Wesleyan University before returning to his alma mater, Princeton. A popular teacher and a fine scholar—his study *Congressional Government* (1885) was a highly respected work—he was elected president of the university in 1902. In 1910, after fighting a losing battle over plans for a graduate school he left the university to run for governor of New Jersey and won. Two years later, thanks in part to a bitter split in the Republican party, he was elected president.

Wilson was an eloquent speaker and a brilliant man. But he was not likable. Arrogant, self-righteous, and cursed with a stubbornness that did not serve him well, he tried to dominate others and compromised only when he felt he had to. His schoolmaster's demeanor did not sit well with many, especially on the Republican side of the aisle in Congress, who bridled at his condescending ways.

The inheritor of Taft's failed Far Eastern policy, Wilson came to power at a critical moment in Chinese history. By 1913 the Manchu dynasty had collapsed and been replaced by a shaky government headed by Yüan Shihkai. Predictably, the various foreign powers with Chinese interests used the opportunity created by China's increasingly chaotic political situation to penetrate further into Manchuria, Xinjiang (Sinkiang), Tibet, Mongolia, and elsewhere.

In considering the Far Eastern situation, Wilson was moved less by his concern for China as a market or an area of political and strategic importance than by a sense of moral outrage. The president learned most of what little he knew about China from missionary accounts of the situation there. These were overwhelmingly critical of the exploitative imperialist powers and supportive of Yüan Shihkai's (Shih-k'ai's) republic. Moved by these accounts as well as his own sympathy for Yüan, whom he mistakenly believed to be struggling to establish a democratic political system, Wilson explained early in his administration that he felt "keenly the desire to help China."[1]

Given these attitudes, it is not surprising that shortly after taking office the new president executed a dramatic shift in America's Far Eastern policy. He described it as a return to the principles first enunciated by John Hay, which he mistakenly believed had been abandoned by Taft and Knox. But there was a difference, for where Hay's policy sprang from a combination of commercial ambition and geopolitical concerns, Wilson's purposes were fundamentally moralistic.

Not a week after his inauguration President Wilson was approached by representatives of the American Group, who were anxious to know his attitude toward future investment in China. During the last months of the Taft administration the six-nation banking consortium had been approached by Yüan's government, which was seeking a loan to help reorganize China's finances and stabilize the regime. As the talks progressed, the American members of the consortium lost interest in the deal. They doubted that a large issue of Chinese bonds would appeal to American investors and were jittery about how the Wilson administration would react to the loan. The bankers told Wilson that they had never been enthusiastic about investing in China. And now, with that nation in chaos, they were even less inclined to do so. They were willing to continue as active participants in the consortium only if Wilson requested their cooperation and guaranteed that the government would stand behind them.

Wilson, who had campaigned against the "special interests," misunderstood the nature of the relationship that had existed between the bankers and the Taft administration. He assumed that the State Department had been fronting for a group of exploitative capitalists anxious to profit at China's expense. Without consulting State Department officials, whom he distrusted, the president withdrew the government's support from the American Group. In a statement to the press he explained that he found the terms of the loan agreement then being negotiated unacceptably exploitative, dangerously close to threatening "the administrative independence of China itself."[2] Wilson thus ended the group's involvement in the consortium and, not incidentally, destroyed the only vehicle at hand for influencing developments in China.

Not long after this Wilson took another dramatic but misguided step, extending diplomatic recognition to Yüan Shihkai's (Shih-K'ai's) government. Tokyo objected that the decision was premature, since China was in a state of political chaos with Sun Yat-sen's Guomindang (Kuomintang) party challenging Yüan and that recognition would "practically amount to interference in favor of Mr Yüan."[3] Others noted that Yuan's was not the sort of government the United States ought to support. It was a republic in name only. Moreover, there was strong reason to believe that Yüan himself had been involved in at least one recent political assassination. But Wilson, anxious to take the moral high ground, ignored all such arguments.

It was one thing to stand on the side of truth, justice, and the open door, a moral exemplar for the Chinese to follow, but quite another to organize a policy that promised positive results. When it came to developing an effective policy, Wilson had nothing to offer. He was strong on rhetoric and moral posturing but weak on performance. In fact, he was not even inclined to pay close attention to Far Eastern developments unless literally forced by circumstances to do so.

THE RETURN OF THE YELLOW PERIL

The spring of 1913, when racial tensions in California produced a renewed crisis with Japan, was one of those moments. Japanese immigration into the Golden State had ended before this. But California's established Japanese population was fifty thousand and growing. The mere existence of a thriving Japanese community, even this relatively small one, was too much for the state's Japanophobes.

The fact that many of California's Japanese residents were acquiring agricultural land seemed particularly threatening to some. Thus Senator James D. Phelan warned that if something was not done his state would soon become nothing more than a "Japanese plantation." The California legislature responded by enacting the Webb Alien Land Act, which forbade those "unqualified for citizenship" from owning land in California.[4]

Wilson, who shared Taft's antipathy for the Japanese and opposed their immigration on racial grounds, did nothing to discourage California's lawmakers from passing the Webb Act. A few days after its passage, however, he was jolted by a strong note from Tokyo objecting to the Webb Act and asking that Japanese immigrants living in the United States be guaranteed the same rights as resident aliens from other countries.

The Japanese protest was firmly stated, but there was nothing in it that should have caused a panic. Yet the military jumped to the conclusion that war was imminent. The Army and Navy Joint Board urged Wilson to redeploy ships from Chinese waters to the Philippines and to strengthen American land forces there as well as in Hawaii. Admiral Bradley Fiske, who seems to have believed that Hawaii and the Philippines were in immediate danger, warned the president that "war was not only possible but even probable."[5]

Wilson refused to make any military preparations on the ground that such movements would promote hysteria at home and might be viewed as provocative in Tokyo. The president's decision should have been final. But the Joint Board leaked its views to the press, setting off a minor panic. The members of the board may have assumed that the public hysteria would force Wilson to follow their advice. But they had badly misjudged their man. Infuriated, he dissolved the board and pursued a diplomatic settlement with Japan.

By the end of May 1913, tensions had eased, and the war scare was over. But kind words and conciliatory gestures had not resolved the basic problem. The Webb Act was still the law in California, and Tokyo remained displeased that Japanese citizens were not accorded the same rights as other resident aliens in the United States.

World War I came as a heaven-sent opportunity to the Japanese. With Europe in turmoil, Tokyo moved quickly first to strengthen its position on the Asian continent and then to establish itself as the paramount power in China. Japan began by joining the Allies and seizing Germany's holdings in Micronesia, at Qingdao (Tsingtao) on Kiaochow Bay, and on the Shandong (Shantung) Peninsula. Next, to assure hegemony in China, Tokyo forwarded to Beijing (Peking) a peremptory note listing twenty-one demands separated into five groups. The first four of these groups were intended to secure Japan's position on the Shandong Peninsula and in other areas it claimed as spheres of influence. These were rough equivalents to the sort of concessions that European imperialists had claimed elsewhere in China. But the fifth group was quite different. The concessions Tokyo demanded here were clearly aimed at transforming China into a Japanese protectorate.

Though the Japanese warned Beijing not to reveal the nature of these demands, Chinese officials leaked them to Western diplomats, hoping to win support. Paul Reinsch, the American minister in China who was very pro-Chinese, urged the administration to take a strong stand against Japan. Under ordinary circumstances Wilson would no doubt have taken the diplomat's advice. But the president, who was then preoccupied by a deepening crisis with Mexico and the dangerous European situation, had no time for China. He left the issue in the hands of Secretary of State William Jennings Bryan.

Bryan, who unlike the president admired and trusted the Japanese, sent a note objecting to Tokyo's fifth category of demands. At the same time, however, in a remark that seemed to indicate the United States was backing away from the open door, he admitted that "territorial contiguity" created "special relations" between Japan and China.[6] When the Japanese assured the secretary that their differences with Beijing were in fact not very great, he backed still further away, leaving both Tokyo and Beijing with the impression that the United States had no quarrel with Japan's China policy.

After receiving strident complaints from Paul Reinsch in Beijing about Bryan's bungling, Wilson himself took over the direction of Far Eastern policy. In a move that no doubt puzzled and confused the Japanese, who on the basis of their dealings with Bryan could only have concluded that the United States was willing to acquiesce in their China policy, he sent a firm warning to Tokyo in the form of a strong reiteration of the open door policy with special reference to maintaining the territorial integrity as well as the sovereignty of China.

Not long after receiving Wilson's warning, Tokyo in fact did abandon its claims under the fifth group of the twenty-one demands. Japan did so, however, not because of American objections but in response to a strong protest from its British ally and as a result of opposition from elder statesmen inside the Japanese power structure who believed that the attempt to turn China into a protectorate went too far.

At this point, with little hope of any further help from Britain and nothing more substantive than rhetoric coming out of Washington, Beijing came to terms with Japan. An agreement signed by the two Asian nations confirmed Japan's claims to its spheres of influence in Manchuria and China proper and tightened the economic ties that bound China to Japan's growing empire.

Aware of the importance of gaining great power approval for its expanded position in China, Tokyo next launched a carefully orchestrated diplomatic offensive that netted it most of the support it required. In 1916, Britain, Russia, and France all recognized Japan's paramount position in China. Only one important power with Far Eastern interests refused to go along. The last word from Washington on this subject came in identical notes sent to Beijing and Tokyo, in which the president refused to recognize any agreements that either violated the principles of the open door or limited American treaty rights in China.

Wilson thus identified the United States as the sole obstacle standing between Japan and the achievement of its aims in China. Such a policy might have been acceptable if Wilson had been willing to back up his words with force. But he wasn't. Since Japan viewed its interests on the Asian continent as vital and worth fighting for, Wilson's policy left the United States frustrated and, some argued, humiliated. Theodore Roosevelt once explained that an old cowboy saying, "Never draw unless you mean to shoot," was sound advice in diplomacy. [7] Wilson followed another line of reasoning—that the United States ought always to stand for moral principles. Unhappily, however, to take a moral stand, as he did in this case, did China no good and contributed to the worsening relationship between Japan and America.

In April 1917, the United States entered World War I against the Central Powers and became in effect Japan's ally. Nevertheless, relations between the two countries remained in a state of disarray. Suspicions were rife. Some inside Japan's ruling elite believed that Japan and the United States were headed for a showdown over control of the western Pacific and China. They argued that Washington would use the war as a pretext to strengthen its military and naval forces in the Pacific in preparation for war with Japan.

A number of American policy makers in the State Department and the military were thinking along similar lines. Convinced that Japan and the United States were destined someday to clash, the Navy's General Board concluded that the United States should develop a naval force capable of controlling the western Pacific, an area that was, in a manner of speaking, Japan's backyard. To achieve that end, the board recommended the construction of a fleet no less than twice the size of Japan's.

All the war talk notwithstanding, Washington and Tokyo were both anxious to improve relations. With that in mind, Viscount Kikujiro Ishii and Secretary of State Robert Lansing, who had replaced Bryan at the State Department, opened negotiations in August 1917. But the talks hit a snag almost immediately. Both sides wanted better relations. But neither Washington nor Tokyo was prepared to make the necessary concessions. Wilson's most trusted adviser, Colonel Edward House, urged the president to recognize Japan as more or less preeminent in China. Otherwise, he thought, trouble was certain. "Japan is barred from all the undeveloped places of the earth, and if her influence in the East is not recognized as in some degree superior to that of the Western powers, there will be a reckoning."[8] But Wilson, who remained sympathetic to China and committed to a rigid interpretation of the open door policy, was unprepared to make any such concession. Nor could he, for domestic political reasons, satisfy the Japanese on the questions of immigration and land ownership in California. As for the Japanese, they wanted nothing less than an American recognition of their "paramount interests" in China.

Though it soon became clear that no basis existed for a substantive agreement, neither side wanted to admit this publicly. And so the diplomats drafted a deliberately vague, ambiguous accord. Under the terms of the Lansing-Ishii Agreement of 1917 the United States and Japan reaffirmed their joint commitment to the open door in China and to China's territorial integrity and independence. At the same time, however, the United States recognized that Japan had certain unspecified "special interests" in China.[9] Because the meaning of this phrase went unexplained, each side was able to interpret the agreement quite differently. Secretary Lansing understood that the agreement settled nothing. He and Viscount Ishii made that clear in a secret protocol to the agreement in which they agreed to maintain the status quo in China until after the war, when, presumably, further negotiations would take place. The two nations had merely agreed to put off until another time their contest over the future of China and the Pacific.

WILSON'S CARIBBEAN INTERVENTIONS

During the presidential election campaign, Latin Americans thrilled to Woodrow Wilson's rhetoric, to his denunciation of dollar diplomacy and Republican imperialism. But Wilson behaved in much the same way as his predecessors. Nor was he averse to using force to achieve his ends. On the contrary, his criticism of Republican tactics notwithstanding, he intervened in the Caribbean more frequently than either Roosevelt or Taft.

Nicaragua's problems had by no means been resolved by the time Wilson assumed office. The Díaz government, which, it will be recalled, came to power with more than a little help from Taft and Knox, was virtually bankrupt. The salaries of government employees had not been paid in months, and the government's creditors were demanding payment of long-standing debts. The government's problems, of course, encouraged rival political factions to think in terms of a coup.

Wilson and Bryan believed that financial aid was the key to internal peace in Nicaragua and did just what Taft and Knox would have done. The secretary worked with the Díaz regime and a group of New York bankers to arrange the necessary loan. Though the bankers did finally agree to extend a loan, it was not nearly enough to resolve Nicaragua's ongoing problems. Bryan then tried another approach. The Taft administration had earlier negotiated a treaty with Nicaragua that granted the United States control over Nicaragua's canal route, a naval base in the Gulf of Fonseca and a lease on the Corn Islands. In return the United States had agreed to pay Nicaragua $3 million. This 1911 agreement had been rejected by the Senate. But Bryan now revived the project in the form of the Bryan-Chamorro Treaty of 1914. He wasn't so much interested in the strategic advantages it offered the United States as the economic aid it could provide to the Nicaraguans. The Bryan-Chamorro Treaty as finally ratified by the Senate was a major disappointment to the Wilson administration. The $3 million it produced did next to nothing to resolve Nicaragua's financial problems. Political instability there remained a serious problem as well.

Just how much of a problem this was, and how determined the Wilson administration was to maintain order in Central America, became clear in 1916 when Nicaragua was scheduled to hold presidential elections. Wilson's commitment to democratic principles notwithstanding, the State Department interceded to block the efforts of antigovernment candidates and secure the election of General Emiliano Chamorro, a man who was popular in Washington because of his pro-American views and his willingness to cooperate closely with the administration. To make certain that no further revolutionary activity followed Chamorro's election, the United States retained an unusually large legation guard in Managua as a symbol of American power and a warning to potential revolutionaries.

In the Dominican Republic, where an American-controlled customs receivership remained in place, Wilson was again confronted by an unstable, not to say chaotic, political situation. He concluded that greater control was needed and that the United States would have to intervene to put all the nation's financial affairs on a sound footing and end internal corruption as well. He pressed the Dominican government for control not only of the customs houses but of all aspects of national finance. This pressure was, of

American marines on patrol in Santo Domingo.

course, an unacceptable intrusion on Dominican sovereignty and was for that reason resisted. Even the Platt Amendment had not gone so far.

After the First World War began, Washington's demands grew more strident. For years American policy makers had been concerned over the possibility that Germany, the only major naval power without a base in the Western Hemisphere, might seek one in the Caribbean. Continued instability in the Dominican Republic seemed an open invitation to German intervention.

By the autumn of 1915 the State Department was no longer asking but demanding that the Dominican government turn control of customs, government finance, and the military over to Washington. Finally, in 1916, an exasperated Wilson landed troops to enforce his demands. His original plan was to disarm the various factions on the island and hold democratic elections—at the point of a gun. The new government would then be required to make all the concessions demanded earlier by the State Department.

This fantastic scheme, clearly a reflection of the president's frustration, led to a complete fiasco. The intervention produced a tidal wave of anti-Americanism in the Dominican Republic that made anything other than continued military occupation of the country impossible. And so the United States Navy ruled there until 1921. Not until 1924 did Washington think it safe to allow real elections.

The republic of Haiti shares the island of Hispaniola with the Dominican Republic. There, revolution had been a way of life as one revolutionary dictatorship followed another in monotonous succession. Elections were farcical and governments uniformly corrupt. A rebellion in early 1914 marked the beginning of an unusually prolonged period of political unrest, during which the Haitian government failed to make the required payments on its foreign debt, much of which was owned by German and French bondholders.

Wilson and Secretary of State Bryan felt they had to take steps to end disorder inside Haiti in order to ensure the continued payment of the republic's foreign debt and eliminate the possibility of foreign intervention there. While they were considering how best to achieve these ends, General Guillaume Sam, the latest Haitian dictator, was overthrown in a coup and fled to the French legation in Port-au-Prince. Before his flight General Sam made one very serious mistake. He ordered the execution of 167 political prisoners. The next day an organized mob broke into the French legation, dragged General Sam into the street, and literally hacked him to pieces. This was in July 1915, by which time the war in Europe was eleven months old. Unwilling to give either France or Germany an opportunity to intervene and perhaps remain in Haiti, President Wilson sent in the marines.

After order had been restored, the United States Navy supervised presidential elections and forced the newly created Haitian government to agree to a treaty that granted Washington control of its customs houses, its finances, and the military. The treaty also gave the United States the Platt Amendment right to intervene militarily in Haitian affairs to defend the terms of the treaty and Haitian independence and to protect lives and property on the island. This 1915 agreement marked the beginning of a fifteen-year period during which American forces remained in Haiti, a constant reminder that Haitian independence was more myth than reality.

Following the acquisition of the site for the Panama canal, the purpose of three successive administrations was to forge a policy that would be beneficial not only to the United States but to Caribbean and Central American states as well. Had they succeeded, the United States would have profited from an expanding regional trade, improved investment opportunities, an end to European intervention, and greater security for the Panama Canal. The Caribbean peoples would have benefited from peace and improved economic and social conditions.

Though in the short run it appeared that dollar diplomacy had succeeded in the Dominican Republic, it soon became clear that stability could not be achieved by economic means alone. And when the United States was confronted with the choice of leaving the peoples of Central America and the Caribbean free to fight things out among themselves or intervening with military force to establish order, policy makers in Washington invariably chose the latter course. There was always a good reason for this. Sometimes American economic interests seemed threatened. On other occasions intervention was considered a strategic necessity. But no matter how the United States justified its behavior, it was clear that the peoples of Central America and the Caribbean were free only in a nominal sense and that their sovereignty was limited by the strategic and economic needs of the United States.

MEXICO, THE FORGOTTEN REVOLUTION

For more than three decades, from 1876 until 1910, Mexico was governed by Porfirio Díaz. It was a period of relative stability and economic progress for the country. But it was not a time that the great mass of the Mexican people remember fondly. Foreigners and a small group of elitists controlled Mexico's land and resources, while most of its fifteen million people lived as landless peasants in a feudal condition.

By 1910, the Díaz dictatorship was on its last legs, threatened by an accumulation of discontents at all levels of Mexican society. As the presidential elections of that year approached, Díaz found himself on the defensive, challenged by a number of opposition leaders. These men had emerged from the shadows of Mexican politics after the dictator himself thoughtlessly suggested in an interview with an American newspaperman that he believed Mexico was ready for democracy.

Among those hoping to bring down the dictator, none was more prominent than Francisco de Madero. Idealist, dreamer, and mystic, Madero headed the Anti-Reelection party. A practicing spiritualist who believed that he was in contact with the great minds of the past, this slight, frail-looking man thought he had been chosen to bring about a major revolution not only in Mexico but perhaps throughout the world.

When it became clear during the election campaign that Madero was attracting support, Díaz had him arrested, tried on charges of sedition, convicted, and imprisoned. With Madero out of the way, the old man himself went on to an overwhelming victory at the polls. But Díaz paid a high price for having made a mockery of the elections. Once it became clear that honest elections were impossible, revolution became inevitable.

The spark that kindled this astonishing event came when Madero escaped from his prison cell and fled to San Antonio, Texas, where he took control of a revolutionary junta headquartered there. Safe on the American side of the Rio Grande, he issued a revolutionary manifesto and announced that November 20, 1910, was to be the day on which the Mexican people would rise and destroy the Díaz tyranny.

On the appointed day uprisings against the government did take place in numerous parts of the country. The movement, which gained momentum in the months that followed, was never very large. But the men who led it, Francisco Villa and Emiliano Zapata among them, were skillful guerrilla fighters who kept the government on the defensive while draining its strength. Díaz, now nearly eighty, was too old to lead. And the government, lacking strength and substance, collapsed like a house of cards. On May 25, 1911, Díaz resigned and went into exile.

Madero was an easy winner in the presidential elections that followed.

But it soon became clear that though he had been an appealing symbol in the struggle against Díaz, he was ineffective as a national leader.

Along the road to power, Madero promised labor reforms, a free system of education, judicial and agrarian reform, and the creation of a truly democratic political order. In fact, however, he seems to have been primarily interested in implementing political reforms. On the other hand, many of those who backed his cause including Emiliano Zapata in Morelos, Francisco Villa in Chihuahua, Alvaro Obregón in Sonora, and to a lesser extent Venustiano Carranza, were leaders of a social revolution that had attracted the support of workers, peasants, and a large number of middle-class Mexicans as well. Madero was unprepared to lead this genuinely revolutionary movement. But neither could he contain it. Mexico therefore continued in a revolutionary condition.

THE AMERICAN REACTION TO REVOLUTION

The Taft administration, like other foreign governments with interests in Mexico, at first greeted the Mexican Revolution calmly. From a distance Madero's movement appeared to be nothing more than an attempt by one elite to seize political power from another. Foreign economic holdings did not seem to be threatened. But as it became clear that Madero could not control the forces he had helped set in motion, that attitude changed. During the Díaz years, Americans had invested in excess of $1 billion in the country. Now that investment was at risk, as were the lives of some fifty thousand Americans resident in Mexico. Taft reacted to the escalating danger by urging those Americans who could to leave Mexico immediately. He also mobilized a force of twenty thousand, deploying it near the border. Naval forces cruised in Mexican waters, their marine contingents ready for action in the event that a landing should prove necessary. But Taft hoped to avoid intervention. Mexico was a large country, and the violence was widespread. Intervention would be expensive and probably ineffective.

The president's fondest hope was that Madero would be able to create a stable government without American interference. To aid in the endeavor, he declared an embargo on the sale of weapons to Mexico, a policy that substantially reduced the flow of arms to rebel forces and favored Madero. In the months that followed Madero did strengthen his hold over parts of his sprawling country. But still the revolution continued, with American lives and property increasingly at risk.

By the autumn of 1912, Taft was clearly out of patience. He explained to Secretary of State Philander Knox that he thought "we ought to put a little dynamite in" a note about to be sent to Mexico City "for the purpose of stirring up that dreamer who seems unfitted to meet the crisis in the country of which he is President." In December, State Department officials threatened the Mexican foreign minister with military intervention "if the ongoing killing of Americans and the destruction of American property did not stop."[10]

Henry Lane Wilson, the American minister in Mexico, urged the president to topple the Madero regime. Wilson was not the only one thinking such thoughts. By this time Britain and Germany, the other powers with important economic interests in Mexico, also believed that Madero would have to go. Still, Taft delayed. He was a cautious man, made more so by warnings from Secretary Knox that Wilson was apparently exaggerating the danger in order "to force this government's hands in its dealings with the Mexican situation."[11]

On February 10, 1913, the final crisis of the Madero regime came when fighting broke out between government forces and a rebel force led by Felix Díaz and General Bernardo Reyes. Mexico City became a war zone, and the diplomatic quarter was caught in the cross-fire. In the midst of the battle, Minister Wilson decided that the time had come to seek Madero's resignation. He told a group of diplomats meeting with him in the American legation that "Madero is crazy, a fool, a lunatic, and must be declared legally incapable of exercising his duties."[12] Though uninstructed, Wilson went to the Presidential Palace and, speaking for himself as well as the German, British, and Spanish ministers, demanded that Madero step down. But the president refused, and the battle for Mexico City continued.

A week after the fighting in the city began, the government's fate was sealed when General Victoriano Huerta, who commanded the government's forces, informed Henry Lane Wilson that he was going to overthrow Madero. Wilson, acting without instructions as he would throughout the crisis, made no objection. Thus it was with Wilson's tacit approval that Madero and his cabinet were taken prisoner. Huerta's next objective was to end the fighting in the city. Again he turned to Wilson, and again the minister did not disappoint him. At Wilson's invitation Huerta and the rebel leader, Felix Díaz, met in the American embassy, where a compromise was hammered out that left Huerta as the provisional president of Mexico. By mediating between Huerta and the rebels, Wilson in effect sanctioned the agreement. Thereafter Huerta must have believed that he was acting with American support.

Among Huerta's remaining problems was the question of what to do about his prisoner, the former president. As before, he asked Wilson's advice. The envoy's enigmatic response, which has sometimes been interpreted as authorization for Madero's assassination, was that Huerta "ought to do that which was best for the peace of the country."[13] Two days later, in the dark of night, while ostensibly being transferred from one prison to another, Madero was murdered.

Unmoved by this bloody business, Minister Wilson urged the administration to extend immediate recognition to the new government. Mexico's internal affairs, he believed, even when they involved the assassination of a deposed president, were none of America's business. The United States wanted a government in Mexico that was able to protect American lives and property, and Huerta had a better chance of accomplishing this than anyone else.

If Wilson was indifferent to Madero's fate, the American people were shocked and outraged by his murder. For the Taft administration to recognize Huerta even before he had washed the blood from his hands would not serve Republican party purposes. With little time remaining before Woodrow Wilson took the oath of office, Taft and Knox preferred to leave this messy business unresolved.

WILSON AND HUERTA

Victoriano Huerta was an affront to everything Woodrow Wilson held sacred. The self-righteous American president made it clear from the beginning that he would "never recognize a government of butchers."[14] More significant, he became obsessed by the idea that Huerta must be driven from power.

Practical men, including those with Mexican interests, leaders of the American colony in Mexico, and even Wilson's closest personal adviser, Colonel Edward M. House, argued that Huerta should be recognized because he stood the best chance of establishing a stable government in Mexico. But Wilson rejected that view, arguing that there were times when in order to do what was morally correct the United States might have to sacrifice its interests. Thus he told an audience in Mobile, Alabama, "We must show ourselves friends by comprehending their [Latin America's] interests whether it squares with our own interest or not."[15]

Wilson did not believe that it was enough to be against Huerta. He hoped to guide Mexico toward the creation of a democratically elected government that would operate on constitutional principles. The president's purpose, he once explained to an English visitor, was to "teach the Latin American Republics to elect good men."[16]

Wilson also believed that it was the duty of the United States to spread the gospel of free enterprise to Mexico as well as other underdeveloped lands. Because of his beliefs, he had little use for Venustiano Carranza's Constitutionalists or others such as Villa and Zapata, who represented the real revolutionary force at work in Mexico. Huerta would have to go. But Wilson hoped to replace him with a moderate who was committed to democratic rule and free enterprise, someone who would accept guidance from Washington and protect American propertied interests.

In August 1913, Wilson began a diplomatic offensive intended to bring Huerta down. He sent the former governor of Minnesota, John Lind, as his special emissary to Mexico with an offer to mediate between Huerta and Carranza. But what Wilson called mediation was in fact an invitation for Huerta to resign. The president proposed a military truce to be followed by free elections in which Huerta would not be a candidate. Wilson had a warning for the Constitutionalists, too. He demanded that Carranza fight "with a ballot and not with the gun" and made it clear that he would refuse to recognize any government produced by a revolution.[17]

Huerta not only rejected Wilson's proposal; he held fraudulent elections, after which he had himself proclaimed president of Mexico. The old general, who understood that his action would infuriate Wilson, did not take this step lightly. He was being strongly backed by London and the British minister in Mexico City, Sir Lionel Carden. British companies had vital interests in Mexico, especially in oil. From the Foreign Office's point of view, Huerta seemed more likely to protect those interests than the revolutionaries who opposed him.

Like Huerta, Carranza also rejected Wilson's proposal for mediation and free elections. The Constitutionalist leader suspected, no doubt correctly, that Wilson wanted to be rid of him, too. Certain that Wilson's ultimate ambition was the creation of a satellite government in Mexico City, he did not intend to be played like a pawn on Washington's chessboard.

Wilson's failed effort at "mediation" had one unexpected result: it strengthened Huerta's position inside Mexico, where anti-Americanism was rife. This development had no effect on Wilson, however, who stubbornly persisted in seeking the dictator's removal. He implemented an embargo on the sale of arms to Mexico and sought to convince the European powers to join him in isolating Huerta by withholding recognition.

Berlin quickly agreed to follow Wilson's lead in Mexico. Downing Street, on the other hand, hung back. The Royal Navy, which was then converting from coal to oil, was becoming more dependent on Mexican oil. Moreover, other British investments in Mexico had to be protected. At length, however, after tapping into alternative sources of petroleum and winning assurances from Wilson that the United States would "protect all foreign property in Mexico during the civil war," Britain's foreign secretary, Sir Edward Grey, agreed to follow Washington's lead in Mexico.[18] Given the tense European situation, at the time American friendship meant far more to London than its connection with General Huerta.

Wilson complemented his attempts to isolate Huerta diplomatically with secret offers of support to the Constitutionalists. But in return, he demanded that following Huerta's departure the Constitutionalists agree to the creation of a provisional government, to be followed swiftly by democratic elections.

Carranza wanted no part of such an arrangement. He informed Wilson's emissary that he would use force against any American incursions into Mexico and would make no commitments regarding Mexico's political future. He wanted diplomatic recognition and renewed access to American arms and ammunition, nothing more. Stunned by this peremptory rebuff, Wilson refused to extend recognition to Carranza's provisional government. He did, however, raise the arms embargo. It was a marriage of convenience. The Constitutionalists, after all, were the only force inside Mexico capable of driving Huerta from power.

Wilson expected that as a result of his exertions Huerta would soon have no choice but to resign. But, though the Constitutionalists were stronger than before, their advance south was slow. Meanwhile Wilson's interference in Mexico's internal affairs had done much to strengthen Huerta, who, as winter gave way to spring, 1914, showed no signs of running for cover. The president now awakened to the unhappy truth. His blustering and pressure tactics had placed his and his country's credibility on the line. Now Huerta *had* to go. But the only way left to accomplish that seemed armed intervention. And Wilson was emotionally unprepared to take that last drastic step.

THE MARINES TAKE VERACRUZ

In April 1914, Tampico, an oil refining center on the Pánuco River just a few miles from the Gulf of Mexico, was tense and excited. A battle seemed certain to take place there between a garrison loyal to Huerta and a Constitutionalist force massing near the town. Tampico was also the port of call of an American naval squadron commanded by Admiral Henry T. Mayo, whose job it was to protect American lives and property there.

On the morning of April 9, 1914, the crew of a U.S. Navy whaleboat put in at a dock that had been declared off limits by the commander of the Tampico garrison. The American sailors were loading drums of gasoline on to their boat, when they were arrested by a Mexican patrol and marched to a nearby prison. There, a ranking officer freed the men, who were returned to the wharf with his apologies. They finished their work and returned to their ship. The whole affair took less than an hour.

That would have been that but for Admiral Mayo's insistence that this insult to the Stars and Stripes—the whaleboat was flying a flag fore and aft—should not go unnoticed. He demanded that General Morelos Zaragosa, who commanded at Tampico, discipline the officer who arrested his men, forward a written apology, and "hoist the American flag on a prominent position on shore and salute it with twenty one guns."[19] Zaragosa, no fool, asked Mexico City for instructions.

General Huerta was willing to court martial the officer who made the arrests and forward a written apology to Mayo. But he could not under duress fire a salute to the American flag without undermining his political strength at home. His nationalist credentials would have been down the drain.

Huerta's refusal to fire that salute gave President Wilson an opportunity to increase the pressure. With Congress and the public firmly behind him, he ordered the entire Atlantic fleet to Tampico. The navy was ordered to blockade Mexican ports, cutting Huerta off from much-needed military supplies being shipped in from Europe, until he fired those twenty-one guns in honor of Old Glory.

The president was forced to change his plans at the last minute when the State Department informed him that because an official state of war did not exist it would be a violation of international law to interdict the arms traffic between Mexico and Europe. An illegal blockade would undoubtedly produce serious problems for the administration with a number of Huerta's arms suppliers, including Britain and Germany. At the same time, Wilson learned of the imminent arrival at Veracruz of the German merchant ship *Ypiranga* carrying a cargo of arms and ammunition. The only way to deny Huerta these weapons while avoiding difficulties with the Germans was to seize the *Ypiranga*'s cargo after it had been unloaded and before it could be shipped to Huerta's forces. It was for this purpose that Wilson ordered the marines ashore at Veracruz.

On April 20, 1914, several hundred marines and naval personnel went ashore in the Mexican port city. The initial landing went without incident because the Huertista commander there agreed not to resist. But as the Americans moved outward from the wharf area, they encountered small-arms fire from civilians and a number of overzealous naval cadets in the city. The fighting continued throughout the day, until Veracruz had been secured. When it ended eighty Americans had been killed or wounded. The Mexicans suffered more than three hundred casualties.

Wilson was shocked. Convinced of the righteousness of his cause, he had expected that the American invaders would be treated as liberators. He became even more flustered when not only Huerta but Carranza, too, denounced the invasion and demanded an immediate troop withdrawal. It is not surprising, then, that when Argentina, Brazil, and Chile offered to mediate between Mexico and the United States, he leapt at the opportunity while insisting that American troops would remain in Veracruz until an agreement was signed.

The so-called ABC Mediation, for the initials of the three countries that served as mediators, began on May 20, 1914, at Niagara Falls, New York, and settled nothing. Wilson continued to insist that the purpose of the talks should be to end Huerta's rule and lay the groundwork for free elections in Mexico. But Huerta didn't want free elections. Neither, for that matter, did Carranza, who was winning the war and seemed likely to achieve power by the sword. "The First Chief," as Carranza called himself, was in fact so uninterested in what happened at the conference that he at first refused to send a delegation. When he relented, it was only to hold secret talks with the American delegates there. But nothing came of these discussions either. Carranza steadfastly denied Wilson what he most wanted—control over the Mexican Revolution. In the end the delegates to the conference framed some face-saving protocols and adjourned having achieved nothing.

While the talks went on, the war did, too. And with some unexpected (and unwanted) help from the Americans, the Constitutionalists finally drove Huerta from power. The cost of the war and General Huerta's dependence on printing press money to meet his growing financial needs had placed the Mexican economy in jeopardy even before the landing at Veracruz. The continued American control of the customs houses there cut Huerta off from an important source of scarce revenues. The result was even more paper money. By July, government issued currency was worthless, and the economy was in a tailspin. Beset by overwhelming problems both on the battlefield and in the counting house, the old general at last resigned and went into European exile.

Wilson imagined that once Huerta was out of the way he would be able to play honest broker in Mexico, arranging for the creation of a new government based on democratic principles, committed to the free enterprise system, and willing to protect foreign property. When Mexico continued in a revolutionary condition, with the various factions fighting each other, the president, anxious to keep Carranza from attaining complete control of Mexico, called for the creation of a coalition government and warned that continued instability would leave the United States no choice but to "decide" for itself "what means should be employed to help Mexico save herself."[20]

This threat of intervention netted the president little save the anger and resentment of Zapata and Carranza, both of whom wasted no time throwing the president's warning back in his face. Zapata's brother, Eufemio, was particularly vehement: "We are not afraid to defend our country . . . even if they [the Americans] send millions of soldiers. We will fight them, one against hundreds."[21]

Of the major Mexican revolutionary leaders, only Francisco Villa responded affirmatively to the president's call for a coalition government and an end to the fighting. But by this time he had failed in an attempt to seize power, been outmaneuvered politically by the Constitutionalists, and been outgeneraled by Alvaro Obregón. Villa was at the time penned up in northern Mexico, an irritant but no longer a threat to Carranza's leadership.

Though Woodrow Wilson had no strong positive feelings for Francisco Villa, he liked Carranza even less. "We do not wish the Carranza faction to be the only one to deal with in Mexico," Secretary Lansing wrote. "Carranza seems so impossible that an appearance, at least, of opposition to him will give us the opportunity to invite a compromise of factions."[22] For this reason the Wilson administration lent its support to Villa while continuing to insist on the creation of a broadly based coalition government for Mexico.

Unhappily for Wilson, compromise was not in the cards. Before the end of 1915, Villa, with fewer than five hundred soldiers left in his command, was reduced to fighting a guerrilla war against Carrancista forces. Under these circumstances Wilson finally and reluctantly extended de facto recognition to Carranza's government.

A SECOND INTERVENTION

Washington's decision to recognize the Carranza regime came as a shock to Francisco Villa, who charged that in return for recognition and a $500 million loan, Carranza had sold out to the United States. "The price of these favors," he alleged, "was simply the sale of our country by the traitor Carranza."[23] Convinced of this, Villa redirected his guerrilla activities away from Carrancista forces and against Americans. In January 1916, his men

General Francisco Villa (second from the left) provoked an American military intervention in Mexico by a raid on Columbus, New Mexico, in which several Americans were killed. The intervention led to a crisis between President Woodrow Wilson and President Venustiano Carranza of Mexico that almost resulted in war.

slaughtered sixteen American mining engineers working in Sonora. Then, on March 9, four hundred of his raiders crossed the border into New Mexico. They rampaged through the streets of the town of Columbus, shooting anyone in sight until they were driven off by a cavalry unit stationed there.

Villa's was a clever strategy. He assumed that the Columbus raid would result in an American intervention in Mexico. If Carranza allowed American forces to enter the country unopposed (which Villa thought he might feel compelled to do to maintain his secret arrangement with Washington), he would be proven to be a traitor to the revolution. If he resisted, it would mean a war with the United States that would destroy his power.

With the American public and the Republican opposition demanding action, Wilson had no choice but to intervene. He promised to send troops into Mexico but temporarily held off, hoping that Carranza could be convinced to request American aid against Villa. But that was a forlorn hope. At length Wilson acted without Carranza's consent. And so, for the second time in two years an American force, this time six thousand strong under the command of General John J. ("Black Jack") Pershing, invaded Mexico, bent on trapping Villa.

The American intervention proved to be an enormous bonus for Villa, whose popularity soared in 1916. Whereas his force had been reduced almost to the vanishing point not long before, by the end of the year he commanded an army of ten thousand men. Meanwhile Carrancista troops grew restless, more ready to join Villa than to aid the Americans in hunting him down. As one observer wrote: "The general sentiment among the rank and file of the revolutionary (Carrancista) forces is one of sympathy with Villa. They openly express their admiration for his adventure and their regret for not having been with him."[24]

With six thousand American soldiers racing about in a country where anti-Americanism was rampant, incidents were bound to occur. Not a month after Pershing's troops crossed the border, an American patrol was attacked by a mob that included a number of Mexican government soldiers. Two Americans and forty Mexicans were killed in the fray. Carranza, reacting to growing internal pressures, demanded that Pershing's force withdraw immediately. But Wilson, who was under similar pressure, refused to budge until Villa was brought to justice. Two months later in June 1916, the situation took an even more dangerous turn when a small American force clashed with a larger body of Mexican troops. Twelve Americans were killed in this affray, and twenty-three were taken prisoner.

With the two nations poised on the brink of war, Wilson demanded the return of the prisoners and, to make certain that Carranza understood the gravity of the situation, mobilized the national guard. He even drafted a message to Congress asking for the authority to occupy northern Mexico. But he soon thought better of it and never delivered that message. There was little popular support for a full-scale war with Mexico. Moreover, it seemed very likely that the United States might soon be dragged into the European conflict. Under the circumstances, a war with Mexico had to be avoided. When Carranza made a friendly gesture, releasing the American prisoners and proposing a negotiated settlement to the crisis, Wilson quickly agreed.

The Mexican-American conference, which convened in September 1916 in Atlantic City, only served to accentuate the chasm dividing Mexico and the United States. Washington, continuing to treat Mexico as if it were simply another banana republic, insisted that Carranza guarantee to protect the lives and property of Americans doing business in Mexico and recognize America's right to intervene militarily if the Mexican government should fail or be unable to do so. Carranza rejected this astonishing demand out of hand and refused to discuss any political issues until all American forces had been withdrawn from Mexican territory.

The Mexican-American talks reached total deadlock in late December 1916. What happened next was largely dictated by European developments. In mid-January 1917, the Imperial German government announced the resumption of unrestricted submarine warfare. This decision made American intervention in the European war inevitable. Wilson then had little choice but to withdraw General Pershing's force from Mexican soil. The last troops left on February 5, 1917. But Mexican-American relations remained in a state of disarray. The adoption of the Mexican constitution of 1917, which asserted the government's right to expropriate foreign holdings, only exacerbated tensions.

General John J. ("Black Jack") Pershing led the American force that entered Mexico to track down Francisco Villa and his men. They failed and were subsequently withdrawn in 1917, when it became clear that the United States would soon become involved in the European war.

The year 1917 was epochal in Mexican history. Not only did the country receive a new reform constitution, but Carranza won an overwhelming victory in the first free elections since Madero's time. Of course, none of this was the result of Woodrow Wilson's repeated interferences in Mexico's internal affairs. When all was said and done, "moral imperialism" had not influenced in any positive way the course of Mexican history.

ENDNOTES

1. *The Cabinet Diaries of Josephus Daniels, 1913–1921*, ed. E. David Cronan (University of Nebraska Press, Lincoln, Neb., 1963), p. 17.
2. Woodrow Wilson, quoted in Arthur Link, *Woodrow Wilson and the Progressive Era* (Harper and Row, N.Y., 1954), p. 83.
3. Quoted in Warren I. Cohen, *America's Response to China: A History of Sino-American Relations* (Columbia University Press, N.Y., 3rd ed., 1990), p. 73.
4. James D. Phelan, quoted in Arthur Link, *Woodrow Wilson, The New Freedom* (Princeton University Press, Princeton, N.J., 1956), p. 289.
5. Admiral Bradley Fiske, quoted in *ibid.*, p. 297.

6. Secretary of State William Jennings Bryan to the Japanese Ambassador, March 13, 1915, *Foreign Relations of the United States, 1915* (Washington, 1924), pp. 105–11.

7. Theodore Roosevelt to William Howard Taft, December 22, 1910, *The Letters of Theodore Roosevelt*, ed. Elting E. Morison (Harvard University Press, Cambridge, Mass., 1951), VII, p. 190.

8. Edward M. House, quoted in Charles E. Neu, *The Troubled Encounter, The United States and Japan* (John Wiley and Sons, N.Y., 1975), p. 92.

9. Lansing-Ishii Agreement, quoted in A. Whitney Griswold, *The Far Eastern Policy of the United States* (Harcourt Brace and Co., N.Y., 1938), p. 216.

10. Quoted in Walter V. and Marie Scholes, *The Foreign Policies of the Taft Administration* (University of Missouri Press, Columbia Missouri, 1970), p. 95.

11. Philander Knox, quoted in *ibid.*, p. 96.

12. Henry Lane Wilson, quoted in Kenneth Grieb, *The United States and Huerta* (Lincoln, Nebraska, 1969), p. 16.

13. Scholes, *Foreign Policies of the Taft Administration*, p. 101.

14. Wilson, quoted in Arthur Link, *Woodrow Wilson and the Progressive Era*, p. 109.

15. Woodrow Wilson, quoted in *ibid.*, pp. 117–18.

16. Wilson, quoted in *ibid.*, p. 119.

17. Wilson, quoted in Friedrich Katz, *The Secret War in Mexico: Europe and the U.S. and the Mexican Revolution* (University of Chicago Press, Chicago, Ill., 1981), pp. 168–69.

18. Quoted in *ibid.*, pp. 189–90.

19. Admiral Mayo, quoted in Howard F. Cline, *The United States and Mexico* (Harvard University Press, Cambridge, Mass., 1953), p. 156.

20. Wilson, quoted in Robert E. Quirk, *The Mexican Revolution, 1914–1915* (University of Indiana Press, Bloomington, Ind., 1960), pp. 256–57.

21. Eufemio Zapata, quoted in Katz, *The Secret War in Mexico*, p. 299.

22. Robert Lansing, quoted in *ibid.*, p. 300.

23. Francisco Villa, quoted in *ibid.*, p. 306.

24. Anonymous, quoted in *ibid.*, p. 308.

SUPPLEMENTARY READING

The most recent and most complete bibliography of works dealing with American foreign relations is Richard Dean Burns, ed., *Guide to American Foreign Relations Since 1700* (Santa Barbara, Cal. ABC-Clio, 1982). This work is carefully annotated and amazingly complete for works written before 1980. The five-volume series, *Foreign Affairs Bibliography* (Washington, Council on Foreign Relations 1933–1976), is also carefully annotated. The first of these volumes was published in 1933, the last in 1976. Though dated, Samuel Flagg Bemis and Grace G. Griffin, eds., *Guide to the Diplomatic History of the United States, 1775–1921* (Washington, 1935), is still useful. See also Frank Friedel, ed., *Harvard Guide to American History* rev. ed., 2 vols. (Cambridge, Mass., Belknap Press, 1974). Numerous historical journals are likely to include articles dealing with American foreign relations. See the *American Historical Review*, *Diplomatic History*, the *International History Review*, the *Journal of American History*, and the *William and Mary Quarterly*.

THE AGE OF THE AMERICAN REVOLUTION

There are many fine overviews of the diplomacy of the American Revolution. The standard work is Samuel Flagg Bemis, *The Diplomacy of the American Revolution*, (Bloomington, Ind., University of Indiana Press, 1957). Arthur

Burr Darling's *Our Rising Empire, 1760–1803* (New Haven, Conn., Yale University Press, 1940) surveys a wider time span but has good chapters on the revolutionary era. Alfred L. Burt's older study, *The United States, Great Britain, and British North America* (New Haven, Conn., Yale University Press, 1940) is still useful. Richard W. Van Alstyne, *Empire and Independence: The International History of the American Revolution* (N.Y., John Wiley and Sons, 1965) puts extra emphasis on the European side of the struggle. The most recent and in many ways the best of the general histories of the diplomacy of the Revolution is Jonathan Dull, *A Diplomatic History of the American Revolution* (New Haven, Conn., Yale University Press, 1985).

The ideological aspect of American diplomacy in the revolutionary era is discussed at length in Felix Gilbert, *The Beginnings of American Foreign Policy* (Princeton, N.J., Princeton University Press, 1961). Another important source is Bernard Bailyn, *The Ideological Origins of the American Revolution* (Cambridge, Mass., Harvard University Press, 1967). Economic issues are discussed in Vernon Setser, *The Commercial Reciprocity Policy of the United States* (Philadelphia, Pa., University of Pennsylvania Press, 1937) and Curtis Nettles, *The Emergence of a National Economy* (N.Y., Harper and Row, 1962).

One of the turning points in the revolutionary struggle came when France and America forged an alliance in 1778. All of the general surveys treat this alliance with great care. More specialized studies include Edward S. Corwin, *French Policy and the American Alliance of 1778* (Princeton, N.J., Princeton University Press, 1916). In spite of its age, the Corwin book still has much to recommend it. A fine study of more recent vintage is William Stinchcombe, *The American Revolution and the French Alliance* (Syracuse, N.Y., Syracuse University Press, 1969).

The negotiations leading to the treaty of peace signed in Paris in 1783 have also attracted the attention of many scholars. Again, one should consult the survey histories, especially the work of Jonathan Dull. In addition Richard B. Morris, *The Peacemakers: The Great Powers and American Independence* (N.Y., Harper and Row, 1965) is essential. A more recent work that includes many fine essays is Ronald Hoffman and Peter J. Albert, eds., *Peace and the Peacemakers, The Treaty of 1783* (Charlottesville, Va., University of Virginia Press, 1986).

The major figures involved in the diplomacy of the period have all received careful attention. The standard work on Benjamin Franklin remains Carl Van Doren, *Benjamin Franklin* (N.Y., The Viking Press, 1938). See also Gerald Stourzh, *Benjamin Franklin and American Foreign Policy* (Chicago, Ill., University of Chicago Press, 1954), and, for a far different view, Cecil B. Currey, *Code Number 72: Ben Franklin Patriot or Spy?* (Englewood Cliffs, N.J., Prentice-Hall, 1972). The standard biography of John Adams is Page Smith, *John Adams* (Garden City and N.Y., Doubleday, 2 vols. 1962). See also James Hutson's fine *John Adams and the Diplomacy of the American Revolution* (Lexington, Ky., University of Kentucky Press, 1980). John Jay is admirably dealt with in Morris, *The Peacemakers*. For the role played by Arthur Lee, see Louis

Potts's fine biography, *Arthur Lee, A Virtuous Revolutionary* (Baton Rouge, La., Louisiana State University Press, 1981).

The Confederation period has not attracted great interest on the part of scholars. However, the works by Burt and Darling already mentioned deal with this period. The best general history of the era, Merrill Jensen's *The New Nation: A History of the United States During the Confederation, 1781–1789* (N.Y., Alfred A. Knopf, 1950), has an important foreign policy component. Abraham D. Sofaer, *War, Foreign Affairs and Constitutional Power: The Origins* (Cambridge, Mass., Ballinger Publishing Co., 1976), and Frederick W. Marks III, *Independence on Trial: Foreign Affairs and the Making of the Constitution* (Scholarly Resources, Wilmington Del., 1986), are both first-rate works. Paul Varg, *The Foreign Policy of the Founding Fathers* (Lansing, Mich., Michigan State University Press, 1963), has an important essay on the subject.

THE FEDERALIST ERA, 1789–1801

The Federalist period was a time of prolonged crisis as the Washington administration attempted to steer clear of the European wars. The standard work on Anglo-American relations for the period, including the Confederation, is Samuel Flagg Bemis, *Jay's Treaty, A Study in Commerce and Diplomacy* (New Haven, Conn., Yale University Press, 1962). Other important works include Bradford Perkins's important *The First Rapprochement: England and the United States, 1795–1805* (Philadelphia, Pa., University of Pennsylvania Press, 1954); Jerald A. Combs, *The Jay Treaty: Political Battleground of the Founding Fathers* (Berkeley, Cal., University of California Press, 1970); and J. Leitch Wright, Jr., *Britain and the American Frontier, 1783–1815* (Athens, Ga., University of Georgia Press, 1975).

Relations with Spain are covered in Samuel Flagg Bemis, *Pinckney's Treaty: America's Advantage From Europe's Distress* (New Haven, Conn., Yale University Press 1926); Arthur P. Whitaker, *The Spanish-American Frontier, 1783–1795: The Westward Movement and the Spanish Retreat in the Mississippi Valley* (Boston, Mass., Houghton-Mifflin, 1927); and Whitaker's *The Mississippi Question, 1795–1803: A Study in Trade, Politics and Diplomacy* (N.Y., Appleton-Century, 1934). A more general study is Lester D. Langley, *Struggle for the American Mediterranean: United States European Rivalry in the Gulf-Caribbean, 1776–1904* (Athens, Ga., University of Georgia Press, 1975).

For Franco-American relations see Alexander DeConde, *Entangling Alliance: Politics and Diplomacy under George Washington* (N.Y., Scribner's, 1958); Louis M. Sears, *George Washington and the French Revolution* (Detroit, Mich., Wayne State University Press, 1960); Lawrence S. Kaplan, *Jefferson and France: An Essay on Politics and Political Ideas* (New Haven, Conn., Yale University Press, 1967); Harry Ammon, *The Genet Mission* (N.Y., W.W. Norton and Co., 1973); and Albert Hall Bowman, *The Struggle for Neutrality: Franco-American Diplomacy During the Federalist Era* (Knoxville, Tenn., University of Tennessee Press, 1974).

Many biographies are of considerable importance in studying the foreign policy of the era. Especially useful are Douglas Southall Freeman, *George Washington* (N.Y., Scribner's, vol. VI, 1954; VII, 1957); John C. Miller, *Alexander Hamilton and the Growth of the New Nation* (N.Y., Harper and Row, 1959); Dumas Malone, *Jefferson and the Ordeal of Liberty* (Little, Brown and Co., 1962); Gerald Stourzh, *Alexander Hamilton and the Idea of Republican Government* (Stanford, Cal., Stanford University Press, 1970); and Jacob E. Cooke, *Alexander Hamilton* (N.Y., Scribner's, 1982). Biographies of lesser figures that also should be consulted include Robert Ernst, *Rufus King: American Federalist* (Chapel Hill, N.C., University of North Carolina Press, 1968), and Gerard Clarfield, *Timothy Pickering and the American Republic* (Pittsburgh, Pa., Pittsburgh University Press, 1980).

The standard work on the quasi-war with France is Alexander DeConde, *The Quasi-war: The Politics and Diplomacy of the Undeclared War with France, 1797–1801* (N.Y., Scribner's, 1966). Important studies of the presidency of John Adams include Manning J. Dauer, *The Adams Federalists* (Baltimore, Md., Johns Hopkins University Press, 1953), and Steven G. Kurtz, *The Presidency of John Adams* (Cranbury, N.J., A.S. Barnes and Co.,1961). William Stinchcombe, *The XYZ Affair* (Westport, Conn., Greenwood, 1980), supersedes everything else on that important subject. Marvin Zahniser, *Charles Cotesworth Pinckney: Founding Father* (Chapel Hill, N.C., University of North Carolina Press, 1967), deals with a figure of importance in the diplomacy of the period. Peter P. Hill, *William Vans Murray; Federalist Diplomat: The Shaping of Peace with France, 1797–1801* (Syracuse, N.Y., Syracuse University Press, 1971), is also important.

THE JEFFERSONIAN ERA

Even though it is now considered out of date, Henry Adams's *History of the United States during the Administrations of Jefferson and Madison*, (N.Y., Scribner, 9 vols., 1889–1909), remains the place to start. Dumas Malone's two volumes, *Jefferson the President: First Term, 1801–1805* (Boston, Mass., Little, Brown and Co., 1968) and *Jefferson the President: Second Term, 1805–1809* (Boston, Mass., Little, Brown and Co., 1974) are more accurate and no less brilliant. Irving Brant, *James Madison: Secretary of State, 1800–1809* (Indianapolis, Ind., Bobbs Merrill and Co., 1953) is also indispensable.

Studies of Anglo-American relations for these years abound. Among the very best are Bradford Perkins, *Prologue to War: England and the United States, 1805–1812* (Berkeley, Cal., University of California Press, 1961), and Reginald Horsman, *The Causes of the War of 1812* (Cranbury, N.J., A.S. Barnes and Co., 1962). On the subject of impressment, see James F. Zimmerman, *Impressment of American Seamen* (N.Y., Columbia University Press, 1925). The best study of America's relations with France in this period is Clifford L. Egan, *Neither Peace Nor War: Franco-American Relations, 1803–1812* (Baton Rouge, La., Louisiana State University Press, 1983).

The Barbary wars are dealt with in Raymond W. Bixler, *The Open Door on the Old Barbary Coast* (N.Y., Pageant Press, 1959), and James Woodress, *A Yankee's Odyssey: The Life of Joel Barlow* (Philadelphia, Pa., Lippincott, 1958). Two more recent works are especially useful. See David H. Finnie, *Pioneers East: The Early American Experience in the Middle East* (Cambridge, Mass., Harvard University Press, 1967), and James A. Field's important study, *America and the Mediterranean World, 1776–1886* (Princeton, N.J., Princeton University Press, 1969).

The Louisiana purchase has attracted a good deal of attention. Among the best studies are E. Wilson Lyon, *Louisiana in French Diplomacy, 1759–1804* (Norman, Ok., University of Oklahoma Press, 1934), and Alexander DeConde, *This Affair of Louisiana* (N.Y., Scribner's, 1976). See also George Dangerfield, *Chancellor Robert R. Livingston of New York, 1746–1812* (N.Y., Harcourt Brace and Co., 1960), and Harry Ammon, *James Monroe* (N.Y., McGraw-Hill, 1971).

The War of 1812 has attracted more than its share of attention. Many of the titles listed above should be consulted. Beyond those, one should consider Samuel Flagg Bemis, *John Quincy Adams and the Foundations of American Foreign Policy* (N.Y., Alfred A. Knopf, 2 vols., 1949). Irving Brant's two volumes, *James Madison: The President, 1809–1812* (Indianapolis, Ind., Bobbs Merrill, and Co., 1956) and *James Madison: Commander in Chief, 1812–1836* (Indianapolis, Ind., Bobbs, Merrill and Co., 1961), are also essential. Raymond Walters, Jr., *Albert Gallatin: Jeffersonian Financier and Diplomat* (N.Y., Macmillan, 1957) is an excellent biography of a central figure. Roger H. Brown offers a provocative interpretation of the American decision to fight in *The Republic in Peril: 1812* (N.Y., W.W. Norton and Co, 1971). Bradford Perkins, *Castlereagh and Adams: England and the United States, 1812–1823* (Berkeley, Cal., University of California Press, 1964) is by far the best study of its kind and completes the author's trilogy on Anglo-American relations in the early years of the republic. The most recent study of the war, and one of the more notable, is J.C.A. Stagg, *Mr. Madison's War: Politics, Diplomacy, and Warfare in the Early American Republic, 1783–1830* (Princeton, N.J., Princeton University Press, 1983).

On the conduct of the war itself, see Harry L. Coles, *The War of 1812* (Chicago, Ill., University of Chicago Press, 1965). See also J.C.A. Stagg, *Mr. Madison's War*, which has excellent chapters on military operations.

The history of the Monroe Doctrine has attracted the interest of large numbers of scholars. The place to begin is still Dexter Perkins, *The Monroe Doctrine, 1823–1826* (Cambridge, Mass., Harvard University Press, 1927). Other important studies include Edward H. Tatum, *The United States and Europe, 1815–1823* (N.Y., Russell and Russell, 1967); George Dangerfield, *The Era of Good Feelings* (N.Y., Harcourt Brace and World, 1952); John A. Logan, *No Transfer: An American Security Principle* (New Haven, Conn., Yale University Press, 1961); and Ernest R. May, *The Making of the Monroe Doctrine* (Cambridge, Mass., Belknap Press of Harvard University Press, 1975). Nor can one ignore Bradford Perkins, *Prologue To War*, already noted, or the many biographies of important figures of the period. Most notable are Bemis's biography of John Quincy Adams and Ammon's biography of James Monroe. See also John H. Powell, *Richard Rush: Republican Diplomat, 1780–1859* (Philadelphia, Pa., University of Pennsylvania Press, 1942).

For the Florida question, see Philip C. Brooks, *Diplomacy and the Borderlands: The Adams–Onis Treaty of 1819* (Berkeley, Cal., University of California Press, 1936), and Robert Rimini, *Andrew Jackson and the Course of American Empire, 1767–1821* (N.Y., Harper and Row, 1977). For Latin America see J. Fred Rippy, *Rivalry of the United States and Great Britain over Latin America, 1808–1830* (Baltimore, Md., Johns Hopkins University Press, 1929); Charles C. Griffin, *The United States and the Disruption of the Spanish Empire, 1810–1822* (N.Y., Columbia University Press, 1937); and, preeminently, Arthur P. Whitaker, *The United States and the Independence of Latin America, 1800–1830* (N.Y., W. W. Norton and Co., 1964).

THE AGE OF MANIFEST DESTINY

By far the best study of this period, not likely to be superseded, is David M. Pletcher, *The Diplomacy of Annexation: Texas, Oregon and the Mexican War* (Columbia, Mo., University of Missouri Press, 1973). Another work of the highest order that deals with expansionism in the period is Charles G. Sellers, *James K. Polk, Continentalist: 1843–1846* (Princeton, N.J., Princeton University Press, 1966). A more recent study of this period is Norma Lois Peterson, *The Presidencies of William Henry Harrison and John Tyler* (Lawrence, Ks., University of Kansas Press, 1989).

Historians have long debated the meaning and significance of the concept of Manifest Destiny. The more important studies of this ideological question are Albert K. Weinberg, *Manifest Destiny: A Study of Nationalist Expansionism in American History* (Chicago, Ill., Quadrangle Books, 1963); Henry Nash Smith, *Virgin Land: The American West as Symbol and Myth* (Cambridge, Mass., Harvard University Press, 1970); Norman A. Graebner, *Empire on the Pacific: A Study of American Continental Expansion* (N.Y., Ronald Press, 1955); and Frederick Merk, *Manifest Destiny and Mission in American History* (N.Y., Alfred A. Knopf, 1963).

For Anglo-American relations in this period, see Frederick Merk's *The Oregon Question: Essays in Anglo-American Diplomacy and Politics* (Cambridge, Mass., Harvard University Press, 1967). See also Wilbur D. Jones, *The American Problem in British Diplomacy* (Athens, Ga., University of Georgia Press, 1958); Kenneth Bourne, *Britain and the Balance of Power in North America, 1815–1908* (Berkeley, Cal., University of California Press, 1967); and Howard Jones, *To the Webster-Ashburton Treaty: A Study in Anglo-American Relations, 1783–1843* (Chapel Hill, N.C., University of North Carolina Press, 1977).

The diplomacy of the Mexican War is best covered in two books previously noted—Pletcher, *Diplomacy of Annexation*, and Sellers, *Polk*. Other studies of note include Eugene D. P. Fuller, *The Movement for the Acquisition of All Mexico, 1846–1848* (Baltimore, Md., Johns Hopkins University Press, 1936); Joseph W. Schmitz, *Texan Statecraft, 1836–1845* (San Antonio, Tx., the Naylor Co., 1941); Glenn W. Price, *Origins of the War with Mexico: The Polk-Stockton Intrigue* (Austin, Tx., University of Texas Press, 1967); Seymour V. Connor and Odie B. Faulk, *North America Divided: The Mexican War* (1971); Neal Harlow, *California Conquered: War and Peace on the Pacific, 1846–1850* (Berkeley Cal., University of California Press, 1982); and Ernest M. Lander, Jr., *Reluctant Imperialists: Calhoun, the South Carolinians, and the Mexican War* (Baton Rouge, La., Louisiana State University Press, 1984). For the war from the Mexican side, see José Fernando Ramirez, *Mexico during the War with the United States,* ed. Walter V. Scholes, (Columbia, Mo., University of Missouri Press, 1950). See also Gene M. Brack, *Mexico Views Manifest Destiny, 1821–1846* (Albuquerque, N.M., University of New Mexico Press, 1975). Other aspects of the war are covered in John H. Schroeder, *Mr. Polk's War: American Opposition and Dissent, 1846–1848* (Madison, Wis., University of Wisconsin Press, 1973), and Frederick Merk, *Slavery and the Annexation of Texas* (N.Y., Alfred A. Knopf, 1972).

For an overview of the developing American interest in China, see Foster Rhea Dulles, *China and America: The Story of Their Relations since 1784* (Princeton, N.J., Princeton University Press, 1946); Te-kong Tong, *United States Diplomacy in China, 1844–1860* (Seattle, Wash., University of Washington Press, 1964); and a more recent work, Robert A. Hard, *The Eccentric Tradition: American Diplomacy in the Far East* (N.Y., Scribner's, 1976). More specialized works of interest include John K. Fairbank, *Trade and Diplomacy on the China Coast: The Opening of the Treaty Ports, 1842–1854* (Stanford, Cal., Stanford University Press, 1953); Clifton J. Phillips, *Protestant America and the Pagan World: The First Half Century of the American Board of Commissioners for Foreign Missions, 1810–1860* (Cambridge, Mass., Harvard University Press, 1969); Edward V. Gulick, *Peter Parker and the Opening of China* (Cambridge, Mass., Harvard University Press, 1973); and Peter W. Fay, *The Opium War, 1840–1842: Barbarians in the Celestial Empire in the Early Part of the Nineteenth Century and the War by Which They Forced Her Gates Ajar* (Chapel Hill, N.C., University of North Carolina Press, 1975).

Two fine overviews of Japanese-American relations are William L. Neumann, *America Encounters Japan: From Perry to MacArthur* (Baltimore, Md. Johns Hopkins University Press, 1963) and Foster Rhea Dulles, *Yankees and Samurai: America's Role in the Emergence of Japan, 1791–1900* (N.Y., Harper and Row, 1965). Commodore Matthew C. Perry's exploits in Japan are amply covered in Arthur Walworth, *Black Ships Off Japan: The Story of Commodore Perry's Expedition* (N.Y., Alfred A. Knopf, 1946) and Samuel Eliot Morison, *"Old Bruin": Commodore Matthew C. Perry* (Boston, Mass., Little, Brown and Co., 1967).

For Central American issues, see William O. Scroggs, *Filibusters and Financiers: The Story of William Walker and His Associates* (N.Y., Macmillan, 1916); Albert H. Carr, *The World of William Walker* (N.Y., Harper and Row, 1963); and Mario Rodriguez, *A Palmerstonian Diplomat in Central America:*

Frederick Chatfield, Esq. (Tucson, Ariz., University of Arizona Press, 1964). Cuban issues are discussed in Basil Rauch, *American Interest in Cuba, 1848–1855* (N.Y., Columbia University Press, 1948); Philip S. Foner, *A History of Cuba and Its Relations with the United States* (N.Y., International Publishers, 2 vols., 1962–1963); and Hugh Thomas, *Cuba: The Pursuit of Freedom* (N.Y., Harper and Row, 1971).

On southern interest in the Caribbean see Amos A. Ettinger, *The Mission to Spain of Pierre Soulé, 1853–1855* (New Haven, Conn., Yale University Press, 1932); Robert E. May, *The Southern Dream of a Caribbean Empire, 1854–1861* (Baton Rouge, La., Louisiana State University Press, 1973); Donald D. Spencer, *Louis Kossuth and Young America: A Study of Sectionalism and Foreign Policy, 1848–1852* (Columbia, Mo., University of Missouri Press, 1977); Charles H. Brown, *Agents of Manifest Destiny* (1980); James T. Wall, *Manifest Destiny Denied* (Washington, D.C., University Press of America, 1982); and Robert E. May, *John A. Quitman, Old South Crusader* (Baton Rouge, La., Louisiana State University Press, 1985). Other biographies of importance include Ivor D. Spencer, *The Victor and the Spoils: A Life of William L. Marcy* (Providence, R.I., Brown University Press, 1959), and Roy F. Nichols, *Franklin Pierce: Young Hickory of the Granite Hills* (Philadelphia, Pa., University of Pennsylvania Press, 1958).

There are surprisingly few good general histories of Civil War diplomacy. But a fine one is David P. Crook, *The North, the South and the Powers, 1861–1865* (N.Y., John Wiley and Sons, 1974). See also Philip Van Doren Stern, *When the Guns Roared: World Aspects of the American Civil War* (Garden City, N.J., Doubleday, 1965). Southern diplomacy is brilliantly described by Frank L. and Harriet Chappell Owsley in *King Cotton Diplomacy: Foreign Relations of the Confederate States of America* (Chicago, Ill., University of Chicago Press, 2d. ed., 1959).

Franco-American relations during the Civil War have been carefully detailed in Lynn M. Case and Warren F. Spencer, *The United States and France: Civil War Diplomacy* (1970). Another important work is Henry Blumenthal, *A Reappraisal of Franco-American Relations, 1830–1871* (Chapel Hill, N.C., University of North Carolina Press, 1959).

For relations with Britain during the Civil War see Ephraim D. Adams, *Great Britain and the American Civil War* (N.Y., Russell and Russell, 2 vols., 1925); Two studies by Norman B. Ferris are *Desperate Diplomacy: William H. Seward's Foreign Policy, 1861* (Knoxville, Tenn., University of Tennessee Press, 1976), and *The Trent Affair: A Diplomatic Crisis* (Knoxville, Tenn., University of Tennessee Press, 1977). See also Gordon H. Warren, *Fountain of Discontent: The Trent Affair and the Freedom of the Seas* (Boston, Ma., Northeastern University Press, 1981). Other special studies of interest include Stuart L. Bernath, *Squall Across the Atlantic: American War Prize Cases and Diplomacy* (Berkeley, Cal., University of California Press, 1970), Frank J. Merli, *Great Britain and the Confederate Navy, 1861–1865* (Bloomington, Ind., Indiana University Press, 1970); and Warren F. Spencer, *The Confederate Navy in Europe* (Tuscaloosa, Ala., University of Alabama Press, 1983).

Biographical studies include Martin B. Duberman, *Charles Francis Adams* (Boston, Ma., Houghton-Mifflin and Co., 1967); Glyndon G. Van Deusen, *William Henry Seward* (N.Y., Oxford University Press, 1967); and David Donald, *Charles Sumner and the Rights of Man* (N.Y., Alfred A. Knopf, 1970).

THE BEGINNINGS OF INSULAR IMPERIALISM

There are a number of studies that are important for the entire period from the end of the Civil War to the turn of the century. Charles S. Campbell, *The Transformation of American Foreign Relations, 1865–1900* (N.Y., Harper and Row, 1976), is especially notable for the balance it provides between economic and other factors in explaining American expansionism. Another, briefer study that tries for balance is Robert Beisner, *From the Old Diplomacy to the New, 1865–1900* (Arlington Heights, Ill., Harlan Davidson, Inc., 2d. ed., 1986). Two general studies are extremely important. William A. Williams, *The Roots of the Modern American Empire: A Study of the Growth and Shaping of Social Consciousness in a Marketplace Society* (N.Y., Random House, 1969) is a work filled with insight. Walter LaFeber, *The New Empire: An Interpretation of American Expansion, 1860–1898* (Ithaca, N.Y., Cornell University Press, 1963), is another work of major importance.

There are several good studies of policy makers in this period. Of particular importance are Allan Nevins, *Hamilton Fish: The Inner History of the Grant Administration*, rev. ed., 2 vols. (N.Y., Dodd, Mead, and Co., 1957), and Ernest N. Paolino, *The Foundations of American Empire: William Henry Seward and U.S. Foreign Policy* (Ithaca, N.Y., Cornell University Press, 1973). See also Alice F. Tyler, *The Foreign Policies of James G. Blaine* (Minneapolis, Minn., University of Minnesota Press, 1927); Allan Nevins, *Grover Cleveland: A Study in Courage* (N.Y., Dodd, Mead and Co., 1934); Edward Younger, *John A. Kasson: Politics and Diplomacy from Lincoln to McKinley* (Iowa City, Iowa, Iowa State Historical Society, 1955); Michael J. Devine, *John W. Foster: Politics and Diplomacy in the Imperial Era, 1873–1917* (Athens, Ohio, Ohio University Press, 1981); and Charles W. Calhoun, *Gilded Age Cato: The Life of Walter Q. Gresham* (Lexington, Ky., University of Kentucky Press, 1988).

For Mexico and Latin America, see Dexter Perkins's two volumes, *The Monroe Doctrine, 1826–1867* (Baltimore, Md., Johns Hopkins University Press, 1933), and *The Monroe Doctrine, 1867–1907* (Baltimore, Md., Johns Hopkins University Press, 1937). Other important studies include Charles C. Tansill, *The United States and Santo Domingo, 1798–1873: A Chapter in Caribbean History* (1938), and Alfred J. and Kathryn A. Hanna, *Napoleon III and Mexico: American Triumph over Monarchy* (Chapel Hill, N.C., University of North Carolina Press, 1971). The Alaska purchase is discussed in two studies: Archie W. Shiels, *The Purchase of Alaska* (Anchorage, Alaska, University of Alaska Press, 1967), and Ronald J. Jensen, *The Alaska Purchase and Russian American Relations* (Seattle, Wash., University of Washington Press, 1975).

For the later years of the century, see especially David M. Pletcher, *The Awkward Years: American Foreign Policy under Garfield and Arthur* (Columbia, Mo., University of Missouri Press, 1962); John A. S. Grenville and George B. Young, *Politics, Strategy and American Diplomacy: Studies in Foreign Policy, 1873–1914* (1966); Milton Plesur, *America's Outward Thrust* (DeKalb, Ill., Northern Illinois University Press, 1971); Emily S. Rosenberg, *Spreading the American Dream: American Economic and Cultural Expansion, 1890–1945* (N.Y., Hill and Wang, 1982); and Richard Welch, Jr., *The Presidencies of Grover Cleveland* (Lawrence, Ks., University of Kansas Press, 1988). Naval affairs are discussed in Kenneth J. Hagan, *American Gunboat Diplomacy and the Old Navy, 1877–1889* (Westport, Conn., Greenwood Press, 1973); Benjamin F. Cooling, *Benjamin Franklin Tracy* (Hamden, Conn., Anchor Books, 1973); and Frederick C. Drake, *The Empire of the Seas* (Honolulu, Hawaii, University of Hawaii Press, 1984).

For Latin American affairs, see Herbert Millington, *American Diplomacy and the War of the Pacific* (N.Y., Columbia University Press, 1948); Frederick B. Pike, *Chile and the United States, 1880–1962: The Emergence of Chile's Social Crisis and the Challenge of United States Diplomacy* (Notre Dame, Ind., Notre Dame University Press, 1963); and Joyce S. Goldberg, *The Baltimore Affair: United States Relations with Chile, 1891–1892* (Lincoln, Neb., University of Nebraska Press, 1986).

For Pacific affairs, see William A. Russ, Jr., *The Hawaiian Revolution, 1893–1894* (Selinsgrove, Pa., Susquehanna University Press, 1959); Ralph S. Kuykendall, *The Hawaiian Kingdom, 1874–1893* (Honolulu, Hawaii, University of Hawaii Press, 1967); Merze Tate, *Hawaii: Reciprocity or Annexation* (East Lansing, Mich., Michigan State University Press, 1968); and Paul Kennedy, *The Samoan Tangle: A Study in Anglo-German-American Relations, 1878–1900* (Dublin, Ireland, Irish University Press, 1974).

THE AGE OF EMPIRE, 1899–1917

There are many fine studies of American imperialism in the late nineteenth century. Aside from those already noted, see Julius W. Pratt, *Expansionists of 1898: The Acquisition of Hawaii and the Spanish Islands* (Baltimore, Md., Johns Hopkins University Press, 1936); Ernest R. May's two fine books, *Imperial Democracy: The Emergence of America as a Great Power* (N.Y., Harcourt Brace and World, 1961) and *American Imperialism: A Speculative Essay* (N.Y., Atheneum, 1968); H. Wayne Morgan, *America's Road to Empire: The War with Spain and Overseas Expansion* (N.Y., John Wiley and Sons, 1965); Richard Hofstadter, *The Paranoid Style in American Politics and Other Essays* (N.Y., Alfred A. Knopf, 1966); and David Healy, *U.S. Expansionism: The Imperialist Urge in the 1890's* (Madison, Wis., University of Wisconsin Press, 1970). See also Lewis Gould's excellent *Presidency of William McKinley* (Lawrence, Ks., University of Kansas Press, 1980).

The anti-imperialist movement is discussed in Robert L. Beisner,

Twelve against Empire: The Anti-Imperialists, 1898–1900 (N.Y., McGraw-Hill, 1968); Daniel B. Schirmer, *Republic or Empire: American Resistance to the Philippine War* (Cambridge Mass., Schenkman Pub. Co., 1972); Hans L. Trefousse, *Carl Schurz* (Knoxville, Tenn., University of Tennessee Press, 1982); and Kendrick Clements, *William Jennings Bryan, Missionary Isolationist* (Knoxville, Tenn., University of Tennessee Press, 1983).

Anglo-American relations in the period have attracted the attention of many scholars. Among the best books on the subject are A. E. Campbell, *Great Britain and the United States, 1895–1903* (London, England, Longman's, 1960); R. G. Neale, *Great Britain and United States Expansion: 1898–1900* (East Lansing, Mich., Michigan State University Press, 1966); Bradford Perkins, *The Great Rapprochement: England and the United States, 1895–1914* (N.Y., Atheneum, 1968); and Edward P. Crapol, *America for Americans: Economic Nationalism and Anglophobia in the Late Nineteenth Century* (Westport, Conn., Greenwood, 1973).

Policy makers of this period, preeminently Theodore Roosevelt, have received a great deal of attention from historians. Some of the best are Howard K. Beale, *Theodore Roosevelt and the Rise of America to World Power* (Baltimore, Md., Johns Hopkins University Press, 1956); David H. Burton, *Theodore Roosevelt, Confident Imperialist* (N.Y., Farrar, Straus, Cudahy, 1968); Raymond A. Esthus, *Theodore Roosevelt and the International Rivalries* (Seattle, Wash., University of Washington Press, 1970); and John Milton Cooper, Jr., *The Warrior and the Priest: Woodrow Wilson and Theodore Roosevelt* (Cambridge, Mass., Belknap Press of Harvard University Press, 1983). See also Richard Leopold, *Elihu Root and the Conservative Tradition* (Boston, Little, Brown and Co., 1954); Kenton J. Clymer, *John Hay: The Gentleman as Diplomat* (Ann Arbor, Mich., University of Michigan Press, 1975); Henry F. Pringle, *The Life and Times of William Howard Taft* (N.Y., Farrar and Rinehart, 1939); Walter V. Scholes and Marie V. Scholes, *The Foreign Policies of the Taft Administration* (Columbia, Miss., University of Missouri Press, 1970).

China policy has a vast literature. See, for example, Paul A. Varg, *The Making of a Myth: The United States and China, 1897–1912* (East Lansing, Mich., Michigan State University Press, 1968); Jerry Israel, *Progressivism and the Open Door: America and China, 1905–1921* (Pittsburgh, Pa., University of Pittsburgh Press, 1971); Michael Hunt's two studies, *Frontier Defense and the Open Door: Manchuria in Chinese-American Relations, 1895–1911* (New Haven, Conn., Yale University Press, 1973); and *The Making of a Special Relationship* (N.Y., Columbia University Press, 1983); Delbert L. McKee, *Chinese Exclusion versus the Open Door Policy, 1900–1906: Clashes Over China Policy in the Roosevelt Era* (Detroit, Mich., Wayne State University Press, 1976); and Charles Vevier, *The United States and China, 1906–1913: A Study of Finance and Diplomacy* (New Brunswick, N.J., Rutgers University Press, 1955). See also Thomas J. McCormick, *China Market: America's Quest for Informal Empire* (Chicago, Ill., University of Chicago Press, 1967), and Marilyn B. Young, *The Rhetoric of Empire: American China Policy, 1895–1901* (Cambridge, Mass., Harvard University Press, 1968).

Japanese-American relations are discussed in Fred H. Harrington, *God, Mammon, and the Japanese: Dr. Horace N. Allen and Korean American Relations, 1884–1905* (Madison, Wis., University of Wisconsin Press, 1944); Roger Daniels, *The Politics of Prejudice: The Anti-Japanese Movement in California and the Struggle for Japanese Exclusion* (Berkeley, Cal., University of California Press, 1962); Charles E. Neu, *An Uncertain Friendship: Theodore Roosevelt and Japan, 1906–1909* (1965); and in Akira Iriye, *Pacific Estrangement: Japanese and American Expansion, 1897–1911* (Cambridge, Mass., Harvard University Press, 1972).

For Caribbean and Panama policy, see Dana G. Munro, *Intervention and Dollar Diplomacy in the Caribbean, 1900–1921* (Princeton, N.J., Princeton University Press, 1964); Sheldon B. Liss, *The Canal: Aspects of United States–Panamanian Relations* (Notre Dame, Ind., Notre Dame University Press, 1967); Lester D. Langley, *The Cuban Policy of the United States: A Brief History* (N.Y., John Wiley and Sons, 1968); and David G. McCullough, *The Path between the Seas: The Creation of the Panama Canal 1870–1914* (N.Y., Simon and Schuster, 1977). See also Warren G. Kneer, *Great Britain and the Caribbean, 1901–1913: A Study in Anglo-American Relations* (East Lansing, Mich., Michigan State University Press, 1975). The United States's role in Cuba is discussed in David F. Healy, *The United States in Cuba, 1898–1902* (Madison, Wis., University of Wisconsin Press, 1963); James H. Hitchman, *Leonard Wood and Cuban Independence, 1898–1902* (The Hague, the Netherlands, Nijhoff, 1971); and in Louis A. Perez, Jr., *Cuba between Empires, 1878–1902* (Pittsburgh, Pa., Pittsburgh University Press, 1983).

The place to begin any study of Woodrow Wilson's interventionist policies is with three works by Arthur Link: *Woodrow Wilson and the Progressive Era* (N.Y., Harper and Row, 1954), *Wilson the Diplomatist* (Princeton, N.J., Princeton University Press, 1957), and *Wilson, The Struggle for Neutrality, 1914–1915* (Princeton N.J., Princeton University Press, 1960).

In addition to many of the titles listed above that deal with Wilson's Far Eastern policy, see Tien-yi Li, *Woodrow Wilson's China Policy, 1913–1917* (Kansas City, Mo., University of Kansas Press, 1952); Roy W. Curry, *Woodrow Wilson and Far Eastern Policy, 1913–1921* (N.Y., Bookman Associates, 1957); and Burton F. Beers, *Vain Endeavor: Robert Lansing's Attempt To End the American-Japanese Rivalry* (Durham, N.C., Duke University Press, 1962).

For Caribbean affairs, see Hans Schmidt, *The United States Occupation of Haiti, 1915–1921* (New Brunswick, N.J., Rutgers University Press, 1971); David Healy, *Gunboat Diplomacy in the Wilson Era: The U.S. Navy in Haiti, 1915–1916* (Madison, Wis., University of Wisconsin Press, 1976); Lester D. Langley, *Struggle for the American Mediterranean: United States–European Rivalry in the Gulf-Caribbean, 1776–1904* (Athens, Ga., University of Georgia Press, 1976).

There is an extensive literature dealing with U.S.-Mexican relations during this period. See especially Howard F. Cline, *The United States and Mexico* (N.Y., Atheneum, 1963); R. E. Quirk, *An Affair of Honor: Woodrow Wilson and the Occupation of Veracruz* (Lexington, Ky., University of Kentucky Press, 1962); Kenneth Grieb, *The United States and Huerta* (Lincoln, Neb.,

University of Nebraska Press, 1969); P. Edward Haley, *Revolution and Intervention: The Diplomacy of Taft and Wilson with Mexico, 1910–1917* (Cambridge, Mass., Massachusetts Institute of Technology Press, 1970); Larry D. Hill, *Emissaries to a Revolution: Woodrow Wilson's Executive Agents in Mexico* (Baton Rouge, La., Louisiana State University Press, 1973); Jules Davids, *American Political and Economic Penetration of Mexico, 1877–1920* (N.Y., Arno Press, 1976); and Friedrich Katz, *The Secret War in Mexico: Europe and the U.S. and the Mexican Revolution* (Chicago, Ill., University of Chicago Press, 1981).

ILLUSTRATION CREDITS

We gratefully acknowledge the following sources for permission to reprint the illustrations that appear in this text on the pages listed:

The National Archives: pp. 1, 6, 13, 15, 20, 30, 41, 60, 66, 73, 77, 93, 102, 109, 111, 132, 146, 164, 196, 200, 203, 204, 208, 225, 247, 263, 266, 268, 269, 270, 272, 277, 281, 282, 296, 300, 319, 329, 331.

The State Historical Society of Mississippi: pp. 158, 168, 217.

The Library of Congress: pp. 153, 176, 178, 189, 220, 255, 298, 304, 312.

INDEX